LOLLARDS AND THEIR BOOKS

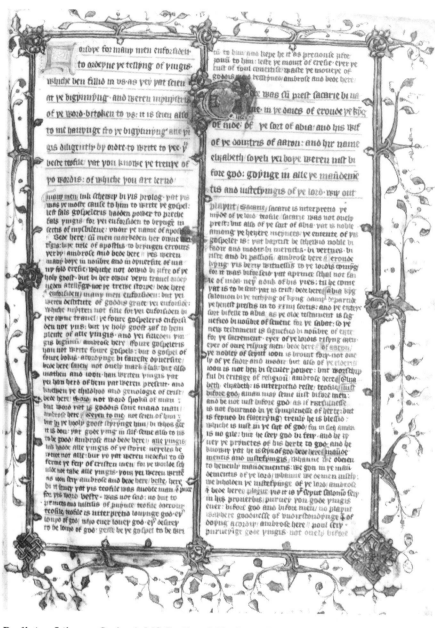

Bodleian Library Oxford, MS Bodley 243, f. 1ʳ. Opening of the shorter version of the *Glossed Gospels* on Luke.

LOLLARDS AND THEIR BOOKS

ANNE HUDSON

THE HAMBLEDON PRESS
LONDON AND RONCEVERTE

Published by The Hambledon Press

35 Gloucester Avenue, London NW1 7AX (U.K.)

309 Greenbrier Avenue, Ronceverte
West Virginia 24970 (U.S.A.)

ISBN 0 907628 60 5

British Library Cataloguing in Publication Data

Hudson, Anne
    Lollards and their books. − (History series; 45)
    − (Literature series; 3)
    1. Lollards − History
    I. Title II. Series. III. Series
    273'.6   BX4901.2

Library of Congress Cataloging in Publication Data

Hudson, Anne, 1938-
    Lollards and their books.

    Includes bibliographical references and index.
    1. Lollards − Addresses, essays, lectures.
    2. Wycliffe, John, d. 1384 − Addresses, essays, lectures.
    I. Title
    BX4901.2.H83   1985   284'.3   85-5571
    ISBN 0 907628 60 5

Printed and Bound in Great Britain by
Robert Hartnoll Ltd., Bodmin, Cornwall

CONTENTS

List of Illustrations   vii

Foreword   ix

Acknowledgements   xiii

Abbreviations   xv

1   Contributions to a History of Wycliffite Writings   1

2   A Lollard Compilation and the Dissemination
of Wycliffite Thought   13

3   A Lollard Compilation in England and Bohemia   31

4   A Neglected Wycliffite Text   43

5   The Debate on Bible Translation, Oxford 1401   67

6   John Purvey: A Reconsideration of the Evidence
for his Life and Writings   85

7   A Lollard Mass   111

8   The Examination of Lollards   125

9   Lollardy: The English Heresy?   141

10   A Lollard Sect Vocabulary?   165

11   Some Aspects of Lollard Book Production   181

12   A Lollard Quaternion   193

13   The Expurgation of a Lollard Sermon-Cycle   201

14   Observations on a Northerner's Vocabulary   217

15   'No Newe Thyng': The Printing of Medieval
Texts in the Early Reformation Period   227

16   Appendix: Additions and Modifications to
a Bibliography of English Wycliffite Writings   249

Index   253

Index of Manuscripts   261

PERMISSIONS

Acknowledgement is due to the following institutions, by whose permission the illustrations are produced: Brno University Library (6); Durham University Library (9); London, the British Library (4, 7, 8, 10); Oxford, the Bodleian Library (1, 2, 3); Oxford, the Warden and Fellows of Merton College (5).

LIST OF ILLUSTRATIONS

Bodleian Library Oxford, MS Bodley 243, f. 1^r.   Frontispiece
Opening of the shorter version of the *Glossed
Gospels* on Luke.

Bodleian Library Oxford, MS Bodley 277, f. 302^r.
Miniature from the border of a copy of the later
version of the Wycliffite Bible, showing a figure with
a bishop's mitre but animal's feet.   facing xvi

Bodleian Library Oxford, MS Bodley 448, f. 128^v.
Part of the 'Intermediate' version of the *Floretum/
Rosarium*; the entry for *luxuria* ends with a quotation
from Wyclif's *De Mandatis*.   facing 1

London, British Library MS Harley 401, f. 7^r.
Opening of the *Floretum* text.   30

Merton College Oxford MS 319, f. 41^r. Roundel from
an initial in a copy of Netter's *Doctrinale* book V,
chapter 17, showing the burning of books (presumably
Wycliffite books).   31

Brno University Library MS Mk 28, f. 126^r. Opening
of the *Opus Arduum*.   66

London, British Library MS Harley 2324, f. 45^v.
The Lanterne of Li3t.   124

London, British Library MS Cotton Titus D. i, f. 4^r.
The Thirty-Seven Conclusions of the Lollards.   164

Durham University Library MS Cosin V. iii. 6, f. 6^r.
Lollard dialogue between a knight and a clerk.   192

London, British Library MS Harley 1203, f. 64^r.
Lollard tract on Matthew 7. 15.   216

FOREWORD

The papers that are included in the present volume were published between 1971 and 1983, whilst I was engaged in the editing of Wycliffite texts. Those texts appeared in *Selections from English Wycliffite Writings* (Cambridge, 1978) and in *English Wycliffite Sermons* i (Oxford, 1983). Because the first chapter of the introduction to the latter edition supersedes it, the paper that was printed in *Medium Ævum* xl (1971) under the title 'A Lollard Sermon-Cycle and its Implications' has not been reproduced here. With the exception of the first and last chapters, the papers have been reprinted without alteration save for adjustment of the cross references; in the case of the two exceptions, I took advantage of the necessity to reset the material to add a few more recent bibliographical references concerning Lollard texts. I have also added a note to chapter 8, to draw attention to a further manuscript of the procedural material and lists of questions which I discovered shortly after the publication of the original paper. The fact that the remainder is unaltered should not, of course, be taken to imply that it could not now be improved: though I do not think that there are any statements that I now believe to be incorrect, there are certainly places where I should now want to alter the emphasis or to shift the inferences drawn, and many points at which I should want to add new references both from my own study and, more importantly, from the subsequently published contributions of others.[1] But that would be to write a new book, not to produce a collection of reprints. I hope indeed to redress balances, and to add more material in a full study of these Wycliffite texts on which I am at present engaged.

A glance through the titles of the various chapters, let alone any perusal of their content, will reveal that I have used the terms 'Wycliffite' and 'Lollard' as synonyms. This has been done deliberately, in full awareness of the tendency of historians in the middle of the century and after to distinguish the two, reserving 'Wycliffite' for the academic followers of the Oxford heretic and using 'Lollard' for the more popular adherents of the period between 1384 and the 1530s, whose knowledge

---

1   In particular attention should be drawn to the two important new papers included in Margaret Aston's book, *Lollards and Reformers: Images and Literacy in Late Medieval Religion* (The Hambledon Press, London, 1984) where are also reprinted her earlier papers. References to these latter have here, for reasons of space, been left unaltered.

of Wyclif such historians considered to be slight. The distinction appears to me to be misguided. The first use of the term *Lollardi* in relation to English heretics appears to be that of Henry Crumpe in 1382, who used the word to describe his fellow academics in Oxford who favoured Wyclif's views; opponents of Wyclif down to the time of Netter and later used the terms *Wyclevistae* and *Lollardi* as equivalents; the two words are also found interchangeably in Hussite Bohemia. Equally, though there was clearly a wide gap between men such as Nicholas Hereford, Philip Repingdon and John Aston on the one hand and most of the suspects investigated in, for instance, bishop Alnwick's campaign against heresy in the Norwich diocese between 1428 and 1431, it is far from evident whether, let alone where, any useful line can be drawn between the 'academic Wycliffite' and the 'popular Lollard'. Hereford, Repingdon and Aston are all known to have gone on 'preaching tours' outside the university, propagating Wyclif's ideas to a relatively uneducated audience; conversely, the Norwich diocese group declaredly had access to books, was in contact with heretics in other parts of the country, and was instructed by the far from ignorant William White. A number of the papers in the present collection are concerned with the means by which a heresy which originated in the university of Oxford found its way far beyond its bounds. If the papers more recently published seem to favour the term 'Wycliffite', it is because I have become more convinced in the course of my work that the ideas and the methods of the texts I have investigated can be traced back to Wyclif, even though they may have been modified or developed further over the passage of time.

Since I began work on Wycliffite texts I have incurred many debts, debts to institutions and to individuals. For financial aid it is a pleasure to acknowledge help from Lady Margaret Hall, Oxford, from the University of Oxford and, most munificently at the present time, from the British Academy. The staff of many libraries have been most patient with my importunate requests; in particular those who work behind the desk in Duke Humfrey's Library in the Bodleian deserve my especial gratitude. To three scholars who have died in the last few years I want to record my debt: to Eric Dobson, to Beryl Smalley and perhaps most of all to Neil Ker, whose astonishing memory and acute observation were matched by an immense generosity with information. Many other friends, colleagues and correspondents have given me material, opinions and encouragement; to all I owe much. Any selection must be invidious, but, if I limit myself to a further three living scholars, then my debt is probably greatest to Norman Davis, Margaret Aston and Pamela Gradon: to Norman Davis for his constant belief that my efforts about Wycliffite texts were worthwhile and for his readiness to read and to correct, to Margaret Aston for discussing many points by letter and for her generosity to a non-historian who might be regarded as trespassing on territory outside her competence, and to Pamela Gradon for her willingness to become involved in Wycliffite matters and to discuss them endlessly.

ACKNOWLEDGEMENTS

The articles reprinted here appeared first in the following places and are reprinted by the kind permission of the original publishers.

1 & 16   *Notes and Queries* ccxviii (1973), 443-53, under the title 'Contributions to a bibliography of Wycliffite writings'.

2   *Journal of Theological Studies* N.S. xxiii (1972), 65-81.

3   *Journal of Theological Studies* N.S. xxv (1974), 129-40.

4   *Journal of Ecclesiastical History* xxix (1978), 257-79.

5   *English Historical Review* xc (1975), 1-18.

6   ©1981 by The Regents of the University of California. Reprinted from *Viator*, xii (1981), pp. 355-380, by permission of The Regents.

7   *Journal of Theological Studies* N.S. xxiii (1972), 407-19.

8   *Bulletin of the Institute of Historical Research* xlvi (1973), 145-59.

9   *Studies in Church History* xviii (1982), 261-83.

10   *So meny people longages and tonges: Philological Essays in Scots and mediaeval English presented to Angus McIntosh*, ed. Michael Benskin and M.L. Samuels (Edinburgh, 1981), 15-30.

11   *Studies in Church History* ix (1972), 147-57.

12   *Review of English Studies* N.S. xxii (1971), 451-65.

13   *Journal of Theological Studies* N.S. xxii (1971), 435-42.

14   *Middle English Studies presented to Norman Davis*, ed. Douglas Gray and E.G. Stanley (Oxford, 1983), 153-74.

15   *Five Hundred Years of Words and Sounds for E.J. Dobson*, ed. E.G. Stanley and Douglas Gray (Cambridge, 1983), 74-83.

ABBREVIATIONS

The following list covers abbreviations used in some or all of the ensuing chapters. Because of the different styles of periodicals and publishers, there may be minor differences in punctuation and typography from that shown below.

BIHR	*Bulletin of the Institute of Historical Research* (London, 1923-)
BJRL	*Bulletin of the John Rylands Library* (Manchester, 1903-)
CHB	*The Cambridge History of the Bible* (Cambridge, 1963-70).
CSer	*Camden Series* (London, 1838-)
CYS	*Canterbury and York Society* (London, 1907-)
EETS	Early English Text Society; OS Original Series; ES Extra Series; SS Supplementary Series; where no indication of series is given, the Original Series is implied.
Emden (O)	A.B. Emden, *A Biographical Register of the University of Oxford to 1500* (Oxford, 1957-9)
EHR	*English Historical Review* (London, 1886-)
HL	C.J. Hefele and H. Leclercq, *Histoire des Conciles* (Paris, 1907-35)
JEH	*Journal of Ecclesiastical History* (London, 1950-)
JTS	*Journal of Theological Studies* (London, 1899-)
Knowles, *RO*	David Knowles, *The Religious Orders in England* (Cambridge, 1948-59)
MAE	*Medium Aevum* (Oxford, 1932-)
MED	Middle English Dictionary, ed. H. Kurath, S.M. Kuhn *et al.* (Ann Arbor, 1952-)
PL	*Patrologia Latina*, ed. J.P. Migne (Paris, 1841-)
PBA	*Proceedings of the British Academy* (London, 1903-)
RES	*Review of English Studies* (Oxford, 1925-)
RS	*Rolls Series* (London, 1858-1911)
SCH	*Studies in Church History* (London, 1964-)
STC	*A Short-Title Catalogue of Books printed in England, Scotland and Ireland and of English Books printed abroad 1475-1640*, ed. A.W. Pollard and G.R. Redgrave (London, 1926); Second revised edition of section I-Z by W.A. Jackson, F.S. Ferguson and K.F. Pantzer (London, 1976).
Wilkins	*Concilia Magnae Britanniae et Hiberniae A.D. 446-1717*, ed. D. Wilkins (London, 1737)

Bodleian Library Oxford, MS Bodley 277, f. 302^r. Miniature from the border of a copy of the later version of the Wycliffite Bible, showing a figure with a bishop's mitre but animal's feet.

Bodleian Library Oxford, MS Bodley 448, f. 128ᵛ. Part of the 'Intermediate' version of the *Floretum/Rosarium*; the entry for *luxuria* ends with a quotation from Wyclif's *De Mandatis*.

CONTRIBUTIONS TO A HISTORY
OF WYCLIFFITE WRITINGS

It has been the misfortune of Wyclif and his followers to arouse great emotions, whether of admiration or opprobrium, and to remain little read. The fault does not lie entirely on the side of the critic: despite the undoubted interest of Wyclif's ideas, these ideas were often expressed in repetitive and tendentious argument in difficult scholastic Latin; his English followers, despite the vernacular in which they mostly expressed themselves, inherited their master's repetitiousness and often wrote for initiates of the sect in a form of expression that a modern reader finds hardly less opaque. The pioneer study of Wyclif's own Latin writings was done in the nineteenth century: Shirley's *Catalogue of the Original Works of John Wyclif* was published in 1865, and formed the basis for the editions of the Wyclif Society between 1883 and 1921; in 1924 Loserth, perhaps the most energetic of the editors for the Society, produced a revision of Shirley's Catalogue.[1] Since then study of the Latin writings has flagged, apart from the series of articles by Professor S. Harrison Thomson and others adding manuscripts to Loserth's list and attempting to date some of the philosophical tracts,[2] and apart from editions of a few, mostly short texts.[3] The only substantial modification to the corpus of writings known to survive has been the identification by Miss Beryl Smalley of sections of Wyclif's commentary

---

[1] J. Loserth, revision of Shirley's *Catalogue of the Extant Latin Works of John Wyclif* (London [1924]); this is still the best guide to the corpus of Wyclif's Latin writings though certain texts there included should be excised following the article of S. H. Thomson in *Speculum*, iii (1928) pp. 382–91. [Loserth's list has now been superseded by W. R. Thomson, *The Latin Writings of John Wyclif: an Annotated Catalog* (Toronto, 1983)]

[2] See the articles by Thomson, Stein and Reeves cited in *A Manual of the Writings in Middle English 1050–1500*, ed. J. Burke Severs, II (Hamden, Conn., 1970), p. 519. It is still possible to add manuscripts to the lists of those of Bohemian origin, notably from the collections in the Prague Metropolitan Chapter and in Brno University Library; it is likely that no definitive list can be made until further Czech collections have been catalogued.

[3] Notably the editions of the *Summa de Ente* by S. H. Thomson (Oxford, 1930) and of the *De Trinitate* by A. D. Breck (Boulder, 1962).

super totam Bibliam in English manuscripts.[4] The English writings that Shirley included in his *Catalogue* have fared even worse this century: following the efforts of Arnold and Matthew in the last third of the nineteenth century, only a few minor tracts have been printed and the background to the texts so neglected that the possible value of the English tracts for the historian of Lollardy has been almost entirely ignored.[5] A glance through a recently published bibliography of the writings assigned to Wyclif and his followers reveals how little work has been done on them in the last fifty years.[6] The purpose of the present paper is to add some evidence concerning the transmission of Wyclif's ideas to the Lollards of the late fourteenth and fifteenth centuries, and to amplify the material concerning the preservation of Lollard texts.[7]

Wyclif's own writings are notoriously badly preserved in manuscripts of English origin: of the twelve tracts making up the *Summa Theologie* five do not survive in England, and there is no manuscript here of the *De Eucharistia* or *Trialogus*. For all of these, as for well over a half of Wyclif's total output, we are dependent upon Bohemian transcripts made during the Hussite period.[8] Apart from the manuscripts of the *Postilla super totam Bibliam*, few English manuscripts can be added to the list assembled by Loserth: most significant are MS. Gonville and Caius Cambridge 337/565, important primarily for its copies of the *De Composicione Hominis* and *De*

---

[4] "John Wyclif's *Postilla super Totam Bibliam*", *Bodleian Library Record*, iv (1953), pp. 186–205, and "Wyclif's *Postilla* on the Old Testament and his *Principium*", *Oxford Studies Presented to Daniel Callus O.P.* (Oxford Historical Society, 1964), pp. 253–96; the content of the text has been surveyed by G. A. Benrath, *Wyclifs Bibelkommentar* (Berlin, 1966). Two of the Bohemian manuscripts that Benrath was unable to see, Prague University III.F.20 (523) and VIII.F.9 (1563), are almost certainly parts of an originally single volume, or a companion set; the first contains the commentary on the four gospels (not omitting Luke as Benrath, p.388, implies), the second that on the Pauline espistles, Acts and the canonical epistles.

[5] T. Arnold, *Select English Works of John Wyclif* Oxford, 1869–71) 3 vols. and F. D. Matthew, *The English Works of Wyclif hitherto unprinted* (E.E.T.S. o.s. 74, 1880). A notable exception to the general tendency amongst historians to ignore the vernacular material is M. Aston's "Lollardy and Sedition 1381–1431", *Past and Present*, xvii (1960), pp. 1–44.

[6] See *Manual* (above f. 2), pp. 354–80, 517–33; the section is by S. H. Thomson and E. W. Talbert; a review of the whole volume by the present writer will appear in *Medium Ævum*. [xliii (1974), pp. 199–201.]

[7] New editions of the vernacular writings associated with Wyclif and the Lollards, other than the biblical translation, are being prepared; until the work is completed, with a careful analysis of the doctrinal content, it is premature to produce a definitive list of Wycliffite texts. For this reason the material pp. 249–52 does not aim to extend the corpus of English Lollard writing listed in the *Manual*.

[8] For the date at which Wyclif's writings reached Prague see especially F. Šmahel, " 'Doctor evangelicus super omnes evangelistas': Wyclif's Fortune in Hussite Bohemia", *Bulletin of the Institute of Historical Research*, xliii (1970), pp. 16–34, and the many references there given.

Dominio Divino otherwise unrecorded in England,[9] and MS. Wisbech Museum 8 containing, along with English Lollard sermons to be mentioned below, the short polemical *De Mendaciis Fratrum* and *Descriptio Fratris*.[10] Much work remains to be done on the availability of Wyclif's writings in England after his death. Certainly sufficient remained in Oxford in 1410 to be worth burning at Carfax in the presence of the chancellor of the university.[11] In 1407 the Czech scholars Nicholas Faulfiš and George Kneyhnicz obtained copies at Braybrook in Northamptonshire and Kemerton in Gloucestershire, and checked their texts in Oxford.[12] The link between these places may have been Robert Lychlade, expelled from Oxford in 1395 for teaching heretical views in the university and elsewhere (though restored in 1399), by 1402 rector of Kemerton and in the same year executor to the will of Dame Anne Latimer, wife of the Lollard knight Sir Thomas Latimer of Braybrook.[13] As well as the documentary evidence and the references in medieval library catalogues for manuscripts that did not survive the efficient destruction here,[14] there are signs that systematic attempts were made in England to render the complexities of Wyclif's Latin writings more accessible to the interested preacher. Dr. Wilks has recently sought to show that the band of "poor preachers", deduced from references in the Latin writings by Cannon but dismissed by McFarlane, was a central

---

[9] See S. H. Thomson, "A Gonville and Caius Wyclif Manuscript", *Speculum*, viii (1933), pp. 197–204; a manuscript of the *De Mandatis* unmentioned by Loserth is Cambridge University Library Ii.3.29.

[10] For the *De Eucharistia Confessio* in Trinity College Cambridge B.14.50 see S. H. Thomson, "John Wyclif's 'Lost' *De Fide Sacramentorum*", *Journal of Theological Studies*, xxxiii (1932), pp. 359–65, Thomson missed the fact that the manuscript also contains the *Descriptio Fratris* (f. 20).

[11] As recorded by Gascoigne, *Loci e Libro Veritatum*, ed. J. E. Thorold Rogers (Oxford, 1881), p. 116.

[12] See the annotations to their manuscript, now Vienna 1294, of the *De Veritate Sacre Scripture*, *De Ecclesia* and *De Dominio Divino*. For details about them, and about Wyclif's other Oxford followers, see A. B. Emden, *A Bibliographical Register of the University of Oxford to A.D. 1500* (Oxford, 1957–9), 3 vols.

[13] For Lychlade's career at Oxford and Kemerton, see Emden, *Oxford*, II. 1184; K. B. McFarlane, *Lancastrian Kings and Lollard Knights* (Oxford, 1972), p. 214 fn. 1 mentions the will but does not appear to have identified Lychlade with the man expelled from Oxford for Lollardy. (McFarlane's book is a posthumous collection, this part deriving from 1966.)

[14] A full collection of the evidence remains to be made; episcopal registers and secular documents provide frequent references. For material from medieval library catalogues see, for instance, John Bale, *Index Britanniae Scriptorum*, ed. R. L. Poole and M. Bateson (Oxford, 1902), pp. 264–74; F. M. Powicke, *The Medieval Books of Merton College* (Oxford, 1931), p. 76; M. R. James "Catalogue of the Library of Leicester Abbey", *Transactions of the Leicestershire Archaeological Society*, xix (1936–7), pp. 408, 427; xxi (1940–1), p.17.

part of Wyclif's thought through a large part of his career.[15] If this band were ever anything more than an idea in the reformer's mind, it should be possible to trace, not only its activities,[16] but also texts and aids to study intended for its use. Two such aids to study can readily be identified. The first is the provision of analyses, that is a guide, chapter by chapter, to some of the longer works of Wyclif. Five of these survive in England, to the philosophical tracts *De Universalibus* and *De Tempore*, and to three sections of the *Summa Theologie*, the *De Mandatis, De Veritate Sacre Scripture* and *De Simonia*.[17] Since these in identical form are found in Hussite copies, it is likely that the comparable analyses existing in Bohemia to all the other sections of the *Summa* apart from the brief *De Statu Innocencie* also go back to English sources.[18] That the summaries are not merely English but also authorial is suggested by the Prologue prefixed to the surviving insular analysis of the *De Mandatis*, where the writer speaks of himself as the author of the tract.[19] More ambitious was the second aid to study: the provision of indexes, detailed alphabetical guides to the contents of a tract, with reference by chapter or sermon number and by subdividing letter, the last presupposing the annotation of the text with marginal letters and the transmission of these from copy to copy. Three such indexes are known to survive in English manuscripts: one to the *De Mandatis* in MS. Cambridge University Library Ll.5.13, a second to the *Opus Evangelicum* in MS. Trinity College Dublin C.1.23, and a third to the *Sermones Quadraginta* in

---

[15] M. Wilks, "*Reformatio Regni*: Wyclif and Hus as Leaders of Religious Protest Movements", *Studies in Church History*, ix (1972), pp. 109–30; H. L. Cannon, "The Poor Priests: a Study in the Rise of English Lollardry", *Annual Report of the American Historical Association for the Year 1899* (Washington, 1900), i, 451–82; K. B. McFarlane, *John Wycliffe and the Beginnings of English Nonconformity* (London, 1952), p. 101.

[16] These are mentioned by, for example, Henry Knighton and the St. Albans chronicler; given the partial reinstatement of their trustworthiness by McFarlane, *Lollard Knights*, pp. 221–6, on the existence of support for the movement amongst the landed gentry, it seems time to reconsider the recent tendency to regard their observations about the poor preachers as hysterical and over-exaggerated.

[17] MS. Gonville and Caius 337/565 has analyses of the two philosophical tracts and of *De Mandatis*, MS. Lincoln Cathedral 159 of the two philosophical tracts, MS. Trinity College Dublin C.1.23 of *De Tempore*, MS. Trinity College Dublin C.1.24 of *De Veritate* and *De Simonia* and MS Trinity College Cambridge B.16.2 of the *De Universalibus*.

[18] MSS. Vienna 4523 and 5204 have that of the *De Universalibus* and MS. Vienna 4316 of the *De Tempore*; analyses of parts of the Summa appear in MSS. Vienna 1294, 1339, 1340, 1341, 1343, 1622, 3927, 3933, 3937, 4504, 4514, 4515, 4536; MSS. Prague University Library III.B.5, III.F.11, X.D.11, X.E.9; MSS. Prague Metropolitan Chapter B.53, C.38 and C.73. They have mostly not been printed, presumably since the editors of the individual works thought them lacking in authority.

[19] See Thomson's article cited in fn. 9 above, pp. 201–2.

MS. Lambeth 23.[20] More numerous indexes, covering all the major theological writings of Wyclif and two philosophical tracts, survive in Bohemian manuscripts; some are there ascribed to Peter Payne, the fugitive Lollard who played a major part in Prague after 1415,[21] and it has been conjectured that Payne may be responsible for all.[22] If this is correct, he may well merely have amplified indexes brought from England, since the fuller index to the *De Mandatis* found in the Hussite manuscripts nonetheless makes use of the same arbitrary chapter subdivisions as those in the English manuscript.[23] Apart from these two aids to study, analyses and indexes, there is a third compilation that seems to have sprung from a similar aim and background: this is the *Floretum Theologie*, abbreviated as the *Rosarium Theologie*, known in twenty-four English and the same number of Bohemian manuscripts. The *Floretum* contains within its alphabetical *tituli* some 180 quotations from Wyclif, many of them very lengthy; it must have been compiled between 1384, since the *Opus Evangelicum*, only completed shortly before Wyclif's death in that year, is extensively used, and 1396, the date given by a scribal colophon in MS. Harley 401. Elsewhere I have sought to demonstrate that this compilation was one method by which Wyclif's doctrine, originating in a university setting, may have been disseminated to the ordinary parish priest.[24]

[20] Although other English copies of all these works survive, none has either index or marginal subdividing letters.

[21] For Payne see Emden, *Oxford*, III.1441–3 and references there given, to which may be added F. M. Bartoš, *M. Petr Payne diplomat husitské revoluce* (Prague, 1956). The attribution to Payne occurs in MS. Prague University Library X.E.11, with the dates 1432 and 1433, a manuscript consisting entirely of Wyclif indexes; similar manuscripts, though without Payne's name, are MSS. Prague Metropolitan Chapter C.118 and Vienna 1725.

[22] S. H. Thomson, "A Note on Peter Payne and Wyclyf", *Medievalia et Humanistica*, xvi (1964), pp. 60–3; a number of details there given require correction. An example of these indexes is that to the *De Mandatis* printed in the Wyclif Society edition (that to the *De Ecclesia* printed from MS. Vienna 1294 is atypical because of its brevity; the fuller version is in MSS. Prague University X.E.11 and Prague Metropolitan Chapter C.118). The index to the treatment of biblical passages, found in MSS. Prague University IV.G.27 and Vienna 4522, presupposes the existence of the same indexing subdivisions but at present cannot be shown to go back to English antecedent.

[23] Since the insular and continental indexes to this text are based on the same original, it is obviously difficult to prove from the content of the index that one is an amplification of the other; the congruence of subdivision is a better indication of this. Unfortunately, no Hussite index to the *Opus Evangelicum* or *Sermones Quadraginta* survives; an index must have existed to the *Sermones super Evangelia Dominicalia* and *Sermones super Epistolas* since marginal subdivisions are found in Wolfenbüttel MS. Helmstedt 565.

[24] See "A Lollard Compilation and the Dissemination of Wycliffite Thought", *Journal of Theological Studies*, N.S. xxiii (1972), pp. 65–81; further material, particularly about the Bohemian manuscripts, is to be found in "A Lollard Compilation in England and Bohemia". [See below pp. 13–42.]

Turning from Wyclif's own writings, it is noticeable that little attention has been paid to the surviving Latin texts by his followers. Perhaps the most interesting of these is the commentary on the Apocalypse, known from its opening words as the *Opus Arduum*. No manuscript of this is known to survive in England, a fact that perhaps accounts for its neglect, but thirteen copies survive abroad, mostly in Czech libraries.[25] A colophon, found complete in two and partially in a third manuscript, records that the text was completed in prison on 7 April 1390 after having been begun about Christmas of the previous year; the date is confirmed by references within the text.[26] That, despite its present distribution, the text originated in England is shown by the exclusively English affairs to which allusion is made, the preoccupation with the persecution of Lollards and the Dispenser crusade, and the references to the destruction of books in Oxford and Salisbury.[27] Worked into the flexible frame of a biblical commentary is a full statement of Lollard beliefs, theological and political. For this and for the considerable amount of evidence concerning the contemporary treatment of the sect, the *Opus Arduum* deserves study as a source of primary importance. A number of shorter Lollard writings also penetrated to Bohemia, many of them lost in England. A discussion of the honour due to images, listed by Shirley as a work of Wyclif, was certainly written by one of his followers since it refers to texts by Wyclif as those of another person; equally, however, it is likely to be English from the exclusively insular material of the rest of the manuscript.[28] Perhaps more interesting, since it represents a topic less frequently found in Lollard writings is a *posicio* written by a disciple of Wyclif: "Sex raciones ad probandum quod ad regem secularem pertinet punire clericos scilicet mortaliter peccantes".[29] From the

---

[25] Brief details about the texts are to be found in F. Bartoš, "Lollardský a Husitský Výklad Apokalypsy", *Reformační Sborník*, vi (1937), pp. 112–4; A. Molnar, "Apocalypse xii dans l'interprétation hussite", *Revue d'histoire et de philosophie religieuses*, xlv (1965), pp. 212–31; B. Ryba, "Strahovské Zjevenie Český husitský výklad na Apokalypsu . . .", *Strahovská Knihovna*, i (1966), pp. 7–29. Manuscripts are Brno University Mk 28 and Mk 62; Prague University III.G.17 and V.E.3; Prague Metropolitan Chapter A.117, A.163, B.48/1, B.48/2, B.82/2; Vienna 4526; 4925; Karlsruhe Landesbibliothek 346; Naples Bibl. Naz. VII A 34 (the last two I have not seen).

[26] The colophon is in MSS. Brno Mk 28 and Prague University V.E.3; part only in MS. Prague Metropolitan Chapter A.117. The attribution to a Master Richard in MS. Brno Mk 62 should not be taken too seriously in view of the late date of the copy (1444). The date is confirmed in the discussion of Rev. xx (MS. Brno Mk 28 f. 201).

[27] For the crusade cf. MS. Brno Mk 28 ff. 154v, 181; the reference to the destruction of books is in the explanation of Rev.xii.5 (MS. Brno Mk 28 f. 174v). For the significance of the allusions to persecution cf. below, p. 448.

[28] Shirley *Catalogue* revised Loserth no. 27; see MS. Prague University X.E.9 ff. 210v–214. The author described himself as "quidem ruralis simplex discipulus" of Wyclif.

[29] MSS. Prague University X.E.9 ff. 206–207v, Vienna 3928 ff. 189–90 and Vienna 3932 ff. 155v–156.

nature of the subject, the discussion does not mention any specific time or place. But the author gives away his nationality by his citation of the clauses of a coronation oath to support his view; these clauses correspond precisely to those of Richard II's oath as that is recorded by the chroniclers.[30] Even more surprising to find in a Bohemian context is the satirical poem concerning the 1382 "Earthquake" Council at Blackfriars in London: a Hussite manuscript now in Vienna preserves this Latin text complete with its English "O and I" refrain.[31] As further study is made of the numerous Hussite manuscripts in libraries in Czechoslovakia and elsewhere, it is possible that more texts of English Wycliffite origin will come to light; in the case of writings that do not contain specific contemporary reference, the disentanglement of material written by Wyclif's English followers from that composed by his Bohemian disciples is not always an easy matter.[32]

Whilst the Latin Lollard writings are in most cases much better preserved in Bohemia than in England, for the English texts we are entirely dependent upon the manuscripts that escaped the episcopal suppression here. That a large amount was destroyed appears not only from the accounts of confiscation, but also from the reference in trials to books and texts no longer extant.[33] The most impressive survivor is, of course, the Wycliffite translation of the Bible: even the list of 230 manuscripts recently published by Dr. Lindberg can be supplemented.[34] Until further work is done on the dating and textual relations of these manuscripts, it is difficult to assess the

[30] See P. E. Schramm, trans. L. G. Wickham Legg, *A History of the English Coronation* (Oxford, 1937), p. 236, for references to the chroniclers.

[31] MS. Vienna 3929, ff. 223v–225; the text is printed by T. Wright, *Political Poems and Songs* (Rolls Series 1859–61), I, 253–63 from British Museum MS. Cotton Cleopatra B.ii. The Vienna manuscript contains otherwise copies of several of Wyclif's own texts. The refrain appears usually in the form "wyt a o and a I" (cf. R. L. Greene, "A Middle English Love Poem and the 'O-and-I' Refrain-Phrase", *Medium Ævum*, xxx (1961), pp. 170–5). [A further copy of the poem appears in Bodleian Library MS. Digby 98, f.195 verso to recto, on a leaf added to the manuscript. It is briefly mentioned in P. R. Szittya, '"Sedens super Flumina" a fourteenth-century poem against the Friars', *Mediaeval Studies*, xli (1979), p. 31.]

[32] As, for example, with the *Posicio discipuli M. Johannis* and its reply concerning the Eucharist in MSS. Vienna 3929, ff 250–261, and Vienna 4527, ff. 194v–209; in both manuscripts the other contents are largely Wyclif's own writings.

[33] See J. A. F. Thomson, *The Later Lollards 1414–1520* (Oxford, 1965), pp. 242–4 and the present writer "Some Aspects of Lollard Book Production", *Studies in Church History*, ix (1972), pp. 156–7. [See below pp. 181–92.]

[34] C. Lindberg, "The Manuscripts and Versions of the Wycliffite Bible", *Studia Neophilologica*, xlii (1970), pp. 333–47; to this can be added Cambridge University Library MSS. Add. 6681, 6682, 6683 and 6684. The only English Wycliffite manuscript that seems to have reached Hussite territory is the copy of the New Testament translation in Dresden (Lindberg no. 182); that in Wolfenbüttel (Lindberg no. 153) only went abroad in the seventeenth century.

varied arguments about the responsibility for the translation.[35] But it seems clear that the evidence for the search both for an authorative Latin text and for a satisfactory method of translation must imply the existence of scholarly effort in a protected centre for some considerable length of time. Similar implications can be drawn from the state of the text of the Lollard sermon-cycle printed by Arnold a hundred years ago. In an appendix to this article [pp. 249–50] is set out a list of the manuscripts that are now known to contain the whole or part of this cycle of 294 sermons (item 7 in appendix). I have described the complex arrangements of these sermons elsewhere;[36] the textual relations of the manuscripts, in so far as these can be deduced, suggest both that a large number of copies must have been lost and that there must have been the most careful supervision of the writing and correction of the manuscripts. If the production was organized, so also the conclusion seems inescapable that the sermons were intended for a well-informed audience, sharing common assumptions with the writers and capable of elucidating the brief allusions found.[37] The *Opus Arduum* throws some light on the production of Lollard sermons. Elaborating on Revelations xii. 5, the writer interprets the man-child born to the woman clothed with the sun as the fruit of study of the scriptures. This, he states, the bishops are currently endeavouring to destroy by their order to burn "omnes libros scilicet omelias ewangeliorum et epistolarum in lingua materna conscriptos". But, the writer adds, however much the devil strives through the bishops to stamp out such knowledge, the effort will be of no avail: not all such books have been destroyed, and the place of those that have been burnt will rapidly be taken by others "quia non omnes libri tales sunt destructi, sed loco eorum alii iam de nouo conscripti sunt, ut in brevi (Domino fauente) patebit, ipsis multum forciores".[38] It would be tempting, given the ferocity of the surviving sermon-cycle, to identify this with the replacements here described; but, even if proof of this is lacking, the *Opus Arduum* descriptions of persecution of the sect may indicate that the sermon-cycle has been dated too late by

[35] See the material listed by Muir in *Manual*, pp. 548–9, to which must be added more recently S. L. Fristedt, "New Light on John Wycliffe and the First Full English Bible", *Stockholm Studies in Modern Philology*, N.S. iii (1968), pp. 61–86; ibid. *The Wycliffe Bible*, Part II, Stockholm Studies in English, xxi (1969); H. Hargreaves, "The Wycliffite Versions", *The Cambridge History of the Bible*, II, ed. G. W. H. Lampe (Cambridge, 1969), pp. 387–415; C. Lindberg, *MS. Bodley 959*, vol. 5, Stockholm Studies in English, xx (1969), note pp. 90–8, 329–39.

[36] "A Lollard Sermon-Cycle and its Implications", *Medium Ævum*, xl (1971), pp. 142–56.

[37] The sermons rarely explain Lollard tenets or give detailed reasons for the rejection of current thought; much more frequently they merely refer to views in a vocabulary that is obviously familiar to the readers. Consequently, in the edition by Arnold which lacks any elucidatory notes, the sermons are often unintelligible to a modern reader.

[38] MSS. Brno University Mk 28,f. 174v; Prague University V.E.3, f. 95r–v.

recent critics.[39] The *Opus Arduum* is firmly dated as 1389-90, and the similarity of its references to those in the sermons makes a date after 1400 for the latter unnecessary; on other grounds an earlier date would be preferable. The importance of this sermon-cycle can be seen, not only from the number of the surviving manuscripts, but also from the adaptation of some of its sermons by another writer, an adaptation known from three further manuscripts.[40]

Apart from the Bible and this sermon-cycle, Lollard vernacular writings are not very well preserved, though additions can be made to the list recently published by Thomson and Talbert (see appendix below). Yet, as more work is done on these texts, it is possible again to discern traces of an organized attempt to disseminate Wycliffite views. Parallel to the differing arrangements of the sermons, are found at least three redactions of the Glossed Gospels, described by Dr. Hargreaves;[41] these again would seem to have been intended to fit differing needs amongst the Lollard community. Two versions are known of several tracts: thus, for instance, the text known as "The Clergy May Not Hold Property" has been printed from a manuscript where it is a straightforward argument in ten chapters with appended Latin authorities; but it also exists with some modifications in the form of an extended sermon.[42] This latter is interesting, since the wording makes it clear that the preacher was itinerant:

> Now siris the dai is al ydo and I mai tarie you no lenger, and I haue no
> tyme to make now a recapitulacioun of my sermon. Netheles I purpose to
> leue it writun among you, and whoso likith mai ouerse it . . . And certis, if
> I haue seid ony thing amys, and I mai now haue redi knouleche therof, I
> shal amende it er I go, and if I haue such knouleche herafter, I shal with
> beter will come and amende my defautis.[43]

[39] E. W. Talbert, "The Date of the Composition of the English Wyclifite Collection of Sermons", *Speculum*, xii (1937), pp. 464–74, dates the sermons between *c*. 1376 and *c*. 1412; similar limits were set by M. W. Ransom, "The Chronology of Wyclif's English Sermons", *Washington State College Research Studies*, xvi (1948), pp. 67–114. It must be reiterated, against the views expressed in both these articles, that there is nothing whatever in the textual history of the sermons that would support the idea of publication over such a long period of time; given the circumstances of medieval publication, not to mention the situation of the Lollards, it seems reasonable to conclude from this that the sermons were not written over such an extended time.

[40] See appendix no. 11; a definition of the standpoint of the redactor will not be possible until a critical edition of the source sermons is complete.

[41] See *Manual*, p. 545, for material on these texts, to which should be added Hargreaves' paper, fn. 35 above, where details are given of MS. York Minster XVI D.2, pp. 407–8.

[42] Matthew (above f. 5), pp. 359–404 from MS. Lambeth 551; the sermon version is found in the four other manuscripts listed in the appendix no. 85.

[43] British Museum MS. Egerton 2820, f. 116r–v.

It is also worth remarking that two manuscripts of this sermon are in the same hand.[44]

The attempt to assign authors to the English writings is, I would suggest, doomed to failure and largely futile. Wyclif is almost never mentioned by name, or by his Latin title of *Doctor Evangelicus*, in the manuscripts (an exception to this is found in the case of works dependent upon the Latin *Floretum* or *Rosarium*);[45] none of the English writings are ascribed by a medieval hand to Purvey.[46] The need for concealment no doubt led to the suppression of explicit attribution, but it would seem that there may have been deliberate anonymity intended: these were the writings not of an individual preacher but of "true men", "poor priests", members of "Christ's sect" spreading the *doctrina evangelica* "grounded in holy writ".[47] This is not to say that these anonymous texts never derive from Wyclif's Latin writings. Some of the sermons of the cycle mentioned above are dependent upon Wyclif's sermons, though not so closely as has sometimes been implied;[48] similarly, there is a vernacular reduction of Wyclif's *Dialogus* and *De Officio Regis*.[49] The complexities of relationship, however, between the Latin tracts of Wyclif and his followers, on the one hand, and the vernacular treatises on the other are only confused by ill-founded speculation connecting the last with known disciples. Further, it is clear that the Lollards were often in open dispute with orthodox thinkers and that therefore the writings of these latter may throw light on textual problems of Lollard tracts: the questions in *Jack Upland*, found also in Woodford's *Responsiones ad Quaestiones LXV*, are a

[44] MSS. Egerton 2820 and Cambridge University Library Dd.14.30 (2).
[45] Only one of the manuscripts of the sermon-cycle contains any medieval ascription to Wyclif (Bodleian MS. Douce 321), though MS. New College Oxford 95 has the colophon "Magister Johannes Wy" added to its copy of some of the Canticles commentaries (Arnold, III, 48–81); one of the few other manuscripts having Wyclif's name is British Museum MS. Harley 2385, ff. 3, 5r,v, attached to *Manual* nos. 13, 43 and 15.
[46] The ascription of works to Purvey rests upon his designation by Netter as *librarius Lollardorum* (*Doctrinale Fidei* (Venice 1757–9, reprinted Gregg 1967), III, 732); Netter quotes from Purvey's works but no systematic attempt to identify these passages has been made.
[47] The English phrases are recurrent through the sermon-cycle described above, the Latin derives from the *Opus Arduum* which also contains the translation of the others; the vocabulary goes back to Wyclif himself who frequently describes himself as *quidam fidelis*.
[48] For instance by the cross reference to the English sermons found in the Wyclif Society editions of the Latin *Sermones* and by H. B. Workman, *John Wyclif* (Oxford, 1926), II, 206–13.
[49] The first is in MS. Trinity College Dublin C.5.6, ff. 154v–161; the second in Bodleian MS. Douce 273, ff 273, ff. 37v–53. [The second has now been edited by J.-P. Genet as the first text in *Four English Political Tracts of the Later Middle Ages* (Camden Society Fourth Series, xviii (1977), pp. 1–21.]

case in point.[50] Here they were only following the tradition established by Wyclif: an interesting instance is the interchange between William of Rymington, prior of Salley Cistercian house in Yorkshire, and Wyclif.[51] Rymington had written a *Tractatus* containing 44 conclusions directed against Wyclif; Wyclif replied in the *Responsiones ad XLIV Conclusiones, sive ad Argucias Monachales*; shortly after Wyclif's death Rymington in his turn answered with a dialogue between *Catholica Veritas* and *Heretica Pravitas*.[52] Apart from the intrinsic interest of this series, the last dialogue has some interest as defining the beliefs of the *Wycliffistae* shortly after their leader's death, a definition written, unlike those of Netter, without the benefit of hindsight.

Finally, it is from the texts that some of the best evidence comes for the survival of Lollard ideas through the fifteenth century and into the period of the Reformation. Trials of heretics continued throughout this time and the phraseology of the suspects' evidence, curtailed though it is by the schematic form of the episcopal records, frequently recalls that of the early Lollards.[53] Professor Dickens has shown how difficult it is in certain expressions of opinion to distinguish Lollardy from Lutheranism.[54] A number of manuscripts of Lollard works dating from the very end of the fifteenth or early sixteenth centuries survive: for instance, MS. Bodley 540, MS. Cambridge University Library, Ff. 6.2, MS. Corpus Christi College Cambridge 100, British Museum MSS. Add. 10047, 15580 and MS. New College Oxford 320.[55] More indicative of serious interest are the printed texts that appeared in the first half of the sixteenth century: the vernacular tract on the translation of the Bible was printed abroad twice about 1530, the *Lanterne of Lyyt* in England at the same time; about six years later another

---

[50] See below appendix 95; comparison of the Latin with the vernacular reveals that the sixteenth-century printed edition must have used a good text, and provides evidence for the redating of *Jack Upland*.

[51] For Rymington see Emden, *Oxford*, III, 1617, and references there given.

[52] Rymington's two works are found in MS. Bodley 158; the sequence of texts is MS. Bodley 158, ff. 199–217 (with material on f. 187 inserted on f. 205), Wyclif's *Responsiones (Opera Minora*, pp. 201–57, no English manuscript surviving), MS. Bodley 158, ff. 188–97.

[53] For example the abjuration of Thomas Bykenore clerk in 1443 (Salisbury register Ayscough f. 53v) "that holi chirche catholike is congregacioun of trewe men wiche only schul be saued", which is Wyclif's *congregatio omnium predestinatorum* with the addition of the Lollard *true men*; or the contrast between Christ, sold by Judas for thirty pence, and the sales of Christ's body by contemporary priests for half a penny, found in *The Order of Priesthood* (Matthew, p. 167/3ff.), in fifteenth-century trials (e.g. Ely register Gray f. 131 of 1457, Lincoln register Chedworth f. 12v of 1457) and in a York trial of 1528 (York register Wolsey f. 131v).

[54] A. G. Dickens, *Lollards and Protestants in the Diocese of York 1509–1558* (London, 1959).

[55] For the first three see *Manual*, nos. 52, 95 and 55; for the last three are manuscripts of the Wycliffite Bible.

English printer issued *Jack Upland*; the Prologue to the Wycliffite Bible was printed by John Gough in London in 1540; the puzzling *Wycklyffes Wycket* was published first in 1546 and was reissued three times in 1548, 1550 (?) and 1612.[56] Interest in Lollard personalities as well as Lollard thought was shown by the printing, probably in Antwerp in 1530, of the accounts of the trials of William Thorpe and Sir John Oldcastle; the latter was reissued in 1544.[57] In the case of the edition of *Jack Upland* it would seem that the printer had available a better manuscript than any now surviving;[58] the *Wycket* is not known in manuscript form.

Much remains to be done on the origins and history of the Lollard movement. A recent critic has suggested that it may never be possible to trace the early stages satisfactorily. But so far only an arbitrary section of the evidence has been investigated; historians have confined their attention almost exclusively to documentary sources, sources which of their very nature are hostile to the movement. Certainly, before the Latin and English texts written by the Lollards can satisfactorily be used by historians, much textual and interpretative study must be done. But these texts, I would suggest, provide the "new material . . . of a kind and quantity so far unsuspected", whose existence McFarlane doubted.[59] Its value lies in the confirmation and amplification of the other sources, and in particular in its evidence concerning the organization and resources of the sect.

[56] For all of these save the Prologue to the Wycliffite Bible see *Manual*, nos. 55, 94, 95, 8, and appendix below; the Prologue (not listed under the later *Manual* section, pp. 547–50), is STC 3033. For all of these see Mrs. Aston's article cited in the appendix no. 55; for ownership of Lollard books in the early sixteenth century, see particularly J. Fines, "Heresy trials in the diocese of Coventry and Lichfield, 1511–12", *Journal of Ecclesiastical History*, xiv (1963), pp. 160–73, and I. Luxton, "The Lichfield Court Book: a Postscript", *Bulletin of the Institute of Historical Research*, xliv (1971), pp. 120–25.

[57] See *Manual*, nos. 101 and 102, with additions for the first below.

[58] See Heyworth's edition (*Manual*, no. 95) for arguments concerning the independence of the early printed text; its authority is shown by the Latin *Responsiones* that were unknown to Heyworth. The Latin text is to be edited by Fr. E. Doyle, who identified the questions as those of *Jack Upland*.

[59] McFarlane, *Lollard Knights*, p. 142.

2

A LOLLARD COMPILATION AND THE
DISSEMINATION OF WYCLIFFITE THOUGHT

ONE of the most recurrent, and most elusive, ideas in the accounts of the Lollard movement has been that of the band of poor preachers, who are said to have taken Wyclif's ideas from their original Oxford setting to the common people in the various districts of England. Early historians were convinced of the existence of such priests, and were also sure that Wyclif had instigated their first organization.[1] The preaching expedition in the Winchester diocese in 1382 undertaken by Hereford, Aston, Alington, and Bedman, with other unnamed followers, provides certain evidence of concern to spread Wyclif's views before his death;[2] the chroniclers refer to later, and more popular preaching, references which can be borne out by material in the episcopal registers.[3] How far Wyclif himself organized the preaching is more obscure, though a community of vocabulary between the heresiarch's own writings and the texts of the early Lollards may suggest a closer link than some recent critics have been prepared to allow.[4] The reason for the early historians' convictions about the poor preachers is easy enough to see: how otherwise can one explain the passage from Wyclif's Latin writings, designed for and circulated in a university environment, to the ordinary Lollard of the fifteenth century, whose only language was English? The recent tendency to doubt the close connection between Wyclif and Lollardy has been partly

[1] The only early systematic attempt to discuss the matter is that by H. L. Cannon, 'The Poor Priests; a study in the rise of English Lollardry', *Annual Report of the American Historical Association for the year 1899* (Washington, 1900), i, pp. 451–82; this was drawn on by writers such as H. B. Workman, *John Wyclif* (Oxford, 1926), ii, pp. 201–20, 325–404.

[2] *Wykeham's Register*, ed. T. F. Kirby (Hampshire Record Society, 1896–9), ii, pp. 337–8.

[3] For instance Henry Knighton, *Chronicon*, ed. J. R. Lumby (Rolls Series, 1889–95), ii, pp. 184–5; *Continuatio Eulogii*, ed. F. S. Haydon (Rolls Series, 1858–63), iii, pp. 355; Thomas Walsingham, *Historia Anglicana*, ed. H. T. Riley (Rolls Series, 1863–4), ii, pp. 53, 188–9; *Fasciculi Zizaniorum*, ed. W. W. Shirley (Rolls Series, 1858), pp. 275–6; Waltham register (Salisbury), ff. 222–223^v.

[4] All references to Wyclif's Latin works are to the editions of the Wyclif Society (1883–1921) unless otherwise stated. For Wyclif's own references see *Sermones*, i. 179/8–13, 281/1–9, ii. 279/1–8, iii. 73/29–32; *De Daemonio Meridiano* (*Polemical Works* ii) 424/17–425/5; *Dialogus*, 10–11. For Lollard usage, the sermon-cycle printed by T. Arnold, *Select English Works of John Wyclif* (Oxford, 1869–71), i. 209/5 ff., ii. 359/23 ff. provides examples.

a result of the apprehension of this problem;[1] if the existence of such priests is denied, then it is very difficult to see how the connection could be made. Yet these recent views do not altogether convince: the list of questions that formed the basis for investigation of Lollardy, set out in different forms in three episcopal documents of the first half of the fifteenth century, all concern matters traceable to Wyclif's own writings, involve terminology that he had made notorious, and ideas that he had rendered suspect.[2] The views of the majority of fifteenth-century Lollards, apart from the small number of cases showing admixture of wilder ideas, are clearly traceable to the heresiarch, however popularized and debased the form in which they are actually expressed.[3]

One possibility for the resolution of this problem has not hitherto been explored: the passage of ideas could have been through books, as well as through persons. The purpose of this paper is to give an account of a group of these books. The books in question are a collection of what, for want of a better term, must be described as 'alphabetical, theological common-place books'; this, to a modern reader, hardly gives an idea of the ambitious nature of a compilation that, in its longest form, would extend in print to about a thousand pages. The books go under the title of *Floretum* or *Rosarium Theologie*; to some extent the titles appear to be interchangeable, though this is not true of all the manuscripts.[4] It is not my aim here to untangle all the ramifications of textual relations between the manuscripts; such a study could be written only after complete collation and, though some refinements of argument would doubtless emerge, it seems questionable whether it would essentially alter the interpretation of the compilation's nature. The manuscripts are very numerous and are found in England and in Bohemia. The latter are obviously Hussite productions, though derived from England. It is with the English texts that I am here concerned. The English manuscripts, eighteen in all, fall roughly into three groups: a full version, containing some 509 entries and generally entitled *Floretum*; an intermediate version, containing the same number of entries but with their content altered and somewhat reduced, called,

---

[1] K. B. McFarlane, *John Wycliffe and the Beginnings of English Nonconformity* (London, 1952), pp. 121 ff.; M. E. Aston, 'Lollardy and Sedition 1381–1431', *Past and Present*, xvii (1960), pp. 1–44; J. Crompton, 'Leicestershire Lollards', *Transactions of the Leicestershire Archæological and Historical Society*, xliv (1968–9), pp. 11–44.

[2] Polton register (Worcester), pp. 113–14; British Museum MS. Harley 2179, ff. 157–157ᵛ; Bekynton register (Bath and Wells), opening 95.

[3] Cf. J. A. F. Thomson, *The Later Lollards 1414–1520* (Oxford, 2nd edn., 1967), pp. 239–50.

[4] The confusion appears particularly in the Bohemian manuscripts (see below, p. 20 n. 4).

when given a title, *Rosarium sive Floretus Minor* (hereafter described as 'Intermediate' version); thirdly, a reduced version, containing some 303 entries only, many of which are shortened in comparison with the foregoing two versions, and generally entitled *Rosarium*. The three versions are connected, not merely by their titles, but also by their shared possession of common material. No entry-title is found in the Intermediate or *Rosarium* version that is not included in the *Floretum*; further, although the material under the individual title varies to a considerable extent, there is a great amount of shared text found in all three versions. The nature of the material will be described below, but some idea of the type of the compilation may be seen from the first ten titles of the *Floretum*: *absolucio, abominacio, abstinencia, abusio, accepcio, accidia, accusacio, Adam, addicio legis, adiutorium*. The combination of interests shown in this group, biblical figures, moral and theological vices and virtues, ecclesiastical theory and practice, is typical of the work as a whole. Under each heading is assembled a variety of material: references to, and short quotations of, relevant scriptural passages, citation of patristic and later writers, and frequent references to canon law. All these authorities are cited by exact reference, author, work, book, chapter or section, as relevant, and often within chapter by some subdivision such as 'iuxta finem'; precise identification of the passage of canon law is invariable. The exactness, and multiplicity, of reference is noteworthy: there can be no question of reliance upon memory even for the biblical quotations. This precision is found in all manuscripts of all three versions, save in the very rare instance where an individual scribe miscopied his exemplar.

The interest of the compilation for the student of Wyclif and the Lollards lies in the fact that all three versions quote a number of passages on the authority of 'Doctor Euangelicus'. This is, of course, Wyclif's Latin title. The passages can be found, and found quickly because of the compiler's consideration in providing exact references, in Wyclif's Latin writings. The extent of the compiler's debt to Wyclif is greatest in the case of the *Floretum*: here some 170 passages have the name 'Doctor Euangelicus' (or *D.E.* as it is sometimes abbreviated) attached. Moreover, many of these passages are of considerable length: quotation of over a page in the printed edition is by no means uncommon.[1] That the actual compiler was a sympathizer of Wyclif's, to put it no more strongly at this point, is clear at any rate from the Prologue attached

---

[1] For instance, in the *Floretum* and Intermediate versions appear quotations of length from *De Mandatis* under *taciturnitas* (pp. 404/13–405/13), *timor* (pp. 83/26–85/22), *verba* (pp. 427/7–428/16), *ymagines* (pp. 156/15–158/17), and from the *Op u:Evangelicum* under *visio Dei* (i. 51/38–53/14).

to some manuscripts of the *Floretum*: here the author announces his intention of providing 'pauperes sacerdotes', who are 'propter penuriam pecunie libros emendi impediti', with 'istam facilem compilacionem domesticam pro fidei domesticis'[1] intended to assist them in preaching to the people, their prime duty. All the Lollard vocabulary is found here. Though this Prologue does not accompany the Intermediate or *Rosarium* redactions, the citation there, even in the shortest text, of a large number of passages acknowledged to be by Wyclif must be evidence of the Lollard instigation of the version and its copying. In some of the manuscripts later medieval readers observed the dangerous nature of the material: a marginal annotator in MS. Harley 401 commented (f. 96ᵛ) 'iste Doctor Euangelicus fuit Johannes Wyclyff Caue ergo'.

Before looking more closely at the Wyclif passages, it is useful to make some comment on the English manuscripts.[2] They may be set out as follows:

(*a*) *Floretum*: *inc.* (Prologue) Jesu Christo domino nostro pastorum principe ...(Text) *Absolucio* Dominus noster Jesus Christus dixit beato Petro ...; *expl. Zizania* ... crescere vsque ad messem dicit dominus noster Jesus Christus.

Manuscripts: British Museum Harley 401 (with Prologue and title), dated 1396; Royal 8 D. ii, ff. 50–100 (without Prologue or title), ends incomplete under *circumcisio*; Bodley 55 (with Prologue and title).

(*b*) '*Intermediate*' *version*: *inc.* (no Prologue) *Absolucio* dicitur tripliciter...; *expl. Zizania* ... crescere vsque ad messem dicit dominus noster Jesus Christus.

Manuscript: Bodley 448 (no medieval title).

(*c*) *Rosarium*: *inc.* (no Prologue) *Absolucio* dicitur tripliciter ...; *expl. Zelus* ... et omne opus pravum.

Manuscripts: Cambridge University Library li. 6. 19; Gonville and Caius College Cambridge 217/232 (ends incomplete under *ypocrisis*), and 232/118; Trinity College Cambridge B. 14. 44 (ends incomplete under *ypocrisis*), and O. 7. 30; Bodley 31, Bodley 626 (ends incomplete under

---

[1] MS. Harley 401, f. 1. The Prologue also appears in MS. Bodley 55, f. iii, but is so badly damaged by damp that it is mostly illegible; a copy was made by Langbaine and appears in MS. Langbaine 5, pp. 163–4, but comparison with the Harley manuscript makes it possible to see that the transcript is rather an inaccurate one.

[2] For the continental manuscripts see below, p. 20 n. 4. Four of the Bodleian library manuscripts were noted, though their nature was not perceived, by H. G. Pfander, 'The Medieval Friars and some alphabetical reference-books for sermons', *Medium Ævum*, iii (1934), pp. 19–29; six manuscripts of the *Rosarium*, again without indication of their associations, are listed by F. Stegmüller, *Repertorium Biblicum Medii Aevi* (Madrid, 1940–61), vi. no. 10080. MS. Harley 401 was described, and its contents understood, by S. Harrison Thomson, *Latin Bookhands of the Later Middle Ages 1100–1500* (Cambridge, 1969), plate 103.

malum), Bodley 803, ff. 39–177, Bodley Rawlinson c. 5; University College Oxford 95 (begins incomplete in *adversitas*); British Museum Harley 3226, Harley 4884, ff. 150–294ᵛ; Worcester Cathedral Library Q. 15, and Q. 68.

For the following study comparison of all the manuscripts was made with reference to their entries, subject and order, the presence of the Wyclif quotations, and content of certain subjects such as *absolucio*, *ecclesia*, *eucharistia*, and marginalia. The basis of study has been a small number of manuscripts: Harley 401 and Bodley 55 for the *Floretum*, Bodley 448 for the 'Intermediate' version, and Bodley 31 and University College Oxford 95 for the *Rosarium*. In ensuing references the title of the entry has been used rather than folio numbers since the former is common to all manuscripts in the version, the latter only to a particular manuscript.

The relation of the three versions to each other is not a simple one. As has been said, the *Rosarium* contains no title not also found in the *Floretum*; but, although this would suggest a simple reduction of the former from the latter, the content of the material under each title does not confirm this simplification. Although some references are retained, there has been considerable re-writing in the reduction: thus all the references in the entry for *ecclesia* in the *Rosarium* are to be found in one section of the longer entry on the same subject in the *Floretum*, but the setting of the quotations is different. More importantly, further citations from authorities have been added in the *Rosarium*. This also applies to Wyclif: the *Rosarium* redactor must have had access to Wyclif's Latin works (or to extracts from them, acknowledged to be Wyclif's) outside the *Floretum*. Thus new Wyclif quotations are added under the headings of *fides*, *Maria*, and *martires*.[1] The position of the Intermediate version is also a complicated one. At first sight, it appears to be merely the *Floretum*, without Prologue and having a different incipit to the first item, since otherwise the entries cover exactly the same ground as the *Floretum*. Further investigation, however, shows that matters are not so simple. Though some items exactly correspond to the equivalent *Floretum* entry, others are re-organized and re-written. Thus, at the beginning of the work, the entries for *absolucio* in the two versions are entirely distinct, those for *abominacio* are in complete agreement, whilst the third, for *abstinencia*, is introduced in the Intermediate version by some sentences not in the *Floretum* but then continues with material common to both. A few quotations from Wyclif are omitted in the Intermediate version, but again the redactor

---

[1] Under *fides* to *Sermones*, ii. 123/25–9, under *Maria* to *De Mandatis*, p. 127/28 ff., under *martires* to *De Civili Dominio*, i. 295/16 ff.

must have had access to the heresiarch's writings independently since, for instance under *excommunicatio*, new quotations are introduced.[1] One must, therefore, conclude that, though the basic work of compilation was done only once, activity on it must have continued for some time and probably by several people, and that this activity, like the original work, must have been in a centre having access to a considerable bulk of Wyclif's writings.

It should further be mentioned that variation is found between manuscripts of the same version. The text of the *Rosarium* in the majority of manuscripts seems to be fairly stable, with only the minor variation explicable in terms of scribal error. But MS. Trinity College Cambridge O. 7. 30 represents a fuller version with some sixty extra entries not found in any other known manuscript of the *Rosarium*. The state of this text confirms the supposition that the process in these compilations was one of gradual reduction rather than of progressive amplification.[2] Similarly in the *Floretum* there are differences between the version in MS. Harley 401 and that in MS. Bodley 55, differences that show intentional interference. Thus a reference under *statuta* in MS. Harley 401 to the parliament held at Gloucester in 1378 is missing in MS. Bodley 55.[3] In quotations from Wyclif also there is discrepancy: a reference under *adoracio* in MS. Harley 401 is lacking in MS. Bodley 55, but conversely a quotation under *excommunicatio* (not that mentioned above, p. 70) in MS. Bodley 55 is not in MS. Harley 401.[4] The state of Harley 401 may give some clue about the origin of this sort of variation. The margins have been annotated by a number of hands, two of which provide additional Wyclif references, again quoting passages and giving exactly similar precise identification.[5] It would seem once more that we have to do with Lollard sympathizers, knowledgeable in Wyclif's Latin writings.

The body of Wyclif's writings available to the compiler and the various redactors was quite a large one. There is, as would be expected from the aim announced in the *Floretum* Prologue, a predilection for the didactic or exegetical, rather than the philosophical or polemical, writings. In all three versions are found quotations from the Latin

---

[1] From *De Civili Dominio*, i. 277/11 ff.

[2] The manuscript contains the characteristic *Rosarium* quotations from Wyclif under *fides*, *Maria*, and *martires* though also retains from the longer versions the Wyclif quotations for *derisio*, *dies*, *genuflexiones*, *grex*, *juga*.

[3] MS. Harley 401, f. 298ᵛ.

[4] Under *adoracio* to *De Mandatis*, p. 161/7–32; under *excommunicatio* to *Sermones*, i. 238/35–239/3.

[5] Thus one annotator on f. 192 under *munus* refers to *Sermones*, iv. 502/4 ff.; a second on ff. 204–5 adds two passages from the *De Mandatis*, pp. 261/9–15 and 248/22–249/14 to the entry for *oracio*.

sermons, Sunday Gospel, Proprium and Commune Sanctorum, and
Sunday Epistle sets and the *Sermones Mixti*, the *De Civili Dominio*, the
Opus Evangelicum, and, most frequently, the *De Mandatis*. In the
Floretum and the Intermediate version are also found quotations from
the *Dialogus*, the *De Officio Pastorali*, *De Symonia*, *De Apostasia*, and
De Paupertate Christi.[1] In the Intermediate and *Rosarium* versions is
a passage from the *Trialogus*.[2] The references given are always correct
(or in isolated cases can be put right in an individual manuscript by
reference to another) and precise: thus the number of a sermon and its
series is given in reference to the liturgical *Sermones* series, the text
on which an observation from the *Opus Evangelicum* occurs, the chapter
of other tracts; more detailed references, such as *in primis*, *ad finem*,
or indexing by letter (for which see further below), are correct. Of the
170 passages from Wyclif quoted in the *Floretum* only two remain
baffling. Passages cited by Wyclif from other writers, such as the extensive quotation from Augustine and Chrysostom in the *Opus Evangelicum*,
are included within the 'Doctor Euangelicus' section by the paragraph
markings though their ultimate source is acknowledged.[3] The text of
the Wyclif quotations is very accurately produced, when the passages
are compared with the printed editions. Occasional variants are found,
but these are usually of a comprehensible kind, and may sometimes
be preferable to the printed readings. This possibility is important in
the case of some of the texts quoted, the *De Civili Dominio*, *De Paupertate Christi*, and the *Trialogus*, of which no insular copy is known to
survive and where the text has necessarily been printed from Bohemian
Hussite transcripts.[4] The quotations here allow checking of the accuracy

[1] To *Dialogus*, pp. 51/15–52/19 under *sacerdotes*; *De Officio Pastorali* (ed.
G. V. Lechler, Leipzig, 1863), p. 10/13–26 under *renunciare*; *De Symonia*,
pp. 61/6–62/2 under *symonia*; *De Apostasia*, pp. 113/25–30, 32–5, 114/33–7
under *veritas*; *De Paupertate Christi* (*Opera Minora*), p. 71/1–23 under *regere*.

[2] *Trialogus* (ed. G. V. Lechler, Oxford, 1869), p. 135/11–18 under *fides*.

[3] For instance, under *peccata* in the *Floretum* the compiler correctly notes
'Doctor Euangelicus recitans Lincolniensem' for *Opus Evangelicum*, i. 282/30–
283/3.

[4] W. W. Shirley's *Catalogue of the Extant Latin Works of John Wyclif* revised
by J. Loserth (London, 1925) can be amplified by reference to a number of
more recent articles listed in E. W. Talbert and S. Harrison Thomson's bibliography in *A Manual of the Writings in Middle English 1050–1500*, fasc. ii, ed.
J. Burke Severs (Hamden Conn., 1970), p. 519, and further from library catalogues. For *De Civili Dominio* two more manuscripts are now available, Paris
Bibliothèque Nationale fonds lat. 15869 and Florence Laurentian Plut. xix
cod. xxxiii (last chapter only); the same Florence manuscript provides another
copy of the *Trialogus*, of which a short extract is also found in Brno University
Library Mk 109; an incomplete text of *De Paupertate Christi* exists in Vatican
Borghese 29.

of the continental tradition. Similarly, the single insular manuscript of the liturgical *Sermones*, *Dialogus*, *De Symonia*, *De Apostasia*, and *De Officio Pastorali* tracts may usefully be checked for the passages cited here.

The date and milieu in which these compilations originate can to some extent be assessed. MS. Harley 401 of the *Floretum* redaction is dated at the end 1396. This is probably the date of the completion of the scribe's work and not of the original compilation, but it provides a *terminus ante quem*. A *terminus post quem* is provided by the use in all redactions of the *Opus Evangelicum*, a work clearly dated on internal evidence in the year 1384 and probably finished only very shortly before Wyclif's death on 31 December of that year.[1] The twelve years between these two dates provide a suitable period: before the mention of Wyclif, even under his Latin by-name, would inevitably lead to heretical investigation,[2] even if copying of his works were severely discouraged, and when the Lollard movement still had the interest of certain secular men able to provide the finance for the type of work and the size of manuscript involved here.[3] The continental manuscripts are, of course, Hussite productions and, in some cases, are attributed to Bohemian authors and said to have been completed in the second decade of the fifteenth century.[4] They do, however, witness to the importance that was attached to the compilation, since copies of all three versions were thought worth taking to Prague.

The lengthy and frequent quotation from Wyclif's Latin writings

[1] See Loserth's introduction to his edition, i, p. v.

[2] For the continuance of interest in Wyclif after his disappearance from Oxford see J. A. Robson, *Wyclif and the Oxford Schools* (Cambridge, 1961), pp. 218–46. The fact that Arundel in 1408 saw fit to promulgate the highly unpopular inquiry into Oxford books and teachers (D. Wilkins, *Concilia Magnae Britanniae et Hiberniae* (London, 1737), iii. 318–19) suggests that questions that Wyclif had raised were by no means dormant yet.

[3] Cf. McFarlane, *Wycliffe*, pp. 146, 174–8; for the financing of vernacular manuscripts see *Medium Ævum*, xl (1971), pp. 142–56.

[4] Twenty-three manuscripts are known to exist abroad, all in Prague or Brno save two copies of the *Rosarium* in MSS. Pommersfelden 186 and Wroclaw University 1302. From the catalogues of the Prague and Brno libraries it is possible to ascertain that MSS. Prague University 819 (V. B. 2), 1441 (VIII. B. 5), 1744 (IX. D. 6), Prague Metropolitan Chapter 451 (C XXXII), 461 (C XXXVII. 4), 659 (D XCII. 2) and Brno University Mk 35 are copies of the *Floretum*; Prague University 694 (IV. E. 14), and Brno University Mk 28 of the Intermediate version; Prague University 994 (V. H. 17), 1982 (X. H. 4), 2228 (XII. G. 17), Prague Metropolitan Chapter 658 (D XCII. 1), 684 (D CXIV), 685 (D CXV) of the *Rosarium*. Details are not sufficient for decision to be made about MSS. Prague University 133 (I. C. 41), 751 (IV. G. 19), 1454 (VIII. B. 18), 2365 (XIII. F. 27), Prague Metropolitan Chapter 582 (D XVI) and 674 (D CV).

would suggest that the compilation must originate in a centre not far removed from the university. This is amply confirmed by the other authorities cited. The list of theological writers quoted in the *Floretum* and the Intermediate version is an impressive one: as well as the usual patristic authorities, Augustine, Ambrose, Jerome, Gregory, Basil, Chrysostom, Gregory Nazianzen, Origen, Cyprian, Leo, Bede, Cassian, and Cassiodorus, are found more recent authorities, Peter Lombard, Lyra, Bernard, Hugh and Richard of St. Victor, Peter Comestor, William of St. Amour, Hugh of St. Cher, Peter of Blois, and Holcot. Secular writers have a smaller part: Aristotle and Seneca represent the classical period, Boethius the early medieval period, whilst Higden's *Polychronicon* is used for an account of the origin of tithes. Aquinas is represented by a few passages from the *Summa Theologiæ*;[1] much more frequent is the citation of the *Compendium Theologicae Veritatis* of 'Thomas', a work now known not to be by Aquinas but one which circulated in the medieval period under his authority.[2] As has been said, a large amount of canon law is quoted; alongside direct quotation appear some citations of the commentators, Guido de Baysio, Hostiensis, Joannes Andreae, Guilielmus [de Monte Lauduno] on the *Clementines*.[3] Two more recent theological authorities are of more significance: FitzRalph's name appears in the entry for *exequie* and Grosseteste is frequently represented by references to his Dicts and other works. The reverence in which both these authors were held by Wyclif and the Lollards amply explains their appearance.[4]

The exactitude of reference found in the Wyclif citations is exactly paralleled with all these other authors, and with the large number of biblical passages cited under each entry. The scholarship of the compiler is revealed also by the register that is found in some manuscripts of the *Floretum*.[5] This provides an alphabetical list of all the

---

[1] Under *mercator, obediencia, peccatum, sortilegium, superbia*, and *votum*.

[2] Printed under Bonaventura's name in the collected edition published Rome, 1588–96, vol. viii; almost the whole of this work must be quoted at one point or another of the *Floretum*.

[3] Guido de Baysio, the Archdeacon, is cited in the *Rosarium* under *privilegium* and in the margin of MS. Harley 401 beside *missa*; the other three appear in the *Rosarium* under *iurisdiccio*.

[4] Grosseteste's Dicts (see S. Harrison Thomson, *The Writings of Robert Grosseteste* (Cambridge, 1940), pp. 214–32) are cited regularly by number; also referred to are the sermons (under *prelacia*) and the spurious *De Oculo Morali* (under *prosperitas*). For the Lollard honour given to FitzRalph, leading to his designation as 'St. Richard', see the unprinted text in MS. Harley 1203, ff. 64–91 and Arnold iii. 281/13, 412/21, 416/20.

[5] MSS. Harley 401, ff. 1–6ᵛ, Bodley 55, ff. iii–viiᵛ; also Prague University 819, ff. 1–10ᵛ, Prague Metropolitan Chapter 451, ff. 259ᵛ–64ᵛ, 461, ff. 2–8, Brno University Mk 35, ff. 254ᵛ–8.

main entries with the number of each, together with a large quantity of proper names from the Bible, often with an explanation of their meaning, giving references to the entries in which these persons or places are mentioned. These references also provide a subsection, in the form *li.* plus number, or a letter indication of position, or sometimes both; thus, to give an instance of the last, the entry *Abel luctus vel miserabilis 222 li. 2a* is to be found under entry 222 *Libido* subsection 2 part a. In MS. Harley 401 the subsections are regularly marked in the margin of the entry, the entry number being at the start of each; no letter subdivision is provided. In MS. Bodley 55, though this initial register is included, the entry numbers are only supplied in a modern hand and no subsection numbering is found; the manuscript was apparently never finally completed. In the Register are also given cross-references in the case of main entries: thus § *Ymagines titulo 506, 237* refers to *ymagines*, entry 506, and *mandatum primum*, item 237. At the end of the entries themselves are some cross-references to other relevant entries.

The methods by which these large compilations were built up must be reserved for separate study, but a few points are relevant to the present paper. It seems clear that the compilers must have used indexes to many of the works on which they drew. Most interesting to the matter here is that indexes to Wyclif's Latin writings were obviously put to good account. These indexes have been used by some editions in the Wyclif Society, though all those printed have come from continental manuscripts. Many of them are detailed; their nature can be seen from a few entries from the index to the *De Ecclesia*: 'An presciti qui habent fidem sunt de ecclesia et predestinati in mortali sunt tunc extra ecclesiam?', 'Precaria accipitur dupliciter', 'Papam non tenemur credere esse caput ecclesie', each followed by chapter number and letter subdivision. Clearly this type of index would greatly lighten the task of the compilers of the *Floretum*. One insular manuscript of the *De Mandatis*, the work perhaps most frequently cited in the *Floretum*, preserves such an index. This is MS. Cambridge University Library Ll. 5. 13; the index is similar, but not identical, to that printed in the Wyclif Society edition from a Prague manuscript.[1] Comparison of the index with the *Floretum* shows that two-thirds of the latter's references to the *De Mandatis* could have been simply obtained by looking up the relevant entry in the index. Similarly, a somewhat more modest index to the *Opus Evangelicum* found in MS. Trinity College Dublin C. 1. 23

---

[1] Edition pp. 537–67 from Prague Metropolitan Chapter 462; MS. C.U.L. Ll. 5. 13, ff. 112–29ᵛ. Other English manuscripts of the *De Mandatis*, C.U.L. Ii. 3. 29, Trinity College Cambridge B. 15. 28, Gonville and Caius College Cambridge 337/565, Bodley 333 and Magdalen College Oxford 98, have no index.

would supply a similar proportion of the references to that work. Simple association would provide the remainder, as for instance the passage from *Opus Evangelicum* cited under *vicarius* in the *Floretum* but listed under *papa* in the index.[1] No surviving manuscript of the *Sermones* appears to have such an index, but it seems certain from references within these compilations that one must originally have existed.[2] Going beyond Wyclif, it again seems certain that indexes were used. The indexes to the homilies on Matthew ascribed in the medieval period to Chrysostom, such as those in MSS. Bodley 743, ff. 112^v–127^v, or Bodley 709, ff. ii–xvii^v, correspond closely to the references in the *Floretum*; similarly, the index to the Dicts of Grosseteste in MSS. Bodley 798, ff. iv–xi, and Bodley 830, ff. iv^v–xi, would simply provide many citations used.[3] The same situation can be found with other patristic authorities. A biblical index, one such as that found in MSS. Bodley 627 and 688, was also obviously used, together with a classified handbook to canon law. Though in some ways the agreement with such indexes diminishes the individuality of the compilation, it also points to the scholarship of the enterprise.

From all the evidence it would, I think, be difficult to dispute that the compilation originated from the minds of university men; nor does it seem likely that the work was drawn together in the first place outside Oxford. The number and range of authorities used could hardly be available outside the university, except in the larger monasteries which, from internal references showing complete Wycliffite condemnation of *religiones privatae*, are ruled out. The sympathies of the compilers are clear: they agree entirely with Wyclif's most extreme condemnations of contemporary church government and policy, they share his view of the church as *congregatio omnium predestinatorum* and use his terminology concerning the *presciti*.[4] The entry on the pope is unfavourable, though not so outspoken as might be expected. The truncated nature of the entry even in MS. Harley 401, where it occupies

---

[1] MS. Trinity College Dublin C. 1. 23, p. 419; the index is not present in the other English manuscript, Trinity College Cambridge B. 16. 2.

[2] To the manuscripts listed by Loserth in his revision of Shirley's *Catalogue* nos. 34–7, can be added Wolfenbüttel Helmstedt 306 and 565 (see H. Kühn-Steinhausen, 'Wyclif-Handschriften in Deutschland', *Zentralblatt für Bibliothekswesen*, xlvii (1930), pp. 625–8).

[3] It is not suggested that these particular indexes were used by the compiler of the *Floretum-Rosarium*, but only that this *type* of index must have been available.

[4] See the entries for *ecclesia, predestinacio, presciencia,* and, amongst others, *frater, obediencia, prelacia, sacerdos,* and *religio*; the Wycliffite condemnation of images and pilgrimages is amply reflected in the entries for *ydolatria, ymagines,* and *peregrinacio*.

only a single page as compared with eight for *prelacia*, leads to the suspicion that it may already have suffered expurgation. A rapid review of the more disreputable events of the papacy in its first thousand years of existence is given from the chronicle of Martinus Polonus; the tone of disapproval is clear, but the expected discussion of the theory of the papal office and jurisdiction is lacking. Wyclif is not mentioned by name in the entry on the Eucharist; the material is somewhat ambiguous, but the Wycliffite view seems implied by the condemnation of the Occamist explanation concerning the annihilation of the substance of bread. Despite the abbreviation in the *Rosarium* version, leaving only some twenty quotations from Wyclif, the Wycliffite standpoint is still perfectly clear.

Here then is a compilation that could act as a handbook of Wycliffite thought. Is there any evidence that it did actually fulfil this function? Fortunately, evidence is available that enables a positive answer to be given to the question. This evidence may be divided into two groups. First is the testimony of the manuscripts. As has been said, there are eighteen manuscripts surviving in England, a number that, given the wholesale destruction of Lollard books in the fifteenth century, must imply considerable circulation.[1] In addition to these eighteen Latin manuscripts, there is a single copy of a Middle English translation of the *Rosarium*, complete with its references to the 'Doctor Euangelicus'. The translation is an accurate one, and all the citations with their details are transcribed. The manuscript, Gonville and Caius College Cambridge 354/581, can be dated palaeographically in the late fourteenth century;[2] linguistically it is somewhat confused, confirming the occasional mistake that would suggest it is a copy of an earlier exemplar and not the translator's own manuscript, showing north-eastern and south-east Midland features. The purpose of the translation cannot be doubted: to make the material available to the large number of Lollard sympathizers, including lower clergy, whose only language was English. In this version, as in the Latin *Rosarium*, the reader is struck particularly by the preponderance of material from canon law, cleverly cited to turn the instrument of the ecclesiastical hierarchy against its makers.[3]

---

[1] The medieval provenance of only one is known: the copy of the *Rosarium* in MS. Worcester Cathedral Q. 15 belonged to the medieval library there (N. R. Ker, *Medieval Libraries of Great Britain* (London, 2nd edn., 1964), p. 213).

[2] M. R. James, *A Descriptive Catalogue of the Manuscripts in the Library of Gonville and Caius College* (Cambridge, 1907–14), i. 400–400*; I owe the dating to the help of Dr. Ian Doyle.

[3] A neat instance of the distortion is seen under *predicacio* (f. 103ᵛ) where *Decretals* v. vii. 13 (§ 6) is cited against unauthorized preaching, but the writer then notes that this must be modified in the light of the scriptural example of Moses, sent by God but not by men.

It is clear that, though some of Wyclif's most scathing words were reserved for the practitioners of canon law, his followers recognized that they could not hope to oust the system but must endeavour to convert it to their own ends;[1] the Egyptians in this compilation are shown to have been effectively spoiled.

The second type of evidence is in many ways the more satisfactory. It may be illustrated from a manuscript of the early fifteenth century, now Trinity College Cambridge B. 14. 50. From the make-up of the quires, the manuscript is clearly of two parts, the first (ff. 1–25ᵛ) being quires of mixed parchment and paper, the rest (ff. 26–70) only parchment; this is confirmed by the hands. From the contents, however, the two parts belong together. The Lollard origins of the second part have long been recognized: it contains two tracts, one on the legitimacy of Bible translation into the vernacular, the other ascribed by a modern critic to Purvey, a treatise against worship of images and a dialogue against the friars.[2] The rest of the volume has been neglected. In the first part appear notes for sermons, first on the dominical gospels and then on gospels for certain saints' days; these are followed by various notes. Amongst these is found the short *Descriptio Fratris* ascribed, as in the continental manuscripts from which alone hitherto it has been known, to Wyclif:

Pseudofrater degens in hoc seculo est diabolus incarnatus cum adinuentis suis signis sensibilibus, desponsatus ad seminandum discordias in militante ecclesia ex summa cautela sathane machinatus. Hoc doctor euangelicus.[3]

The notes for sermons are instructive. Some are very brief and merely give indications of possible topics for discussion arising from the liturgical text for the day. Others are more detailed. One (ff. 3–3ᵛ) for the second Sunday after Trinity provides a quotation from the sermon for the same occasion in the standard Lollard sermon-cycle.[4] The text is Luke xiv. 16 *Homo quidam fecit cenam magnam*:

Here may be touchid of þis greet soper-makyng. And for 4 causis þis soper is gret: for þe lord is greet þat makiþ þis soper, so þat no man but he may make siche a soper; also þe peple is greet and many; also þe mete

---

[1] See the frequent quotation of canon law in *An Apology for Lollard Doctrines* (ed. J. H. Todd, Camden Society, 1842) and *The Lanterne of Liȝt* (ed. L. M. Swinburn, E.E.T.S. 151, 1917).

[2] See the description in M. R. James, *The Western Manuscripts in the Library of Trinity College Cambridge* (Cambridge, 1900–4), i. 457–9; the manuscript was much used by M. Deanesly, *The Lollard Bible* (Cambridge, 1920), who printed ff. 26–34 (pp. 437–45, 461–7).

[3] *Polemical Works*, ii. 409, here f. 20; it is no. 90 in Loserth's revision of Shirley's *Catalogue*.   [4] Arnold, i. 4/11–17.

is preciouse siþ Crist is al maner of mete and drynk þat þei sopen wiþ; also þe tyme of sittyng at þis soper is wiþouten ende.[1]

The whole of the second sentence is an exact quotation from the English sermon, the wording ensuring that it derives from the vernacular sermon and not from its Latin source.[2] Other notes add similar summaries.[3] Here then are Wyclif and the Lollard sermons brought together by a single preacher. Also in these same notes are references to the *Rosarium*: the preacher notes 'seke in Rosarie' for material concerning prayer and, for the exposition of the miracle of the feeding of the four thousand, 'seke in Rosarie of þes loues'.[4] The references are sensible ones: if the entries for *oracio* and *panis* are consulted, plenty of relevant material is provided for the preacher. The second part of the manuscript, despite its different format and scribe, clearly belongs with the first in interest even if not in origin. Amongst the Latin texts, found after the English tracts already mentioned, are Wyclif's *De Eucharistia Confessio*[5] and also passages taken straight from the *Rosarium*: the passages are from the entries on *possessio, mendicacio, edificacio, elemosina, predicacio,* and *ymagines*.[6] The end of this last shows erasure of two letters following *hoc*: the first was clearly *d*, the second is completely illegible. Comparison with the *Rosarium* reveals the reason for the erasure: the letters were *d.e.*, the authority 'Doctor Euangelicus' concluding a citation from the *De Mandatis*.[7]

Here then, in a single volume, are brought together the *Rosarium*, quotation from Wyclif outside the *Rosarium*, and the standard Lollard sermon-cycle, in a handbook clearly the work of a Lollard preacher. The use of the *Rosarium* has plainly been appreciated: it can provide the preacher with material for his sermons, and it can also furnish him with authorities designed to support certain Wycliffite standpoints.

---

[1] The rest of the note, not printed here, contains a brief summary of Arnold, i. 4/17–6/32.   [2] *Sermones*, i. 228/34 ff.

[3] The notes for sermons for 4 and 6 Trinity (ff. 4–4ᵛ) bear a general resemblance to the sermons in Arnold, i. 9–12, 14–17; not all the notes are derived from this single source.   [4] f. 2 for 4 Easter and f. 4ᵛ for 7 Trinity.

[5] Loserth's revision of Shirley's *Catalogue* no. 21; it was printed by S. Harrison Thomson, 'John Wyclif's "Lost" *De Fide Sacramentorum*', *J.T.S.* xxxiii (1932), pp. 361–5.

[6] The headings of the *Rosarium* are not retained; thus the passage from the *possessio* entry is headed here (ff. 58–60) 'Contra temporalia clericorum', the *mendicacio* entry (ff. 60ᵛ–62ᵛ) 'Contra mendicacionem fratrum', the *edificacio* entry (ff. 62ᵛ–64ᵛ) 'Contra edificaciones fratrum et aliorum', the *elemosina* entry (ff. 64ᵛ–65) 'Nota quod homines non deberent elemosinas dare fratribus', the *predicacio* entry (ff. 65ᵛ–66) 'Contra mendicacionem fratrum propter predicacionem verbi Dei', and the *ymagines* entry (ff. 68ᵛ–70) 'Contra modernam adoracionem ymaginum'.   [7] *De Mandatis*, pp. 157/19–158/17.

Amongst the vernacular Lollard manuscripts are a number of collections of biblical and patristic texts; some of these can be shown to derive from the compilations here discussed. For proof of derivation obviously reference such as that in the manuscript described above is needed; but if a sequence of authorities for a topic is cited, without ascription but in the same order as in the *Floretum* or *Rosarium*, it seems reasonable to assume a connection. Obviously, this rules out the more intelligent Lollard who used the compilations with greater skill, selecting references from different places and altering the order of citation; but only on this criterion does it seem possible to eliminate the possibility of coincidental agreement. A number of vernacular texts can be shown to fulfil this requirement, and it is likely that more will be found. Thus the text known as 'Of Antecristis songe in chirche', extant in MS. Trinity College Dublin C. 5. 6 (ff. 124–6) and as part of a longer text in MSS. Trinity College Dublin C. 3. 12 and Corpus Christi College Cambridge 296, derives its lengthy patristic citations from the *Floretum* entry for *cantus*.[1] A text headed 'Antecrist', preserved in MSS. Harley 272 (f. 155^v) and Norwich Castle Museum 158. 926 4g. 3 (ff. 119^v–120^v), derives from the first section of that entry in the *Rosarium*. The authorities quoted in 'Of byndynge and assoillynge' in MS. Cambridge University Library Ii. 6. 55 (ff. 35^v–41^v) derive from the entry on *absolucio* in the *Rosarium*. Similarly, some texts in MS. Bodley Eng. th. f. 39 rely on the *Floretum*, drawing from the sections on *ymagines*, *miracula*, *antichristus*, *peregrinacio*, and *clericus*. In the first of these a quotation from Wyclif's *De Mandatis* is included, here referred to in the margin as 'Oxonie: libro de mandatis' and the author described in the text as 'a wrshipful doctour'.[2] More perspicacious use of the *Floretum–Rosarium* is, as has been said, difficult to prove, but it is to be suspected in the case of *The Lanterne of Li3t*.[3]

That other compilations, similar to those described here, circulated amongst Wycliffites seems highly likely; certainly it is to be suspected that some sort of biblical index, its selection showing a Wycliffite slant,

---

[1] The longer text is printed in F. D. Matthew, *The English Works of Wyclif hitherto unprinted* (E.E.T.S. 74, 1880), pp. 188–96.

[2] The manuscript was edited by E. P. Wilson (Oxford B.Litt. thesis, 1968), though without realization of the sources mentioned here; the passages reliant upon the *Floretum* are ff. 7–8, 9–9^v, 11^v–12^v, 13–14^v, and 48–48^v. It should be noted that the text on ff. 37–8 'þe Ei3te Condicions of Mawmetries þat men vsen aboute Ymagis' is also found in MS. Trinity College Cambridge B. 14. 50, ff. 34–5, the manuscript discussed above.

[3] It is easy to divide the text into sections with headings such as those used for the entries in the *Floretum–Rosarium*. Of the large number of patristic quotations some can be found in the relevant sections of the compilations, but it is more difficult to find a sequence that fulfils the criterion above.

circulated amongst Lollards such as Walter Brut, whose erudition has aroused considerable surprise amongst modern commentators.[1] Quite apart from the help of such compilations to the preacher or to the suspect on trial, it is likely that they were used in the Lollard 'schools' of which the episcopal records give clear evidence. The continuance of these schools through the fifteenth century is shown by the material for 1428–31 from the Norwich diocese preserved in Bishop Alnwick's casebook, now Westminster Cathedral MS. B. 2. 8, that for the Coventry area of 1511 and that for the Canterbury diocese in the same year;[2] all contain similar references to schools in which Lollard doctrines were taught. The importance attached to these schools is shown by one heretic in 1485, who held that it was necessary for a man 'ad exercendum scolas per vnum annum antequam cognoscat rectam fidem'.[3] The vocabulary of the *Floretum* and *Rosarium* often presupposes a group of 'familiares', cognizant of the nuances implied: the 'poor priests' preaching to the 'fidei domestici', condemning the 'religiones privatae' as 'ungrounded' in scripture. It is significant that a passage from Wyclif is introduced in the *Floretum* as the observation of 'quidam fidelis', another as from 'quidam fidelis euangelicus'.[4] Here is used for Wyclif himself the terminology used in the standard Lollard sermon-cycle for the Lollards: there the introduction of a remark with the words 'true men say' or 'true priests think' is regularly an indication that a Lollard belief follows.[5] The combination of evidence, from within the *Floretum–Rosarium* and its translation, and from the notes in MS. Trinity College Cambridge B. 14. 50, is, I think, overwhelming: here we have a handbook, drawn up by university followers of Wyclif for

---

[1] *Registrum Johannis Trefnant* (Hereford), ed. W. W. Capes (Canterbury and York Society, 1916), pp. 278–365; for comments McFarlane, *Wycliffe*, pp. 135–8.

[2] The Coventry cases are recorded in Lichfield Record Office B/C/13; an account of the manuscript is given by J. Fines, 'Heresy Trials in the Diocese of Coventry and Lichfield, 1511–12', *Journal of Ecclesiastical History*, xiv (1963), pp. 160–74. The Canterbury material is in the Warham register (Lambeth), ff. 159–75ᵛ.

[3] Hales register (Lichfield), f. 166ᵛ; the heretic came from Coventry.

[4] MS. Harley 401, ff. 26ᵛ and 29: under *antichristus* a reference apparently to *De Christo et suo Adversario Antichristo* (*Polemical Works*), ii. 680/10 ff., and *archidiaconi* a quotation from *De Mandatis*, pp. 382/13–384/2.

[5] The origin of the term is probably 2 Cor. vi. 8 'ut seductores et veraces', as would appear from the sermon on this text, Arnold, ii. 271/15 ff. 'for Goddis servauntis shulen have a name of þe world þat þei disseyven men, and ȝit þei shulen holde treuly þe sentence of Goddis lawe'. This passage also accounts for Pecock's observation that the Lollards call each other *knowun men* (*The Repressor of over much blaming of the Clergy*, ed. C. Babington (Rolls Series, 1860), i. 53), since the following phrase 'sicut qui ignoti, et cogniti' is explained 'as þei weren not knowun of men, but as aungels þat camen fro hevene'.

Lollards, relying upon the Latin writings of the 'Doctor Euangelicus' but also upon the jargon of the sect, designed for, and used by, sympathizers outside the Latin and university milieu in which the ideas originated.

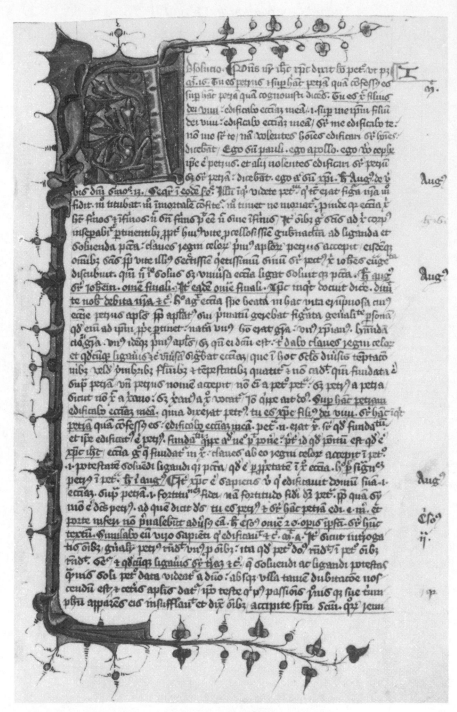

London, British Library MS Harley 401, f. 7^r.
Opening of the *Floretum* text.

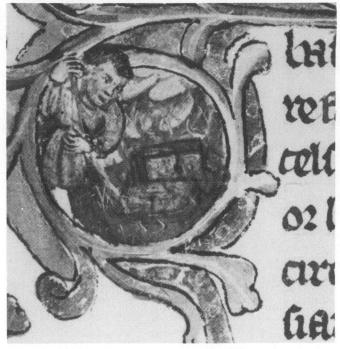

Merton College
Oxford MS 319,
f. 41^r.

Roundel from
an initial in a
copy of Netter's
Doctrinale book
V, chapter 17,
showing the
burning of books
(presumably
Wycliffite books).

3

A LOLLARD COMPILATION IN ENGLAND
AND BOHEMIA

IN a recent paper in this journal an analysis was made of a compilation existing in eighteen manuscripts dating from the end of the fourteenth and the fifteenth centuries;[1] the aim of the paper was to demonstrate the Wycliffite slant of the compilation and to suggest that this compilation was one of the channels through which the ideas of Wyclif passed from their university origins to the parish clergy and the ordinary Lollard. Consideration was deliberately limited to manuscripts of English origin. The purpose of this note is to add some information on more English manuscripts, and to give a brief account of the fortunes of the compilation in Hussite Bohemia.

To the list of English manuscripts given in the original paper can now

[1] 'A Lollard Compilation and the Dissemination of Wycliffite Thought', *J.T.S.* N.S. xxiii (1972), pp. 65–81. See above pp. 13-29.

be added five more, two of the *Floretum*, two of the *Rosarium*, and one containing a mixed text.[1] The most important aspect of this is that the *Floretum*, which by its greater length and far more numerous quotations from Wyclif is of greater significance for the spread of the heresiarch's thought, can now be shown to have been more widely known. The two manuscripts are Leicester Wyggeston Hospital 10 D 34/16, a straight-forward copy of the *Floretum* without the preface, and Salisbury Cathedral library 36, a text complete with index and preface. Both have minor divergences from the text presented by MS. Harley 401, the most interesting being the omission of the reference to the Gloucester parliament in 1378 found under *statuta*; neither have the final rubric of Harley 401 giving the date 1396. The Salisbury copy was given to the library by Thomas Cyrcetur, a canon of the cathedral from 1431 until his death in 1453 and a notable benefactor of the library.[2] It is apparently in his hand that an inscription has been added on f. 342[v] at the end of the text 'Nomen auctoris M. Johannes Wympol cuius anime propicietur dominus'.[3] The copy seems originally to have been intended for, or possibly even belonged to, Lincoln College Oxford, since an inscription recording this ownership is partially erased and then completed by the record of Cyrcetur's gift to Salisbury.[4] A further copy of the *Floretum* is known to have belonged to another Oxford college: in three medieval lists of the books in the library of All Souls' reference is found to a manuscript with a constant second folio catchword, described once as *Rosarium theologie*, once as *Floretum theologie* and once as *Flores*

---

[1] For references to the Leicester, Salisbury, and two Shrewsbury manuscripts, and for descriptions of the last two, I am indebted to the great kindness of Dr. Neil Ker.

[2] For his life see A. B. Emden, *A Biographical Register of the University of Oxford to A.D. 1500* (Oxford, 1957–9), i. 531–2; see also E. Maunde Thompson, *Catalogue of the Library of the Cathedral Church of Salisbury* (London, 1880), p. 9, and N. R. Ker, 'Salisbury Cathedral Manuscripts and Patrick Young's Catalogue,' *Wiltshire Archaeological and Natural History Magazine*, liii (1949), p. 171.

[3] In default of supporting authority, this ascription cannot be taken too seriously; Emden does not record this name as that of a *magister* at either Oxford or Cambridge.

[4] The gift by Cyrcetur is recorded on the third initial flyleaf recto, above which is still legible 'Liber [   ] lincoln oxon'; on the verso is the Salisbury *ex libris* inscription. The same re-direction appears in Salisbury Cathedral MS. 81, a Bible also donated by Cyrcetur. The surviving medieval catalogues of Lincoln College date from 1474 and 1476, and hence Salisbury 36 does not appear in them (see R. Weiss, 'The Earliest Catalogues of the Library of Lincoln College', *The Bodleian Quarterly Record*, viii (1937), pp. 343–59). In view of the interest of Richard Flemyng, founder of Lincoln, in questions of heresy (see Emden, *Oxford*, ii. 697–9), it is ironic that this compilation should apparently have been intended for its library.

theologie.[1] Whilst the *Floretum* is elsewhere described as the *Rosarium*, the latter is not elsewhere called without qualification the *Floretum*; Dr. Ker's suggestion that the text was the longer work seems therefore most reasonable. The two further copies of the *Rosarium* are Jesus College Cambridge MS. 73[2] and Shrewsbury School MS. X.[3] Both are basically straightforward copies of the text, though each has a few additions suggesting that their scribes had access to copies of the *Floretum* as well as using the *Rosarium* exemplar. The Jesus College manuscript has four extra entries not normally found in the text, each inserted not in the correct alphabetical place but at the end of the block of entries for the relevant initial; the third, in the entry for *sequi Christum*, includes the usual *Floretum* reference to Wyclif's *De Mandatis*.[4] The Shrewsbury copy is rather more divergent from the usual pattern. In the first place, three sections are missing, material from *fama* to *fides* probably because of a defect in the scribe's exemplar, material from *humilitas* to *inuidia* and from *mandata* to *miraculum* because of a loss of leaves from this manuscript, leaving the entries at either end incomplete. Secondly, some forty-four extra titles have been added, in blocks at the end of the initial letter in question; these do not overlap entirely with the extra entries in the Jesus College manuscript, nor do they correspond with the additional material noted in Trinity College Cambridge MS. O.7.30.[5] Quite a large proportion of these extra entries are very short, providing only biblical references for the matter in question, but a few, such as those for *fidelitas* and *pax*, derive partly from the *Floretum*.

The fifth manuscript is Shrewsbury School MS. XXIII, a confusing manuscript which contains a muddled blend of the *Floretum* and *Rosarium*.[6] The order of the items is often unalphabetical, but this cannot always be corrected by the supposition of displaced or misbound leaves or quires; some sections of the text, whether *Rosarium* or *Floretum*, are missing, apparently by the deliberate act of the scribe since the gaps do not correspond to the ends of leaves. Basically, re-arranging the items into alphabetical order and omitting those sections that belong to neither *Floretum* nor *Rosarium*, the sections taken

[1] See N. R. Ker, 'Records of All Souls College Library 1437–1600', *Oxford Bibliographical Society* 1971, pp. 6, 38, 52, 129.

[2] M. R. James, *A Descriptive Catalogue of the Manuscripts in the Library of Jesus College Cambridge* (Cambridge, 1895), pp. 110–11.

[3] The only description so far published is that by S. Leighton, 'The Early Manuscripts belonging to Shrewsbury School', *Transactions of the Shropshire Archaeological and Natural History Society*, 2nd Series, ix (1897), p. 296.

[4] *De Mandatis*, pp. 269/25–270/10; all references to Wyclif's Latin works are to the editions of the Wyclif Society (1883–1921) unless otherwise stated.

[5] *J.T.S.* N.S. xxiii (1972), p. 70. See above p. 18.

[6] Described briefly in the article cited above (n. 3), p. 299.

from the former are from *absolutio–concepcio*, *debita–fraus*, *maceracio–medicina*, *misericordia–preceptum*, and those from the latter are *fures–lex*, *sapiencia–zelus*. In addition, two blocks of extra entries were inserted (ff. 43–44ᵛ, 138ᵛ–141ᵛ), at apparently arbitrary places and out of alphabetical order. Some of these overlap with entries already present in the text, as *epiphania*, *scandalum*, or *papa*, others provide new titles, such as *emulacio* or *homicidium*. It does not appear that these extra entries have anything to do with the *Floretum* text as that is known from other manuscripts, nor are any references to Wyclif found. The general appearance of the manuscript would suggest that its scribes regarded it as a commonplace book, to which sporadic additions were made.

Mention must be made of one further English manuscript, Lincoln Cathedral MS. 241.[1] This again is not a straight text of either compilation. It begins as the *Floretum* without the preface, but then contains an eclectic and rearranged selection of entries with additions peculiar to itself. Even within the *tituli* that are in correct *Floretum* position discrepancies from the usual text appear, though the Wycliffite slant of the entries remains evident. It would appear that the manuscript represents an independent reduction of the *Floretum*, but one which bears witness to the sympathetic interest that the text excited.

The additional manuscripts of the *Floretum* and *Rosarium* in England support the view that these compilations were influential in the spread of Wycliffite thought. The area, however, in which Wyclif's ideas were more widely effective was, of course, Bohemia. With the vexed question of the degree of Hus's dependence upon Wyclif we are not here concerned;[2] anyone, however, who looks at the manuscripts of Wyclif's writings preserved in the libraries at Prague and Vienna cannot doubt the popularity of the English reformer's writings in Bohemia in the period after 1390. Whilst this popularity has long been acknowledged, less work has been done on the transmission of English Lollard texts to Bohemia, texts dependent upon Wyclif's ideas but not written by the

---

[1] R. M. Woolley, *Catalogue of the Manuscripts of Lincoln Cathedral Chapter Library* (Oxford, 1927), p. 172. Unlike the Shrewsbury MS. XXIII, this was not a private commonplace book, since correction marks placed frequently on the recto of folios point to scriptorium supervision; second and third hands seem, however, to have taken advantage of gaps left by the original scribe to add material. The selection must have been made from the *Floretum* rather than the *Rosarium* since titles appear that are not found in the latter; all resemblance to either compilation ends on f. 137, after which a further set of similar titles is found.

[2] For a recent view of this question, with references to earlier discussions, see F. Šmahel, ' "Doctor evangelicus super omnes evangelistas": Wyclif's Fortune in Hussite Bohemia', *Bulletin of the Institute of Historical Research*, xliii (1970), pp. 16–34.

master himself. Discussion of most of these must be reserved for another occasion; but it would emerge that the compilation at present under review was perhaps the most widely spread Lollard text that emigrated to Bohemia. The position as it is known at present shows the following manuscripts:[1]

(a) *Floretum*: Prague University V.B.2 (819), VIII.B.5 (1441), VIII.B.18 (1454), IX.D.6 (1744); Prague Metropolitan Chapter C.32 (451), C.37/4 (461), D. 92/2 (659); Brno University Mk 35.

(b) 'Modified' version: Prague University IV.E.14 (694), XIII.F.27 (2365); Klosterneuburg 369.

(c) *Rosarium*: Prague University IV.G.19 (751), V.H.17 (994), X.H.4 (1982), XII.G.17 (2228); Prague Metropolitan Chapter D.16 (582), D.92/1 (658), D.105 (674), D. 115 (685); Prague National Museum X.D.11; Brno University Mk 28; Pommersfelden 186; Vienna Nationalbibliothek 4492.

(d) Shortened *Rosarium*: Prague Metropolitan Chapter D.114 (684).

[The identification of the compilations in Prague University I.C.41 (133) and in Wrocław University 1302 with the *Rosarium* is incorrect.][2]

In the two types that descend straight from English antecedents, (a) and (c), there is evidence to suggest that in each case the surviving copies descend from a single exemplar. In all the eight copies of the *Floretum* the entries for *gratitudo* and *planete* are missing: in many these omissions are noted by the scribes, who have observed that the numbering of the *tituli* is defective at these points; in some the scribes were aware of the titles of the missing entries.[3] None of the surviving copies of

---

[1] Useful descriptions of the various Czech manuscripts are given in J. Truhlář, *Catalogus Codicum Manu Scriptorum Latinorum . . . in Bibliotheca Publica atque Universitatis Pragensis* (Prague, 1905–6); A. Podlaha, *Soupis rukopisů knihovny Metropolitní Kapitoly Pražské* (Prague, 1910–22); F. M. Bartoš, *Soupis rukopisů Národního Musea v Praze* (Prague, 1926–7); V. Dokoupil, *Soupis rukopisů Mikulovské Dietrichsteinské knihovny, Soupisy rukopisných fondů Universitní knihovny v Brně*, ii (Prague, 1958).

[2] The catalogue title of the first suggests that it is an incomplete text of the *Rosarium* running from *abusio* to *locucio*; despite the existence of two such *tituli* in the present compilations, this is merely coincidental. F. Stegmüller, *Repertorium Biblicum Medii Aevi* (Madrid, 1940–61), vi, no. 10080, lists the second, but the connection if any is very remote. A further manuscript in the Vienna collection, 4488, ff. 11–62, should be mentioned; it begins in the same way as the *Floretum* and ends with *zelum* like the *Rosarium*. Though related to the present compilations, it has been drastically rewritten in a Hussite milieu, using writings of Wyclif not cited in the English version and quoting Czech authors such as Páleč (under *ecclesia*). Since there can be no question of any direct descent from English exemplars, the manuscript is not included in the following discussion.

[3] For instance the rubric in Prague University IX.D.6 'titulus 166 Gratitudo;

the *Floretum* in England lacks either of these entries, but MS. Bodley 448 of the 'Intermediate' version (itself not directly represented in Bohemia) has no entry for *gratitudo*; it is thus possible that this defect derives from an English exemplar. A further peculiarity that may be insular in origin is a note found in all the Bohemian *Floretum* manuscripts at the end of their entry for *papa*: they have only the first paragraph of that entry as found in Harley 401, followed by the instruction 'Nota duas litteras (referring to the indexing subdivisions) infime libri'; none of the manuscripts has the promised material at the end. Salisbury Cathedral MS. 36, however, has the same first paragraph in the usual place, but the second and third at the end of the manuscript (f. 341). None of the Bohemian texts has the reference to the parliament of Gloucester under *statuta*, peculiar to Harley 401. Close collation of the texts would obviously bring out both shared continental features, and idiosyncratic divergences between the manuscripts. One addition certainly of Bohemian origin is a final paragraph added to the entry for *Eucharistia* concerning the necessity for the administration of the sacrament in both kinds to laymen, a paragraph found in all the manuscripts except Prague Metropolitan Chapter C.37/4. No authorities are given for the material, but the source is clearly the utraquist views of the Hussites, an issue that hardly entered English Lollardy. The evidence for the descent of all copies of the *Rosarium* from a single English exemplar is slighter: best indication of this is a rearrangement of the normal alphabetical English sequence *consuetudo–contemplacio–contencio* to *contencio–consuetudo–contemplacio* in all Bohemian manuscripts (except Pommersfelden, which omits the last named.) This irregularity is found in only two English manuscripts, Bodley 31 and Worcester Cathedral Q.68, but the coincidence of this one irregularity, and the absence of other irregularities not shared by all manuscripts of the *Rosarium*, suggests descent from a single English exemplar related to these two.[1] Although Brno University Mk 28 has been placed with the ordinary *Rosarium*, since its text predominantly belongs there, it shares a few characteristics with group (*b*) and will be discussed with those manuscripts.

Of the two types of text not found in England, the last may quickly be dismissed. That the text is basically that of the *Rosarium* may be seen by the presence of Wyclif quotations under *fides*, *Maria*, and

talis titulus deest et debet stare ante titulum grex'; a similar note appears in Prague Metropolitan Chapter D.92/2.

[1] All manuscripts of the *Rosarium* in Bohemia and England share the unalphabetical arrangement *sapiencia–sanguis* (save Trinity College Cambridge O.7.30), and *liberalitas–lepra* (save Bodley 626 and Harley 4884.)

martyr which are distinctive of that version.[1] On the other hand, as well as the omission of a number of the usual *Rosarium* entries, the Wyclif quotations usually found under *avaricia, lucerna, sabbati, temptacio, uox,* and *ymago* are lacking although the *tituli* themselves are present. The gaps in the entries do not correspond to omissions in any of the known English manuscripts; it is, therefore, not provable that this shortened version originated outside Bohemia.

More interesting is the version that I have described as 'modified'. From the information provided by the catalogues these manuscripts appear to have the type of text presented in England by Bodley 448, since the *incipit* and *explicit* agree; investigation of the manuscripts themselves shows this to be misleading, though the nearest relation to the version known in England remains the 'Intermediate' type. The three manuscripts differ in some details, but share sufficient characteristics to be regarded as a group. A handful of about eight entries present in Bodley 448 are omitted in all three Bohemian texts; conversely, three new entries appear in the latter, for *meditacio, questio,* and *renunciacio*. More important is the frequent and drastic reduction: the shortening of the entry for *mandata* from the five folios in Bodley 448 to a single column in these three manuscripts is the most dramatic instance, but the scale is not untypical. Consequent upon this is the elimination of many of the Wyclif quotations found in Bodley 448. There are few Wyclif quotations that are peculiar to the 'Intermediate' version, but the three Bohemian manuscripts of the 'Modified' group share with Bodley 448 a handful of quotations not found in any manuscripts of the *Floretum* though present in the *Rosarium*.[2] The Bohemian manuscripts, however, have some additional *Rosarium* quotations not present in Bodley 448.[3] It would seem reasonable to regard the 'Modified' text as a shortened version of the 'Intermediate' type, conflated with the *Rosarium,* though whether this alteration was carried out in England or Bohemia remains unclear. Brno Mk 28 is basically a manuscript of the ordinary *Rosarium,* but from *s* onwards has been partially conflated with a text of this group so that items, for instance *secte* and *seculi* with their

---

[1] See *J.T.S.* N.S. xxiii (1972), p. 69. See above p. 17.

[2] For instance the references to *De Civili Dominio* i. 276/28 ff. under *excommunicacio* and to the *Trialogus* (ed. G. V. Lechler, Oxford, 1869), p. 135/11–18 under *fides*. These Bohemian manuscripts have a number of drastic rearrangements of entries, notably in the letters *f, i, l,* and *s*; they share with Bodley 448 the unalphabetical sequence *gaudium–galline*. They also lack, with Bodley 448, the *Floretum* Wyclif quotations under *adoracio, iuramentum, ius, mors, obediendia,* and *rex*.

[3] Neither the *Floretum* nor Bodley 448 have the references to *Sermones* ii. 123/25 ff. under *fides* and to *Sermones* ii. 18/5 ff. under *prelacia* found in all *Rosarium* manuscripts and also in this group.

Wyclif quotations, not found in the *Rosarium*, appear here. It should be noted that Prague University XIII.F.27, Klosterneuburg 369, and Brno Mk 28 have the usual *Floretum* preface added at the end.

The most that can be proved about these Bohemian texts is that a single exemplar of both the *Floretum* and the *Rosarium* must have been taken from England, and that in all probability an exemplar of the 'Intermediate' version similar but not identical to that in Bodley 448 or a copy of the 'Modified' version came from the same source. The most interesting question is, of course, the date at which these Lollard compilations were brought to Bohemia. Only one manuscript of the *Floretum* is precisely dated: Prague University V.B.2 in 1413. Rather more information is found in manuscripts of the *Rosarium*: two are dated 1417, three others 1418, 1419, and 1420 respectively;[1] the last three are the dates when the scribes finished work. Of the 'Modified' version two are dated: Prague University XIII.F.27 in 1419 and Klosterneuburg 369 much later in 1443. Though most of this evidence merely shows the dissemination of the compilation and not its entry into Bohemia, the colophons to two of the *Rosarium* manuscripts offer more information. Prague University IV.G.19 ends 'Explicit liber Rosarii sive Minoris Floreti pronuncciatus per reverendum Magistrum Mathiam licenciatum in collegio Caroli in lectuario theologorum a.d. 1417', of which Prague Metropolitan Chapter D.16 offers a fuller version 'Explicit rozarium aut parvus floretus sacre theologye pronunciatus per reuerendum licenciatum Mathiam in colegio Karuly et in lectuario theologorum et finitus in vigilia Margarethe et penultima die mensis Julii et hoc sub anno domini 1417 hijs licenciatus in artibus Et cetera Jacobi de Skroward' (the final name is apparently that of the scribe). Support for these rubrics is given by the old catalogue of Prague University Library where V.H. 17 was ascribed 'Magistro Matthiae'.[2] These rubrics have been understood by some scholars to imply that the author of the *Rosarium* was one Mathias.[3] But two objections to this

[1] The two dated 1417 are discussed below; the others are Prague National Museum X.D.11, Brno Mk 28, and Prague University X.H.4 respectively. These dates fit in well with the manuscripts of Wyclif's own writings known in Bohemia, in so far as these are dated. Though some of Wyclif's ideas were known in Prague well before 1400 (see particularly E. Stein, 'Mistr Mikuláš Biceps', *Věstník královské České společnosti nauk Třída Filosoficko–Historicko–Jazykozpytná Ročník 1928* (1929), p. 43), the dissemination of his work seems to be concentrated in the period 1400 to 1420.

[2] See the catalogue (above, p. 35 n. 1), no. 994 and J. Truhlář, 'Dva staré katalogy knih kolleji Pražských,' *Věstník České Akademie*, xiii (1904), pp. 98–105.

[3] See F. M. Bartoš, 'Ze studií husitských', *Časopis Matice Moravské*, lxi (1937), pp. 215–17, and the description of Brno University Mk 28 (above, p. 35 n. 1).

arise: first, that the text originated in England and hence can have no fundamental connection with the Charles University in Prague; secondly, that *pronunciatus* implies not the act of composition but the delivery or publication of a text. Mathias, then, was not the author of the *Rosarium* but the man who, in accordance with the well-attested practice in Prague before and during the Hussite period, dictated the text to an assembled group of scribes, many of whom were more probably scholars than professionals.[1] Humble though this task may seem, Master Mathias's part in the history of the compilation may have been important. His name is connected with three other manuscripts, where the similarity in the form of the rubric suggests that the same man was involved. The least informative of these is Prague University Library VIII.B.8, where a copy of Grosseteste's *Dicta* is concluded 'per Mathiam baccalaur' in collegio Karoli reportatum', the date given being 1414.[2] More interesting is Brno University Mk 28, where the scribe of the *Rosarium* dated his work 1419; the second item in the manuscript is the Lollard Apocalypse commentary, usually known from its opening words as *Opus Arduum*, whose final colophon reads 'Pronuncciatum Prage per Mathiam Baccalarium dictum Engliss. Reportatum vero per Martinum de Verona sub anno domini 1415, finitum III feria post festum Egidii'.[3] The colophons of these two manuscripts and of the *Rosarium* copies give a comprehensible sequence: in 1414 and in 1415 Mathias was described as *baccalarius*, by 1417 he was a master; all three works with which his name is associated are texts of Lollard origin or of particular interest to the Lollards. With the third manuscript the evidence is less satisfactory since the colophon no longer remains: an old librarian stated that Prague University Library VIII.F.16 (1570) contained 'Matthiae Engliss de Hnaticz Summulae collectae de libris

[1] The provisions of 1367, repeated in 1390, recorded in *Monumenta Historica Universitatis Carolo-Ferdinandeae Pragensis* (Prague, 1830–2), i. 13–14, 40–2, make it clear that this practice was well established before Hus. For its continuation in the Hussite period see F. Šmahel, 'Le mouvement des étudiants à Prague dans les années 1408–1412', *Historica*, xiv (1967), p. 60.

[2] Though Grosseteste's writings were, of course, known in Bohemia before 1400, it is clear from the number of manuscripts in Prague dating from the first half of the fifteenth century (see S. Harrison Thomson, *The Writings of Robert Grosseteste* (Cambridge, 1940), pp. 292–3) that the interest of Wyclif and Hus gave considerable impetus to the study of the earlier writer.

[3] Discussion of this important text must be deferred to another occasion. Brief material is available in F. Bartoš, 'Lollardský a husitský výklad Apokalypsy', *Reformační sborník*, vi (1937), pp. 112–14; A. Molnar, 'Apocalypse xii dans l'interprétation hussite', *Revue d'histoire et de philosophie religieuses*, xlv (1965), pp. 212–31; B. Ryba, 'Strahovské Zjevenie, Český husitský výklad na Apokalypsu . . .', *Strahovská knihovna*, i (1966), pp. 7–29.

Johannis Wiclif et Johannis Thartis'.[1] The manuscript is now defective, but contains four texts of philosophical material to which this description could well apply.

Provided, however, that the Mathias of the *Rosarium* manuscripts can be identified with the Mathias Engliš of the Brno *Opus Arduum*, it is possible to discover more of the possible history of the compilation in Bohemia. Mathias Engliš has been traced in a number of Hussite missions from 1424 to 1440, and it has been suggested that he was the representative of the Hussite church sent to Constantinople to negotiate with the Eastern church in 1451.[2] Under his original name, Mathias de Hnátnice, he is recorded as being admitted a bachelor at the Caroline university in Prague in 1412.[3] Most interesting, however, for the present question is the origin of his by-name Engliš. He was certainly not like Peter Payne (known in Bohemia as Peter Engliš) of English origin, since he came from Hnátnice, a small village in eastern Bohemia. Nor, so far as can be ascertained at present, can his name be found in any English records.[4] But he was associated with Nicolas Faulfiš, the Czech scholar who, with George of Knychnicz, made copies in England of Wyclif's *De Ecclesia*, *De Dominio Divino*, and *De Veritate Sacre Scripture*, which they took back to Bohemia together with the testimonial letters in favour of Wyclif, supposedly provided by the university of Oxford, and a chip of stone from Wyclif's tomb.[5] The association between Faulfiš and Mathias de Hnátnice can be traced to 1409, when Mathias lent Faulfiš some money; this loan he attempted to retrieve from Faulfiš's family after the latter's death in 1411.[6] Unfortunately, the legal records reveal nothing of the reasons for the acquaintance of the two men, but it is interesting that along with Mathias in the proceedings appear the names of two prominent Hussites, Simon of Tišnov and John of Jesenice. The most reasonable interpretation of the by-name Engliš would seem to suggest that either Mathias had himself visited England, or that he was particularly interested in manuscripts from that source,

[1] See the catalogue (above, p. 35 n. 1), no. 1570.

[2] F. M. Bartoš, 'A Delegate of the Hussite Church to Constantinople in 1451–1452', *Byzantinoslavica*, xxiv (1963), pp. 287–92 and xxv (1964), pp. 69–74; this supersedes Bartoš's earlier notes 'Ze studií husitských', *Časopis Matice Moravské*, lxi (1937), pp. 215–17 and 'Husitský diplomat Matěj Engliš', *Jihočeský sborník historický*, xxi (1952), pp. 114–15.

[3] *Monumenta* (p. 139 n. 1), i. 419.

[4] I am grateful to Dr. Emden for confirming that the name does not appear in Oxford records.

[5] See Emden, *Oxford*, ii. 670–1; also F. M. Bartoš, 'Husův přítel z Českých Budějovic', *Jihočeský sborník historický*, xix (1950), pp. 43–4.

[6] See the records printed in *Archiv Český*, xxxvi (Prague, 1941), pp. 440–1 and *Archiv Český*, xxviii (Prague, 1912), p. 649.

perhaps obtaining them through Faulfiš. In either case, Mathias's associations with central figures in the Hussite movement suggest that the *Rosarium*, and with it the *Floretum* (given the frequent colophons indicating knowledge of the connection between the texts), must have circulated with some authority in the movement. This suggestion is supported by an enigmatic note in the same Brno Mk 28 copy of the *Rosarium*: at the end of the entry for *crux* the scribe seems to have realized that he was running out of paper, so he noted that he would add, instead of the full text, six entries not part of the original 'et est edicio (sic) M. Jo. Hus, quam materiam eciam, invenietis in Bethleem perietibus, insinuatam per Magistrum Johannem Hus ibidem procuratam'. *Bethleem* is, of course, the Bethlehem Chapel in Prague where Hus preached from 1402 until 1412. The six entries, for *creare*, *credere*, *remittere*, *obediencia*, *excommunicacio*, and *symonia*, follow the usual pattern of the *Floretum–Rosarium*, with biblical and patristic quotations;[1] it would, therefore, seem reasonable to accept the colophon's implication that they were inserted into a copy of the compilation. Whether the scribe was correct in asserting that they were the work of Hus is less important than the evidence that the compilation was known and studied within his circle.

The final stage in the history of the compilation belongs exclusively to the field of Hussite studies: whether it was used by Hus himself or by his followers, whether it extended its influence to the more extreme Taborite party, whether it was translated in whole or in part into Czech, are questions that cannot be answered here. But it is clear from the number of copies of the *Floretum–Rosarium* that are already known that both in England and in Bohemia the work was very widely disseminated. It is likely also that in both countries more manuscripts will be found, in libraries not properly catalogued as yet and also in more familiar places hidden under the vague terminology of 'compilation' or 'distinctiones'. Netter referred to the *author Floreti* as Wyclif's *discipulus*[1] and clearly appreciated the nature of the *Floretum* as a handbook of Wycliffite thought, and as a collection of authorities with which to support that viewpoint. The latter may appear the less interesting to a modern critic, but the frequent citation of just such authorities by texts as far apart as English Lollard collections in Bodleian MS. Laud Misc. 210 and Durham University MS. Cosin V.v.1 and the Latin tracts of

[1] *Doctrinale Fidei Catholicae* (Venice, 1757–9), ii, cols. 793, 834 and 837 (bk. v, caps. 136 and 145); parts of the entry for *confessio* are quoted. The editorial suggestion there that the author of the *Floretum* was Peter Payne is unacceptable, both from the date of the compilation and from the complete absence of Payne's name from Bohemian copies where, had there been any connection with him, it would certainly appear.

Hus, such as his *De Libris Hereticorum Legendis*, shows how useful this could be.[1] That such a compilation should exist and attain wide circulation in England and Bohemia is not surprising: it will be far more surprising should no further similar texts be discovered.

[1] *Magistri Iohannis Hus Opera Omnia* xxii, *Polemica*, ed. J. Eršil (Prague, 1966), pp. 21–37.

4

A NEGLECTED WYCLIFFITE TEXT

M odern accounts of the Wycliffite movement and of the beliefs of its adherents have been based for the most part upon records compiled by opponents. Most obviously hostile are the episcopal registers and documents, though these have the advantage of being relatively prolific and almost always dated and localised; inevitably, secular records about the movement become more ample as Lollardy was identified with sedition. The surviving chronicles, such as those of Knighton or Walsingham, were largely written by members of those orders that Wyclif castigated throughout his teaching. The picture constructed from these records has sometimes been filled out with details from overtly hostile and polemical texts such as Netter's *Doctrinale*. Given such sources, it is hardly surprising that the accounts appear incomplete, even at times incoherent and contradictory. Episcopal registers, as has been suggested elsewhere, present only fragmentary records of the views they condemned; polemical authors, and even chroniclers, often wrote with hindsight, an advantage to their own argument, but a disqualification to their usefulness as historical sources.[1] Particularly in the case of Lollardy, where increasing opposition from the ecclesiastical hierarchy was reinforced after about 1400 by suspicion of treason so amply confirmed in the Oldcastle revolt, late texts are peculiarly unreliable. McFarlane, in his posthumously published lectures, suggested that many aspects of the movement 'are irremediably hidden from us', unless 'new material is found of a kind and quantity so far unsuspected'.[2] One source of material that McFarlane knew but did not care to use provides a great deal of evidence: a large body of texts survives written by the Lollards themselves. Much of it is in English, but its primary historical insufficiency is that most of it is undated, unlocalised and anonymous. There is, however, one text, strangely ignored by all English historians

[1] See 'The Examination of Lollards', *Bulletin of the Institute of Historical Research*, xlvi (1973), 145–59, especially 151–2; 'The Debate on Bible Translation, Oxford 1401', *English Historical Review*, xc (1975), 1–18. See below 125–39 (especially 131–2) and 67–84.

[2] K. B. McFarlane, *Lancastrian Kings and Lollard Knights*, Oxford 1972, 141–2; the lectures as published date from 1966.

save one, that cannot be dismissed on these grounds:[3] it is in Latin, and is precisely dated at a peculiarly important period in the growth of the Lollard movement.

The text is a commentary on the Apocalypse, called from its opening words *Opus Arduum*, and its date is succinctly given in the final colophon to two MSS.: 'Explicit quoddam opus breue et debile super Apokalipsim Iohannis, inchoatum circa Natale Domini et, aliquando mense interposito, aliquando quindena nonnunquam ebdomada et multis diebus interruptis, completum feria quinta in ebdomada Pasce proximo sequentis anni domini $M^occclxxxx^o$ in carcere'.[4] This date is confirmed by references within the commentary, references not confined to these two MSS. but obviously original. At the beginning of his exposition of chapter v the author states that the world has aged by 1389 years since the birth of Christ, and the same date is given in chapter xiii in a discussion of the merits of the two warring popes; in chapter xx, however, the author writes that 'sumus in anno ab incarnacione $M^occc^oxc^o$'.[5] It would appear that between the writing of the commentary on chapter xiii and that on chapter xiv the author learnt of the death of Urban vi, since in the former chapter, and in material up to that point, the two popes mentioned are Clement vii and Urban vi, but in chapter xiv the writer discusses whether 'ex quo Vrbanus sextus iam mortuus est, in quo omnia misteria antichristi fuerunt impleta, numquid eciam mortuus sit antichristus?'[6] Urban died at Rome on 15 October 1389, but news of this might well not have reached a man in prison in England for several months. That the colophon's assertion of the author's imprisonment is correct is fully borne out by the text: in the prologue the writer asserts that he has been in prison for three years or more, whilst later in the exposition of chapter x he defiantly comments 'non est mihi verisimile quod vnquam ista et consimilia scripsissem contra antichristum et suos, nisi ea occasione qua se putabant michi excludere viam, scilicet me incarcerando ne vnquam agerem aliquid contra eos'.[7] The author states his native language to be English, mentions the earthquake in London in 1382 (during the

[3] No mention of the text here discussed is found in H. B. Workman, *John Wyclif*, Oxford 1926, K. B. McFarlane, *John Wycliffe and the Beginnings of English Nonconformity*, London 1952 or M. Lambert, *Medieval Heresy*, London 1977, 217–71. The text was studied by Mrs. M. Aston for her article 'Lollardy and the Reformation: Survival or Revival?', *History*, xlix (1964), 156–7; I am much indebted to Mrs. Aston for telling me that she did not intend to publish further on the text and for discussing this paper with me.

[4] All quotations from the *Opus Arduum*, unless otherwise stated, are from MS. Brno University Mk 28, here fol. 216; punctuation and capitalisation have been modernised, but the spelling of the MS. has not been normalised. I am grateful to the librarians of the various collections in which MSS. of the work have been preserved, and particularly to Dr. V. Dokoupil of Brno University Library.

[5] Fols. 150, 181, 201.

[6] Fol. 186; the question is part of a long comment on xiv.20.

[7] Fols. 127, 164^v; cf. also fols. 130^v and a similar claim on fol. 141: 'quamuis antichristi tortores nituntur claudere ora ewangelicorum eos incarcerando, tunc dant eis maximam oportunitatem studendi et scribendi contra eum, cuius oppositum credunt ipsi'.

Blackfriars' Council at which Wyclif's opinions were condemned), and repeatedly discusses the Flanders crusade of bishop Despenser.[8] From the views expressed, which I shall discuss below, it is plain that the author was an adherent of Wyclif. To clinch the matter, the writer often states that his own punishment is part of the persecution by ecclesiastics who defame the opinions of him and his like and revile them 'ut Lolardi'.[9] Henry Crumpe had used the appellation as a term of abuse in 1382; in the present text it retains its abusive nature, regarded with dislike by the sect itself as well as by its opponents.[10]

The reason for the neglect of this text by modern critics lies in the distribution of the MSS: all thirteen are found in continental libraries, mostly in the areas where Hussite thought prevailed, whilst none has so far been identified in England. The final colophon quoted above is found in two MSS., Brno Mk 28 and Prague University Library V.E.3; a third, Prague Metropolitan Chapter A.117 contains the opening of it, as far as 'mense interposito etc.'[11] The first of these continues to explain that the text was *pronunciatum* at Prague by Matthias Engliss, and is now *reportatum* by Martin of Verona in 1415; it is probably the earliest of the surviving MSS. Matthias Engliss is otherwise known as Matthias of Hnadnice, acquainted with Nicolas Faulfiš who came to England in 1407 to obtain copies of Wyclif's writings; Matthias is also found as the 'publisher' in Prague of the Lollard *Rosarium*.[12] Only one other MS. of the *Opus Arduum* is dated: this is Brno Mk 62, and the date given at the end, 1444, refers to the copying.[13] Paleographically the other MSS. belong to the fifteenth century, apart from that in Karlsruhe Badische Landesbibliothek 346 which is of the early sixteenth century.[14] The usual form of the commentary is a continuous text, in some cases preceded or followed by a

[8] Fols. 161^v, 174^v; fols. 155^v–156; the Flanders crusade fols. 132–3, 146, 154^v, 160^v, 178, 181, 188 etc.

[9] Fols. 136^v, 153, 157^v, 161^v, 179, 181^v; the significance of these passages will be discussed below.

[10] See M. Aston, 'Lollardy and Sedition, 1381–1431', *Past and Present*, xvii (1960), 36 n.1; for later use of the term by Wycliffites, where it is applied to Christ and his apostles see *Selections from English Wycliffite Writings*, Cambridge 1978, no. 17/151–2.

[11] For descriptions of these MSS., and of others mentioned below in the same collections, see V. Dokoupil, *Soupis rukopisů Mikulovské Dietrichsteinské knihovny, Soupisy rukopisných fondů Universitní knihovny v Brně*, ii, Prague 1958; J. Truhlář, *Catalogus Codicum Manu Scriptorum Latinorum...in Bibliotheca Publica atque Universitatis Pragensis*, Prague 1905–6; A. Podlaha, *Soupis rukopisů knihovny Metropolitní Kapitoly Pražské*, Prague 1910–22.

[12] See F. M. Bartoš, 'A Delegate of the Hussite Church to Constantinople in 1451–1452', *Byzantinoslavica*, xxiv (1963), 287–92 and xxv (1964), 69–74; also my paper 'A Lollard Compilation in England and Bohemia', *Journal of Theological Studies*, NS xxv (1974), 132–40. See above 34–42.

[13] For the rest of the colophon in this MS. see below, 56.

[14] *Die Handschriften der Badischen Landesbibliothek in Karlsruhe iv: Die Karlsruher Handschriften*, i, Wiesbaden 1970, no. 346; also H. Kaminsky et al., 'Master Nicholas of Dresden, The Old Color and the New', *Transactions of the American Philosophical Society*, NS lv (1965), 33.

transcription of the biblical book on which it is based: in this form it is found in the five MSS. so far mentioned and also in Prague Metropolitan Chapter A.163, B.48/1, B.48/2, B.82/2, Vienna 4526, Vienna 4925 and Prague University Library III.G.17, the last of which is seriously abbreviated. In one MS., Naples Bibl.Naz.VII.A.34, the biblical text forms the main item on each page, and extracts from the commentary are crammed into the margins and between the lines; such an arrangement is certainly a secondary one.[15] In most of these MSS. the other contents are Wycliffite or, more particularly, Hussite, but there seems to have been no attempt to alter the English text to suit Bohemian concerns: no reference is made to the Hussite preoccupation with utraquism, and no tampering to update the accounts of the papacy is found.[16] For the purposes of this paper I have used principally Brno Mk 28 and Prague University Library V.E.3, though I have checked in all the other MSS. any passages that could have bearing on date or origin. In default of a critical edition the relative value of the various MSS. remains unclear, but nothing in my study of the work leads me to doubt the sufficiency of these two.[17]

The text continued to be used on the Continent beyond its simple copying. A fragment of a Czech translation has been found in a binding in the Strahov library at Prague; several Hussite preachers and commentators drew on the text for exegesis, as Molnar has traced.[18] More interesting from a Wycliffite viewpoint is the fact that an abridged version of the *Opus Arduum* was printed in 1528 at Wittenberg with a preface by Luther.[19] Luther says that the MS. of the text came to him 'e Sarmaticis Liuonicisque regionibus' (sig.A.2), but it is not entirely clear how closely he had studied the work: his preface does not make clear the English origin of the text, though this is evident from his printed version, and the editorial dating unhappily selected an error, an error which

---

[15] See the catalogue by C. Cenci, *Manoscritti francescani della Biblioteca Nazionale di Napoli*, i, Florence 1971, no. 212; the text ends incomplete on fol. 90^v in chapter xiii.

[16] For instance in Brno Mk 62 the *Opus Arduum* is accompanied by Wyclif's *Dialogus, De Fundacione Sectarum, De Perfectione Statuum* and an extract from *De Ecclesia*; Karlsruhe 346 contains various works by Nicholas of Dresden. Compare the usual addition of a paragraph on utraquism to the distinctio *Eucharistia* in the *Floretum* in Hussite copies mentioned in my paper referred to above (n. 12), 36 .

[17] Save in the lack from both MSS. of any commentary to chapter vii. 9–17, an omission noted in the Prague University Library MS., fol. 66 margin. All of the MSS. except those in Brno are listed by F. Stegmuller, *Repertorium Biblicum Medii Aevi*, Madrid 1940–61, but divided under two entries, nos. 4870 and 5118; the reference under the former to Prague Metropolitan Chapter A.108 should be deleted. Stegmuller under 4870 also listed a MS. from sale catalogue number 7 (no date) of Jacques Rosenthal, Karlstrasse 10, Munich; from the details there under no. 1008 it is not clear that the text was the *Opus Arduum*.

[18] For the first see B. Ryba, 'Strahovské Zjevenie, Česky husitský výklad na Apokalypsu...', *Strahovská knihovna* i (1966), 7–29; for the second A. Molnar, 'Apocalypse xii dans l'interprétation hussite', *Revue d'histoire et de philosophie religieuses*, xlv (1965), 212–31.

[19] The title of the work in Luther's edition was *Commentarius in Apocalypsin ante Centum Annos editus*; for some comments see Mrs. Aston's paper (n. 3 above), 156–7, and Molnar, art. cit., 214–15.

could have been identified as such from matter only a page later as well as from conflicting evidence from other parts of the work.[20] The MS. used for this edition was similar to, though not identical with, the abbreviated Prague University Library MS. III.G.17; from both a number of specifically Wycliffite references had been removed, though both are still recognisably of that origin. Also from this branch of the stemma is the version in the Naples MS. It would appear that Luther's MS. derived from an earlier stage, since the expurgation is less far-reaching.[21] Luther's edition was known to John Bale; to Bale return must be made in discussing the possible authorship of the original work.

Before considering the historical value, and authorship, of the *Opus Arduum*, it is worth looking further at the nature and sources of the commentary. Like many before him, the Lollard author used the obscurities and enigmatic statements of the Apocalypse as convenient excuses for the discussion of contemporary questions. He protests that his main interest is with the literal sense of scripture, but his understanding of 'literal sense' is that of Lyra whom he quotes 'sensus literalis scripturarum...non est ille qui per uoces in mente significatur, sed qui per res significatas intelligitur'.[22] By such a method the door open in heaven of chapter iv.1 (fol. 145), for instance, is holy scripture by which men can come to a vision of the secrets of heaven; the seven angels of chapter xv.6 (fol. 187[v]) are 'vniuersi predicatores ewangelici contra antichristum et collegas', the seven plagues that they bear are 'omnes vindictas antichristo et suis inferendas', the temple from which they come 'id est de secreto in quo prius latitabant vacantes studio scripturarum et contemplacioni'. Inevitably the commentary cannot present a logically structured account of its author's opinions, since, despite many digressions, the dominant structure is that provided by the biblical narrative; because of this certain views recur, particularly those concerning antichrist, whilst others which the author may have considered equally important are only touched on. There are, however, a number of occasions when the reader suspects the intrusion of structural devices foreign to a strict commentary. Thus in chapter ii (fols. 132[v]–133), on the dubious excuse of verse 3, is given a set of authorities and then six numbered reasons why bishops should not take part in war; again, in the same chapter, following verse 17, appears a long digression (fols. 136–

[20] The English origin is evident from, for instance, fols. 59–59[v], 67[v]; on fol. 170 the marginal note selected the date 1357 from an error in the edition, and this is erroneously corrected at the end to 1338 (fol. 195[v]), but on fol. 170[v] the correct date 1390 appears (as also fol. 122[v] where the date appropriate to the beginning of the text, 1389, is given).

[21] For instance Luther preserves a comment on vernacular books with only minor alteration at xii.4 (Luther edition fol. 110[v]), completely omitted in the Naples MS. and partially omitted in Prague University III.G. 17; all, however, have identical omissions at ii.17, vi.4, x.4, xi.2; the text of all three is identical in the section omitted in the two MSS. primarily used here (above, n. 17) and plainly derives from a Lollard exemplar.

[22] See fol. 168, quoting Lyra on Judges ix; for Wyclif's allusion to this same definition see G. Benrath, *Wyclifs Bibelkommentar*, Berlin 1966, 304 n. 837.

137^v) condemning the friar's views on the Eucharist and on vernacular scriptures. In chapter xi, where the plagues of verse 6 are equated with the ten plagues of Egypt and these in turn are said to result from neglect of the ten commandments (with fine disregard for chronology), there appears a long diatribe on the friars' contempt for each of the commandments; it seems likely that this was originally a separate treatise, a type of work well known amongst Lollard texts.[23] Even more plainly an intrusion is a section in chapter xx where the author reverts to the phrase of xix.16 'Rex regum et Dominus dominantium' to introduce the question whether 'Christo iure hereditario pertinebat regnum David temporale?' The form of the discussion (fols. 204^v–206^v) makes it clear that a university determination is being incorporated into the commentary.[24] Technical terminology of a similar source is also used to discuss whether the clergy can take legal action in a temporal cause (fols. 143–4), and to inveigh against appropriations (fols. 170–71).

The learned background of the text indicated by these digressions is confirmed by the sources the author quotes.[25] At the beginning of the text he rather misleadingly asserts that his chief source is the *Glossa Ordinaria* (fols. 127^v–128), which he will amplify by reference to some 'modern' postillators. Certainly he quotes from the *Glossa* occasionally, but he has extensive recourse to a wide variety of texts by Augustine, Jerome, Chrysostom (and pseudo-Chrysostom), Gregory and Bede. Other ancient writers, Ambrose, Orosius, Origen, Eusebius, Josephus, Haymo and the *Vitae Patrum*, are used more sparingly. The references given are usually to author and work only, rarely a more precise location; in this, and in the paucity of citations from canon law, the *Opus Arduum* differs from the Lollard *Floretum* or *Rosarium*.[26] Of more recent authors Bernard is quoted

---

[23] Fols. 168^v–71; the friars' preaching of fables is seen as an offence against the second commandment, indulgences against the fourth, the licentiousness of the priesthood against the sixth, and, at great length, appropriations, ecclesiastical patronage and simony against the tenth. The connexion between plagues and commandments is made in a short paragraph often appended to the *Floretum* (e.g., MS. Harley 401, fol. 334^v), but this discussion is much longer. For other discussions see T. Arnold, *Select English Works of John Wyclif*, Oxford 1869–71, iii. 82–92, the Wycliffite addition to *The Lay Folks' Catachism*, ed. T. F. Simmons and H. E. Nolloth, EETS 118 (1901), 33–59, and A. L. Kellogg and E. W. Talbert, 'The Wycliffite *Pater Noster* and *Ten Commandments*', *Bulletin of the John Rylands Library*, xlii (1960), 363–77.

[24] The section is completely omitted from Luther's edition and from the abbreviated Prague University Library MS. III.G.17 (the Naples MS. has broken off before this point), but there is no reason to suppose that it was not a part of the original text: the vocabulary is the same, and the debate follows on from earlier discussion of the temporal claims of the clergy. The section is the last of four questions discussed, the first concerning vocal praise in heaven, the second on images and the third on how God can inflict perpetual pain in hell.

[25] A full investigation of the text's sources cannot be undertaken here; the comments that follow concern the writer's major declared debts and possible influence from Wyclif.

[26] For the more accurate references of the *Floretum* see 'A Lollard Compilation and the Dissemination of Wycliffite Thought', *Journal of Theological Studies*, NS xxiii (1972), 65–81. Canon law is used at one point, in typical Wycliffite fashion, to show how it refutes the views of the friars on the Eucharist (fol. 162^v). See above 13-29.

some five times, Peter of Poitiers, Peter Comestor, Anselm, Richard of St. Victor and Thomas of Hales less often. The chronicles of William of Malmesbury and Martinus Polonus are also used. Grosseteste is cited four times, in each case with approbation; most interesting is the writer's explanation for the discrepancy between his own views on the friars and those of Grosseteste, where he justifies the latter by pointing to the gradual degeneration of the orders from their ideals 'hiis modernis temporibus' (fol. 140).[27] A tract alleged to be by Robert Kilwardby is quoted in chapter x,[28] and three chapters earlier the favourite of Wyclif and the Lollards, 'Parisiensis' *De Fide et Legibus*, is cited (fol. 157ᵛ).[29] FitzRalph is not quoted, but his opposition to the friars and the ensuing legal case at Avignon are discussed.[30] Grosseteste and FitzRalph are described in typical Lollard fashion as saints, the failure of the papacy to effect their sanctification being adversely compared to papal readiness to canonise at random any who have supported curial claims.[31] Four Franciscan authors are mentioned though not quoted. The first is abbot Joachim of Fiore whose view that the gospel law has been superseded by the law of the Spirit is condemned in chapter iii (fol. 143ᵛ); even if one may suspect that the *Opus Arduum* is indebted to the Joachite tradition of Apocalypse commentary, its author is apparently unaware of his inheritance.[32] The other three are mentioned in a particularly interesting passage in chapter xii: the author alleges that the bishops have caused the destruction in Oxford and Salisbury of the works of 'Willelmi Occam contra papam Romanam, fratris Iohannis de Ripsissa, fratris Petri Iohannis super Apokalipsim' (fol. 174ᵛ). John of Rupescissa (de Roquetaillade) and Peter John Olivi were both Spiritual Franciscans, influenced by Joachite thought, and because of their views about the poverty of their order congenial to the Lollard writer. Olivi's commentary on the Apocalypse now survives in only two copies, one in Paris and the other in Rome, but the survival of his commentary on St. Matthew's

---

[27] The works quoted are Grosseteste's commentary on the *De Celesti Hierarchia* (fol. 126ᵛ) and the *De Mystica Theologia* (fol. 129) of pseudo-Dionysius, and the *Dicta* (fol. 150ᵛ). Hussite writings and transcripts usually cite Grosseteste as *Lincolniensis*, but the insular origin of the present text is shown in the use of his personal name as well (fol. 140).

[28] The incipit is given as 'Status predicatorum'; such a text is not included amongst the works of Kilwardby by P. Glorieux, *La Faculté des Arts et ses maitres au xiiie siecle*, Paris 1971, no. 411.

[29] See Workman, *John Wyclif*, i. 342.

[30] Fols. 147ᵛ, 162, 171ᵛ, 180.

[31] Fol. 147ᵛ; for Lollard sanctification see Arnold, op. cit., iii. 459/1, 467/17, and the mention of 'sanctus Ricardus qui gessit hoc negocium quod ego nunc habeo contra fratres' in Nicholas Hereford's Ascension Day sermon in 1382, reported in MS. Bodley 240, fol. 848ᵛ.

[32] For the influence of Joachim in fourteenth-century England see M. W. Bloomfield, *Piers Plowman as a Fourteenth-century Apocalypse*, New Brunswick 1961, 157–60, and M. E. Reeves, *The Influence of Prophecy in the Later Middle Ages*, Oxford 1969, 81–8; for his influence on English Apocalypse commentaries see B. Smalley, 'John Russel O.F.M.', *Recherches de théologie ancienne et médiévale*, xxiii (1956), 277–320, and 'Flaccianus *De Visionibus Sibyllae*', *Mélanges offerts à Étienne Gilson*, Toronto and Paris 1959, 552–4.

gospel in MS. New College Oxford 49, an English MS. of c. 1400, supports the implication that his works could have been familiar in Wycliffite circles.[33] Ockham is occasionally quoted by Wyclif.[34] The author does not identify here the texts of Rupescissa; either the *Prophetiae* or the *Vade mecum in tribulatione* contain material which might have appealed to the Lollards, but it is possible that texts no longer surviving, or not now attributed to Rupescissa, were in the author's mind.[35] Associated with these three Franciscan authors as suffering the same fate at the bishops' hands is William of St. Amour. William's anti-fraternal views were obviously sympathetic to the Lollards: Wyclif quoted him, and passages from his *Collectiones Sacrae Scripturae* are included in the *Floretum* and *The Lanterne of Light*; Netter regarded William as one of Wyclif's chief mentors.[36] From the phraseology of the *Opus Arduum* it is clear that the writer associated the destruction of these authors' texts with the persecution of his own sect.

Wyclif himself is not quoted, at any rate by name. Amongst Wyclif's *Postilla super totam Bibliam* is, of course, a brief commentary on the Apocalypse: Dr. Benrath has suggested that, despite its biblical position, this section was written fairly early, in 1371. As would be expected from this date, Wyclif's comments contain little that is tendentious, and it is, therefore, not surprising that the invectives of the *Opus Arduum* have no parallel there. More significant is the fact that uncontroversial interpretations in the later work differ from those in Wyclif's commentary: thus the twenty-four seats and elders of chapter iv.4 are in Wyclif 'omnes cathedrales ecclesias' and 'vniuersitas episcoporum qui debent esse senes etate et moribus',[37] whilst in the *Opus Arduum* they are 'omnes libri canonici ueteris testamenti qui sunt xxiiii computando Ruth et Neemiam pro libris per se' and 'omnes doctores antiqui testamenti et noui, qui per xii prophetas et xii apostolos principaliter designantur' (fol. 145ᵛ). Although a full comparison of the two texts would doubtless produce some parallels, selective contrast makes it plain that the Lollard author

---

[33] See D. L. Douie, *The Nature and the Effect of the Heresy of the Fraticelli*, Manchester 1932, 81–119, and R. Manselli, *La 'Lectura super Apocalipsim' di Pietro di Giovanni Olivi*, Rome 1955. Bale owned a copy of the Apocalypse commentary before 1553 (see H. McCusker, 'Books and Manuscripts formerly in the possession of John Bale', *The Library*, 4th series xvi (1935), 159 no. 249).

[34] For Wyclif's view of Ockham see *De Veritate Sacre Scripture*, i. 346/21–354/12 (all references are to the editions of the Wyclif Society unless otherwise stated), *De Ordinatione Fratrum* (*Polemical Works*, i), 92/2, 94/13 and 95/15.

[35] The two texts were printed by E. Brown, *Appendix ad Fasciculum Rerum Expetendarum...ii*, London 1690, 494–508; for these and other works see J. Bignami-Odier, *Études sur Jean de Roquetaillade*, Paris 1952, and Reeves, op. cit., 225–8, 321–5.

[36] *De Ordinatione Fratrum* 92/4. The *Collectiones Sacrae Scripturae* (*Opera Omnia*, Constance 1632, 462) is quoted in the *Floretum* under *edificacio* and in the *Lanterne of Light*, ed. L. M. Swinburn, EETS 151 (1917), p.38/3–14. For Netter's assertion see *Doctrinale Fidei Catholicae...*, ed. B. Blanciotti, Venice 1757–9, iv. 3, 22 (references to Netter are by book and chapter).

[37] Benrath, op. cit., 9; see MSS. Bodley 716, fols. 162–162ᵛ and Magdalen College Oxford 55, fol. 241ᵛ.

did not draw on Wyclif's work to any extent, and that any parallels probably spring from common use of an earlier work. After the *Postilla* Wyclif wrote little on the Apocalypse, despite drawing on it not infrequently for a biblical quotation to clinch some argument. Exceptions to this paucity are mostly amongst the sermons, where the liturgy provided lessons from the Apocalypse. Chapter i of the *Opus Arduum* is paralleled by *Sermones*, IV no. 21, iv by *Sermones*, III no. 33, vii by *Sermones*, IV no. 22, xx by *De Solutione Sathanae* (*Polemical Works*, ii. 385–400), and xxi by *Sermones* IV no. 63; in each case the Wyclif work does not deal with the whole chapter.[38] But amongst all these instances there are no significant parallels; a few self-evident similarities of interpretation are found, but no verbal echoes in the later work and few general resemblances. Though the *Opus Arduum* reeks of the preoccupations and polemics of Wyclif, the master seems to have contributed nothing to the detailed exegesis of the text.

There is, however, one apparently overt reference to Wyclif. Elaborating on the description of the locusts in chapter ix.8, the writer refers to earlier attacks on episcopal temporalities 'sicut temporibus W. de Sancto Amore, et sancti Ricardi Armocani (i.e. FitzRalph), nunc cum eis contra alios tendendo ut modo, et contra istos instarent ut dicunt aufferendo eis temporalia sua, si tamen Wicleff nichil nouisset contra eos' (fol. 162). Luther's edition generalises the last clause to 'fideles nihil mouissent', but, despite this and the omission of the clause in the other two abbreviated texts, the sentence obviously requires mention of a proponent of disendowment later than William of St. Amour or FitzRalph. There is no reason to question the evidence of the majority of MSS.[39] Less clear is the possibility that Wyclif is referred to elsewhere in the text. Some of the commentator's remarks seem to be particularised in a way that suggests the initiated were intended to see greater significance in them than a casual reader. Thus, in chapter xiv.6 '*et uidi alterum angelum* predicatorem aliquem missum a Christo ad ewangelizandum contra antichristum *volantem* mole[m] terrenorum a se remouentem, *per medium celi*, id est per mediam ecclesiam non percialiter vni ecclesie sed equaliter omnibus, predicantem et docentem in circuitu quam ecclesiam uerbis et exemplis secum trahit ad conuersacionem ewangelicam et doctrinam, *habentem* ex iniuncto Christi ewangelium eternum, non in primitiua ecclesia seruandum tamen sed eciam moderna' (fol. 183).[40] Earlier in chapter viii verse

[38] Perhaps the most interesting case is the parallel with *De Solutione Sathanae*, a work of Wyclif's last years; despite a review of some of the same topics, there is no close parallel of exegesis.

[39] Apart from the abbreviated versions mentioned, only one MS. (Prague Metropolitan Chapter A.117, fol. 69^v) does not entirely confirm the reading: in the text it has the name 'Wilhelmus' but the margin has a rubricated 'Wycleff'. The scribe of Brno Mk 28 and correctors of Prague University V.E.3 and of Karlsruhe 346 wrongly anticipated Wyclif's name in the first part of the sentence as the expansion of 'W.'.

[40] There are a number of similar passages, for instance fol. 185: '*et alter angelus* quilibet zelator et predicator ewangelice ueritatis desiderans iudicium extremum in quo manifestabitur omnibus ueritas doctrine sue contra antichristum'.

13 an even more pointed observation is found '*et uidi et audiui uocem vnius aquile* cuiuslibet veri doctoris ewangelici qui, sicut aquila corporaliter ita mente, conspicit a longinquo que iam dicta sunt mala, et que adhuc futura sunt ecclesie, et circumuolat vniuersalem ecclesiam scribendo aut docendo misteria huius prophetie' (fol. 161). Whilst the casual reader could interpret *ewangelici* in this sentence as 'evangelical', even merely 'christian', the intelligent sympathiser would perceive the introduction of Wyclif's by-name, *Doctor Evangelicus*.[41] Elsewhere too it is tempting to see ambiguity in the words *doctrina evangelica*—both the simple 'gospel teaching' and, for the initiated, 'the teaching of the Doctor Evangelicus'.[42] The Hussite appellation of Wyclif as the fifth evangelist is perhaps anticipated here.[43] The material is difficult to interpret, and the impression made by continuous reading impossible to convey in summary, but the conviction grows that elusive observations of this kind are more pointed than they may appear out of context.

This conviction is strengthened by the author's undoubted use of other parts of the Lollard vocabulary, vocabulary that is found abundantly in the vernacular standard sermon-cycle and in other shorter works; some of the elements of this sect language are mentioned by hostile chroniclers or polemicists.[44] Right-minded men are the *fideles*: 'multi fideles in isto tempore antichristi firmi in doctrina ewangelica' (fol. 164^v), who are defined earlier and more fully (fol. 158): 'Soli illi fideles Christi sunt qui doctrinam ewangelicam iuxta porcionem status sui quam corde credunt, opere implent et eam publice confiteri propter timorem antichristi non dimittunt. Omnes illi infideles sunt habendi qui, quamuis corde credant ewangelio, factis tamen negant, aut cum oporteat examinari ab antichristo aut aliquo vicariorum suorum cuiusmodi sunt omnes abusionibus pape heresibus et blasphemiis fauentes contra conscienciam suam et doctrinam ewangelicam sibi parent'. The *fidelis predicator* preaches *lex*

---

[41] The date of the by-name's origin is unclear. It was certainly well established by 1395 when it was used to refer to the author of the *Trialogus* in the *Twelve Conclusions of the Lollards* (see *English Historical Review*, xxii (1907), 297); similarly it is the regular appellation in the *Floretum* which must antedate 1396. Knighton in his *Chronicon*, written c. 1390–95, described the Wycliffites as *doctores Evangelicae*, ed. J. R. Lumby, Rolls Series 1889–95, ii. 186, presupposing the name for Wyclif. It is regularly used in MSS. of Wyclif's works, whether of English origin (as Trinity College Dublin C.1.23) or Hussite (as Vienna 4343, 4505).

[42] Thus ix.4 (fol. 163^v): '*dicentem* uocem scilicet *vj^{o}angelo* cuicumque predicatori ewangelico qui *habebat tubam*, id est doctrinam ewangelicam contra antichristum declarandam quia non solum Iohannes sed omnes precones Christi preteriti temporis premouerunt nos qui sumus tempore antichristi quid facturi sumus contra eum, *solue quattuor angelos*, id est, tu predicator... predica ut sibi caueant electi ne decipiantur ab eis per antichristum'.

[43] See F. Šmahel, '"Doctor evangelicus super omnes evangelistas": Wyclif's Fortune in Hussite Bohemia', *Bulletin of the Institute of Historical Research*, xliii (1970), 25 and n. 3.

[44] For the terminology see *Journal of Theological Studies*, NS xxii (1971), 457–8; with the *fidelis predicator* compare Knighton, ii. 179 '*trewe prechoures*' and 188 'falsos fratres vocantes, seipsos veros praedicatores et evangelicos'; for other elements of this vocabulary compare Pecock, *Repressor of Overmuch Blaming of the Clergy*, ed. C. Babington, Rolls Series 1860, i. 36, 53 and Netter, vi. 33. See below 207-8.

ewangelica rather than *fabulae*, as do the *male secte*, the men of *religiones privatae* whose faith is grounded not in the gospel but in the provisions of men; similarly, 'fidelis predicator apprehendit sensum huius prophetie et aliarum contra antichristum; non debet tamen thesaurum abscondere quacumque occasione, sed omni tergiuersacione postposita ipsum docere et publice predicare et aduocare coram clero et populo' (fol. 166ᵛ). Because the message of the gospel must not be hidden, the true preacher will use the vernacular language whether for speaking or writing (fol. 161ᵛ); the fundamental cause of all the errors in the contemporary Church is seen to be ignorance of the Bible (fol. 143ᵛ). But there is opposition to this use of the vernacular: 'docent eciam isti falsi fratres quod gradu laici quamuis litterati non debent studere scripturam sacram, nec eam habere in lingwa materna nec alias informare' (fol. 136).[45] The most explicit account of the persecution that follows upon attempts of the writer and his sect to educate the laity in the gospel appears in the commentary to chapter xii.5 (fol. 174ᵛ): '*Preparat se eciam ad deuorandum filium matris ecclesie*, id est fructum per scripturarum studium conceptum destruere, quod iam patet, quantum in eo est impletum per generalem mandatum prelatorum ad comburendum, destruendum et condemnandum omnes libros, scilicet omelias ewangeliorum et epistolarum in lingwa materna conscriptos, suggerendo quasi non liceat nobis Anglicis legem diuinam habere in nostro wlgari, quod tamen omnibus Ebreis, Grecis et Latinis est commune. Et propterea qui sint diaboli in hac causa discipuli spirituales facile patet, quia fratres huius negocii procuratores erant capitanei et preduces. Sed quamuis ad hec quantum potuit per se et per suos laborauit diabolus, non tamen perfecit, quia non omnes libri tales sunt destructi, sed loco eorum alii iam de nouo conscripti sunt ut in tempore breui, Domino fauente, patebit, ipsis multum forciores. Et propterea subdit et *peperit*, scilicet ecclesia, *filium masculum*, quia sicut masculus in vigore prestat femelle, sic libri tardius conscripti sunt prioribus contra antichristum et fautores suos multum validiores'. The assertion of the destruction of Lollard books accords well with the story told by Knighton of the confiscation of books from William Smith of Leicester, books 'quos in materna lingua de evangelio, et de epistolis et aliis episcopis et doctoribus conscripserat, et ut fatebatur per annos octo studiose conscribere laborauerat'; this confiscation occurred in 1389.[46] More interesting is the *Opus Arduum*'s certainty that new books have been written to take the place of those lost, and that these are more outspoken

---

[45] For the discussion of this question see my paper cited above (n. 1). The defence of vernacular scriptures was not at this date the prerogative of the Lollards, and the author of the *Opus Arduum* seems to have been ahead of his time in identifying the opposition with the friars. There are, as will be discussed below, other topics on which the author seems to have been very perceptive in his understanding of incipient difficulties.

[46] Knighton, ii. 313; it should be noted that these MSS. cannot have contained the Wycliffite Bible, since this would not have been described as 'de...aliis episcopis et doctoribus'. Knighton dates the confiscation as 1392, but Courtenay's register shows this to be incorrect: see J. H. Dahmus, *The Metropolitan Visitations of William Courtenay*, Illinois 1950, 164–7.

than the old. All this points to an author at the centre of the Wycliffite movement, and confirms the indirect evidence of the vernacular MSS. concerning the organisation perfected in the early years of the sect.[47]

Who then was the author of the *Opus Arduum?* In many respects the question is trivial: the author withholds his name, and would seem to do so deliberately, for there are many places where revelation seems not merely natural but almost inevitable.[48] The text is the work of a representative *fidelis predicator*, and, as Knighton commented, all members of the Wycliffite sect became alike in ideas, manner and speech.[49] Much time and ink has been spent in fruitless speculation on the authorship of Lollard texts, and it is ironic that the one early tract whose author is identifiable and of significant status, *The Two Ways* by Sir John Clanvowe, should be of virtually no interest either in its ideas or its contemporary reference.[50] With whatever reluctance, however, one is led into consideration of the question by the enticements of the author's leading statements. From the material discussed so far it is obvious that the author was a Lollard of university background, acquainted with the activities and language of the movement, and imprisoned from about 1387 until at least Easter 1390. He mentions only three places by name: London, Oxford and Salisbury. The first of these is unhelpful; the second is only interesting in that it is coupled with Salisbury, a less obvious choice, as the places where the books of Ockham, Rupescissa, Olivi and William of St. Amour have been destroyed (fol. 174^v). Salisbury is again mentioned as the location of a miracle that occurred in October 1389 (fol. 148).[51] The author refers by name to two of his other writings, both mentioned twice: the first is *De Antichristo* (fol. 196) or *Dialogus de Antichristo* (fol. 167^v), said to be in the vernacular; the second is *De Abusiuis* (fols. 167^v and 190), whose subject seems to have been much the same, since the writer comments that he has there shown that the pope is antichrist. There are also vaguer references to writings *alibi* (fols. 151, 163^v), and demonstrations he has made *in aliis* (fol. 176); he also affirms his

[47] See 'A Lollard Sermon-Cycle and its Implications', *Medium Aevum*, xl (1971), 142–56; the case there made could now be much more strongly supported.

[48] As for instance in the concluding section of his prologue, where the author compares his own position with that of the original recipient of the vision (fol. 127), or in the last verses of the final chapter (fols. 215^v–216) where he recommends his work.

[49] Knighton, ii. 186–7: 'acsi essent de uno gignasio educati et doctrinati ac etiam de unius magistri schola simul referti et nutriti', their master forming them 'eadem identitate spiritus sui ... et conformitate unius loquelae'.

[50] See Workman, op. cit., especially i. 329–32; M. Deanesly, *The Lollard Bible*, Cambridge 1920, especially 252ff. *The Two Ways* has been edited by V. J. Scattergood, *The Works of John Clanvowe*, Cambridge 1975, 57–80; see the comments of McFarlane, *Lollard Knights*, 199–206.

[51] The story concerns the release of two *falsi monetarii* from sentence of death following prayers on their behalf to the Virgin Mary; the date is 'in festo sancti Hugonis', presumably the translation of St. Hugh as the greater saint on 6 October; see *Breviarium ad Usum insignis ecclesiae Sarum*, ed. F. Procter and C. Wordsworth, Cambridge 1879–86, iii. 890.

intention of writing further on the question of ecclesiastical temporalities 'de hiis, vita comite, lacius allibi disputare propono' (fol. 206ᵛ). The most tantalising indication of authorship comes in the commentary to the penultimate chapter, verse 2: '*ego ergo Iohannis*, et non ego W. nisi secundarie, *vidi civitatem*' (fol. 207ᵛ). Six of the MSS. have the initial alone, one has 'Wi.', another 'Wij.' and a third, the Brno MS. normally transcribed here, 'Vilhelmus'; four, including Luther's text, omit the phrase.[52] It is difficult to see any sense in the comment unless the second name were that of the commentator, speaking the words, as it were, after the evangelist. From the evidence it would seem that 'W.' has considerable authority, but that 'Vilhelmus' may be a conjectured expansion. It may be prudent to reflect that, since it is inherently probable that all these continental copies descend from a single English exemplar taken to Hussite Bohemia, the initial could possibly be an error in that exemplar. It is important, when examining claims that have been advanced for the author, to note that the one initial that would be improbable in the sentence is 'J', the one name that would make the sentence unintelligible is *Johannes*.

There are, further, two problems that any consideration of authorship must face. First, how could a man in prison have access to such a wide variety of books? The quotations are far too numerous and long to suppose that they derive from memory. The apparent parallels with the examinations of Walter Brut and William Thorpe are not exact: Brut was composing answers at the request of bishop Trefnant and might, therefore, have been allowed books for their preparation; Thorpe, though he refers to a number of the fathers and to canon law, quotes only infrequently and briefly.[53] Both were concerned to show ordered justification of their views and not, as with the *Opus Arduum* author, to compose an attack. Obviously it is possible that a commentary begun in prison should have been expanded when the author was released. But, apart from the digressions mentioned above, the text reads as a homogeneous whole; and, given the joy with which the author comments on the frustration of the bishops' intentions with regard to Lollard books, one would expect, had the text been completed in freedom, that a similarly exulting observation would have been made. The text itself leads one to accept at face value the information of the final colophon. The second, and related, problem is how the text was 'published'. If one accepts that the author was still in prison when he completed his

[52] 'Wi.' is found in Prague Metropolitan Chapter A. 163, 'Wij.' in the same library A.117; the four that lack the name are Metropolitan Chapter B.48/1, B.82/2, Prague University Library III.G.17 and Luther's edition; the Naples text is defective by this stage.

[53] For the second set of Brut's answers see *Registrum Johannis Trefnant*, ed. W. W. Capes, Canterbury and York Society (1916), 285–358; for Thorpe's examination see the modernised edition by A. W. Pollard, *Fifteenth Century Prose and Verse*, London 1903, 101–67. Thorpe's references could all have come from a single roll which, from other trial evidence, Lollards often carried to counter attacks on their beliefs.

commentary, how was even a single copy smuggled out to a sympathetic receiver who would either disseminate it himself, or pass it on to one who would? Here the parallel with Thorpe's text is closer. Even allowing for the relatively comfortable circumstances enjoyed by some medieval prisoners, it seems unlikely that a man incarcerated for heretical views, whether established or as yet only keenly suspected, would have been allowed the means to write his views freely or, having done so, would have been permitted to pass his text to a sympathiser.[54]

Three names have hitherto been proposed as author. First the annotators of three MSS. state the text to be by Wyclif himself; this is manifestly impossible from the dates that are embedded in the commentary.[55] Secondly Brno Mk 62, dating from 1444, ascribes the text to a 'Magister Richardus'; Bartoš, on the basis of this, suggested Richard Wyche.[56] But the first recorded encounter of Wyche with the ecclesiastical authorities was in 1401, when he was arrested in Northumberland where he was preaching; no mention was made in the ensuing trial of any previous investigation for heresy, let alone of a three year imprisonment on that account.[57] Wyche was burnt for heresy in 1440, and it seems rather unlikely that he would have been at the centre of the Lollard movement as early as 1387.[58] The suggestion, only supported by one late and inexplicit ascription, can safely be rejected. A more difficult candidate is John Purvey, first put forward by Bale, and supported by various later writers, none of whom appears, however, to have had evidence beyond that of Bale.[59] The first possible indication that Bale knew the commentary is in his *The Ymage of both Churches*, publicly available by 1546, though apparently well under way by 1543.[60] There Bale includes in his list of authorities (sig. A.7ᵛ) 'Author a centum annis Anglus libro i', with no incipit.[61] In 1548 Bale in his *Illustrium Maioris*

---

[54] For literary works undertaken in prison compare the familiar instances of Charles of Orleans or Sir Thomas Malory; in both these cases their offences were completely unconnected with anything they wrote or would have need of in their writing.

[55] In MSS. Vienna 4526, 4925 and Naples; all are late medieval hands.

[56] F. M. Bartoš, 'Lollardský a Husitský Výklad Apokalypsy', *Reformačni Sborník*, vi (1937), 112–14.

[57] For the various sources concerning this episode in Wyche's career, see M. G. Snape, 'Some Evidence of Lollard Activity in the Diocese of Durham in the early fifteenth century', *Archaeologia Aeliana*, 4th series xxxix (1961), 355–61.

[58] See *Calendar of Close Rolls*, 1435–41 (1937), 385–6.

[59] For instance T. Tanner, *Bibliotheca Britannico-Hibernica sive De Scriptoribus*, London 1748, 609.

[60] *A Short-Title Catalogue...1475–1640*, ed. A. W. Pollard and G. R. Redgrave, London 1926 (hereafter cited as STC), lists the first edition as no. 1297 ([1548?]); no. 1299 printed by Wyer is certainly of 1550. For the earlier datings see L. P. Fairfield, 'John Bale and the Development of Protestant Hagiography in England', in *J.E.H.* , xxiv (1973), 149 n. 4.

[61] Mrs. Aston, *History*, xlix (1964), 157 n. 32, connects this with the explanation of Apocalypse xiii.18 given by Bale (pt. ii, sig. K.7): Bale states that one interpretation of the number 666 'was found out by a certaine vnnamed disciple of John Wyckleffe'. Mrs. Aston takes both to refer to the *Opus Arduum*. But, in fact, the interpretation bears no resemblance to either Luther's printed commentary on the verse (fol. 124), or to the full *Opus Arduum* (fols. 181ᵛ–182).

Britanniae Scriptorum . . . Summarium attributed to John Purvey a 'Commentarium in Apocalypsim li. 1' with the incipit 'Ioannes Apostolus et Euangelista'; this is the incipit of the second prologue to Luther's edition (sig. A.7ᵛ–A.8).[62] However, in the *Scriptorum Illustrium Maioris Brytanniae Catalogus*, published in Basle in 1557–9, though the title of the work remains the same, the incipit appears as that of the text of Luther's edition: 'Apocalypsis, quasi diceret, Non deb.'. Bale added a more specific note, mentioning Luther's edition, noting the autobiographical details (but not the initial, since this was lacking from the print), and commenting that the work derived 'ex magistri Vuicleui lectionibus publicis'.[63] No indication is given of why Bale associated the work with Purvey, or of the reason for the change in incipit. It should be noted first that there is no evidence to suggest that Bale knew the text in any form other than Luther's edition, and second that Bale had discovered from Netter the idea that Purvey was 'librarius' of the Lollard movement and had written tracts himself.[64] There are a number of objections to Bale's association of the *Opus Arduum* with Purvey. The most obvious is that Purvey's Christian name, Johannes, is the one that is impossible in the apparently autobiographical remark. Secondly, despite Knighton's inclusion of Purvey's views under the year 1382, the first known trial of Purvey was in February 1401 when he was said to be 'nuper suspectus, infamatus, accusatus et manifeste convictus'; as with Wyche, there is no mention of earlier imprisonment.[65] Thirdly, the only books attributed by name to Purvey at any date near to his lifetime are not assimilable to those mentioned in the *Opus Arduum*: Netter mentions a *Libellus de Oratione* and *De Compendiis Scripturarum, paternarum doctrinarum et canonum*. The multitude of other works that have in recent times been ascribed to Purvey result more from a dislike of anonymity than from any positive evidence in favour of his authorship.[66] Bale's assertion that the

[62] STC, 1295, another edition 1296; fols. 181–181ᵛ; the appended note indicates, though not with particular reference to the Apocalypse commentary, that Purvey wrote 'adversus Satane synagogam' and that he identified this with the Church of Rome—not an unusual view amongst the Lollards. Bale added a muddled and partially incorrect sentence about Purvey's later history.

[63] Op. cit., 541–3. Purvey does not appear in Bale's *Index Britanniae Scriptorum*, ed. R. L. Poole and M. Bateson, Oxford 1902. Bale's brief biography of Purvey inserted into a blank space in MS. e Musaeo 86, f. 62 (the MS. of *Fasciculi Zizaniorum*) provides no help about his writings. Bale's own annotated copy of his *Summarium* is now Edinburgh University Library MS. Laing 651, but unfortunately contains no comments on the Purvey entry.

[64] See Bale's reference to Netter, *Catalogus*, i. 542; for Netter's observation see *Doctrinale*, vi. 117.

[65] Knighton, op. cit., ii. 178–80; McFarlane, *Lollard Knights*, 149 n. 3 notes that Knighton 'grouped too many incidents in which Wycliffe, Swinderby, and other Lollards were concerned within a single year for the accuracy of his dating to be accepted'. The events of 1401 are recorded in *Fasciculi Zizaniorum*, ed. W. W. Shirley, Rolls Series (1858), 400–407.

[66] *Doctrinale*, ii. 70, 73; vi. 13, 17. For discussion of some works attributed to Purvey, see my paper cited in n. 1 above and *Selections from English Wycliffite Writings*, Cambridge 1978, introductory notes to nos. 2, 3, 6, 24 and 27. I hope to publish elsewhere a full study of Purvey's career and possible writings. See below 85-110.

commentary derives from Wyclif's lectures is puzzling: despite similarities in some of the interests, the *Opus Arduum* deals with questions, such as images and biblical translation, that came to the fore after Wyclif's death, and the style is very different from that of Wyclif. Unless new evidence, either about Purvey or concerning the source of Bale's attribution, appears, it seems reasonable to reject Purvey as improbable.

Beginning afresh from the evidence of the *Opus Arduum*, one looks for a man of university education and interests, who was imprisoned between 1387 and 1390, and whose initial may have been W.[67] Several candidates possible on the last count can be eliminated because they are known to have been at liberty during the crucial three years: William Smith, who anyway lacked the necessary education,[68] William Swinderby and Walter Brut.[69] The last certainly revealed in his trial a deep interest in the Apocalypse, but his comments bear little resemblance to the *Opus Arduum*. William Thorpe claimed acquaintance with Wyclif's early followers in Oxford when he came before Arundel in 1407 but, whilst he admitted to having been examined by bishop Braybrook of London in 1397 (an admission confirmed from ecclesiastical records), he did not mention earlier imprisonment, nor authorship of an Apocalypse commentary.[70] Given Thorpe's exuberant self-revelation, it seems safe to exclude him from further consideration. An intriguing possibility is William James, a fellow of Merton for many years, and one whose name was recurrently linked with Lollardy. In 1382 he publicly defended Wyclif's view of the Eucharist; in 1394 and 1395 orders were given for his arrest and production before the king's council in chancery on 20 December 1395; in 1420 he recanted his heresy before archbishop Chichele. He certainly had the necessary education, but there is no evidence concerning his whereabouts in the years 1387–90.[71]

If the enigmatic, and possibly misleading, authorial note is left aside, and the more certain evidence of date considered, the name of Nicholas Hereford comes forward. After his escape from the papal prison in

[67] Some candidates, such as William Taylor and William White, seem not worth consideration since the evidence suggests that their involvement with the Lollard cause was later than the dates here in question.

[68] Knighton, op. cit., ii. 180–83, 190–91, 313; for the date see above, n. 46. See further J. Crompton, 'Leicestershire Lollards', *Transactions of the Leicestershire Archaeological and Historical Society*, xliv (1968–9), 19ff.

[69] Trefnant register (above, n. 53), 231–78 and 278–359 respectively; for Swinderby's earlier career in Leicester see Knighton, ii. 189–97 and Crompton, loc. cit. It appears that Swinderby spent the years 1387–90 preaching on the Welsh marches, where he came into contact with Brut.

[70] See the modernised edition noted above, n. 53, and *Selections* (above, n. 66) no. 4; the investigation by Braybrook is confirmed by John Lydford's book, ed. D. M. Owen, Devon and Cornwall Record Society, NS xx (1975), nos. 206 and 209.

[71] References for James's career are collected in A. B. Emden, *A Biographical Register of the University of Oxford to A.D. 1500*, Oxford 1957–9, ii. 1012–13. His name is not found in the college records between 1384 and 1391, but the material is not complete and the evidence is negative anyway. Netter, *Doctrinale* v. 26 has an undated story of James's blasphemous behaviour at mass.

Rome, Hereford returned to England, where renewed proclamations for his arrest were published.[72] He was captured in January 1387, and imprisoned first in the town gaol at Nottingham. On 1 February an order was granted allowing the transfer of Hereford to custody in Nottingham castle. The request for the move had come from Sir William Neville, warden of the castle, who was listed by Walsingham amongst the Lollard knights. Neville urged the transfer of Hereford 'because of the honesty of his person', and guaranteed that his prisoner should not 'walk abroad, nor preach errors, nor publish unlawful sermons contrary to the faith of the Church'.[73] Hereford recanted by the end of 1391, and by then was said to have become as ardent in his opposition to heretical views as he had previously been in their support.[74] Information about the interval between February 1387 and the recantation is scant and not wholly consistent. Walsingham, under the year 1387, tells a story of how Hereford endeavoured to dissuade a dying Lollard priest from oral confession, urging him that confession to God alone was sufficient. This anecdote is located at Shenley manor, the home of Sir John Montague, another of Walsingham's Lollard knights. Chronologically, if Walsingham is right in dating the story in 1387, this must have come after Hereford's arrest; yet Shenley was in Hertfordshire, far from Nottingham castle to which Hereford was committed.[75] Knighton, on the other hand, says that Hereford was imprisoned soon after his return to England in 1387 by the archbishop of Canterbury; this assertion gains some support from a comment of Thorpe's dated twenty years later.[76] Courtenay's episcopal register does not record the imprisonment, though it would seem likely from some notes in that register that matters of heresy were set out in a separate book, 'in quaterno de heresibus', a book now sadly lost.[77] What does seem plain from these fragmentary and somewhat

[72] See references in Emden, op. cit., ii. 913–15; Workman, ii. 131–7, 336–9, though some details in the latter need correction and attribution of English works, other than biblical translation, to Hereford is largely hypothetical.

[73] *Calendar of Close Rolls 1385–9* (1921), 208; the instrument for Hereford's arrest is printed in full by F. D. Logan, *Excommunication and the Secular Arm in Medieval England*, Toronto 1968, 193. See *Lollard Knights*, 198–9 for comments on the arrest and transfer by McFarlane.

[74] *Calendar of Patent Rolls 1391–6* (1905), 8; Hereford acted as one of the bishop's assessors in the trial of Walter Brut in October 1393 (Trefnant register, 359, 394–401).

[75] Walsingham, *Historia Anglicana*, ed. H. T. Riley, Rolls Series (1863–4), ii. 159–60; the story was copied into the notebook of the Carthusian William Mede; MS. Bodley 117, fols. 32–32ᵛ. In *Ypodigma Neustriae*, ed. H. T. Riley, Rolls Series (1876), 348 Walsingham described Montague as, amongst the Lollard knights, 'vesanior omnium'.

[76] Knighton, ii. 174; the information comes after a general review of Hereford's career under the year 1382. Thorpe (edition cited above, n. 53) 165 states that Hereford was imprisoned by the archbishop of Canterbury, but does not give a date.

[77] Lambeth register Courtenay fol. 34ᵛ has three marginal notes 'Respice quaestiones dampnatas in quaterno de heresibus contentas', 'Respice litteras restitucionis domini Philipi Repyngdon in octauo folio quaterni de heresibus contentas', 'Respice litteras restitucionis magisti Johannis Ayshton in octauo folio quaterni de heresibus contentas'; there is no trace of any of these three amongst surviving material.

conflicting details is that Hereford on his arrest had the interest of at least
two of the Lollard knights, and that they were prepared to offer him some
public protection. Some aspects of the *Opus Arduum* could be explained if
Hereford, in these circumstances, were its author. In the first place, with
such guardians it is not so difficult to explain the writer's access to books
and his freedom to write; nor is it impossible to suppose that the Lollard
knights might have connived at the release of the commentary to a
sympathiser at large. Secondly, in 1382 Hereford had appealed from the
judgment of Courtenay to the pope; Urban VI, on his arrival in Rome,
however, confirmed the condemnation and committed Hereford to life
imprisonment.[78] Such a decision would explain the extreme vehemence
of the *Opus Arduum* author's hatred for Urban VI, vehemence that
culminates in the question already quoted 'ex quo Vrbanus sextus iam
mortuus est, in quo omnia misteria antichristi fuerunt impleta, numquid
eciam mortuus sit antichristus?'[79] After Hereford's recantation two
significant statements appeared. First, an anonymous Lollard wrote to
upbraid Hereford as a renegade; he wrote in Latin, reproached Hereford
for his bad grammar and pronunciation, and cited canon law against
him. If Hereford were the author of the *Opus Arduum*'s observations
about persecution and the reaction of the *fidelis* to that persecution, the
Lollard would, indeed, have had cause for his bitter reproaches and have
had double reason for calling Hereford the leader of the Nicolaitans
(Apoc., ii. 6,15).[80] Secondly, the king issued a statement of public
protection for Hereford: this was claimed to be needed because Hereford
in his new-found orthodoxy 'is sued maliciously by his enemies in divers
temporal courts with a view to his imprisonment and to prevent him
further resisting their depraving doctrine'; the complainants were
ordered to forward their claims to the king and council.[81] This strange
wording would suggest that Hereford's enemies were of considerable
political independence, who thought that they could reverse the
advantages gained by the established Church from the heretic's recantation. As with the letter of the anonymous Lollard, the anger of these
men would be the more understandable had Hereford recently written in
their defence a text as outspoken as the *Opus Arduum*.

The difficulties of an attribution to Hereford are clear: that the initial
would have to be ignored, or supposed to be an error, and that the text is

[78] See references cited above, n. 72; McFarlane, *Wycliffe,* 112, 126.

[79] Fol. 186, see also fol. 176. Though it is doubtful whether Workman's argument (ii.
314–15) that Wyclif retained a faint confidence in Urban VI can be accepted, it is certainly
true that the polemic of Wyclif's last years was directed against the abuses of the office of
papacy, and particularly against the offence of the existence of two popes, rather than
against the individual failings of Urban (see *Opus Evangelicum,* ii. 169; *Opera Minora* 204,
252 (where 'Urbanus noster' is plainly ironic), 272).

[80] Trefnant register, 394–6; an answer, written on behalf of Hereford by the Dominican
Thomas Palmer, follows, 396–401. Despite the assertion of Deanesly, *The Lollard Bible,* 286
n. 5, there is no reason to attribute the letter to Walter Brut.

[81] *Calendar of Patent Rolls 1391–6* (1905), 8.

not assimilable to Bale's list of Hereford's works.[82] The second of these is not, however, very pressing. Bale does not mention Hereford's involvement in the work of translating the Bible into English, though colophons on two MSS. of the Early Version record evidence in favour of this.[83] A further difficulty is that the author of the *Opus Arduum* regards the bishops as his imprisoners (fols. 153, 157ᵛ), and describes his circumstances as harsh, 'duplici compede cathenatus' (fol. 127), 'compedes non modo ferreos sed calibeos mihi inter ceteros prouiderunt' (fol. 172). It might not be special pleading to suggest that these observations are, like the withholding of his name, deliberate attempts to protect his defenders. Ultimately he is right in supposing that his incarceration is the result of episcopal persecution, whilst the description of his torture is for the eyes of any opponent into whose hands the text might inadvertently fall.

Whether Hereford is accepted or not, it seems clear that circumstances such as his are those that would have enabled the composition of the *Opus Arduum.* Patronage of the kind here suggested by one or two of the Lollard knights is paralleled at exactly the same date by the actions of Sir Thomas Latimer in the case of John Wodard, a Lollard preacher at Chipping Warden. Latimer appears to have successfully defeated the attempts of bishop Buckingham of Lincoln in 1388–9 to bring the preacher to trial. As McFarlane comments, Latimer's 'immunity when the fact of his protection was obvious reveals how little the Lollard knight had to fear. He felt so secure that he did not hesitate to bring an action against the bishop's summoner before the king's justices on assize; and this less that a year after he himself had been cross-examined before the council for his possession of Lollard books'.[84] If Latimer was prepared to act in this fashion in a situation where public knowledge of events was inevitable, and indeed courted, it is quite conceivable that Sir William Neville, Sir John Montague, or another Lollard knight, might be willing to allow a Lollard to write and release an Apocalypse commentary. Their collusion would be especially easy to obtain when this, whatever it might say about the ecclesiastical hierarchy, did not directly incriminate them.

Apart from the question of authorship, perhaps the greatest puzzle of the *Opus Arduum* concerns its purpose. Unlike some of the early Wycliffite texts, it is not apologetic or justificatory:[85] though certain positions are

---

[82] Bale, *Catalogus*, i. 502, lists six works, all without incipit, three of which must date from Hereford's Wycliffite period. None of them has the title of the other works for which the *Opus Arduum* author claims responsibility, though the 'De apostasia fratrum a Christo' clearly dealt with similar subject matter.

[83] See H. Hargreaves, 'The Wycliffite Versions' in *The Cambridge History of the Bible*, ii. ed. G. W. H. Lampe, Cambridge 1969, 400.

[84] See McFarlane, *Lollard Knights*, 194–5.

[85] For instance the *Twelve Conclusions*, in *E.H.R.*, xxii, which must antedate 1395 when they were affixed to various public places in London, *On the Twenty-Five Articles*, Arnold, iii. 454–96, from the reference to Urban vi dating from before his death in 1389, or *Thirty-Seven Conclusions*, ed. J. Forshall, London 1851, that probably date from before 1401.

advanced with supporting authorities and logic, it does not set out to give a full, or fully reasoned, account of the author's views. Nor is the text, like the *Floretum/Rosarium* in Latin or the Glossed Gospels in English, amenable to use as a preacher's handbook.[86] The nearest analogy to the *Opus Arduum* is the vernacular standard Lollard sermon-cycle.[87] Both use biblical texts, though chosen on differing principles, as a starting point for exegesis; polemical material is introduced as the biblical text affords opportunity or, if this is not forthcoming, by more arbitrary digression, but without any attempt at an overall survey of doctrine. Both, further-more, despite their pugnacious tone, seem directed towards an audience of sympathisers. Vocabulary and allusions need not be explained for the uninitiated; arguments begin often not from first principles but from common, and unorthodox, assumptions; the general nature of the opposition needs no definition. Similarly, a major concern of both is with the steadfastness of the sympathisers under persecution. It is tempting to suggest that the books 'multum forciores...multum validiores' that the *Opus Arduum* author describes as having been written after the episcopal destruction of early Lollard books were indeed these sermons. Yet the comparison with the sermons identifies another oddity about the *Opus Arduum*: why, especially given the author's frequent declarations of the need for teaching in the vernacular, was the commentary written in Latin? There is no evidence whatever that it is a translation from English, nor has any trace yet been found of a secondary English version.[88] The answer would seem to be that it was intended for an educated, and in all probability, given the scholastic structures and language incorporated, university audience. This would be in accord with the implications concerning the circumstances of composition proposed above. The author had apparently not yet abandoned the hope that Wycliffite views would prevail in high places; but, whilst the Lollard writers of, for instance, the *Twelve Conclusions* or the later *Disendowment Bill*,[89] looked for support in secular institutions such as parliament, the writer of the *Opus Arduum* was urging university men to rally again in defence of the Wycliffite cause.[90]

Unaffected by these problems, to which only a hypothetical answer is yet available, is the evidence which the text provides about the ideas of

[86] See above, n. 26; for the Glossed Gospels see Hargreaves, art. cit., 407–9.
[87] Printed by Arnold in vols. i–ii of his edition; see further the article cited above, n. 47.
[88] The English Apocalypse commentary that has been regarded as Wycliffite derives from an Anglo-Norman original and owes nothing to the *Opus Arduum*. Two versions exist, one edited by E. Fridner (Lund Studies in English, xxix (1961)), and the other by W. Sauer (Heidelberg thesis, 1971).
[89] See *Selections from English Wycliffite Writings*, nos. 3 and 27.
[90] That this was not a forlorn hope in a lost cause is evident from many pieces of evidence, most notably from the fact that Arundel, in 1407, felt justified in infringing the jealously guarded privileges of the university of Oxford by imposing monthly inquisition by heads of halls into the views on Wycliffite matters held by students in their charge: D. Wilkins, *Concilia Magnae Britanniae et Hiberniae*, London 1737, iii. 318–19.

the Wycliffite movement at a date about five years following the death of its leader. The preoccupations of this writer are not entirely those which one might expect either from a reading of Wyclif's later works or from a study of later Lollard opinions. The Eucharist is only briefly discussed, albeit the interpretation put upon the sacrament is that of Wyclif.[91] There is a review of objections to images and pilgrimages, but these topics are not so dominant as they became in later Lollard texts.[92] The two doctrinal issues that most interested the author are the issues of clerical temporalities and of church government. The first of these is debated with a decidedly legal bias; certain elements normally found in this debate, such as the donation of Constantine, seem not greatly to interest the author, whilst other, less familiar arguments are introduced.[93] In the discussion of both questions Wyclif's ideas of dominion figure much more largely than is the case in most Lollard writing. This, and the consideration of predestination found at other points,[94] groups the *Opus Arduum* with the earlier concerns, concerns of a theoretical and theological cast, rather than with the more practical direction of much later Lollard polemic. The same tendency is evidenced from the castigation of the friars: along with the usual abuse there is an interest in theory, as exemplified in the meticulous way in which the writer establishes that the Minorites violated their own rules concerning money in the expenses they incurred in their refutation of FitzRalph.[95] On the question of the Bible, however, the discussion is both theoretical and practical. The over-riding importance that the author attached to scripture is emphasised throughout the text; the ultimate blasphemy of the church establishment is seen to be their view that 'legem ewangelicam non sufficere pro regimine ecclesie absque decretis paparum et dec-retalibus episcopis, quorum nonnullam doctrinam ewangelicam impugnant expresse' (fol. 176ᵛ). Yet practical action is urged to correct this: scripture must be made available to the people in a language they can understand; even more frequently urged is the duty of every *fidelis* to study, pray about, and, most importantly, teach publicly the truth of the gospel.[96]

Two contemporary situations seem to have preoccupied the writer. The

[91] See fols. 136ᵛ, 148, 162ᵛ; in the first is found the contention that the Wycliffites alone maintain the faith of *Ego Berengarius*.

[92] See fols. 157, 165, 204; for the recurrence of disapproval of images in Lollard trials see J. A. F. Thomson, *The Later Lollards 1414–1520*, Oxford 2nd ed. 1967, passim.

[93] For these arguments see above, 49.

[94] The Church is defined (fol. 173ᵛ) as 'numerus predestinatorum', and there is a fuller statement of Wycliffite belief on the subject earlier (fol. 154); see also fols. 195, 212.

[95] Fols. 180–180ᵛ.

[96] See the earlier discussion of this point, and cf. fol. 168: 'Sic veri predicatores ewangelici, quo magis fuerat indignacio antichristi contra eos, eo instancius laborant, scribendo, predicando, docendo ad ipsius destruccionem et omnium fautorum suorum'. The author also defends lay preaching, and objects to the episcopal insistence upon licenses for preachers (fols. 165ᵛ, 181ᵛ); the bishops, he asserts, send 'ydiotas', not 'doctos in scripturis ... ad predicandum' (fol. 157).

first is the question of the Flanders crusade of bishop Despenser on behalf of Urban VI and against his rival Clement VII. The frequency with which the author recurs to this topic is surprising, given that the crusade took place about six years before the composition of the *Opus Arduum*; it is also perhaps surprising that, with the writer's interest in the relations of Church and State, nothing is said about Despenser's subsequent impeachment.[97] The discussion can hardly derive from an earlier text, originating when the crusade was a topical issue, since the allusions are repetitive and are spread throughout the commentary.[98] The writer appears to see the crusade as a usefully recent exemplification of the many ills he has identified in the Church: the belligerence of the clergy in maintaining their alleged claims, spiritual or temporal, the hypocrisy of the friars who violated their rule by acting as *procuratores* for the crusade when their opposition might have prevented it (fol. 144), the denial by all orders of the precepts of the gospel in their participation, and the falseness of the indulgences offered by Urban VI and Clement VII to their supporters. So frequent are the citations of the crusade, and so outspoken the condemnation of it, that one suspects that either the author or his intended audience had had some personal interest in its course. The second question is the persecution of the writer's own order. The persecution is seen as instigated by antichrist, identifiable as all who do not follow the precepts of the gospel but more particularly as the ecclesiastical hierarchy, and is directed against all who impugn their way of life.[99] Those preaching against clerical abuses 'incarcerantur, affligun-tur, vel ne predicent prohibentur omnes veri precones ewangelici...tam et hereticum clamant et Lolaldum merito comburendum' (fol. 157ᵛ). More extreme is the statement earlier in the text 'nunc autem tanta est persecucio induta contra aduersarios antichristi ut uel combustioni tamquam heretici uel carceri perpetuo tamquam paricide deputentur' (fol. 128ᵛ). At first it would seem that the author states that burning is already the penalty for obduracy as a Lollard, but closer examination of the wording shows that this is never quite the case. There is obviously knowledge that death is a possible punishment, knowledge that could have come from awareness of this eventuality on the continent, but it is nowhere stated that such punishment has been exacted in England.[100] As

---

[97] See particularly fols. 132–3, 146ᵛ, 154ᵛ, 181, 188; for an account of events following the crusade see M. Aston, 'The Impeachment of Bishop Despenser', *Bulletin of the Institute of Historical Research*, xxxviii (1965), 127–48.

[98] Knighton, ii. 178 mentions a sermon of Aston against the crusade in 1383. The way in which discussion of the crusade is worked into the commentary here throughout is in marked contrast to the obviously excrescent structures examined above, 47-8.

[99] Fols. 158, 167ᵛ, 194ᵛ; the writer (fols. 141–141ᵛ) urges attempts to convert the persecutors, and recognises (fol. 157ᵛ) that persecution is not always the worst fate that can befall a group.

[100] See fols. 161ᵛ, 164, 171, 180ᵛ, 181ᵛ, 195; typical are the rather vague terms used in fol. 160: 'sic nunc plures ewangelici a papa Romano et vicariis suis uariis generibus mortis occiduntur, et multo plures talium occisi erunt ab eis. Ista doctrina wlgata et

Richardson pointed out, though *De Heretico Comburendo* was only enacted in 1401, there is clear evidence in the chroniclers and in documents that the death penalty for heresy was both canvassed by orthodox ecclesiastics and feared by Wycliffites from at least 1388 onwards.[101] One of the proponents of this penalty was indeed bishop Despenser of Norwich, the arch-enemy from the Flanders crusade.[102] The evidence of the *Opus Arduum*, since it is firmly dated, is of interest for the Lollard sermon-cycle: here very similar statements about persecution are found, statements that have led some critics to date the whole of that cycle, or some parts of it, after 1401; such a dating is for other reasons difficult, and from this testimony can be shown to be unnecessary.[103]

The importance of the *Opus Arduum* lies in the evidence it provides about the Wycliffite movement some six years after its founder's death. The form of the commentary, and the interpolations within it, make it clear that academic interests had not yet been submerged to the needs for popular preaching. Similarly, as has been suggested, the conjunction of the use of Latin rather than English with the address to an already converted audience indicates the author's confidence of finding sympathetic academic readers. With hindsight we can see a steady popularisation of Wycliffite ideas, beginning in Wyclif's lifetime and continuing with increasing momentum after Arundel's constitutions and the Oldcastle revolt. But to this Wycliffite in the late 1380s the trend was apparently by no means clear, let alone inevitable. The absence of MSS. of English origin and its non-appearance in refutations such as Netter's *Doctrinale* might suggest that the author had miscalculated his audience. But this is not a necessary conclusion. The complete loss of English MSS. of so many of Wyclif's writings testifies to the effectiveness of suppression. If the arguments about composition advanced above are accepted, 'publication' must have been hazardous; if the author were Hereford, he in his speedily-found orthodox zeal might well have assisted in the suppression of his own work. Despite this suppression, the text that the Hussites copied presents indispensable information for the historian. Perhaps the most obscure stage in the elusive Lollard movement is that between 1384 and 1401, when Wycliffite ideas spread from the university to the unlearned countryman. In the *Opus Arduum* is reflected the view of one Wycliffite about the situation of the Church, his own sect and the possibility of reform, during that crucial but obscure phase.

---

constanter aduocata a predicatoribus ewangelicis, de quorum numero absit ut sim ultimus'; or fol. 171ᵛ: 'non statim occidit quos persequitur, sed detinet eos in carceribus ut grauius puniantur'.

[101] H. G. Richardson, 'Heresy and the Lay Power under Richard II', *English Historical Review*, li (1936), 1–28, esp. 20–21.

[102] Walsingham, ii. 189.

[103] See the dates assigned by E. W. Talbert, 'The Date of the Composition of the English Wycliffite Collection of Sermons', *Speculum*, xii (1937), 464–74, and later elaborated by M. W. Ransom, 'The Chronology of Wyclif's English Sermons', *Washington State College Research Studies*, xvi (1948), 67–114.

5

THE DEBATE ON BIBLE TRANSLATION, OXFORD 1401

I

SINCE the publication of *The Lollard Bible* by Miss Margaret Deanesly in 1920, scholars have been aware of the existence of debate about the legitimacy of biblical translation into the vernacular in late fourteenth- and early fifteenth-century England, a debate that was forcibly closed by Archbishop Arundel's Constitutions of 1407. In Appendix II to her book Miss Deanesly printed three texts immediately concerned with the question: a determination by William Butler, a Franciscan friar, dated in the single surviving manuscript in 1401, a second determination by the Dominican Thomas Palmer, and a third text, the only one in English, which Miss Deanesly ascribed to John Purvey.[1] From the evidence produced by Miss Deanesly, the ascription and date of the first alone can be regarded as certain. The single manuscript, Merton College Oxford 68, fos. 202–204^v, concludes with the inscription in the same hand as the text: 'Explicit determinacio fratris et magistri Willelmi Buttiler ordinis minorum regentis Oxoniae. Anno Domini M°CCCC°primo.'[2] Bale mentions amongst Butler's works 'Determinationes contra translationem scripture in linguam vulgarem', though the incipit he gives cannot now be confirmed since the Merton text is acephalous; Bale's information, however, derived from a second manuscript, now lost but in his time in the possession of The Queen's College Oxford.[3] The Palmer determination is much

1. M. Deanesly, *The Lollard Bible* (Cambridge, 1920, reprinted 1966), pp. 401–18, 418–37 and 439–45 respectively; quotations from the first two texts will be from this edition.

2. The text as Deanesly prints it begins on fo. 202; a note at the foot of this leaf states 'Quere principium huius tractatus fo. 119 precedent', but fos. 118–20 are now missing due to the excision of the last three leaves of quire 10. It would seem that the Butler determination must have been added to the manuscript on the empty ends of two quires, since the sequence of texts in the manuscript makes it plain that no displacement has occurred. This is confirmed by the medieval list of contents on the verso of the first parchment flyleaf, where the determination is omitted in the regular sequence but is added at the end, marked 'fo. 119', with a sign for insertion. The hand of the Butler text is not the main hand of the manuscript, though it appears also on fos. 113–117^v in a tractate by John Eyton on usury composed in 1387.

3. John Bale *Index Britanniae Scriptorum*, ed. R. L. Poole and M. Bateson (Oxford, 1902), p. 119; the same information, without the locality of the manuscript, is in *Scriptorum Illustrium Maioris Britanniae . . . Catalogus* (Basel, 1557–9), i. 537. The Merton manuscript has belonged to the college since medieval times; see F. M. Powicke, *The Medieval Books of Merton College* (Oxford, 1931), pp. 206–7.

less satisfactory: the single manuscript, Trinity College Cambridge B.15.11, was written by a Dominican friar from Germany, Cornelius Oesterwik, for an Oxford Dominican John Courteys in 1430; the present text (fos. 42ᵛ–47ᵛ) as Oesterwik left it was anonymous, but a contemporary added the name of Palmer to the head of the tract and the following leaf, and included the tract with the name in the list of contents at the front of the manuscript.[1] No date is assigned to the determination, nor does Bale include the text amongst the writings of Palmer.[2]

The English tract is now known to survive in seven manuscripts, in all of which it is anonymous and undated.[3] Miss Deanesly adduced much detail in an attempt to prove that the author was Purvey, and that the English text was based on an answer delivered by Peter Payne, though written by Purvey, to Palmer's determination; she thought that all three works dated from about 1405. The inclusion of Payne in this hypothesis arose from doubts as to whether Purvey had ever studied at Oxford, and hence whether he could have been in a position to deliver such a reply himself. Despite the tenuous nature of the argument, the conclusions have been widely accepted.[4] The English tract was printed at least twice during the early Reformation period under the title 'A compendious olde treatyse shewynge howe that we ought to haue the scripture in Englysshe'.[5] No light is there cast upon the authorship, though the preliminary material suggests that the text was written 'aboute ye yere of oure lorde a thousande foure hundryd'. Although there has been some rearrangement of the material and a new conclusion has been added, the printed editions contribute almost nothing to our knowledge of the origins of the English text. They probably derive from a mid-fifteenth century revision, to judge from an allusion to the death of Bishop Richard Fleming of Lincoln, itself modified linguistically in the sixteenth century.[6] In the following discussion, the manuscript

1. M. R. James, *The Western Manuscripts in the Library of Trinity College, Cambridge* (Cambridge, 1900–4), i. 473–5; for Oesterwik and Courteys see A. B. Emden, *A Biographical Register of the University of Oxford to A.D. 1500* (Oxford, 1957–9), ii. 1389 and i. 504.   2. Bale *Index* p. 449, *Catalogus* i. 540–1.

3. See the edition by C. F. Bühler, 'A Lollard Tract: on translating the Bible into English', *Medium Aevum*, vii (1938, 167–83); all references will be to this edition.

4. Deanesly pp. 290–4; H. B. Workman, *John Wyclif* (Oxford, 1926), ii. 169; Emden, *Oxford* iii. 1421–2, 1441, 1526–7; also A. B. Emden, *An Oxford Hall in Medieval Times* (Oxford, 1927), pp. 137–8; R. R. Betts, 'Peter Payne in England', *Essays in Czech History* (London, 1969), p. 239 (reprinted from *Universitas Carolina, Historica*, vol. iii (1957)).

5. Deanesly pp. 437–8; see the material in M. Aston, 'Lollardy and the Reformation: Survival or Revival?', *History*, xlix (1964), 154; the version was reprinted by E. Arber, *English Reprints*, xxviii (1871), 170–84. The two reprints are in *A Short-Title Catalogue*, ed. A. W. Pollard and G. R. Redgrave (London, 1926) nos. 6813 (of which the present text forms a part) and 3021; the latter version was issued again as 3022.

6. See Arber's print p. 178 for the reference to Fleming's death in 1431; the amount of modification in the sixteenth century, apart from some modernization of the language, was probably slight.

version alone will be used. The purpose of the present paper is to consider some evidence about the English tract unknown to Miss Deanesly, and to reassess the nature of the debate.

The question of the date of the texts ascribed, on varying grounds, to Palmer and Purvey is, without further evidence, difficult. One limiting factor seems, however, to be clear: the authors of the Latin and English tracts never refer to the legitimacy of biblical translation as a closed argument, settled by recent legislation. Both refer to canon law, as well as to patristic and more recent medieval authorities, for support for their opinions, but it is clear that no definitive legal ruling on the subject is recognized by either. This must suggest that the tracts were written before the promulgation of Arundel's Constitutions in 1407. This *terminus ante quem* is, of course, more convincing in the case of the determination ascribed to Palmer; his position would be infinitely stronger by the addition of reference to such recent and definite legislation, so that it is inconceivable that he would not have alleged it had the Constitution already existed. But even in the case of the English tract one would expect a reference: Lollard writers often cite recent evidence for the worsening state of the church.[1]

II

Deanesly pointed out in her argument that the English tract she ascribed to Purvey also existed in a Latin version, found in Vienna Hofbibliothek MS. 4133; this she thought to be the answer delivered on Purvey's behalf by Payne to Palmer's determination. She called this *De Versione Bibliorum*, a title which has no manuscript justification. The manuscript itself she had not seen, but used the extracts from it printed by Denis.[2] The later editor of the English tract, apparently unaware that it had been published by Deanesly, did not know of this Latin version, and other recent critics have also ignored the point.[3] A study of the complete Vienna tract reveals a number of interesting matters. The manuscript, a composite paper one, of which the tract forms the last item, is of Bohemian origin, as is clear from the script and abbreviations, and appears to date from the first half of the fifteenth century.[4] The contents of the tract, however,

1. The terms of the Constitution on this issue are set out in D. Wilkins, *Concilia Magnae Britanniae et Hiberniae* (London, 1737), iii. 317. For the use of contemporary material by Lollard writers compare the frequent references to Bishop Dispenser's crusade and the indulgences associated with it in, for instance, the *Opus Arduum* (Brno University MS. Mk. 28, fos. 154ᵛ, 178 etc.).

2. Now Österreichische Nationalbibliothek; Deanesly p. 291, n. 1; M. Denis, *Codices Manuscripti Theologici Bibliothecae Palatinae Vindobonensis Latini* (Vienna, 1793–9), i. cols. 843–8.

3. Bühler *art. cit.*; see further E. W. Talbert in *A Manual of the Writings in Middle English 1050–1500*, ii, ed. J. Burke Severs (Hamden Conn., 1970), pp. 369, 529.

4. *Tabulae Codicum Manuscriptorum..in Bibliotheca Palatina Vindobonensi*, iii (Vienna, 1869), 175. The first items are Jerome's commentary on Jeremiah, Lamentations and

make it certain that it originated in England: the author's vernacular, as he often states, is English, the precedents for biblical translation show a detailed knowledge of English versions and contrast is made between contemporary criticism of translation in England and the greater freedom in other countries. At one point he states explicitly that the debate is not about biblical translation in a general context, but only about translation into English.[1] Although the other contents of the manuscript are of patristic and early scholastic date, this tract obviously reached Bohemia along with the multitude of writings by Wyclif himself and his followers.[2]

The Latin version is very much longer than the English tract, and its structure quite different. The opening of the English text, lines 1–93, has no counterpart in the Vienna version; similarly, the conclusion, lines 220–306, is not found in the Latin text. Within the overlapping section there are significant differences: apart from abbreviation, often fairly drastic, in the English text, matter is added.[3] The most interesting addition is the passage (lines 140–3) 'Also a man of Lonndon, his name was Wyring, hadde a Bible in Englische of norþen speche, wiche was seen of many men and it semed too houndred ʒeer olde'.[4] On the other hand, the description of Alfred's translations, drawn mainly from Higden but supplemented from William of Malmesbury, is much shortened, leaving from the lengthy account in the Vienna tract only 'þe kynge ordined opone scolis of diuerse artes in Oxenforde and he turnede þe best lawes into his modor tunge and þe Sawter also'.[5] This abbreviation casts some light on the relation of the two texts: it is obviously likely that the

---

Daniel (P.L. xxiv. 679–900; xxv. 787–92, 491–584), and Honorius Augustodunensis's commentary on Canticles here ascribed to Orosius (P.L. clxxii. 347–496). The last was completed by the scribe in 1418. The text here is in a different hand from the Canticles commentary, but the latter ends on the verso of leaf one of quire 18, the rest of which is filled with the present text. The rubricated chapter numbering has been corrected, apparently by the original scribe, but after the completion of the text.

1. For example fo. 198 'Anglicus noster, Beda venerabilis'; fo. 199 'si propterea non permitteretur ewangelium scribi in Anglico, quia sunt multi tractatus Anglicani continentes hereses et errores...'; fo. 201ᵛ 'forte ne cogaris consequenter concedere istud licere fieri in lingua Anglicana, super qua sola est contencio hiis diebus'.

2. The best recent survey of the transmission of Wyclif's own writings to Bohemia is F. Šmahel, ' "Doctor evangelicus super omnes evangelistas": Wyclif's Fortune in Hussite Bohemia', *Bull. Inst. Hist. Res.* xliii (1970), 16–34, and references there given. Less work has been done on texts by Wyclif's English followers in Bohemia; for selective evidence see my paper 'A Lollard Compilation in England and Bohemia', *Journal of Theological Studies*, N. S. xxv (1974), 129–40. See above pp. 34-42.

3. The material used in the English tract is found on fos. 198–9 of the Vienna manuscript.

4. The identity of this northern version cannot be established. If the writer were inaccurate in describing it as a Bible when he meant only parts of scripture, he might have been referring to the text edited as *A Fourteenth Century English Biblical Version* by A. C. Paues (Cambridge, 1904), see p. lxvii, though his dating does not fit any of the surviving manuscripts.

5. English text lines 146–51; Vienna MS. fo. 198ᵛ; see Higden *Polychronicon* vi, ed. J. R. Lumby (Rolls Series, 1876), 354–6 and William of Malmesbury *Gesta Regum*, ed. W. W. Stubbs (Rolls Series, 1887–9), i. 132–3.

English tract represents an abbreviation of the Latin, since the same reference to Higden is found in both, but the passage is quoted fairly accurately in the Latin but only in epitome in the English. Such a relationship would fit in well with the usual Lollard pattern: a learned work was taken over and abstracted by the English translator. Parallels are the *De Officio Regis* of Wyclif, abbreviated in the English *Tractatus de Regibus*, or the vernacular derivatives of Wyclif's *Dialogus* and *De Officio Pastorali*.[1]

The English tract is a rather formless piece. It opens as if it were intended to be a series of arguments, on the same pattern as the *Twelve* or *Thirty-Seven Conclusions of the Lollards* or as the *Sixteen Points* ascribed by Deanesly, again without substantive evidence, to Purvey[2]: 'Aȝens hem þat seyn þat Hooli Wryt schulde not or may not be drawen into Engliche, we maken þes resouns. First . . ..' But the numeration is lost before the second point is made, and the only formal connecting link is the recurring *also* at the start of each new authority cited. No formal conclusion is drawn, and the text peters out in an anecdote about Arundel's sermon at the funeral of Queen Anne, an anecdote concerning the negligence of prelates rather than biblical translation.[3] The Latin tract is a complete contrast to this: the form is rigidly controlled by the numbering of statements and objections, and concluded by a list of propositions which sum up the preceding arguments. The opening paragraph purports to give the setting for the debate:

Stabilita siquidem translacione Ieronimi tamquam uera in duobus articulis prelibatis, superest ad tertium procedendum, istum videlicet, vtrum sicut Ieronimo licuit ab Hebreo et Greco in Latinum transferre sacrum canonem, ita liceat ipsum in alias lingwas minus principales et famosas transferre. Et quamuis iste articulus in temporibus patrum nostrorum nullatenus in dubium uertebatur, modo uero tam grandis dubitacio oritur super illo quod duo ualentes doctores huius kathedre quasi in ista materia totum tempus lecture sue consumebant; quorum vnus ad articuli partem negatiuam arguebat per aliquot argumenta, alter uero succedens ad articuli partem affirmatiuam arguebat nescio per quot argumentorum uigenarios. Neuter tamen apparuit scole quid uoluit vltimate in materia

1. All references to Wyclif's Latin works, unless otherwise stated, are to the editions of the Wyclif Society (1883–1921); the *De Officio Pastorali* was edited by G. V. Lechler (Leipzig, 1863). The vernacular versions of the first two survive unprinted in, respectively, Bodleian MS. Douce 273, fos. 37ᵛ–53, and Trinity College Dublin MS. C.5.6, fos. 154ᵛ–61; the third was printed F. D. Matthew, *The English Works of Wyclif hitherto unprinted* (E.E.T.S. 74, 1880), pp. 405–57.

2. The first two were printed by H. S. Cronin, *EHR*, xxii (1907), 295–304, and J. Forshall, *Remonstrance against Romish Corruptions* (London, 1851); the last is printed by Deanesly, pp. 462–7.

3. Lines 290–306, concluding 'And he blamed in þat sermoun scharpeli þe necligence of prelatis and of oþer men, in so miche þat summe seiden he wolde on þe morowe leue vp his office of chaunceler and forsake þe worlde, and þan it hadde be þe best sermoun þat euere þei herde'. At the time of this funeral Arundel was archbishop of York and chancellor. Unfortunately, it is not clear whether Arundel was again chancellor whilst the English author was writing, so that more accurate dating is again impossible.

articuli diffinere. In pertractando igitur hunc articulum, sic procedam: primo quidem recitabo quedam argumenta primi doctoris; secundo adiciam plura de propriis ad partem articuli negatiuam; et tertio pro modulo meo soluam argumenta que fiunt ad oppositum articuli antedicti, per que luculenter patebit quid velim sentire circa anticulum pretaxatum.

This introduction raises certain problems. In the first place, it is not clear what the first two questions concerned. The Vienna manuscript contains nothing that could explain this allusion; the preceding article is the commentary of Honorius Augustodunensis on *Canticles*, here ascribed to Orosius, ending on the verso of the first leaf of the last quire; the present text fills the remainder of the final quire, from which certainly nothing has been lost.[1] However, in the light of the following discussion, *iste articulus*, about which *tam grandis dubitacio oritur*, is obviously the legitimacy of biblical translation and the debate engendered by the recent versions of the scriptures. The positions of the two doctors would appear from this introduction to be clear: the first opposed translation, the second produced evidence in favour of it. Neither they nor their audience regarded the matter as a settled one at the end of the debate. The material that follows does not entirely carry through this outline, or the ensuing details of the writer's plan. The first doctor's view is clearly and succinctly set out: the question is announced as 'utrum scriptura sacra est in omnes lingwas interpretanda', and this is answered by thirty arguments against translation, numbered in the margins of the manuscript.[2] Some of the arguments are very brief, being no more than a statement of opinion: thus, for instance, the third states 'uetus testamentum cessauit secundum sensum literalem, sed interpretacio non est nisi secundum sensum literalem, ergo etc.', or the second, more controversially, 'si aliqui deberent [interpretare], precipue deberent esse sacerdotes et inter eos illi qui magis obligantur ad noticiam sacre scripture qui sunt episcopi, sed illi pro hiis diebus sunt insufficientes, ergo etc.'. Others, however, proceed from statements by the fathers or other authorities, and these are quoted at length. Thus, for example, the eleventh argument turns on a statement by Jerome and Lyra's comment on this. Yet others combine both methods: Bacon is quoted in support of the view that 'quod non potest fideliter transferri in uulgare, non debet transferri in uulgare'.[3]

The first doctor makes no summary of his argument, nor does he reiterate his view at the end. According to the opening programme, the second doctor's arguments should follow some further material

1. See above n. 4, p.69. I am indebted to Dr. V. M. Murray for help in transcribing a part of the Vienna text, and to a transcription by Miss M. Dulong (kindly lent by Mr. Neil Ker), against which I was able to check my own.

2. Vienna MS. fos. 195–6.

3. Vienna MS. fo. 195; the text is Bacon's *Opus Tertium* (ed. J. S. Brewer, Rolls Series, 1859), pp. 89–90.

against translation. In fact the author next provides a lengthy discussion on the meaning of the terms *transferre* and *interpretari*, *translator* and *interpres*. The discussion is obviously relevant to the matter in hand, and the author right in observing that many of the arguments advanced by the first doctor had been confused by a lack of distinction between the two terms; it is less clear that these additions clarify matters. The author rightly distinguishes between various senses of *interpretacio*, but his linguistic theory was not quite sophisticated enough to recognize that, whilst interpretation can proceed without translation, translation inevitably involves interpretation. Some of the authorities he cites would suggest that he had appreciated this point, but the conclusion to the section gives away his misapprehension that two languages can be precisely symmetrical: 'tercio modo dicitur translacio fieri, quando ad imitacionem vnius exemplaris in vno ydiomate scribitur eadem sentencia in alio ydiomate.'[1] This ends the digression, but another follows in which the author announces his own view that translation is lawful, even if final demonstration is impossible. The writer's remark here is to be noted:

Hiis taliter premissis, teneo partem questionis affirmatiuam tamquam michi probabilem, nichil temere asserendo; nec aliter intendo in hac materia, seu quauis alia, quam sancta mater ecclesia katholica et Romana sentire. Quod si contingat ecclesiam aliter me docere, aut quod minus bene sapio in quocumque articulo fidem aut mores concernente, profecto sibi obediam indilate.[2]

Such a profession of obedience hardly accords with Deanesly's suggestion that Payne delivered the tract, nor can one readily imagine Purvey endorsing it before his recantation when he might have associated with Payne; its terms should, however, be borne in mind in the following section. The author purposes to continue with material which 'credo, aut saltem coniecturo, esse motiua aliorum qui fauent parti questionis negatiue'; but in fact there follows a lengthy section adducing reasons in favour of biblical translation. At first sight one might conjecture that this passage had been interpolated, or was not originally in this position. But, if the section is an intrusion, it must have been an early one. Most of the English tract is drawn from this part, but it includes a citation from Rolle's Psalter commentary quoted in the Latin text after the author's reversion to his original plan following these reasons.[3] Thus, although there is no sign in the English of the frame, and therefore no certainty that the English redactor knew the whole work, the apparently irrelevant section in

1. Vienna MS. fos. 196–7ᵛ; the author quotes extensively from Bacon, perhaps the most perceptive medieval critic of language but one to whom Wyclif himself rarely refers.
2. Vienna MS. fo. 197ᵛ.
3. English text lines 197 ff.; see Bühler's note for the quotation from Rolle's commentary; Vienna MS. fo. 199.

the Latin version must be regarded as, at most, an early interpolation and, more probably, original.

The return to the original plan is marked by the author 'Dicto de motiuis partis aduerse, respondendum est ad argumenta que fiebant ad oppositum questionis' (fo. 199). There follow thirty sections dealing at length with the thirty arguments advanced by the first doctor. The bias of the author is clear from the extent of these: the statements of the first doctor had taken about five and a half columns in the surviving manuscript, but the answers fill nearly thirty. The authorities alleged by the first doctor are re-interpreted and a large number of contradictory passages brought forward; a concluding section adds some extra authorities in support of the view that the publication of the law of Christ in the vernacular, though to be done with discretion, is legitimate. There is then appended a numbered series of nine propositions in favour of biblical translation. In the Vienna manuscript this list is crammed into the second column of fo. 207^v, extending some way into the lower margin; the scribe had clearly estimated that he could end the text with the quire, but misjudged the length of the material slightly. There is no final colophon, and this absence, together with the smaller number of propositions than had been announced by the first doctor, might lead to the supposition that material had been lost from the end of the text. Evidence exists, however, to show that the Vienna tract is complete.

III

The material so far would suggest that a reappraisal must be made of the relation of the English text to the Latin version, and that Deanesly's assignment of the latter to either Purvey or Payne must be questioned. But the Vienna tract itself does not give any indication of date, beyond the point established by the English version and by Palmer's determination that it must antedate the official restriction on biblical translation in 1407. There is, however, a surviving fragment of a second manuscript of the Latin tract which adds vital, if surprising, information. The fragment is a single leaf, Gonville and Caius College Cambridge MS. 803/807 frag. 36, taken from a binding.[1] The verso is very badly damaged where it was stuck down on to the board, but the recto is quite clear; the hand is an English one of the early fifteenth century, and the text is written in a single column with some correction by the original scribe. From the recto it is clear that the fragment was the final leaf of the text preserved in Vienna MS. 4133, containing the second half of the concluding summary and the ensuing list of nine propositions, of

1. M. R. James, *A Descriptive Catalogue of the Manuscripts in the Library of Gonville and Caius College* (Cambridge, 1907–14), iii. 46; no details are given of the source of the fragment.

which the first four and part of the fifth are legible. Although on the verso the end of the fifth and the other four propositions cannot fully be read, enough is legible for it to be clear that these corresponded to those in the Vienna manuscript, and that no further proposition followed. Since the ninth ends before the middle of the verso, it is clear that nothing has been lost from the Vienna text. The fragment also confirms that the list of propositions should be regarded as an integral part of the text as we have it (even if not of the original debate), and was not added by the Vienna scribe from another source. Within the short passage available, very little difference appears between the two texts.

The main interest of the Caius fragment lies in the colophon on the verso that follows the ninth proposition, a colophon written by the original scribe. The following transcript was made with the help of an ultra-violet photograph:

Explicit tractatus Mag*ist*ri Ricardi Vllerston [   ] de transla [   ]/ [   ] sacre scripture in vulgare editus ab eodem Oxon' [   ] do*mi*ni 1401.

The final figure of the date is not absolutely clear, but from the shape of the stroke there seems no possible alternative; from the material that follows it will appear that such an early date is likely.. The most uncontroversial part of this colophon is the localization of the debate in Oxford; in the Vienna text the English origin is established, and the two protagonists identified as *duo ualentes doctores huius kathedre*, the last term having the possible medieval sense of 'school, faculty'.[1] The existence of debate on this subject in Oxford in 1401 is established by Butler's determination; this latter does not coincide with the Vienna tract in all its arguments, each having some not represented in the other, but there is some overlap of authorities cited that might suggest a common background.[2]

The surprising part of the colophon is, of course, its ascription to Ullerston. Ullerston is otherwise known as a defender of orthodoxy, the author of *Defensorium Dotacionis Ecclesie* against the Lollard attack on endowments, and the compiler of a set of sixteen *Petitiones* for the Council of Pisa in 1408.[3] It seems at first sight very unlikely that such a person would compile the Vienna tract, even if at the time the vernacular translation of the scriptures were not yet formally forbidden. It must be accepted, despite the impersonal expressions

1. Du Cange, *Glossarium Mediæ et Infimæ Latinitatis* (Niort, 1883–7), ii. 226.
2. The patristic authorities, Augustine, Jerome, Gregory and pseudo-Crisostom on Matthew, are so commonplace that it would be unwise to argue from them; perhaps more significant is that both use the *Summa Aurea* of William of Auxerre (Vienna MS. fo. 207ᵛ, Butler p. 411) and pseudo-Dionysius (Vienna MS. fo. 196, Butler p. 405).
3. For Ullerston's career see Emden, *Oxford* iii. 1928–9, and more fully M. M. Harvey, *English Views on the Reforms to be undertaken in the General Councils (1400–1418) with special reference to the proposals made by Richard Ullerston* (Oxford D.Phil. thesis, 1964). I am most grateful to Dr. Harvey for allowing me to consult her thesis, and for commenting on the present paper. The *Petitiones* were printed by H. von der Hardt, *Magnum Oecumenicum Constantiense Concilium* i. pars xxvii (Helmstedt, 1697), cols. 1126–71.

of the prologue, that the second doctor, the supporter of translation, expresses views identical with those of the author; so much is plain both from the greater length of that doctor's arguments and from the expression of the central digressions. Ullerston, if he is indeed the author, must be identified with this unqualified enthusiasm for translation. It should also be observed that the author makes little or no admission of the desirability of episcopal oversight in the process of translation; such an obvious precaution is not overtly mentioned. Furthermore, Ullerston was not one of those who, having dabbled in unorthodoxy, or at any rate in Wycliffite philosophy, at the university, was subsequently converted to contemporary respectability. His *Defensorium Dotacionis Ecclesie* is dated in the surviving manuscripts 1401, the same year as this tract.[1]

Yet it seems unlikely that the ascription is to be rejected. In the first place the colophon is in a form very similar to that of the *Defensorium:*

Explicit tractatus Magistri Ricardi Vllerston Magistri in theologia qui intitulatur Defensorium Dotacionis Ecclesie editus ab eodem Oxon' anno domini M°CCCC° primo.[2]

The arrangement of this tract is very like that of the Vienna text: the author begins with a prologue, couched in terms comparable to those quoted above, proceeds to the arguments against endowment, continues with a digression defining *possessio* and *dives*, and then turns to the arguments he favours on the positive side. A similar reference back to a previous work is found, this time explicitly on the subject of the necessity of manual labour for clerks, and there is again a protestation of willingness to correct under ecclesiastical guidance.[3] Nor is the *Defensorium* a complete vindication of the contemporary church and its status: it is a reasoned account, with full admission of the existence of abuses. The authorities cited overlap to a considerable extent with those of the Vienna tract; this is not surprising in the case of obvious patristic writers, but is more interesting in cases such as Grosseteste, FitzRalph and, particularly, Rolle.[4] Rolle

1. Exeter Dean and Chapter Library MS. 3516, fos. 64–111 and British Museum MS. Lansdowne 409, fos. 39–69ᵛ; I am indebted to Dr. Harvey for information from Dr. J. Catto that there is a third copy in Deutschstaatsbibliothek Berlin MS.Theol. Lat. fol. 580, fos. 375–401ᵛ.

2. Exeter MS. fo. 111, Lansdowne MS fo. 69ᵛ; the latter has a similar explicit to Ullerston's *Petitiones* fo. 137ᵛ.

3. See the prologue Exeter MS. fos. 64ʳ⁻ᵛ. It would be tempting to associate the *Defensorium* and the question mentioned in it 'vtrum omnes clerici corpore validi ad laborem manuum obligantur' with the two previous questions mentioned at the opening of the Vienna tract, were it not that the wording there seems to suggest that the matters under discussion had been more closely related to the text of scripture.

4. Exeter MS. fos. 88ᵛ, 98ᵛ, 104 refer to sermons of Grosseteste, Vienna MS. fo. 198ᵛ to a sermon and fos. 201ᵛ, 207 to his commentary on the pseudo-Dionysius *De Celesti Hierarchia*; Exeter MS. fo. 106ᵛ quotes from FitzRalph's *De Pauperie Salvatoris*, Vienna MS. fos. 197, 203ᵛ from the *De Questionibus Armenorum*. The same passage from Bede's *Historia Ecclesiastica* iii. 26 is quoted in both tracts, Exeter MS. fo. 83, Vienna MS. fo. 205.

is not an author to whom a writer on endowment would naturally turn; he is, on the other hand, an obvious source for arguments in favour of biblical translation.[1] If there is contact in structure and source material between the Vienna tract and the *Defensorium*, Ullerston's later *Petitiones* reveal his appreciation of the validity of certain Wycliffite positions. The titles of some of the sixteen petitions could well be headings for chapters in a Lollard tract: 'Contra Exemtiones', 'Contra Beneficiorum Pluralitates', 'Contra Apostasiam clericorum, sese secularibus negotiis immiscentium'.[2] The third is particularly interesting in the present context 'De legis Christi exaltatione', and one of the observations made recalls the sentiments of the author of the Vienna tract: 'si contingat de legibus loqui, statim de legibus humanis intelligimus, et nequaquam de Evangelio. Quod certe modo in Ecclesia non plus reputatur pro lege, quam versus Catonis aut Senecæ Proverbia.'[3]

It also seems clear that interest in questions which had been raised by Wyclif and which later became identified with Lollardy continued in Oxford up to 1407. The evidence has to be pieced together from slight and often oblique hints, since the 1407 Constitutions made it dangerous subsequently to admit interest or to possess Wycliffite texts; typical is the case of MS. Bodley 716 containing, as Miss Smalley discovered, Wyclif's *Postilla* on the New Testament, written at Oxford in 1403, from which the author's name was subsequently firmly erased.[4] Perhaps the most convincing evidence, however, is that of the Constitutions themselves: the reaction of the university to Courtenay's attempt to obtain the condemnation of Wyclif in 1382 must have made obvious to Arundel that his interference would be bitterly resented as an infringement of the university's privileges (quite apart from any possibility of sympathy with the views to be condemned); that Arundel, notwithstanding, pursued this extreme and unpopular course suggests that he had good grounds for suspicion that Wyclif's views were not regarded with outright hostility, and that the orthodoxy of some members of the

1. Rolle's *De Emendatione Vitae* is quoted Exeter MS. fos. 105^{r-v}, his translation of the Psalter is mentioned in the Vienna tract fo. 198^v and his Latin Psalter commentary quoted fo. 199; for all of these see H. E. Allen, *Writings ascribed to Richard Rolle* ... (London, 1927). Miss Allen discusses the relation of the Latin commentary to the English one pp. 165–92; the latter is known in a number of Lollard redactions. Ullerston later in 1415 used Rolle, and referred to him as an accepted authority, in his commentary on the Canticles (Bodleian MS. Lyell 20, fos. 208, 211^v, 214, 215).

2. Hardt cols. 1144, 1150, 1156.

3. Hardt col. 1140.

4. B. Smalley, 'John Wyclif's *Postilla super Totam Bibliam*', *Bodleian Library Record*, iv (1953), 187–9. From 1382 the authorities had had power to search out and seize books written by Wyclif or his followers (*Calendar of Patent Rolls* Richard II, 1381–5 (London, 1897), p. 153 and, from Archbishop Courtenay's register, Wilkins iii. 166–7), but it seems clear that their efforts were not effective. In 1410 Gascoigne records the burning of Wyclif's books in Oxford (*Loci e Libro Veritatum*, ed. J. E. Thorold Rogers (Oxford, 1881), p. 116).

university was not unimpeachable.[1] Ullerston was a member of The Queen's College, where Wyclif had himself rented a room several times, and where, as Dr. Harvey has pointed out, in Ullerston's residence between 1391 and 1402 there were to be found several men who had been associated with Wyclif. These men included Matthew Willesthorpe and Robert Alington, who had joined with Wyclif in 1381 in depositing a manuscript as surety for a loan,[2] and William Middelworth, expelled with Wyclif from Canterbury Hall in 1369 and bursar of Queen's in 1374–5 when Wyclif was a room-renter there.[3] In September 1401 Queen's paid out money for 'quodam libro de Mandatis Wicliff cum alijs contentis', and Bale records the existence at Queen's of a manuscript containing Wyclif's *De Veritate Sacre Scripture*, *De Blasphemia*, *De Anime Immobilitate* (no incipit given) and *De Statu Innocentie*.[4]

This interest in Wyclif and his writings was not confined to men content to follow him into unorthodoxy, though connections with undoubted heresy can be found. In 1395 Robert Lychlade was expelled from Oxford by the king for teaching heresy; though he was reinstated in 1399, it is interesting to find him in 1402 as an executor to the will of Anne Latimer, widow of Sir Thomas Latimer, and at the same time incumbent of Kemerton, a living connected with Sir William Beauchamp, whose name McFarlane has suggested should be added to those of the Lollard knights.[5] Here is probably the explanation for the three places visited by the Prague men, Faulfiš and Knĕhnic, in 1407, recorded in the annotations to Vienna MS. 1294 containing Wyclif's *De Veritate Sacre Scripture*, *De Ecclesia* and *De Dominio Divino*: Kemerton, Braybrook (the seat of Latimer when he was alive) and Oxford, where they corrected their text of

1. For Courtenay's actions and the university's response see Workman, *Wyclif* ii. 273–93, K. B. McFarlane, *John Wycliffe and the Beginnings of English Nonconformity* (London, 1952), pp. 97–116, and J. H. Dahmus, *The Prosecution of John Wyclyf* (New Haven, 1952), pp. 89–128.

2. Emden, *Oxford*, iii. 2048–9; the manuscript is now British Library MS. Royal 10 E.ii.

3. Emden, *Oxford*, ii. 1279–80. Ullerston may also have come across John Coryngham, examined by Buckingham on a charge of heresy in 1384 (see A. K. McHardy, 'Bishop Buckingham and the Lollards of Lincoln Diocese', *Studies in Church History*, ix (1972), 131–3, 143), through his uncle Roger Coryngham, treasurer of Queen's in 1395–6; John Coryngham himself became a room-renter at Queen's in 1410–11 and 1415–16 (Emden, *Oxford* i. 494), Roger Coryngham later suggested to Ullerston the dedication of the *Petitiones* to Henry V (Harvey, *Ullerston* p. 297 from Magdalen College Oxford MS. 89, fo. 31ᵛ).

4. Queen's College MS. 453 (transcript of the Long Rolls), iv. 476, checked from the roll in question; Bale, *Index* p. 269.

5. Emden, *Oxford* ii. 1184 gives the references for his expulsion, reinstatement and living at Kemerton; K. B. McFarlane, *Lancastrian Kings and Lollard Knights* (Oxford, 1972), p. 214, n. 1 refers to the will, without, apparently, having realized the identity of Lychlade. For the patronage of the living see *V. C. H. Gloucestershire* viii (1968), 216–17 and for Beauchamp McFarlane *Lollard Knights* pp. 166, 214–15. Unfortunately, unless the Robert Smith admitted as rector of Kemerton in 1400 (Worcester reg. Tideman of Winchcomb p. 91) is an *alias* for Lychlade, the episcopal registers do not record the institution.

the first.[1] Other certain Oxford heretics were, of course, William Taylor and Peter Payne, both principals of St. Edmund Hall, a hall which had had the closest links with Queen's.[2] But interest in Wyclif's ideas could be found in orthodox places in the university. The scrapbook of disputations found in Corpus Christi College Oxford MS. 116 deals with matters of philosophy raised by Wyclif and refers to him by name; the scrapbook has been dated between about 1390 and 1410.[3] It is significant that, in referring to the followers of Wyclif, the writer uses the present tense 'Fautores vero istius opinionis ... ut mihi videtur derogantes divine potencie, asserunt...'.[4] One of the most important of the few surviving English manuscripts of Wyclif's writings, Gonville and Caius College Cambridge 337/565 containing the *De Universalibus, De Tempore, De Incarnacione Verbi, De Mandatis, De Statu Innocencie* and the only insular copies of the *De Composicione Hominis* and *De Dominio Divino*, can now be shown to have been in the possession of two Oxford men in the early years of the fifteenth century. An erased inscription on the verso of flyleaf ii contains the names of Henry Bryt, fellow of Queen's in 1403–4 and appearing in the college Long Rolls in several later years,[5] John Mychel, probably the master connected with Exeter College in 1403, and John Gosele, otherwise unknown but presumably also an Oxford man.[6] On textual grounds Professor Harrison Thomson conjectured that the copy of the *De Dominio Divino* made by Faulfiš and Knĕhnic (now Vienna MS. 1294) derived from this Caius manuscript.[7] The case may have been rather more complicated, since the note in Vienna 1294 states that the copy was made at Braybrook, but the closeness of the texts is certainly very striking. Furthermore, though it is later than the debate here in question, Bryt and Ullerston are found together in the records of the Queen's Long Rolls.[8]

The interest of Ullerston himself in Wyclif can be shown clearly, as well as the general Oxford, or even Queen's College, concern. In the *Defensorium* Wyclif is quoted with approval as 'quidam doctor huius cathedre venerandus', with a side-note in both English manuscripts *Wicliff*. Though the passage quoted is an unexceptionable one concerning evangelical poverty, it derives from the controversial

1. *De Ecclesia* was written at Kemerton, fo. 134ᵛ, *De Dominio Divino* at Braybrook, fo. 250ᵛ; for the nature of this copy of this second work see below, n. 7.
2. See Emden, *An Oxford Hall* pp. 125–61.
3. J. A. Robson, *Wyclif and the Oxford Schools* (Cambridge, 1966), pp. 224–31.
4. Fo. 50ᵛ, quoted by Robson, p. 229, n. 1; *cf.* also the passage cited p. 231, n. 1.
5. See Emden, *Oxford* i. 294 and Queen's College MS. 453, iv. 501, v. 3, 19, 67, 100, the last four covering the years 1405–6, 1407–8, 1413–14 and 1416–17. The inscription is not wholly legible even by ultra-violet light, but the names are quite clear.
6. For Mychel see Emden, *Oxford*, ii. 1332.
7. See 'A Gonville and Caius Wyclif Manuscript', *Speculum*, viii (1933), 197–204; Professor Thomson seems to have been unaware of the colophon on the flyleaf, but his statements about the closeness of the texts can certainly be endorsed, a closeness that applies to the original writing and not to the corrections.
8. Queen's College MS. 453, v. 67 for 1413–14.

De Potestate Pape.[1] In the light of all the evidence, therefore, it seems reasonable to accept the Caius colophon. A third copy of the tract on Bible translation, now lost but in the second half of the fifteenth century in the library of the College of the Bohemian nation at Prague, gives limited support: in the catalogue compiled before 1461 appears the entry 'L26 Item tractatus Magistri Richardi de translacione sacre scripture in wlgare ydiomate'. Professor Bartoš suggested that the Master Richard was Richard Wyche, but in the light of the Caius fragment (of which Bartoš was unaware) the surname most probably to be supplied is that of Ullerston.[2] If Ullerston's authorship is accepted, then the 1401 date is also likely to be right. The Queen's Long Rolls give evidence of Ullerston's residence until mid 1402, though they also show him renting a room again in 1403–4 and 1407–8; but, though the later *Petitiones* reveal Ullerston's continuing concern with questions raised by the Wycliffites, the form of the Vienna tract is much more closely allied to that of the *Defensorium* written in 1401, both being clearly directed to an exclusively university audience.

IV

Certain implications follow from the new evidence about the Vienna tract. In the first place, it must be recognized that Miss Deanesly's hypotheses about the authorship and origin of the text are untenable: the author of the tract was Ullerston and not Purvey, the second doctor was also Ullerston and not, as she conjectured, Payne; neither Purvey nor Payne was in Oxford in 1401.[3] Secondly, study of the whole Vienna tract reveals that the English text is by no means so closely related to it as Deanesly suggested; certainly the English depends upon the Latin for the majority of its authorities in the central section, but an entirely new, and much more controversial, frame has been constructed for it. In form it is a typical Lollard production: lists of authorities, biblical, patristic, canonistic and historical, cited in favour of a Lollard viewpoint and given a rough frame, with various subordinate attacks on other polemical

1. Exeter MS. fo. 88, Lansdowne MS. fo. 54ᵛ; *De Potestate Pape* p. 85/8–14, a statement which, as Wyclif himself comments, he elaborated on elsewhere (*e.g. De Civili Dominio*, iii. 119/34 ff.).

2. For the catalogue see J. Bečka and E. Urbánková, *Katalogý Knihovna Koleji Karlovy University* (Prague, 1948), plate 66, col. 144; F. M. Bartoš, 'Hus, Lollardism and Devotio Moderna in the Fight for a National Bible', *Communio Viatorum*, iii (1960), 247–54, especially pp. 248, 252 (Bartoš knew the Vienna tract from Denis only, and his remarks in consequence need modification).

3. Emden, *Oxford*, iii. 1526–7, 1441–3. The defender of biblical translation in the Vienna tract admits that heresy exists in English manuscripts (above n. 1, p.70); with the rejection of the association with Purvey and Payne this becomes much easier to explain, as a reference to already extant Lollard literature.

targets[1]; its use of a source of orthodox origins can be paralleled in the Lollard versions of the *Ancrene Riwle*, Rolle's Psalter commentary or Thoresby's Catechism.[2] Like the rest of such Lollard productions, it is useless to speculate about its authorship. Equally, it can only be roughly dated: its source necessitates a date after 1401, whilst the form of reference to Arundel makes it unlikely that it was written after the archbishop's death in 1414; less certainly the absence of allusion to the prohibition of biblical translation makes a date before 1407 preferable.

There remains the question of the relation of Ullerston's text to the determinations of Butler and Palmer. Despite the identity of date, there is no direct connection between the Vienna tract and Butler's. The latter's six points are distinct from the thirty of Ullerston's opponent and, though a certain amount of overlap must be expected from the identity of subject, the lines of argument are quite different: Butler devotes much more space to the possible adverse effects of translation on the hierarchy of the church, and is more concerned to diminish the importance of the literal sense of scripture than even the opponent of translation in the Vienna tract. Apart from the obvious patristic writers, Butler draws on different authorities, his unusual ones being Peter John Olivi and 'Raby Moysen' or Maimonides.[3] The two texts then are completely independent, albeit both products of the Oxford interest in the question at the turn of the century. It is tempting to conjecture that Butler's determination preceded Ullerston's debate, since the comprehensive nature of the latter suggests that the question had been under discussion for some time.

The text ascribed to Palmer presents more problems. Its form, in the single surviving manuscript, is a muddle, and a less comprehensible one than the superficial confusion of Ullerston's tract. It opens with eighteen tenets defending biblical translation; eighteen points, not regularly answering the first, put the contrary view and this is followed by some additional arguments, numbered in two interwoven and conflicting series; the defender puts forward another five reasons for translation; finally the original eighteen are answered. There is no frame, and the whole has a random appearance as if several arguments on this subject had been fused into one. Its date,

---

1. See, for instance, the texts printed by T. Arnold, *Select English Works of John Wyclif* (Oxford, 1869–71), iii. 267–337, 402–40, or the unprinted material in MSS. Harley 1203, fos. 64–91 or Laud misc. 210, fos. 168–74ᵛ and Durham University Cosin V. v. 1 fos. 175ᵛ–179ᵛ.

2. For the first see J. Påhlsson, *The Recluse, a fourteenth-century Version of the Ancren Riwle* (Lund, 1911); manuscript evidence for the second is summarized by Allen, *Rolle*, pp. 173–6, and for the last (with unacceptable suggestions about authorship) in the edition by T. F. Simmons and H. E. Nolloth (E.E.T.S. 118, 1901), pp. xx–xxvii.

3. Deanesly pp. 404 and 413. The Lollard *Opus Arduum* laments the destruction of texts by Olivi at the end of the fourteenth century (see Brno University MS. Mk. 28, fo. 174ᵛ).

though for reasons already mentioned likely to be before 1407, may well be later than the texts of 1401: the proponents of biblical translation are here identified with the Lollards, whereas in Ullerston's debate, and so far as its material goes also in Butler's, such a position was apparently a neutral one, not yet identified with one party.[1] A date nearer 1407 for this text seems more likely. If the ascription to Palmer is correct, the text probably does not originate in Oxford, since Palmer was prior of the London Dominican convent from 1397 till a date near 1407 and, apart from this tract, there is no evidence of Palmer's presence in Oxford in the first decade of the fifteenth century.[2] But the ascription, resting as it does on the slender evidence of an annotator after 1430, is perhaps questionable. The other works that have been ascribed to Palmer certainly relate to topics in which the Lollards showed interest, but only one can fairly be regarded as his. Merton College MS. 68 contains a treatise *De Originali Peccato* that the scribe attributed 'vt dicitur' to Palmer; but this is a work of Giles of Rome.[3] The same manuscript contains a *Tractatus de Adoracione Ymaginum* again said by the scribe to be by Palmer; this, as Miss Russell-Smith has shown, is with reasonable certainty (and on better manuscript evidence) to be attributed to Walter Hilton.[4] Bale's assignment of these two to Palmer can be shown to derive from his knowledge of this Merton manuscript.[5] The only surviving text whose attribution to Palmer has not been challenged, one not mentioned by Bale, is his defence of Nicholas Hereford in 1393 against the reproaches of a Lollard, following Hereford's recantation.[6] Unfortunately, the subject matter of this is sufficiently different from that of the tract on biblical translation to make any comparison fruitless. Whoever the author of the tract in Trinity College B.15.11 may be, however, the work was certainly not, as Miss Deanesly proposed, the first half of a debate whose second was the Vienna text.

The importance of the new evidence that has come to light lies not only in a fresh ascription of one individual text. Much more significant is the suggestion that questions raised by Wyclif could

1. Deanesly, p. 425: 'Quomodo igitur non errarent simplices idiote circa scripturam, si eam haberent in vulgari idiomate modo, propter malum intellectum Lollardorum...'; *cf.* also p. 421.

2. See Emden, *Oxford*, iii. 1421–2.

3. Merton MS. 68 fo. 23ᵛ; the list of contents does not include this doubt; Powicke, *Medieval Books of Merton College*, p. 206.

4. Merton MS. 68, fos. 18ᵛ–23ᵛ; J. M. Russell-Smith, 'Walter Hilton and a Tract in Defence of the Veneration of Images', *Dominican Studies*, vii (1954), 180–214, see especially pp. 197–9.

5. Bale, *Catalogus*, i. 540–1 and *Index*, p. 449, the latter giving the source of the information. Bale has made the tract against images into two works and has also added to Palmer's name a *De Perigrinatione* beginning 'In materia peregrinacionis' there anonymous (fos. 29–31ᵛ), but elsewhere ascribed to John Sharpe.

6. Found in *Registrum Johannis Trefnant*, ed. W. W. Capes (Canterbury and York Society, 1916), pp. 396–401.

still be debated openly in the early years of the fifteenth century in Oxford, with the implication that the hardening of attitudes, and definition of the bounds of orthodoxy, took place, not at the departure of Wyclif for Lutterworth in 1382, but nearly twenty-five years later under the zeal of Arundel. In 1401 the question of biblical translation could be debated openly, without accusations of heresy being levelled against defenders of the view, and without identification of the proponents of translation as *Wycliffistes*. The fact that later in the fifteenth century tracts of undoubted Lollard authorship were written in defence of the same position as that propounded by Ullerston, and that ownership of vernacular scriptures became a piece of primary evidence in cases of suspected Lollardy, should not be interpreted retrospectively.[1] Just as Wyclif himself put forward many views that originated in orthodox circles, which became outlawed because of their association with his heterodox opinions on topics such as the Eucharist, so many opinions later identified with Lollardy could be questions of neutrality in the early years of the movement.[2] The polarization of opinion came about only gradually. The tracts here discussed point also to the vital period in this polarization. Until more is known about the development of thought and the organization of the early Lollards in the period between Wyclif's death in 1384 and the Oldcastle rising in 1413–14, little will be understood either of the official reaction to political Lollardy or of the survival of Lollard thought through the fifteenth century.[3] Texts such as the reply of William of Rymington to Wyclif's *Responsiones ad xliv Conclusiones*, written shortly after Wyclif's death and therefore free from the benefit of hindsight that must be taken into account when writers such as Netter are used as evidence,

1. For the texts note especially the twelve tracts found together in Cambridge University Library MS. Ii. 6. 26, but compare the views advanced by Trevisa in his *Dialogue between a Lord and a Clerk upon Translation* (ed. A. W. Pollard, *Fifteenth Century Prose and Verse* (London, 1903), pp. 203–8), a dialogue which may also reflect Queen's College discussion of the question (*cf.* D. C. Fowler, 'John Trevisa and the English Bible', *Modern Philology*, lviii (1960), 81–98). Consideration of the relation between Ullerston's tract and the Prologue to the Wycliffite Bible has deliberately been omitted here, in view of the problems in the dating of the versions (see most recently S. L. Fristedt, 'A Note on Some Obscurities in the History of the Lollard Bible', *Stockholm Studies in Modern Philology*, N.S. iv (1972), 38–45 and references there given). For suspicion aroused by possession of Bibles see, for example, the cases investigated by Bishop Chedworth (Lincoln reg. 20, fo. 57ᵛ and 62) in 1462 in the Chilterns, or by Bishop Blythe (Lichfield Record Office B/C/13, fos. 5ᵛ ff.) in 1511–13 in Coventry.

2. The matter of the honour due to images already mentioned is a similar case. Also, though the Lollards came to be regarded as 'Biblemen' not only by Pecock, their view of the source of authority in the church was neither unique nor new; for a balanced survey of this question see H. Oberman, *The Harvest of Medieval Theology* (Cambridge Mass., 1963), pp. 361–93 and references there.

3. *Cf.* the view proposed by M. Aston, 'Lollardy and Sedition 1381–1431', *Past and Present*, xvii (1960), 1–44; McFarlane's conclusion, *Lollard Knights*, pp. 141–2, that the stages by which Lollardy developed may never be ascertainable, seems unduly pessimistic when a large amount of evidence, in the texts written by and against the Lollards, in English as well as in Latin, remains uninvestigated.

have been oddly ignored.[1] The documentary sources have been finely combed for material on the crucial period, even if episcopal registers may still yield evidence; but this paper may suggest that the texts of the time may yet produce facts to alter the picture of the early years of Lollardy and official orthodoxy.

1. See MS. Bodley 158, fos. 188–97; the original text of Rymington is on fos. 199–217 (plus fo. 187 which has material properly belonging on fo. 205); Wyclif's answer is printed in *Opera Minora*, pp. 201–57. The text is briefly discussed by Workman, *Wyclif*, ii. 122–3, and by J. McNulty, 'William of Rymyngton, Prior of Salley Abbey', *Yorkshire Archaeological Journal*, xxx (1931), 245–7.

6

JOHN PURVEY: A RECONSIDERATION OF THE EVIDENCE

FOR HIS LIFE AND WRITINGS

In the criticism of Lollard texts one name constantly recurs: John Purvey has been credited with the composition of a very large proportion of the surviving material. Early critics linked Purvey's name with that of Wyclif as authors of vernacular texts, but, while modern skepticism has argued that it is unlikely, on grounds of time if for no other reason, that Wyclif had any share in the actual composition of such texts, the same caution has not extended to the attributions to Purvey.[1] To take two recent instances: in 1975 a historian argued against Wyclif's association with the Bible translation that has usually taken his name, but, though dismissing near contemporary evidence on that score, went on to observe without query, "The text underwent a process of continuous revision which in due course led to the Purvey version in the 1390s";[2] similarly, in 1977 another historian spoke without hesitation of "the discrepancies between [Purvey's] pre-1401 treatises and the errors he abjured in 1401" as the result of pressure on "the naturally scholarly and moderate Purvey."[3] The time has perhaps come for a new look at the evidence. In the following investigation the material will be divided into four, strictly chronological, sections: first, the evidence that can be taken as contemporary with Purvey; then, the statements that, while not made completely without the benefit of hindsight, come from sources whose authors could have known Purvey; thirdly, the testimony of Reformation writers; and fourthly, the additions made by critics from the seventeenth century onwards. Though there are some connecting links between all four groups, it will be seen that a development occurs so surprising that the man of the fourth section is hardly recognizable as the man of the first.

---

[1] For attribution of English works to Wyclif see W. W. Shirley, *A Catalogue of the Original Works of John Wyclif* (Oxford 1865) 31-49; the whole section was omitted in J. Lechler's revision of this (Oxford 1927). In pt. 2 of the *Manual of the Writings in Middle English 1050-1500* (Hartford, Conn. 1970) 522-523 a section is still headed "Works Generally Ascribed to Wyclyf," but the preceding introduction (356-362) expresses doubts of the correctness.

[2] M. Wilks, "Misleading Manuscripts: Wyclif and the Non-Wycliffite Bible," *Studies in Church History* 11 (1975) 160.

[3] M. D. Lambert, *Medieval Heresy: Popular Movements from Bogomil to Hus* (London 1977) 246; Lambert took his comments, as his notes acknowledge, from M. Deanesly, *The Lollard Bible* (Cambridge 1920; repr. 1966), for which see section IV below.

I. CONTEMPORARY RECORDS

In this category is included only documentary material, and not the evidence of the chroniclers who, at least in the story of Purvey, can readily be shown to be writing in the knowledge of events that occurred after the year in which they entered the facts. With Purvey, two types of documentary evidence are available: episcopal registers and secular pronouncements. From these two only a very limited amount of information can be recovered. First, the Lincoln register of Bishop Buckingham records on 13 March 1377/8 letters dimissory for the admission to ordination for all priestly ranks of a John Purvey of Lathbury (Bucks). Since in the later document of Purvey's trial he is said to be of the Lincoln diocese, it is reasonable to accept that the Purvey here is the same man as the heretic.[4] The next appearance in evidence of this category is in 1387 when John Purvey is named, alongside Nicholas Hereford, John Aston, William Swinderby and John Parker, in a mandate sent by Bishop Wakefield of Worcester to his archdeacons, clergy and people; the purpose of the mandate was to prevent the heretical preaching of these men.[5] In May 1388 the Patent Rolls record a commission to the same Bishop Wakefield to search for the books of Purvey, Hereford, Aston and the late John Wyclif, because of their heretical content. The same commission was sent in January 1389 to the bishop of Salisbury and in December 1389 to the bishop of Hereford.[6] By 1387-1388, then, Purvey was known to the ecclesiastical authorities as a significant heretic, worthy of being grouped with Hereford and Aston; he preached unacceptable doctrine, and his name was associated with certain books, presumably, though not declaredly, as their author. It should be noted that Purvey is *not* mentioned in the early series of proclamations against the followers of Wyclif from 1382 onwards: there, Hereford and Aston appear alongside Repingdon and Laurence Bedeman.[7] Nor, as has been observed, is there any trace of Purvey amongst the Oxford records.[8] It cannot, therefore, be proved from this section of the evidence that Purvey knew Wyclif personally. Whether the geographical locations of the 1387-1389 edicts against Purvey are significant is not entirely clear. The mandate of Bishop Wakefield appears to imply that the heretics named had actually preached in the diocese. But the commissions of 1388 and 1389 may be the survivors of a series sent to all bishops, rather than being directed towards areas

[4] Lincolnshire Archives Office (Lincoln Castle), Lincoln register 12, fol. 161; *Fasciculi zizaniorum*, ed. W. W. Shirley, Rolls Series (London 1858) 400; K. B. McFarlane, *John Wycliffe and the Beginnings of English Nonconformity* (London 1952) 119 suggested that he may have been a member of the Purefoy family of Buckinghamshire.

[5] *Wakefield Register 1375-95*, calendared by W. P. Marett, Worcestershire Historical Society n.s. 7 (1972), no. 832.

[6] *Calendar of Patent Rolls 1385-89* (1900) 448, 536; ibid. *1388-92* (1902) 172.

[7] See *Calendar of Patent Rolls 1381-85* (1897) 153; D. Wilkins, *Concilia Magnae Britanniae* (London 1737) 3.158-168; *Wykeham's Register*, ed. T. F. Kirby, Hampshire Record Society (1896-1899) 2.337.

[8] See A. B. Emden, *A Biographical Register of the University of Oxford to A.D.1500* (Oxford 1957-1959) 3.1526-1527.

that the heretics were particularly known to frequent; certainly, however, the south-west, and particularly Bristol on the borders of the Salisbury and Worcester dioceses, was an early center of Lollardy.[9]

From this category of evidence there is then silence for several years. There is no information available between 1389 and 1401, when the episcopal register of Arch-bishop Arundel records the trial of John Purvey.[10] The trial began on Monday 28 February during a meeting of convocation, when seven articles were objected against the suspect, "capellanus, ut asseruit, Lincolnien' dioc' " (fol. 184). Arundel was obviously dissatisfied with Purvey's answers, but was unable to continue the investigation personally in the ensuing few days since he was needed on affairs of state; he therefore assigned Richard [Young] bishop of Bangor and John [Bottle-sham] bishop of Rochester to go on with the examination and discussion of the articles. The trial proper was resumed on Saturday 5 March before Arundel, the two bishops and other clerks; Purvey then made full acknowledgment and renunciation of the articles as heresies. The following day at Saint Paul's cross in London Purvey made public renunciation of the same list of articles, which he read in the vernacular before the bishop of London (Robert Braybrooke), the earl of Warwick, three of the clerks named as present at the trial, and a large number of clergy and people assem-bled there for a sermon. It is not clear from Arundel's register at whose instigation the trial came before convocation. Purvey's investigation follows directly on from the trial of William Sawtre, a case that was declaredly referred by the bishop of Nor-wich, Henry Despenser,[11] but it does not appear that the bishop of Lincoln had sent Purvey forward. No record of investigation appears in the Lincoln register of Bishop Beaufort, and, had the bishop heard the case, the origin of the heretic would presumably have been firmer than is implied by the phrase "ut asseruit."[12]

The seven articles that Purvey abjured are recorded, without the accompanying details of the trial, also in the *Fasciculi zizaniorum*, in Snappe's Formulary and in the collection of documents in British Library MS Royal 8 F.xii.[13] The four records do not differ save in very minor points of wording that do not affect the sense. The first article concerned the Eucharist: that after the consecration the substance of bread and wine remain, not accidents without a subject. The second on confession denied the need for oral confession and private penance and asserted that these were likely to lead to damnation. The third concerned orders: that each predestinate man is a

---

[9] Cf. H. Richardson, "Heresy and the Lay Power under Richard II," *English Historical Review* 51 (1936) 11-12; for heretics in and near Bristol see J. A. F. Thomson, *The Later Lollards 1414-1520*, ed. 2 (Oxford 1967) 20-51.

[10] Lambeth Palace Library, Arundel register 2 fols. 184-185; this section is printed by Wilkins (n. 7 above) 3.260-262.

[11] Lambeth, Arundel register 2 fols. 179v-184; Wilkins 3.255-260.

[12] Lincolnshire Archives Office, Lincoln register 13.

[13] Shirley (n. 4 above) 400-407; Peterborough Registry (on deposit at Northamptonshire County Record Office), Misc. Book 1 Box X643, fols. 141-142; London, B.L. MS Royal 8. F.xii fol. 17r-v. I owe the second reference to the kindness of Dr. Neil Ker; this section was not printed in *Snappe's Formulary*, ed. H. E. Salter (Oxford 1924). In the first two of these the abjuration is undated; in Snappe the place of abjuration is also lacking.

priest and able to administer the sacraments without episcopal ordination; that each holy priest is a bishop and prelate; that whoever is humblest and best fulfills the priestly function is the pope, even if his identity is not known to men. The fourth dealt with the lives of the clergy: that those living evilly hold the keys of hell rather than of heaven, that no Christian is obliged to take count of the censures of such men, that the realm is not harmed by papal excommunication and that, in the event of such excommunication, papal orders need not be obeyed nor the celebration of the usual offices suspended. The fifth claimed that every priest, even if he has no cure of souls, is obliged to preach. The sixth stated that vows of chastity are not binding, and that no prelate should compel their observation. The last condemned Innocent III and the council of Lyons for establishing the doctrine of transubstantiation and ordering annual confession, and stated that papal determinations from that time forward need not be believed unless they are demonstrably founded in Scripture. Leff has pointed out that Purvey in this last has confused the Lateran Council over which Innocent III presided with the 1274 Council of Lyons, a confusion that also appears in the list of heresies extracted by Lavenham to be considered in the next section.[14] Among the seven articles there is only one that is in any way remarkable in Wycliffite thought, the majority being traceable directly to Wyclif and being found in many Lollard writings. The exception is the third, where Purvey went a good deal further than Wyclif in his assertions about the priesthood of all believers.[15]

After this one episode in Purvey's life which is fairly fully documented, the remainder is infuriatingly vague. Arundel's register records that Purvey was admitted as rector of West Hythe on 11 August 1401, and that the place was again vacant by October 1403.[16] Presumably Arundel was sufficiently convinced of Purvey's sincerity in his abjuration to admit him to a living, but the proximity of that living to the archbishop's palace at Saltwood meant that any relapse would not long escape notice. The formulaic nature of the record does not reveal why Purvey relinquished the living. His movements for the next ten years are unknown. In the aftermath of the Oldcastle revolt, however, the name of John Purvey *capellanus* is found. In three of the inquiries in Derbyshire in 1414 he appears along with others as a supporter of Oldcastle: he may not have been a local man, since he is linked with Harley and Morley who fairly certainly came from further south, and the chaplain who stirred up the Derbyshire supporters was clearly William Ederyk.[17] Purvey's name also

---

[14] G. Leff, *Heresy in the Later Middle Ages* (Manchester 1967) 2.579 n. 1; see Shirley (n. 4 above) 383.

[15] Leff 579-580; Leff's account of Purvey's life, though not of his opinions, is largely based on Deanesly and Workman, for which see section IV below.

[16] Lambeth, Arundel register 1 fols. 278, 290v. The normal formula of induction, however, is broken in Purvey's case, since it is recorded that Purvey promised not to preach against the determinations of the church, and acknowledged his danger as a relapsed heretic if he did ("quod ipse non predicabit aliqua sinistra nec determinacioni sancte matris ecclesie contraria et si sic quod habeatur pro relapso in heresim").

[17] Public Record Office (PRO) KB 9.204/1 nos. 60, 61, 63.

appears among a group of Londoners who forfeited their goods for the part that they had played in the Oldcastle rebellion.[18] It will be seen in the next section that there is other evidence that Purvey was still alive for many years after 1403; it seems reasonable to accept that the Purvey of the rebellion documents was the same as the heretic condemned in 1401.[19]

II. NEAR-CONTEMPORARY SOURCES

This category of evidence is more diverse and its reliability much more difficult to assess: common to all of it, however, is a lack of detachment. Though the records used in the previous section all derive from authorities hostile to Lollardy, their purpose is primarily a factual one; they are also dated, and there is no reason to suppose that the date that they allege is other than correct. With the first of the sources in this section the force of this last point becomes evident. Knighton in his *Chronicle* gives a brief account of Purvey, and a list of twelve of his beliefs, under the year 1382.[20] But, since one of the statements he makes is that Purvey lived with Wyclif until the latter's death, it is obvious that this date cannot be taken at its face value. Galbraith argued that this section of Knighton's work was probably written about 1390, and the grouping together under 1382 of Lollard happenings was pointed out by McFarlane.[21] The retrospective nature of the biography of Purvey is confirmed by the fact that Knighton makes him "quartus hæresiarcha" after Wyclif, Hereford and Aston, and introduces him before the accounts of William Smith and of the Lollard knights. The facts that Knighton gives are few: that Purvey was *capellanus simplex*, that he lived in the same house as Wyclif, was intoxicated by his master's views and labored indefatigably to forward them; and that Purvey preached a list of twelve errors in Bristol. Mixed in with this account are some more general observations about Lollard preaching and its terminology, terminology which Purvey obviously used but which, as Knighton makes quite clear, was by no means peculiar to him. Knighton does not state, as some modern critics have alleged, that Purvey lived in Bristol, nor does he give any indication of whether Bristol was a frequent

---

[18] I owe this detail to C. Kightly, "The Early Lollards: A Survey of Popular Lollard Activity in England, 1382-1428," D.Phil. diss. (York 1975) 235, 500; PRO KB 27/616/15(bis) and E 357/24/49. I was able to consult this thesis only after this paper had been completed. Kightly considers Purvey's career, pp. 222-236, 498-500; he accepts most of the views of Deanesly (see section IV below) about Purvey's movements and writings, and hence his account differs substantially from that proposed here.

[19] The standard accounts of Oldcastle's rebellion do not mention Purvey: W. T. Waugh, "Sir John Oldcastle," *English Historical Review* 20 (1905) 434-456, 637-658; J. H. Wylie and W. T. Waugh, *The Reign of Henry the Fifth* (Cambridge 1914-1929) 1.236-292, 3.85-96.

[20] *Chronicon Henrici Knighton*, ed. J. R. Lumby, Rolls Series (London 1889-1895) 2.178-180.

[21] V. H. Galbraith, "The Chronicle of Henry Knighton," in *Fritz Saxl . . . A Volume of Memorial Essays*, ed. D. J. Gordon (London 1957) 136-148; K. B. McFarlane, *Lancastrian Kings and Lollard Knights* (Oxford 1972) 149 n. 3.

haunt of his.[22] The twelve errors are these: the celebration of Mass is a human tradition not founded by Christ; no priest is obliged to say Mass or hours, which are of human invention; any priest can preach without licence; bishops and others hinder preaching lest their sins be made evident; anyone entering private religion renders himself thereby unable to serve God; to give alms to a friar for his sermon is simony; friars should not beg but should gain their sustenance by the work of their hands; excommunication should not stop a priest from preaching nor divert anyone from hearing his sermon; any curate is in a more perfect state than any member of a private religion; literate bishops exhort to preach lest their sins be seen (*sic*); any bishop demanding a fee for consecrating a church, or threatening excommunication if the fee is not paid, is simoniac and himself excommunicate. It is obvious that there has been an error in the transmission of the penultimate error: the sense is the opposite of that required, and contradicts the fourth statement.[23] The second point to be noticed is that these errors bear only a very distant resemblance to those certainly abjured by Purvey in 1401: both recitals of heresy are obviously Lollard, but the similarity does not go much further. Knighton's list contains four articles concerning private religion, a topic not mentioned in the 1401 trial, but omits any consideration of confession or of the question of the priesthood of the predestinate. Knighton's list is largely concerned with practicalities, whereas the 1401 list shows an equal interest in the doctrines underlying practice. Even in the wording of the most obviously shared topic, the Eucharist, the two lists differ: Knighton mentions the celebration of the Mass, the 1401 trial the theological doctrine. It is worth considering that, if one were presented with these two lists *undated*, the trial list would probably be placed earlier than Knighton's because of its more theoretical bias, a bias that it is generally thought that Lollardy lost as time went on.[24] Certainly, faced with these two lists unattributed, one would hardly be tempted to assign them to the same heretic. This implies that Knighton's account of Purvey's beliefs should, like his observations of preaching habits, be seen as a general and not as a particular statement – Knighton is concerned to demonstrate not Purvey's own peculiar ideas but the ideas of the movement to which he belonged. Given this interpretation, it is perhaps also reasonable to treat with caution Knighton's statements about Purvey's life. The stress here is not, surely, upon Purvey as Wyclif's attendant and confidant at Lutterworth (as modern critics have assumed),[25] but upon Wyclif as the fountainhead of all the views that Purvey and his like afterwards preached. Purvey is "invin-

---

[22] All that is said is (Knighton [n. 20 above] 179), "Iste dominus Johannes Purveye prædicavit in Brystowe et publice docuit . . ." (there follow the twelve doctrines). For the asserted residence in Bristol see McFarlane (n. 4 above) 127, Leff (n. 14 above) 2.587, and Kightly (n. 18 above) 223-225, 230-231.

[23] The exact words, found without variation in the two manuscripts (B. L. Cotton Tiberius C.vii fol. 186v and Cotton Claudius E.iii fol. 277v), are "Episcopi litterati et bonæ vitæ hortantur nos ad prædicandum verbum Dei ne eorum peccata videantur;" though the text is clearly wrong, it is not an error that can be put right by the simple insertion or omission of a negative.

[24] See Thomson (n. 9 above) 244ff.

[25] For instance H. B. Workman, *John Wyclif* (Oxford 1926) 2.309.

cibilis discipulus, doctrinamque magistri sui Johannis Wyclyf per omnia et in omnibus executor pervalidus."

Chronologically, the next source of evidence would appear to be the material in the *Fasciculi zizaniorum*. As has already been mentioned, the list of errors abjured by Purvey in 1401 is recorded in this text. Immediately before this in the manuscript is a list of eleven, subdivided errors "libelli Purvey Lollardi, collecti per reverendum magistrum fratrem Ricardum Lavynham Carmelitam." [26] As Crompton has observed, the sole manuscript of the *Fasciculi* must be dated after 1436, but the ascription to Lavenham provides an earlier *terminus ante quem* for the errors. [27] Unfortunately, the date of Lavenham's death is uncertain: early biographers put his death as 1383, but this can be shown to be incorrect by a record in Bishop Braybrooke's London register that states that Lavenham presented three friars for ordination in September 1399. [28] The position of the errors in the *Fasciculi* immediately before the 1401 trial is not necessarily significant, since the ordering of documents in the manuscript is at times far from chronological. [29] Only the *Fasciculi* preserves the Lavenham articles; they are not found in Snappe or in the Royal manuscript. Lavenham's extraction of the errors was a careful piece of work. The evidence is arranged under eleven headings, each of which is then subdivided into between two and fourteen numbered sections; it is, however, not clear whether the book from which the errors came was arranged in this way or whether Lavenham has imposed the order. The text is too long to summarize in detail, but the main headings concern the Eucharist, penance, ordination, the power of the keys and censures, preaching, marriage, vows, the temporalities of the church, the correction of the clergy, the laws and determinations of the church, the condition of the pope and the clergy. In content and in interest the Lavenham errors are closely similar to the 1401 trial articles, taking into account the more limited scope of the latter. The topics of the first five of the 1401 articles correspond to the first five of Lavenham's list, though some of the subdivisions in the latter are ignored in the former; article six in 1401 reproduces closely Lavenham's seventh. The final 1401 article picks up points listed under Lavenham's first, second and tenth errors. On the other hand, despite this similarity, it seems improbable that Lavenham's work was used as the basis for the 1401 trial because topics of certain heterodoxy listed by Lavenham do not appear in the trial material. While Lavenham's

[26] Shirley (n. 4 above) 400-407, 383-399 respectively; Bodleian Library MS e Musaeo 86, fols. 95-96v, 91v-95 (the foliation used is the modern pencil one, incorrect though it is).

[27] J. Crompton, "*Fasciculi zizaniorum*," *Journal of Ecclesiastical History* 12 (1961) 160.

[28] See Emden (n. 8 above) 2.1109-1110. According to Bale, Lavenham was prior of the Bristol Carmelite house; but, as Emden shows, Bale's testimony on Lavenham is in parts certainly erroneous and it is doubtful whether one should attach any significance to this (as McFarlane does [n. 4 above] 127).

[29] For instance the trial of William White in 1428 (Shirley [n. 4 above] 417-432, MS e Mus. 86 fols. 98-101) appears immediately before the trial of Oldcastle in 1413 (Shirley 433-450, MS fols. 101v-105v). Kightly (n. 18 above) 226 and n. 1 argues for a date of 1395 or 1396, but his assumption that Lavenham compiled the list of errors before he became prior of the Carmelite house in London seems unproven.

sixth group may have been ignored as involving technicalities of canon law concerning marriage, technicalities that were not a normal part of Wycliffite belief, it seems improbable that Arundel or his officials would have omitted the heresies concerning the temporalities of the church or those concerning the pope, had these been in any document before them.[30] Purvey would surely have been required to abjure his views on the removal of tithes and dues from the clergy, on the cancellation of payments to the pope and on the annulment of clerical exemption from secular taxation (Lavenham's eighth group), and his view that the pope is antichrist, that the payment of first fruits renders the recipient simoniac and that the Roman curia is the whore of Babylon (Lavenham's eleventh group). It would seem likely therefore that Lavenham's work was not directly connected with the trial; it may consequently date from after that event as probably as from before it. On the other hand, the identity of viewpoint between these two documents is very much closer than between either and Knighton's list. Even in the fuller Lavenham text there is no mention of private religion so prominent in Knighton, even though a Carmelite might have been expected to have been sensitive to this Wycliffite view. As has been mentioned, confusion between the 1215 Lateran Council and the 1274 Council of Lyons appears in Lavenham and the trial articles. This correspondence confirms the suspicions of Knighton's specificity. Two further points should be noted about Lavenham's evidence: first, that the errors are said to derive from a single *libellus*; if this is accurate, the book was presumably either a general survey of Purvey's beliefs or, possibly, a schedule of tenets such as was used by other Lollards and was usually accompanied by authorities to support the tenets.[31] The second point is the reference in the eighth section to a declaration "in quodam alio tractatu" of how the kingdom could be enriched by the removal of temporalities from the clergy. The details of this given by Lavenham agree very closely with the text presented later in 1410 and generally known as the *Lollard Disendowment Bill*.[32] It should, however, be observed that Lavenham does not claim that Purvey was the author of this *tractatus*; it is merely stated that Purvey agreed with its contents, promised prosperity for the kingdom if its recommendations were put into effect and the ruin of the realm if they were not.[33] To this *Bill* a return must be made later.

The next source of evidence is that provided by William Thorpe in his autobio-

---

[30] For a later form of inquiry into Lollard beliefs that mentions these topics see A. Hudson, "The Examination of Lollards," *Bulletin of the Institute of Historical Research* 46 (1973) 153 nos. 8-9 and 155 nos. 7-8. See below 133 nos 8-9 and 135 nos. 7-8.

[31] For a similar survey of beliefs (*not* to be attributed to Purvey!) see the so-called *Apology for Lollard Doctrines*, ed. J. H. Todd, Camden Society (1842); for use of schedules in trials see A. Hudson, "Some Aspects of Lollard Book Production," *Studies in Church History* 9 (1972) 150, 156. See below 184, 191.

[32] See text in A. Hudson, *Selections from English Wycliffite Writings* (Cambridge 1978) no. 27 and notes: the text reappears in section III below, at n. 61.

[33] Shirley (n. 4 above) 393, "De Possessionibus ecclesiæ dicit, 1 Quod ostensum est manifeste in quodam alio tractatu speciali, quomodo rex . . . Ad quod faciendum invocat et hortatur regem, dominos, et communes. Ad idem etiam minatur finalem destructionem vel translationem regni, si non fiat; et promittit exaltationem totius regni et specialiter militiæ, si hoc fiat."

graphical account of his own trial before Arundel in 1407. This account is found in one fifteenth-century English manuscript, and in two Latin manuscripts from Hussite Bohemia; it was also printed in the Reformation period and was familiar to historians such as Bale.[34] Although no record of the trial is found in Arundel's register, the claims that Thorpe makes which can be checked against other sources can be corroborated.[35] About Purvey, Thorpe does not say much. He reports that Arundel taunted him with Purvey's recantation, and with Purvey's avidity for tithes as incumbent of the living near Saltwood; the tense used with regard to this last implies, though it is not clearly stated, that Purvey's activities in this regard no longer continued. Purvey's holding and resignation of the living at West Hythe are established by Arundel's register. It may therefore be reasonable to accept Thorpe's claim that, at the time of his own trial, Purvey "schewiþ now himsilf to be neiþir hoot ne coold."[36] Otherwise Thorpe's testimony is slight. He lists Purvey among Hereford, Repingdon and two less familiar names, Bowland and Geoffrey of Pickering, as his mentors in Wycliffite thought.[37] Purvey is here for the first time found among the early group who knew Wyclif at Oxford, though Thorpe does not explicitly state that Purvey belonged with them. Thorpe also records that Arundel threatened him with imprisonment in the same place in which previously Hereford and Purvey had suffered; from the ensuing conversation, this is Saltwood prison.[38] Though the 1401 trial does not mention this, it would be perfectly credible that Purvey should have been so imprisoned prior to the convocation.

Next comes perhaps the most difficult source to evaluate: Netter in his *Doctrinale*, a source to which may be traced many of the later accretions to the story of Purvey.[39] Netter's great work seems to have been written between 1421 and 1427; as well as his experience in the trials of such notorious Lollards as Oldcastle, William Taylor and William White, Netter obviously had access to a much larger number of Wyclif's Latin works than are now extant in manuscripts of English origin.[40] His testimony therefore commands respect, but its wording deserves scrutiny. Netter

---

[34] Bodleian Library MS Rawlinson C.208; Vienna Nationalbibliothek MS 3936; Prague Metropolitan Chapter MS 0.29; edition published probably in Antwerp in 1530 (S.T.C. 25045). For further details see Hudson (n. 32 above) no. 4; variation between the versions over some of the names of Wyclif's followers does not affect occurrences of Purvey's name. For Bale's knowledge of the text see section III below.

[35] See Hudson (n. 32 above) no. 4, and *John Lydford's Book*, ed. D. M. Owen, Devon and Cornwall Record Society n.s. 20 (1975) nos. 206 and 209.

[36] MS Rawl. C.208 fol. 24.

[37] A modernized version of the [1530?] printing was edited by A. W. Pollard, *Fifteenth Century Prose and Verse* (Westminster 1903) 117, 119, 163; in MS Rawl. C.208 these are fols. 22, 25 and 85v.

[38] Pollard 165; Rawl. C.208 fol. 88.

[39] I have used primarily the edition of Netter's *Doctrinale* by B. Blanciotti (Venice 1757-1759), but have consulted the earlier edition published in Venice in 1571, and some of the manuscripts in England. For the edition used by Bale see below.

[40] See Emden (n. 8 above) 2.1343-1344 for the date of composition; Netter quotes, for instance, from Wyclif's *Trialogus, De Eucharistia* and *De potestate pape* among other texts now available only in Vienna and Prague.

seems to refer to Purvey by name five times, though there are another three references which, because of their similarity to explicit citation of Purvey, can reasonably be added.[41] Most important, Netter quotes from two books that he attributes to Purvey. The first of these is a *De compendiis scripturarum, paternarum doctrinarum et canonum*, a copy of which Netter says he owns, taken from Purvey in prison. In the first chapter of this work, Netter states, the author proves that all priests are obliged to preach; later in the work it is alleged that kings, soldiers and indeed all laymen can preach; in the third chapter it is also argued that preaching is legitimate for women. Purvey, as quoted by Netter, used quotations from canon law, Augustine and Gregory to support these views.[42] The book in question was thus obviously of the type exemplified at its fullest Lollard extent in the *Floretum*; that it was not the *Floretum* itself is, however, proved by another passage where Netter refers to *discipuli* of Wyclif, Purvey *and* the author of the *Floretum*.[43] It is not clear from Netter's references whether the *Compendium* was entirely concerned with preaching, or whether this was merely the subject of the opening chapters.[44] The second work of Purvey's that Netter quotes is a *Libellus de oratione*: the third chapter of this work discussed the question of the length of prayers and chants in the contemporary church, while the fourth examined the reasons for prayer. The method of the work was apparently similar to that of the *Compendium* (and to that of many Lollard works), with patristic quotations to back up the heterodox opinions. A third reference, ascribed to Purvey but not stated to be from the *De oratione*, is probably to this work: its subject was the meaning of the words in Genesis 18.2 "Abraham adoravit eos," that is, the angels that visited his house; Purvey, by Netter's account, took *adoravit* to mean no more than *salutavit*. The matter under discussion, it may be deduced, was the honor due to saints, but this could form part of an argument about whether prayers might be addressed to any other than God.[45] The quotations that Netter gives from these two works, brief though they are, suffice to show that neither is identifiable with any of the multitude of writings later ascribed to Purvey.

Apart from the quotations Netter's testimony is limited to a few descriptions: Purvey is "unus ... magnus authoritate, doctor eximius," "discipulus Wicleffi," "glossator Wicleffi" and "librarius Lollardorum."[46] This does not add much to our knowledge: from other sources it is plain that Purvey disseminated Wyclif's views, and his position in the recitals, from opposing sides, of Knighton and Thorpe would

---

[41] Netter names Purvey in books 2.70, 73, 5.145, 6.13 and 117; book 2.68 refers to "alius glossator" which the 1757 edition glosses as Purvey; 6.17 refers also to a "glossator" in a book *De oratione* (the title of one of Purvey's works), and Bodleian Library MS Bodley 262 fol. 33 expands this by the name "Purvey"; 6.18 refers to the same work as the previous chapter.

[42] Book 2.70, 73; the second of these does not mention the title of the work, but the text is obviously the same as that named three chapters previously.

[43] Book 5.145; for the *Floretum* see A. Hudson, "A Lollard Compilation and the Dissemination of Wycliffite Thought," *Journal of Theological Studies* n.s. 23 (1972) 65-81 and idem, "A Lollard Compilation in England and Bohemia," JTS 25 (1974) 129-140. Above 13-29 and 31-42.

[44] Book 2.73 states that the book taken from Purvey contained three chapters.

[45] Book 6.13, 17; unnamed work quoted in 6.117.

[46] Book 2.70, 73, 5.145, 6.13, 117.

lead one to deduce that he had come to be of some standing in the movement. Whether Netter's "doctor eximius" should be taken to mean that Purvey had a university education seems doubtful; if it is more than an ironic jibe, it could merely mean that Purvey excelled in Lollard learning. By *glossator* Netter clearly means nothing more than "interpreter," one who expounded and elaborated upon his master's teaching; the stress is again upon the derivative nature of Purvey's ideas.[47] The final description, "librarius Lollardorum," the source of so many of the components of the house of cards that will be described in the next two sections, is only given once and is tantalizingly vague. Rather than that Purvey was the author of many Lollard tracts, it more probably means that he was the transcriber or, at most, collector of such works. It should be noted that, despite Netter's expertise in matters Wycliffite, he gives no indication of the range of Purvey's heresies, a range that is much more clearly set out in Lavenham's testimony or in the 1401 trial articles. Similarly, compared with the considerable amount of space devoted to the views of William White,[48] surprisingly little is said about Purvey. It seems reasonable to conclude that Netter's knowledge of Purvey was limited, limited possibly just to the two works that he quotes, and that he had no personal acquaintance with him. As with Knighton, Netter should be treated on the subject of Purvey with some caution.

The last source in this category is very slight. In the trial of John Walcote, a shepherd of Hasleton in Gloucestershire, the suspect claimed to have known Purvey; the trial appears in the Worcester register of Bishop Morgan and is dated 1425. Walcote, despite his humble profession, had been in London and Northampton as well as Bristol, and claimed acquaintance with Swinderby, Taylor, Oldcastle and the London heretic John Claydon. The testimony does not make clear whether Purvey was still living at the time of the trial, nor where or when Walcote had met him.[49]

III. REFORMATION WRITERS

The material in this and the next section is of a different kind from that in the preceding groups: all of it is at best secondary and must be regarded as speculation unless strong reasons are evident for crediting it with more authority. It is, however,

[47] This is very obvious from the way in which Purvey is quoted in many instances immediately after Wyclif, and to similar effect. To take "glossator" as referring to the provider of the glosses found as one stage in the transition from the Early to Late Versions of the Wycliffite Bible (as has been done by S. L. Fristedt, *The Wycliffe Bible* pt. 2, Stockholm Studies in English 21 [1969] lxiii ff. and references) is to assign a more technical meaning to the word than the context in Netter will bear.

[48] See book 6.54, 66, 99, 112-113, 128-129, 140, 156, 164.

[49] Worcestershire Record Office, Worcester register Morgan pp. 168-171; case discussed by Thomson (n. 9 above) 27-28. The relevant section (168-169) reads, "Item quod tu cum hereticis videlicet cum Johanne Beuerlay et cum quodam pellipario ciuitatis London' vocato Claydon ac cum Willelmo Taylour condemnato ad mortem ... communicasti publice et occulte in anime tue periculum non modicum et grauamen et in perniciosum exemplum aliorum. Fatetur articulum et nedum communicauit cum istis vt dixit set eciam cum Willelmo Swynderby, Johanne Puruay et Johanne Oldcastell de heresi et lollardria ad mortem condempnato."

arguable that some of the writers here had access to primary sources now lost to us. If a sixteenth-century writer can be shown to have used sources still available with accuracy and discernment, it may be worth at least keeping an open mind about his statements when their source is no longer extant, provided that those statements are not incompatible with other evidence.

The two writers with whom it is profitable to deal here are John Bale and John Foxe. Bale is the more productive, and the one who published on Purvey first. Bale for a time owned the single manuscript of *Fasciculi zizaniorum*, now Bodleian Library MS e Musaeo 86, and copiously annotated it. As Crompton has observed, the index that Bale provided to the manuscript is listed by him among his own writings in his *Illustrium Magnae Britanniae scriptorum . . . summarium* (fol. 243v), published in Ipswich in 1548; also listed there is the translation of Thorpe's trial which Bale entered into the manuscript (fols. 105v-110v, now ending incomplete). These notes, and probably the rest of Bale's annotations, must therefore have been made between 1540, when the manuscript was dispersed from the dissolved monastic library, and 1547, during Bale's first exile.[50] The annotations are thus Bale's first notes on Purvey. The *Fasciculi* evidence that has been described in the previous section was keenly scrutinized by Bale. Lavenham's articles appear in the manuscript on fols. 91v-95, but for some reason the scribe, having filled the first column of fol. 91v, left the second column blank and continued on fol. 92. Bale filled this second column with notes about Purvey. First he added five references to Purvey from Netter's *Doctrinale*, for which he used the Paris edition of 1521-1532;[51] his quotations are very accurate. Bale then went on, "Iste Joannes Purvey cum Nicolao Herforde doctore theologo, in carcere castri de Saltwode maximis penis astrictus, tandem palinodiam cecinit Londini ad crucem diui Pauli, sub Thomas Arundell Cantuariensi archiepiscopo, anno domini MCCCXCVJ postmodum denuo incarceratus fuit sub Henrico Chycheleye archiepiscopo Cantuariensi anno domini 1421 vt predictus."

[50] See Crompton (n. 27 above) 39-41. Bale certainly knew the text, and probably this, now the only surviving, manuscript, before the Dissolution and before his own defection from the Carmelite order in 1536; this is evident from his notes on Netter, to whom he attributed the *Fasciculi*, in his collections towards a history of his order (see Bodleian Library MS Bodley 73, fols. 56-58, and B. L. MS Harley 3838, fols. 203v-204; for the date of these see L. P. Fairfield, "John Bale and the Development of Protestant Hagiography in England," *Journal of Ecclesiastical History* 24 [1973] 146 n. 4).

[51] Netter (n. 39 above) books 2.70, 73, 6.13, 117, 5.145, cited in that order. The edition of the text from the press of J. B. Ascensius in Paris was in three volumes; the first to be published was "Tomus Secundus" containing book 5 *De sacramentis* in 1521, the second contained book 6 *De sacramentalibus* and came out in 1523, and the last containing books 1 to 4 appeared in 1532. There is an oddity in Bale's references that is hard to explain: his folio numbers agree precisely with these volumes, but he refers to book 5 as volume 3, to book 6 as volume 2. Yet, in addition to the order of publication indicated, book 5 in the print is headed on every verso "Tomi Secundi." Strangely, the edition produced by the press of J. M. de Terra Nova and J. Archarius in Salamanca appeared in the order book 6 (1556) and book 5 (1557); but the date of that edition is too late for Bale's references, and the folios do not agree with his numbers. There is no other known early edition of the text, and in any case the agreement in folio numbers with the Ascensius edition is unlikely to be a coincidence.

This information is found again in Bale's hand on fol. 62 where Purvey appears among the list of Lollards whose biographies are there summarized; it is preceded by one further sentence, "Ioannes Purvey, arcium liberalium Oxonie magister, Wicleui discipulus, glossator, et interpres, vere sincerus theologus ac Latine eruditus, ingenio et eloquio clarus, legisque peritissimus quam plura scripta reliquit posteris." This last sentence is a fair interpretation of the quotations from the *Doctrinale* that Bale gives in his other note, apart from the Oxford association; this is presumably taken from Netter's description *doctor eximius*, quoted by Bale, with the reasonable addition of Oxford because of Wyclif's link with the university. The repeated statement concerning Purvey's imprisonment with Hereford derives from a similar, but less justifiable, extension of a known source, in this case Thorpe's autobiography. Bale, as has been mentioned, had copied into the *Fasciculi* manuscript his translation of this work; the text is now incomplete because of the excision of leaves, but may reasonably be presumed to have been originally a full version. As was remarked in the previous section, Thorpe refers to Arundel's threat of imprisonment in the same place in which Hereford and Purvey had suffered; Thorpe does *not* say that these two men had been there at the same time, but it would not be an unnatural reading of the sentence to take it in that way. Immediately after this threat, Arundel in Thorpe's account mentions the heretic's pleasure at the archbishop's departure from England in 1397, departure which had resulted in Thorpe's release by Bishop Braybrooke.[52] Bale's date for Purvey's imprisonment seems to derive from an over-ingenious interpretation of this sequence of unrelated remarks. This leaves Bale's assertion of the imprisonment of Purvey in 1421. Again this probably derives from Bale's ingenuity in piecing together hints in Netter. Bale quoted the passage from the *Doctrinale*, book 2.73, where Netter refers to the book said to be by Purvey "jam carceribus mancipato surreptum"; Netter's dedicatory epistle for the first four books is addressed to Pope Martin V, but speaks of Henry V as still alive and must therefore have been written before 1422.[53] It would seem that Bale put those two facts together to conclude that Purvey was imprisoned in 1421, and to deduce that, since Purvey's previous imprisonment had been imposed by an archbishop of Canterbury, the second imprisonment would also have been in that prelate's keeping. While it is unlikely that the last deduction is correct, since the very full register left by Henry Chichele does not mention Purvey,[54] Bale may well be correct in understanding Netter's words to mean that the heretic was once more in prison around 1420-1421. Netter acted as assessor in cases of Lollardy for more than one bishop, and might easily have had access to the book either personally or, to judge from the little attention that he pays to Purvey's case, more probably from another assessor.[55]

---

[52] Bodleian Library MS Rawl. C.208 fol. 88r-v.

[53] Netter (n. 39 above) 1757 edition, 1.4.

[54] The register was edited by E. F. Jacob, Canterbury and York Society (1938-1947).

[55] Netter acted under Chichele in the case of William Taylor (ibid. 3.167-168) in 1423, under Alnwick, bishop of Norwich, in the case of William White in 1428 (Shirley [n. 4 above] 417) and earlier in the trial of Oldcastle in 1413 (ibid. 443).

While it seems reasonable to dismiss Bale's statement of Purvey's imprisonment in 1396, it is worth keeping an open mind on this second case.[56]

The same story, together with a list of writings that will be considered below, appears in Bale's *Summarium* published in 1548;[57] the 1421 imprisonment is documented as "ut in utroque opere Vualdenus habet." Oddly, Purvey does not appear in Bale's manuscript notes now edited under the title *Index Britanniae scriptorum.*[58] He reappears in the full *Scriptorum illustrium Maioris Brytanniae . . . catalogus*, published in Basel in 1557-1559 (pp. 541-543). The only substantive change made in the account of Purvey's life here concerns the 1396 imprisonment, where the association with Hereford and the mention of Saltwood have been suppressed. If, however, this was the result of Bale's acquisition of a new source of evidence, there is absolutely nothing to indicate what this was.

Next must be considered the list of writings that Bale attributed to Purvey. In the *Summarium* of 1548 eighteen works appeared, only three of them with incipits. The 1557-1559 *Catalogus* added one item, almost certainly inadvertently omitted in 1548 (for reasons to be shown below), reordered the list and changed one of the three incipits. In the following account the order of 1557 will be followed. The first two works derive straight from the evidence of the *Doctrinale*: they are "Orationem soli Deo esse dirigendam" and "Concordiam scripturarum et canonum."[59] The seventh item, with its incipit, is Purvey's recantation of 1401 at Saint Paul's Cross.[60] The tenth, "Ad regem et concilium," whose incipit is not given, is probably to be associated with a note Bale made in the *Fasciculi* (fol. 94): against the eighth of Lavenham's errors Bale wrote, "Ad parliamentum erant hec data anno domini 1410 et 1414 secundum Fabianum," a reference to the text known as the *Lollard Disendowment Bill*. As has been said, there is a clear similarity between this bill and Lavenham's account, though Lavenham does not assert Purvey's authorship of the bill.[61] Were it not for the incipit given, it might have been more likely that this bill was meant by Bale's sixth item, "Ad parliamentum Anglie"; but the incipit is closer to that of the *Twelve Conclusions of the Lollards*, the manifesto affixed to the doors of Westminster Hall and Saint Paul's in 1395.[62] The *Conclusions* appear in Latin form

---

[56] It was dismissed by Deanesly (n. 3 above) 297 n. 4, on the grounds that the imprisonment is not plainly stated in the *Doctrinale* or the *Fasciculi*; Workman (n. 25 above) 2.169-170 was inclined to accept Bale's testimony.

[57] J. Bale, *Summarium* (1548) fol. 181r-v.

[58] J. Bale, *Index*, ed. R. L. Poole and M. Bateson (Oxford 1902); even more odd, Netter appears there very briefly, with no works named (456).

[59] See above, following n. 41; Bale has expanded the title of the first to fit the nature of the contents as described by Netter.

[60] Incipit "In Dei nomine Amen. Ego Iohannes"; see Shirley (n. 4 above) 400.

[61] See above at n. 32.

[62] Bale (n. 57 above) fol. 181 gives the incipit as "Prima conclusio hæc est quod quando," though the final word is omitted in J. Bale, *Scriptorum . . . catalogus* (Basel 1557-1559) 542; the text proper, as it appears in Shirley (n. 4 above) 360, opens "I. Quod quando ecclesia Angliæ . . . ." Bale noted in the manuscript of the *Fasciculi*, Bodleian Library e Mus. 86 fol. 87, the conjecture that the text was devised by Oldcastle, a conjecture taken up by Foxe (see below). In the *Catalogus* (556-557) Bale included Oldcastle; the first of his alleged works is "Ad par-

in the *Fasciculi*, but Bale's annotations do not associate them with Purvey; if this is the text meant, no reason for Bale's attribution is discoverable. The eighth and ninth items in Bale's list are "Symbolum suæ fidei" and "Pro doctrina Vuicleui," both without incipit. Whether these refer to some part of the *Fasciculi* documentation of Purvey, or whether they are invented titles for books that the *Doctrinale* led Bale to suppose Purvey must have written, is unclear. Leaving aside for the moment the fifth item, there remain ten works in the *Summarium*, eleven in the *Catalogus*, none of them with incipits. Looking at the titles of these, it impinges that many resemble the headings in Lavenham's list of eleven sets of errors, found in the *Fasciculi*; the resemblance is closer in some instances than in others, but all eleven can be fitted against these errors without distortion of either Bale's title or the error.[63] One suspects that Bale has made eleven separate works out of the *libellus* used by Lavenham. That this suspicion is correct is suggested by Foxe: in Foxe's *Commentarii rerum in ecclesia gestarum . . .* (Strasbourg 1554) are given the headings of Lavenham's sets of errors, with the marginal note "Puruei opera," making it plain that Foxe thought of them as separate treatises.[64] It will be shown that Foxe is heavily dependent upon Bale in his treatment of Purvey, and this side-note probably also derives from Bale.[65]

Lastly there is the fifth item in Bale's two lists. The title in both is the same, *Commentarius in Apocalypsim*, but the incipit in 1548 is given as "Ioannes Apostolus et Euangelista," whereas in 1557-1559 it has become "Apocalypsis, quasi deberet, Non deb." The notes to the later work make it plain that this is a commentary on the Apocalypse printed by Luther at Wittemberg in 1528; the 1548 incipit is that of the second prologue to that edition, the 1557-1559 incipit that of the text proper. Bale consulted the work during the preparation of his own commentary on the Apocalypse, the *Ymage of Both Churches*.[66] Elsewhere I have attempted to show that Bale's attribution of this text to Purvey is impossible.[67] Unfortunately,

---

liamentum Angliæ," whose incipit is given as "prima conclusio, quod Anglorum." Neither of the incipits, under Purvey and under Oldcastle, is long enough for the identification of the text to be quite certain.

[63] There are slight alterations in the titles of five of these between the *Summarium* and *Catalogus*, but the reference in each case is clearly to the same work (for instance, in the former are found "De Eucharistiæ profanatione" and "Contra cleri possessiones," changed in the latter to "De profanatione coenae Dominicae" and "Iniustas esse cleri possessiones." These two may be referred to Lavenham's first, "De sacramento eucharistiæ", and eighth, "De possessionibus ecclesiæ," the change to a polemical title reflecting the slant of the material included under the error). The title omitted in the *Summarium* is "De ministrorum conjugio," which is assimilable to Lavenham's sixth, "De sacramento conjugii."

[64] J. Foxe, *Commentaria* (Strasbourg 1554) fol. 43v.

[65] Though possibly from Bale's conversation or his unpublished notes, rather than from interpretation of the *Summarium* (n. 57 above) fol. 181r-v.

[66] See M. Aston, "Lollardy and the Reformation: Survival or Revival?" *History* 49 (1964) 156-157; L. P. Fairfield, *John Bale: Mythmaker for the English Reformation* (West Lafayette, Ind. 1976) 75-85; and K. R. Firth, *The Apocalyptic Tradition in Reformation Britain, 1530-1645* (Oxford 1979) 38-47.

[67] See A. Hudson, "A Neglected Wycliffite Text," *Journal of Ecclesiastical History* 29 (1978) 257-279. See above 43-65.

what is not clear is the reason that led Bale to his conclusion, a conclusion for which the edition itself gives no grounds. Bale certainly scrutinized the *Commentarius* more carefully between 1548 and 1557 than he had done before including it in his earlier work. The *Summarium* has a few comments on the text, but only in the *Catalogus* is it pointed out that the author provides the date of its composition within the text, namely, 1390 when he was imprisoned.[68] This information should have troubled Bale, since it adds a third term of imprisonment to the two that he already has for Purvey; but if it bothered him, the *Catalogus* provides no hint.

When we turn to Foxe, it becomes evident that Bale was his chief source, but equally that Foxe incorporated material that Bale in his published works did not use. Mention has already been made of Foxe's marginal note in his *Commentarii*, the first historical work in which Foxe mentioned Purvey. Also in this work appear the *Twelve Conclusions* and a Latin version of Thorpe's autobiography, both of which could have been derived from the manuscript of the *Fasciculi* when it was in Bale's possession.[69] The account of Purvey in the *Commentarii*, and in Foxe's next historical work, the *Rerum in ecclesia gestarum . . .* (Basel 1559), is otherwise identical with that provided by Bale in his *Summarium*, though Foxe does not repeat the list of Purvey's writings.[70] In the first edition of the *Actes and Monuments* in 1563 the same information about Purvey, under the date 1400, appears along with the headings of Lavenham's articles and a promise to investigate these further at a later time, and with the 1401 trial articles in full.[71] Foxe revised and amplified his *Actes* before the next edition in 1570. Here, immediately after the trial articles is given a full translation of Lavenham's text, followed by the note, "And thus much out of a certaine old written boke in parchment borrowed once of J.B. which boke conteinyng diuers auncient recordes of the vniversitie, semed to haue belong somtimes, to the librarie of the sayd vniversitie: bearing the yeare of the compilyng therof .1396. Whiche computation if it be true, then was it written of him, or that he recanted before Thomas Arundell Archbishop, at Saltwood, where he was impris-

---

[68] The matter is peculiarly teasing, since in every other point of Bale's account it is possible to produce a credible explanation for his statements. This, so far as can be seen, is the one observation about Purvey that does not derive from material that Bale attributed to Netter. While it is unlikely that Bale is right about this Apocalypse commentary, he may well have had better evidence for his assertion than any of the proponents of Purvey's authorship of texts that will be considered in the next section. Bale may have been over-ingenious, but elsewhere in his account of Purvey he did not make anything up; this is significant, for Purvey would have been a suitable candidate for Bale's hagiographic urge (see Fairfield's article n. 50 above).

[69] Foxe (n. 64 above) fols. 43-44 (Purvey), 108-115v (*Twelve Conclusions*), and 116-157 (Thorpe text). For Foxe's works see J. F. Mozley, *John Foxe and His Book* (London 1940); W. Haller, *Foxe's Book of Martyrs and the Elect Nation* (London 1963); and Firth (n. 66 above) 70-110; for the relations between Bale and Foxe in addition F. J. Levy, *Tudor Historical Thought* (San Marino, Calif. 1967) 89-105; and for the *Commentarii*, Aston (n. 66 above) 167-168.

[70] J. Foxe, *Rerum in ecclesia gestarum . . . commentarii* (Basel 1559) 20 (Purvey), 76-79 (*Twelve Conclusions*), 79-96 (Thorpe text).

[71] J. Foxe, *Actes and Monuments* (1563; S.T.C. 11222) 137-140, 140-141, 143-170.

oned."[72] This note is something of a muddle, but presumably results from Foxe's attempt to reconstruct the source of his evidence from notes taken many years previously. The first half of the sentence can reasonably be taken to refer to the manuscript of the *Fasciculi*: much of the material in the first half of the book relates to events or determinations in Oxford, even though the deduction that it belonged to the university is unwarranted. The second part of the sentence can only be understood if it refers solely to the Purvey articles, and not to the manuscript as a whole; against the trial a sixteenth-century hand, but probably not Bale's, had written the erroneous date "1396." Foxe must have had access to the *Fasciculi* before 1553, when Bale abandoned his manuscript collection on going into exile a second time.[73] In fact Foxe's transcription of Lavenham's text, without indication of its source, survives in British Library MS Lansdowne 388, fols. 165-174. In view of Foxe's dependence upon Bale, it is interesting that Foxe never attributes the *Twelve Conclusions* to Purvey; up to the first edition of the *Actes* they are ascribed to Oldcastle,[74] but in the 1570 revision this assignment is removed and nothing else substituted.[75]

After Bale and Foxe little new work seems to have been done on Purvey for some time. The antiquarians and bibliographers of the following centuries, however, took over the story and their publications made it better known. Ussher in his *Historia dogmatica* quoted a passage from Lavenham's articles,[76] and Tanner and Wood repeat the history of Purvey as told by Bale and Foxe.[77] None of these produce any information that could not have been obtained from the two sixteenth-century writers.

IV. THE MODERN PERIOD

If the deductions made in the preceding sections are accepted, the list of Purvey's alleged writings is still very small. To the attributions in Netter and the *Fasciculi* only three texts have been added, the *Disendowment Bill*, the Apocalypse commentary and, possibly in Bale, the *Twelve Conclusions*. Most strikingly, up to this point there has been no association of Purvey with biblical translation. In the medieval testimony

---

[72] Foxe, *Actes and Monuments* (1570; S.T.C. 11223) 649-653; the Thorpe text here appears before the evidence on Purvey, 630-648. The modern editions by S. R. Cattley and revised by J. Pratt (see Mozley [n. 69 above] ix-x) are a rather inaccurate printing of the 1583 fourth edition; the material in the 1837-1841 edition is 3.249-285 (Thorpe), 3.285-292 (Purvey).

[73] See Crompton (n. 27 above) 43. Fairfield (n. 66 above) 90-91 and nn. assigns Foxe's first meeting with Bale to 1548 and points out that the two men lived together in exile in Basel (also idem [n. 50 above] 159-160); Aston (n. 66 above) 168 shows that they also lived together in London.

[74] Foxe (n. 64 above) fol. 107v, (n. 70 above) 76, (n. 71 above) 137.

[75] Foxe (n. 72 above) 605.

[76] J. Ussher, *Historia Dogmatica* . . . , ed. H. Wharton (London 1690) 166.

[77] T. Tanner, *Bibliotheca britannico-hibernica* (London 1748) 609; A. à Wood, *The History and Antiquities of the University of Oxford* (Oxford 1786-1796) 1.493.

that omission may not be significant, since in 1401, the date of our only detailed
evidence on Purvey's views, biblical translation was not forbidden; but the omission
from Bale and Foxe is very striking. These two, like the later Lollards, saw the
prohibition of vernacular scriptures as one of the surest marks of the beast upon the
Roman church, and would certainly have associated the English versions and tracts in
favor of translation (which they certainly knew) with their hero had they found any
hint in their sources. Bale in fact associated the biblical translation with Wyclif
himself, and this was taken up by Fuller, Wharton and Oudin.[78]

The introduction of Purvey's name into the story of the Bible translation came
much later than Bale, and was in the first place declaredly a guess. In 1720 John
Lewis published *The History of the Life and Sufferings of . . . John Wicliffe*; there
some details are given about "*John Purneye* or *Purveye*" derived from Twysden's
edition of Knighton and, without acknowledgment, from either Foxe or Bale on the
1396 and 1421 imprisonments.[79] In the interleaved copy now in the Bodleian Library which Lewis annotated for a second edition is added from Foxe's *Actes*
Thorpe's testimony about Purvey, and, without acknowledgment, the descriptions of
Purvey from Netter.[80] In the following years Lewis was working on his material for
the book eventually published in 1731 under the title *The New Testament, translated
out of the Latin Vulgat by John Wiclif . . . to which is præfixt a History of the
several Translations*. He corresponded on the subject of the history with Daniel
Waterland; some of Waterland's letters have survived. On 17 August 1729 Waterland
wrote to Lewis about the Prologue attached to a few manuscripts of the Wycliffite
Bible.[81] He took an allusion to the revival of a law that no student at Oxford could
incept in theology before completing the full arts course to refer to 1387, and
another allusion to *sleing of quicke men* to refer to the strife between the northerners and southerners in 1388-1389; from this he dated the Prologue to 1388. He noted
a reference to the *last parliament*, but admitted that he had not yet investigated it. [82]
Waterland continued, "Having thus guessed at the *time*, next guess we at the *author*.
And here the first man I fix my eye upon is *John Pervie* (or Purvie). . . . This is the
man I pitch upon, for the translator of the Bible, and the composer of that Prologue." Between these two sentences Waterland mentions Bale, Foxe and Wood and

---

[78] Bale (n. 62 above) 456; T. Fuller, *The Church-History of Britain* (London 1655) 2.142;
H. Wharton, *Appendix ad historiam literaria . . . G. Cave* (London 1689) 53-54; C. Oudin, *Commentarius de scriptoribus ecclesiae antiquis* 3 (Leipzig 1722), 1044-1048. Wharton and Oudin
mention the possibility of Trevisa's association with the translation (for which see D. Fowler,
"John Trevisa and the English Bible," *Modern Philology* 58 [1960-1961] 81-98).

[79] J. Lewis, *History* . . . (London 1720) 218-221; R. Twysden's edition was in his *Historiæ
anglicanæ scriptores decem* (London 1652) 2660-2661.

[80] Bodleian Library, Don.e. 151, facing p. 221; a second edition was in the event published
without alteration posthumously (Oxford 1820).

[81] Bodleian MS Rawlinson D.376, fols. 21-22; printed in *The Works of the Rev. Daniel
Waterland D.D.* (Oxford 1823) 10.359-363.

[82] In the edition of the Prologue by Forshall and Madden (see n. 85 below), these passages
appear on p. 51.

quotes a few of their details; from this it is perfectly certain that Waterland had done no research into Purvey on his own part, but took all he knew from these sources. [83] Waterland then described a monogram on a manuscript in Trinity College Dublin, saying that he had written there for more detail; the letter with the promised information on this appears not to have survived, though Lewis obviously obtained it. [84] When Lewis published his *History* he used all the information sent by Waterland, but all indication of its conjectural nature has entirely vanished. The random guesswork by which Waterland "pitched upon" Purvey has become fact: "It should appear by the Prologue that Pervie translated the whole Bible, and made a glose on the hard places, as namely upon Job and the greater Prophets" (p. 10). From this point onwards the legend of Purvey never looked back.

To review fully the edifice that has been built upon this sandy foundation would be a tedious and fruitless undertaking; only the major investigations are worth scrutiny. The first of these was Forshall and Madden's edition of the two versions of the Wycliffite Bible that appeared in 1850, a work reflecting organization and energy of an amazing kind. [85] Forshall and Madden were fully aware of the shortcomings of Lewis's edition, and of the hurried scholarship of Waterland, his informer, who had mistakenly reversed the order of the two versions of the translation. In their preface they reviewed the evidence of Waterland for both the date and authorship of the Prologue, all of which they seem to have found unsatisfactory. [86] Yet they continue, "That the General Prologue is by Purvey, is capable however of more certain demonstrations." The demonstration that follows is in four stages: (i) a set of parallels of content between the Prologue and the *Thirty-Seven Conclusions*, a Lollard text of which Forshall produced an edition in 1851; [87] (ii) a set of parallels between the *Thirty-Seven Conclusions* and the articles of Purvey's trial, as these appear in the Royal manuscript; (iii) a set of parallels between the *Thirty-Seven Conclusions* and Lavenham's extracts, as these were printed in Foxe's English translation; (iv) a set of biblical quotations from the *Thirty-Seven Conclusions* that are said to agree closely with the Later Version of the Bible translation. From this Forshall and Madden deduced that the *Conclusions* were written by Purvey, and, by virtue of the first stage, that the Prologue was also the work of Purvey. It followed, from the references in the Prologue to the author's own activities in the work of translation, that Purvey was also the originator of the Later Version. This is a tenuous line of argument, and

---

[83] A reference at the end to 'Fox, p. 137 ed. 1' is obscure, since the 1563 edition of *Actes* has nothing relevant on that page.

[84] Dublin, Trinity College MS 75, old press mark A.1.10; see further below at n. 92. Lewis refers to this monogram (n. 79 above) 9-10, with more detail than is found in the extant letters of Waterland.

[85] *The Holy Bible . . . Made from the Latin Vulgate by John Wycliffe and His Followers*, ed. J. Forshall and F. Madden, 4 vols (Oxford 1850); hereafter FM.

[86] FM 1.xxi-xxii, xxiv-xxv.

[87] Under the title *A Remonstrance against Romish Corruptions in the Church* (London 1851), using B. L. MS Cotton Titus D.1; confusingly, the text also goes under the name of *Ecclesiæ regimen*. See Hudson (n. 32 above) no. 24 for further details.

it is easy to attack every stage of it.[88] The passages alleged in stage i are peculiarly unconvincing: all reflect common Lollard ideas, indeed ideas of a general anticlerical bias that can be paralleled as closely in such obviously "non-Purvey" works as *Piers Plowman* and Chaucer's *Pardoner's Tale!*[89] The second and third groups are equally unconvincing, and topics are to be found in the Lavenham and trial articles that are not traceable in the *Conclusions* despite the greater length of that work. Thus the *Conclusions* do not deal with vows, covered in both sets of articles, nor with marriage, a topic discussed at length in Lavenham's set.[90] The last stage obviously proves nothing: as Forshall and Madden admit, the quotations in the *Conclusions* are not taken "with scrupulous accuracy" and, while it is strangely uncommon to find biblical quotations in Lollard works deriving from the Wycliffite Bible, the usage cannot be regarded as peculiar to the originator of that translation.[91] Since Forshall and Madden the alleged monogram in the Dublin manuscript, doubted by those two scholars, has been removed from the evidence.[92] One new detail has accrued from a colophon in one manuscript, Cambridge University Library Ee.1.10, where at Baruch 3.20 appears the note "Here endiþ þe translacioun of N and now bigynneþ þe translacioun of j and of oþere men"; the position of the colophon corresponds to the point at which two other manuscripts, Bodleian Library MSS Bodley 959 and Douce 369 first part, stop and where the second of these has the note "Explicit translacionem Nicholay de herford."[93] But, while the "N" of the Cambridge manuscript may reasonably be amplified by the Douce note, "j" is less helpful: plainly there were many with such an initial other than Purvey.[94] Otherwise the case has not been improved since Forshall and Madden. Yet, even if a few scholars have shown themselves aware of the history of this accretion, neither they nor almost any other writer on the subject have failed to attribute Later Version, General Prologue and *Thirty-*

---

[88] FM 1.xxv-xxviii. A. W. Pollard attacked the logic of FM (n. 37 above) xxi-xxiii, and in his *Records of the English Bible* (London 1911) 1-3, though without specifying details; he himself was anxious to champion the authorship of Trevisa.

[89] For instance FM 1.xxv note y passage 2, with which compare Chaucer's Pardoner's Tale, *Canterbury Tales* C.629-659.

[90] Again, the parallels cited are not close verbal repetitions, but similarities of subject matter such as could be adduced from a dozen other Lollard texts that have never been associated with Purvey. It is also worth observing that the *Thirty-Seven Conclusions* do not confuse the 1215 Lateran Council with the 1274 Council of Lyons, as do both trial and Lavenham articles (see above at n. 14).

[91] The final point in FM 1.xxvii note b end, is again inconclusive: the writer in the *Thirty-Seven Conclusions* mentions a difference between "oon translacioun" and "oure translacioun," both of which he quotes. But, while it is true that "oure translacioun" agrees roughly with the Later Version, *oure* is not a pronoun that can only be used by the author — and, it should be noted, the pronoun is not *my*.

[92] Deanesly (n. 3 above) 378-379 speaks of the monogram with some skepticism; S. L. Fristedt, *The Wycliffe Bible* pt. 1, Stockholm Studies in English 4 (1953) 119-122 disposed of this irrelevance.

[93] See H. Hargreaves, "An Intermediate Version of the Wycliffite Old Testament," *Studia neophilologica* 28 (1956) 130-147, corrected by the same author's section in *The Cambridge History of the Bible* 2, ed. G. W. H. Lampe (Cambridge 1969) 400.

[94] Fristedt (n. 47 above) lxiv-lxv takes the second initial to refer to Wyclif.

Seven Conclusions to Purvey.[95] The translational rules that are found in the final chapter of the Prologue are regularly described as "Purvey's Principles."[96] Shirley in his edition for the Rolls Series in 1858 of the *Fasciculi zizaniorum* added a footnote to the heading of Lavenham's set of errors stating that the *libellus* from which they came was the *Thirty-Seven Conclusions*.[97]

Forshall and Madden added to this group of works a further set. First, in addition to the prologues found in most medieval copies of the Vulgate and translated in the Wycliffite version, some manuscripts add a second prologue to several books of the New Testament. The content of these is more tendentious, and Forshall and Madden commented, "The style is that of Purvey, and it scarcely admits of doubt that they are from his pen." Secondly, because of references within the Prologue to glosses on the Old Testament, these, in those manuscripts in which they are found, were also accredited to Purvey.[98]

The next source is that which seems to have established Purvey as a major author to whom, if in doubt, any Lollard text might be attributed: Margaret Deanesly's *The Lollard Bible*, first published in 1920. An immense erudition went into the production of this book, a book that in many respects is not likely to be superseded for many years; but dislike of anonymity seems to have distorted Miss Deanesly's judgment. She accepted all of the texts attributed to Purvey by Forshall and Madden;[99] she knew the works of Bale and Foxe but alludes to them infrequently. Working from the group of biblical texts, Deanesly added, as Purvey's first effort, the texts

[95] For instance Hargreaves in the papers cited in n. 93 above, pp. 135ff. and 410ff. respectively; Fristedt (n. 92 above) esp. 140-141 in 1956 expressed some caution and emphasized the collaborative nature of the revision, but his paper "The Authorship of the Lollard Bible," *Studier i modern språkvetenskap* 19 (1956) 37 indicated more favor for Purvey's responsibility. A. W. Pollard, *Fifteenth Century Prose and Verse* (n. 37 above) xix-xxiv briefly reviewed the flimsy nature of the case, but his doubts found few readers. McFarlane (n. 4 above) 149, though probably in ignorance of Pollard, had clearly perceived that the evidence for the ascription is slight.

[96] Thus E. W. Talbert, "A Note on the Wyclyfite Bible Translation," *Texas Studies in English* (1940) 29, 34; Fristedt (n. 92 above) passim and "New Light on John Wycliffe and the First Full English Bible," *Studies in Modern Philology* n.s. 3 (1967) 62-63.

[97] Shirley (n. 4 above) 383 n. 1. It is worth noting that R. Vaughan, *John de Wycliffe, D.D.: A Monograph* (London 1853) 358-359 says that the evidence adduced in FM (n. 85 above) on attributions is neither "decisive or forcible," but that no more probable author is known to him. In his earlier *The Life and Opinions of John de Wycliffe* (London 1828) 2.42-51, 415-416 Vaughan says little about Wyclif's disciples by name and talks of the Bible translation as Wyclif's own.

[98] FM 1 (n. 85 above) xxx-xxxi; for these glosses and for evidence that might seem incompatible with common authorship for all these texts see H. Hargreaves, "The Latin Text of Purvey's Psalter," *Medium ævum* 24 (1955) 73-90, and idem, "The Marginal Glosses to the Wycliffite New Testament," *Studia neophilologica* 33 (1961) 285-300.

[99] Deanesly wrote again on this subject later for a public lecture, but this deals in generalities and added nothing to the 1920 statement, though equally it showed no doubts about the views there expressed (see M. Deanesly, *The Significance of the Lollard Bible* [London 1951]). Her prefatory note to the 1966 reprint of *The Lollard Bible* (pp. vii-viii) also altered nothing with regard to Purvey. For acceptance of FM's conclusions see Deanesly (n. 3 above) 266-267, 374-381.

known as the *Glossed Gospels*; these had been attributed by Forshall and Madden to Wyclif.[100] These, according to Deanesly, have to come at the beginning of Purvey's career because they fit into a stage described in the General Prologue as prior to the verbal revision of the literal Early Version; they also used for the biblical text a somewhat revised Early Version translation, still in the unidiomatic style of that stage. In fact, as Hargreaves has shown, there are a number of differing versions of the *Glossed Gospels*; the relations between them, and the direction of the modifications, still need further investigation.[101] But only by a dubious stretching of the words of the Prologue, and with a credulous mind, can it be concluded that they originate from the pen of the author of this latter work. Deanesly used as one further piece of evidence in favor of this identity the appearance of a series of pseudonyms: *simple creature of God* (Prologue), *sinful caitiff* and *poor scribbler* (Gl.G.Matthew), *sinfull caitiff* (Gl.G.Luke), *poor caitiff, simple creature* (Gl.G.John). This usage she took to be a mark of Purvey's authorship. Unfortunately, this cannot be maintained. Deanesly elsewhere referred to the assembly of texts known as *The Pore Caitiff*, many of which employ just such pseudonyms; she rightly dismissed earlier attempts to associate these texts with the Lollards, and even to attribute them to Wyclif; but disingenuously she dismisses the coincidence, "Thus the selection of 'poor caitiff' as a pseudonym by the author must have been merely a coincidence with Purvey's use of similar ones."[102] The dispassionate observer would surely prefer to conclude that the evidence is of no value. While the *Glossed Gospels* certainly fit into the pattern of biblical study described in the General Prologue, and evident from the state of manuscripts of the Early Version such as Bodley 959, there is no reason to attribute them to the author of that Prologue, let alone to Purvey. The complications of revision in them are reminiscent of other early Lollard works, and the scholarly instinct that sent the compiler back from the chief source, the *Catena aurea*, to the authorities upon which Aquinas drew also points to a center of Lollard learning at which more than one enthusiast was active.[103]

Deanesly went on from this point to associate with Purvey more texts on biblical translation. First she added a set of twelve tracts in favor of vernacular scriptures found in one manuscript, Cambridge University Library Ii.6.26, a manuscript of very uncertain orthography and clear textual corruption. As she observed, the tenth tract

---

[100] Deanesly (n. 3 above) 275-282, 376ff.; FM 1.viii-x; they were likewise included amongst Wyclif's English texts by Shirley (n. 1 above) nos. 6-8.

[101] See Hargreaves, "Marginal Glosses" (n. 98 above); idem, *Cambridge History* (n. 93 above) 407-409; and most recently idem, "Popularising Biblical Scholarship: The Role of the Wycliffite *Glossed Gospels*," in *The Bible and Medieval Culture*, ed. W. Lourdaux and D. Verhelst (Louvain 1979) 171-189.

[102] Deanesly (n. 3 above), 275-277, 346-347 and nn. Fristedt (n. 92 above) 139-140 similarly dismisses this evidence. For more recent study of *The Pore Caitif* see M. T. Brady, "*The Pore Caitif*: An Introductory Study," *Traditio* 10 (1954) 529-548.

[103] For discussion of this background to Lollard texts see A. Hudson, "A Lollard Sermon-Cycle," *Medium ævum* 40 (1971) 142-156, and idem, "A Lollard Compilation and the Dissemination of Wycliffite Thought," *Journal of Theological Studies* n.s. 23 (1972) 65-81. Above 13-29.

consists of a large part of the epilogue to the *Glossed Gospel* on Matthew.[104] She does not, however, seem to have realized that several of the other tracts are found elsewhere, some in Lollard contexts but others not. The most significant is the eleventh, which reproduces a part of the prologue provided in the English translation of Robert of Greatham's *Mirror*, a text which, as Deanesly herself remarked, "contain[s], apparently, no Lollard teaching or phraseology." Since the seventh is in large part a version of a paternoster commentary, certainly Lollard but never attributed to Purvey, it is evident that this set of tracts is an anthology on a common subject, but without a common author.[105] Deanesly added one further tract to Purvey's output on the Bible: the text known in a number of manuscripts and printed in 1530 under the title *A Compendyous Olde treatise*, and included by Foxe as an anonymous item in his *Actes and Monuments*. She realized that this was based on part of a Latin tract, though only knew this latter from extracts. I have argued elsewhere that the Latin tract, called by Deanesly *De versione bibliorum* (though it is without title in the manuscript that she knew), is by Richard Ullerston, and have attempted to show that there is no evidence to connect Purvey with any stage of the text's history.[106]

Deanesly accepted Forshall and Madden's attribution of the *Thirty-Seven Conclusions* to Purvey, and tried to add further confessional documents. Her views on the *Twelve Conclusions* are not entirely clear, but she argued strongly in favor of Purvey's responsibility for the *Sixteen Points*, a text found only in a single manuscript, Trinity College Cambridge B.14.50. Her reasons seem to be two: that the document follows immediately on the last mentioned treatise on biblical translation, and that "the noticeably moderate and scholarly character of the articles, combined with the late date of post 1400, strongly suggest it." The first argument disappears with the new evidence about the biblical text. The second is, even on the face of it, weak. Furthermore, such evidence as there is of date would indicate a composition before 1401, since burning is not listed among the persecutions of the Lollards; and, though it is irrelevant to arguments of attribution, the description "moderate" can only come from a superficial understanding of its contents.[107] Out of Netter's statement in the *Doctrinale* that Purvey was *glossator Wicleffi* Deanesly deduced that "Purvey was specially responsible for the translation of Wycliffe's Latin works"; she

---

[104] Deanesly (n. 3 above) 270-274; FM 1 (n. 85 above) xiv-xv had drawn attention to this manuscript and tentatively suggested Wyclif's authorship.

[105] Deanesly 315. The seventh is printed in Hudson (n. 32 above) no. 20 and its relations there discussed. FM 1.xiv had pointed out that the second occurred also in British Library MSS Arundel 254 (fols. 11-12v) and Harley 6333 (fols. 20-21v), to which can be added Trinity College Dublin 76 (fols. 99-100); the sixth exists in B. L. MS Harley 2322, fols. 87-88, and incomplete in Bodleian Library MS Add.B.66, fol. 90; the ninth also in Bodleian Library MS Laud Misc.524, fols. 20v-21. I am indebted to Dr. Valerie Murray for information on these correspondences.

[106] A. Hudson, "The Debate on Bible Translation, Oxford 1401," *English Historical Review* 90 (1975) 1-18; in Foxe (n. 71 above) 452-455. See above 67-84.

[107] Deanesly (n. 3 above) 374-381 and, for the *Twelve Conclusions*, 257-258; on 282 she took the reference in the seventh item of the latter to refer to the *Thirty-Seven Conclusions*, but for this see Hudson (n. 32 above), note to no. 3/90-92. For the *Sixteen Points* see ibid. no. 2 and notes.

therefore added to his output the translation of the *De officio pastorali* (p. 378). Lastly, she suggested, though without any evidence, the tract *Fifty Heresies and Errors of the Friars* (p. 399).[108] With this accumulation of writings it is hardly surprising that Purvey became, in Deanesly's book, the leader of the Lollards (p. 277), making his headquarters in London (p. 283); at the 1401 recantation, we are told, "Lollardy lost its most able champion" (p. 284). But, according to this biography, Purvey did not cease writing Lollard tracts in the superficial orthodoxy of his next years: the *Sixteen Points* illustrate Thorpe's assertion of Purvey's state of mind, "neither hot nor cold" (p. 462).

All of Deanesly's attributions appear to have been accepted by Workman in the narrative of the early years of the Lollard movement that concluded his biography of Wyclif published in 1926. Workman added, on the basis of similarities of language and thought, the texts known as *The Great Sentence of the Curse Expounded* and *Of the Leaven of the Pharisees*.[109] Workman also seems to have been the first critic to mention, albeit with some doubt, the possibility that Purvey might have been the author of the standard Lollard sermon-cycle.[110] Purvey's life here became much fuller: we are told how Wyclif left to his disciples, especially Purvey, the jobs of filling in details in his later Latin compositions, of their translation into English and of their multiplication (2.309); Purvey went on a preaching expedition in the West Country in 1387 (2.163); he was present on 4 August 1394 at the funeral of Queen Anne in Westminster Abbey (2.165).

V. CONCLUSIONS

Further than this there seems no need to go: modern critics have not looked again at the primary evidence, and few have expressed doubts about Deanesly's position. Is the conclusion merely a negative one — that we know almost nothing about Purvey? A little more can, I think, be said. The evidence of the first section, scanty though it may be, points to one conclusion: that Purvey was not among the earliest group of prominent Wycliffites, but came to the fore around 1387 and to trial first in 1401. Of his views Lavenham provides a comprehensive account, though the date at which Purvey held them is unfortunately unclear. So far as the evidence goes, it would seem

[108] Deanesly (n. 3 above) 378 and 399; the first is edited by F. Matthew, *The English Works of Wyclif Hitherto Unprinted*, Early English Text Society 74 (1880) 408-457, the second by T. Arnold, *Select English Works of John Wyclif* (Oxford 1869-1871), 3.366-401.

[109] Workman (n. 25 above) 1.330-331; the first is in Arnold 3.271-337, the second in Matthew 2-27.

[110] Workman 2.196; the cycle was printed by Arnold in vols. 1-2 of his edition. Actually, unknown to Workman, one medieval manuscript might be held to give some support to this attribution. In the manuscript of Snappe's *Formulary* (n. 13 above), immediately after the copy of Purvey's trial articles, appears a list of errors extracted from the ferial and Proprium Sanctorum sermons of this cycle (fol. 142r-v); the errors are easily identified in the sermons from the numbers given. But, despite the juxtaposition, there is no reason to think that Snappe assigned the sermons to the same writer as the previous articles.

that Purvey returned to his heretical position after he had left the living of West Hythe in 1403, but it is not clear that he ever again held any prominent position in the Lollard movement. The documentation here is notoriously scrappy, but, compared with Lollards such as William Taylor, William White or even Thomas Drayton, Purvey's name appears very seldom.[111] Had Purvey been a leader in the Oldcastle revolt, it is odd that nothing is heard about his trial or his execution (which, since he would have been a relapsed heretic as well as a rebel, would surely have followed). The testimony of Knighton and of Netter is difficult to evaluate: both are declaredly partial witnesses and deal here largely in generalities. It is reasonable to accept Netter's quotations, but the rest of his evidence is unsatisfactorily vague. As writings of Purvey I would suggest that the two works attributed by Netter can be accepted; but both of these are now lost. In a sense Bale was right to add the trial articles and, more obviously, the *libellus* (though a single work and not the eleven which Bale made them) used by Lavenham. Bale was also correct in seeing an association, though not necessarily of authorship, between the beliefs of Purvey as retailed by Lavenham and the *Lollard Disendowment Bill*. Further than this it seems to me impossible to go. I see no reason whatever to assign to Purvey any particular association with the Lollard Bible, or with any of the texts advocating vernacular scriptures. The whole snowball of attributions seems to me to reveal a naive dislike of anonymity, and a misunderstanding of the nature of the Lollard movement and of the texts that it originated.

Perhaps the most perceptive observation about the Lollards made by Henry Knighton concerns the way in which they became all alike, alike both in ideas and, more important to the present purpose, in their manner of speech. It is an observation to which Knighton recurs more than once. He notes, significantly in the midst of his comments on Purvey, "Et ita connexæ erant atque concatenatæ opiniones eorum, quod qui istas habuit, habuit et alterius; et qui alterius opiniones habuit, habuit et opiniones istius." That this relates to speech is clear from the fact that it follows Knighton's reference to Lollard use of the terms "trewe prechoures, false prechoures." Later under the same year the similarity, which obviously seemed to him strange, is more fully remarked: even those who have only recently joined the sect "unum modum statim loquelæ et formam concordem suæ doctrinæ mirabiliter habuerunt; et doctores Evangelicæ doctrinæ tam viri quam mulieres materno idiomate subito mutato effecti sunt." It is, he says, as if all had been educated in the same school and instructed by the same teacher who "eos eadem identitate spiritus sui simul aptavit, et conformitate unius loquelæ cum fervore desiderii in suum obsequium inspiravit."[112] Here surely is the explanation for the seeming similarities between various texts: they are attributable not to identity of authorship, but to a common use of a shared vocabulary and a shared method of writing. Study of

[111] For Taylor see A. B. Emden, *An Oxford Hall in Medieval Times*, rev. ed. (Oxford 1968) 124-133; for White and Drayton see Thomson (n. 9 above) 120-131, 173-176 and 24-25, 54, 173-175 respectively.
[112] Knighton (n. 20 above) 2.179, 186-187.

Lollard texts and of other aspects of the movement's history emphasize Knighton's shrewdness here: conventicles, often called schools, existed for the propagation of Wycliffite beliefs, texts were prepared from Lollard handbooks and show, because of their common origin, identical quotations.[113] Knighton's understanding of the *nature* of the Lollard movement, despite mistakes in individual details, was profound; another member of his own community was, after all, Wyclif's Oxford disciple Philip Repingdon. Had Knighton's observations on Purvey been read within the context of his entire account of the movement, a number of misconceptions could have been avoided. Knighton's emphasis falls upon the derivative nature of Purvey's ideas, not on Purvey's creativity, on his discipleship of Wyclif, not on his initiative in the movement. Moreover, Knighton's observations have a wider significance than this single man: they suggest that investigations of Lollardy should concentrate not upon attempts to attribute individual texts to particular authors, but upon a study of the sources and vocabulary of a wide range of texts. Such a study may indeed throw further light on the movement.

[113] For an unusually informative picture of Lollard society, including "schools," see the material edited by N. P. Tanner, *Heresy Trials in the Diocese of Norwich, 1428-31*, Camden Society ser. 4, 20 (1977); for the use of handbooks in the construction of texts see C. von Nolcken, *The Middle English Translation of the Rosarium Theologie*, Heidelberg Middle English Texts 10 (1979) 34-37.

7

A LOLLARD MASS

UNDER the year 1389 Thomas Walsingham in his *Historia Anglicana* gives a brief account of the early Lollards.[1] In particular, he mentions how the heresy spread through the multiplication of Lollard 'priests': the followers of Wyclif claimed 'more pontificum' to ordain more priests. These priests in turn asserted that they possessed all the normal rights of the clergy, including the powers of absolution and of celebration of masses. He continues:

practizaverunt autem istam perfidiam in Diocesi Sarum. Et qui taliter ordinati sunt ab haereticis, sibi cuncta licere putantes, Missas celebrare, divina tractare, et Sacramenta conferre, minime timuerunt. Prodita est haec nequitia per quemdam ab eis ordinatum, qui, stimulatus conscientia, Episcopo Sarum confessus est errorem, apud manerium suum de Sunnyng.

Beside this passage should be placed an entry in the Register of bishop John Waltham of Salisbury (1388–95), an entry that is almost certainly the account given by the 'priest' to which Walsingham here refers.[2] The account is recorded as having been given to bishop Waltham on 3 July 1389 in the chapel of his manor at Sonning. The only detail that the register does not substantiate is that the confession given was the result of the Lollard's own remorse of conscience, a detail that may well be the result of Walsingham's incredulity that anyone could honestly pursue the heresy for long. The interest of the account in Waltham's register is not merely that it substantiates Walsingham's claims: it also provides evidence for two aspects of Lollard history that are particularly obscure, namely the early development of the movement and the nature of Lollard practices, as opposed to Lollard beliefs. The first obscurity results from the sluggishness of the diocesan authorities in organizing their search for *Wycliffistes*, a defect for which Walsingham castigates the bishops.[3] The second aspect can more probably be elucidated. Evidence hitherto largely ignored can be gained from a

---

[1] Thomas Walsingham, *Historia Anglicana* (ed. H. T. Riley, Rolls Series, 1863–4), ii. 188.

[2] Waltham register, ff. 222–223ᵛ; the entry is briefly mentioned by Mrs M. E. Aston, 'Lollardy and Sedition, 1381–1431', *Past and Present*, xvii (1960), p. 13.

[3] Walsingham, ii. 188–9; the stages of action against Wyclif's followers are traced by H. G. Richardson, 'Heresy and the Lay Power under Richard II', *English Historical Review*, li (1936), pp. 1–28.

study of the vernacular sermons and tracts of the Lollards, and documentary material can also yield more information.[1]

The Lollard 'priest' who in 1389 was examined by bishop Waltham was one William Ramsbury, a layman coming, to judge by his name and his area of activity, from Ramsbury in north Wiltshire.[2] He was accused of heretical beliefs and practices. Lollardy is not mentioned by name, but it is clear from the list of accusations that this was the heresy primarily in question. The charges (numbered for convenience in the edition below) 1–6, 8, and 11–12 are obviously Lollard. The views expressed are, for their date, fairly extreme, at any rate as they are set out. Thus, whilst the refusal to venerate images, seen in the twelfth accusation, is a standard charge against Lollards, and is directly traceable to Wyclif's own opinions,[3] the first objection, which denies to any bishop the right of consecration, in its simplification goes beyond the heresiarch's statements.[4] It is possible, however, that the apparent extremity of Ramsbury's views about the Eucharist is due to oversimplification of expression, either on his part or on the part of the recording authority. The denial of transubstantiation is, of course, following Wyclif's view on the subject; but the terms of charge 3 seem to exclude Wyclif's own confession that 'sacramentum eucharistiae est in figura corpus Christi et sanguis'.[5] The complexity of Wyclif's final position on the Eucharist might well have been beyond the comprehension of a layman such as Ramsbury, literate though he declaredly was

---

[1] Recent study of the Lollards has stressed the identification of individuals and communities and, to a lesser extent, the beliefs that were held: J. A. F. Thomson, *The Later Lollards 1414–1520* (Oxford, 2nd edn. 1967); J. Crompton, 'Leicestershire Lollards', *Transactions of the Leicestershire Archaeological Society*, xliv (1968–9), pp. 11–44.

[2] The name appears as *Rammesbury* or *Remmesbury*; I have normalized to the modern spelling. This area of north Wiltshire figures in heresy proceedings again later in 1437 (Nevill register, ii, f. 52), 1485 (Langton register, ii, ff. 35–42), and 1498 (Blythe register, ff. 72ᵛ–79ᵛ).

[3] Objections to the veneration of images, though found before Wyclif, became almost the commonest mark of Lollardy; see Thomson, *Later Lollards*, p. 245. Wyclif's views became increasingly hostile; his opinion is set out very fully in *De Mandatis* (ed. J. Loserth and F. D. Matthew, Wyclif Society, 1922), pp. 153–67.

[4] *De Ecclesia* (ed. J. Loserth, Wyclif Society, 1886), pp. 441 ff., and the comments of M. Wilks, 'Predestination, Property and Power: Wyclif's Theory of Dominion and Grace', *Studies in Church History*, ii (1965), pp. 222–7. Rejection of consecration and ordination is particularly frequent in a set of cases from the Norwich diocese, 1428–31 (Westminster Cathedral MS. B. 2. 8, pp. 245, 250, 319).

[5] *Fasciculi Zizaniorum* (ed. W. W. Shirley, Rolls Series, 1858), p. 106; Wyclif's final views on the sacrament are more fully expressed in his *De Eucharistia* and *De Apostasia*.

('modicam habens litteraturam'); equally, it is quite possible that, in order to bring out the belief in remanence, the accusation suppressed the more ambiguous parts of Ramsbury's views. The difficulties experienced by the examining authorities in obtaining an unequivocal statement about the Eucharist are exemplified in other early cases, such as that of John Aston.[1] The rejection of oral confession and of the priestly powers of absolution is again a simplification of Wyclif's own position, though one that recurs repeatedly in the following century.[2] The fact that Ramsbury could, however, provide biblical justification for his rejection of clerical claims to excommunication suggests that, had Ramsbury's own writings survived rather than only the terse epitome of his accusers, the extremity of his views might be revealed as apparent rather than actual.

Some of the accusations, however, make it clear that Ramsbury had acquired heretical views that did not derive from Wyclif. The seventh, 'that William and his followers have been and are in the true faith and no others', is obviously the normal exclusive claim of the *propheta*, though its terminology may owe something to the jargon of the Lollards, with their 'true men' and 'true priests'. Number 9 could be a popularized form of Wyclif's often-stated objections to *religiones privatae*.[3] Taken in conjunction with accusations 10 and 13–14, however, it is clear that a non-Wyclif element has entered: that of the contemporary continental sect of the Free Spirit, whose more extreme adherents used their asserted freedom from the possibility of sin to justify all forms of immorality.[4] Documentary evidence for the existence of the beliefs of the Brethren of the Free Spirit in England is difficult to trace; the centres of the movement seem to have been in Picardy and the Rhineland, and some have been tempted to deny that the sect ever reached England. But literary sources suggest that Ramsbury's beliefs were not isolated at

---

[1] *Fasciculi Zizaniorum*, pp. 330–3; similarly Oldcastle's prevarication, pp. 438–44. The difficulties of examination well account for the desire of Chichele for a standard form of investigation (*Chichele's Register*, ed. E. F. Jacob (Canterbury and York Society, 1943–7), i. pp. cxxxi–cxxxvii).

[2] Wyclif repeatedly makes clear (*Sermones*, i (ed. J. Loserth, Wyclif Society, 1887), pp. 304–10 and *Opus Evangelicum*, ii (ed. J. Loserth, Wyclif Society, 1896), pp. 10–12) that ignorance of God's absolution is the prime objection to priestly absolution. For the later simplification see the Westminster Cathedral MS. B. 2. 8, pp. 221, 229, 235, etc.

[3] Wyclif's views on the subject are summarized in the last five erroneous conclusions listed in *Fasciculi Zizaniorum*, pp. 281–2.

[4] The most fully documented survey of the sect is that by R. Guarnieri, 'Il Movimento del Libero Spirito', *Archivio Italiano per la Storia della Pietà*, iv (1965), pp. 353–708; see also G. Leff, *Heresy in the Later Middle Ages* (Manchester, 1967), i, pp. 308–407.

this period: Walter Hilton in his *Eight Chapters on Perfection*, written some time between 1383 and 1396, warns his readers against those who claim to have obtained the 'spirit of freedom',[1] whilst the anonymous author of *The Chastising of God's Children*, a text dating from before 1408, takes over a similar warning from Ruysbroek.[2] It is clear, too, that the question asked of Margery Kempe at York, who, it will be remembered, was elsewhere accused of Lollardy, concerning the interpretation of the command 'crescite et multiplicamini' was designed to detect in her any leanings towards the beliefs of the Free Spirit.[3] Obviously, Ramsbury would not have given Margery's acceptable answer, that it concerned the increase of virtues. A further suggestion of English interest in such beliefs, albeit a most puzzling one, is the vernacular translation of the heretical *Miroir des Simples Ames*, puzzling because all the three surviving manuscripts, and the text of the Latin translation subsequently made from the English, are associated with Carthusian houses.[4] The evidence of Ramsbury's beliefs can be added to that of the literary sources to show that, as far apart as York and Wiltshire, the ideas of the Free Spirit were available in England.[5] In other instances, also, these ideas are found in conjunction with Lollardy, though at a later period when Wyclif's own views had been considerably modified by his followers.[6]

[1] Ed. F. Kuriyagawa (Tokyo, 1967), lines 196–212; the text is a translation from a lost original by Lluis de Font, an Aragonese Franciscan friar sent by his order in 1383 to Cambridge to read the Sentences. For Hilton's life see *Dictionnaire de Spiritualité*, fasc. xliv–xlv (Paris, 1968), cols. 525–30.

[2] Ed. J. Bazire and E. Colledge (Oxford, 1957), pp. 138–44; the editors' statements (pp. 53–4, 276) that Ruysbroek's remarks have been altered to fit the Lollards cannot be accepted: the views described have no relevance to that sect but are only understandable as referring to the heresy of the Free Spirit.

[3] *The Book of Margery Kempe*, ed. S. B. Meech and H. E. Allen (E.E.T.S. 212, 1940), p. 121/1–10; the accusation of Lollardy was at Canterbury, pp. 28/28–29/3.

[4] Edition by M. Doiron, *Archivio Italiano per la Storia della Pietà*, v (1968), pp. 243–382; MSS. Bodley 505 and St. John's College, Cambridge, C. 21 belonged to the London Charterhouse, British Museum MS. Additional 37790 was annotated by James Grenehalgh of the Shene Charterhouse; the Latin translation in MS. Pembroke College, Cambridge, 221 was made by Richard Methley, a Carthusian from Mount Grace.

[5] Compare also the account of John Russell, a Minorite from Stamford, recorded in *Chichele's Register*, iii, pp. 91, 98–100; there is no suggestion that Russell had Lollard leanings.

[6] For instance Langdon register (Rochester), f. 94, a case of 1431; Aiscough register (Salisbury), ii, f. 53ᵛ, a case of 1443; Grey register (Ely), f. 131, a case of 1457. Rejection of ecclesiastical ceremony in matrimony is a regular feature of the Norwich diocese group, together with opposition to celibacy; but only one (Westminster Cathedral MS. p. 294) seems to have favoured promiscuity.

The chief interest of Ramsbury, however, lies not in his beliefs but in his account of his 'ordination' and subsequent activities as a 'priest'. His ordination was at the hands of one Thomas Fishbourn and seems to have been performed about 1385. It would be interesting to know more of Fishbourn. He was clearly not the man of the same name who in 1420 became first confessor-general to the newly established Bridgettine house at Syon.[1] Nor is anyone of this name known as one of Wyclif's Oxford followers. It seems most likely that he was not from the Salisbury diocese, or at least not known to reside there, since apparently Waltham made no efforts to pursue him. From his name he may well have come from Sussex, though, to judge by Ramsbury's later area of activity, the Bristol region is also a possibility; in neither case do the surviving bishops' registers provide any information.[2] Despite the unfortunate gaps in these registers, it remains more likely that Fishbourn had received ordination only in the manner that he himself ordained Ramsbury and so, unless he was detected of heresy, would not be recorded in them. The tunic and mantle of russet in which Ramsbury was clad is in precise agreement with Henry Knighton's statement that 'principales pseudo-Lollardi prima introductione hujus sectae nefandae vestibus de russeto utebantur'.[3] A similar description is given by Walsingham, and at a later date a suspect is mentioned as dressed in 'toga de russeto'.[4] The area that Ramsbury had covered in his four years' wanderings was a large one, from Swanage in the south to Malmesbury in the north. All the places mentioned were in the Salisbury diocese, and this may imply that only within the diocese were his activities open to question by this particular bishop, rather than that he had not travelled further. The centre of his activity seems to have been in the north-west of the diocese; although places in the north-east and in the south are mentioned, they are larger places and further apart. In the areas of Warminster and of Chippenham, on the other hand, he visited a large number of neighbouring and small villages. Since these villages are near the border of the Salisbury diocese with those of Bath and

---

[1] Details of his career are most fully recorded in H. Cnattingius, 'Studies in the Order of St. Bridget of Sweden I', *Stockholm Studies in History*, vii (1963), pp. 131–54. Nor is the man here likely to be the same as Thomas Fishbourn mentioned as hearing the submission of William Taylor in 1420 (*Chichele Register*, iii. pp. 159–60).

[2] No registers survive for Chichester from the period 1368–95, nor for Bath and Wells from 1366 to 1407; *Wykeham's Register* (ed. T. F. Kirby, Hampshire Record Society, 1896–9) from Winchester does not mention Fishbourn. Dr. Marett kindly informs me that Wakefield's register at Worcester (1375–95) includes no reference to him.

[3] *Chronicon* (ed. J. R. Lumby, Rolls Series, 1889–95), ii. 184–5.

[4] Walsingham, i. 324; Westminster Cathedral MS. B. 2. 8, p. 286.

Wells in the former case and of Worcester in the latter case, it seems improbable that Ramsbury did not cross into the jurisdiction of these other bishops, even though no record survives. Ramsbury's preaching activities followed the pattern set by the expedition of Hereford, Aston, and others in 1382 in the Winchester diocese,[1] a pattern later to be normal amongst fifteenth-century Lollards.[2] He taught in churches, presumably when the priest in charge was favourable to his views, could be hoodwinked, or was absent, and also in cemeteries. He also propounded his views in taverns, and in more private company 'clanculo in confabulacionibus et potacionibus'.[3] One detail of his penance deserves notice: as well as the usual public abjuration and the less frequent injunction of pilgrimage, Ramsbury was bound to abstain 'ab omnimoda arte mimorum gestis et cantilonis, exceptis hijs que in ecclesijs ad honorem Dei vel alicuius sancti fiunt'. This suggests that Ramsbury had previously used the opportunities afforded by the assembly of large numbers at such spectacles to spread his views.[4]

The form of the mass that Ramsbury used can be seen fairly clearly from the account given. Basically, it followed the orthodox Ordinary of the Mass in the Sarum rite. From the references to the altar, it was performed in church and not outside, as some later Lollards professed to prefer;[5] equally, Ramsbury wore priestly vestments. No mention is made of a sermon, a surprising omission in view both of Ramsbury's own opinion (accusation 11) that preaching was more important than the celebration of masses, and of the normal insistence of Wyclif and his followers on instruction.[6] The sequence of prayers used and of actions performed is straightforward, apart from two inversions: the *Adiutorium* stands before the Confession, instead of being in its normal medieval position after the Absolution, and the *Agnus Dei* apparently

[1] *Wykeham's Register*, ii. 337–8.
[2] For instance, the Bristol group in 1420 recorded in Morgan's register (Worcester), pp. 33–8, and a commission of Bowet (York), i, f. 305 of 1411. The evidence could be greatly enlarged.
[3] Cf. Lincoln Diocesan Records Vj/o, f. 6, a record of Repingdon's visitation of the Leicester archdeaconry in 1413 (quoted by Crompton, 'Leicestershire Lollards', p. 39).
[4] Lollard disapproval of *histriones* is seen in the text from British Museum MS. Additional 24202 printed by T. Wright and J. O. Halliwell, *Reliquiae Antiquae* (London, 1841–3), ii, pp. 42–57.
[5] For instance, some of the Norwich group (Westminster Cathedral MS. B. 2. 8, pp. 227, 234, 285); Thomas Cole in 1460 in Bekynton's register (Bath and Wells), opening 249^b; John Edward in 1490 in Langton's register (Salisbury), ii, f. 39.
[6] The insistence is well illustrated by the 294 sermons of the standard Lollard cycle (see *Medium Ævum*, xl (1971), pp. 142–56).

preceded the fraction of the bread.[1] The omission of the *Gloria*, and that
of the Creed, is not likely to be on doctrinal grounds.[2] The specified
excision of prayers after the Absolution, presumably those concerning
the blessing and censing of the altar, however, may result from Lollard
beliefs; these prayers, like that over the chalice following the Offertory,
would have been repugnant to Ramsbury as unscriptural and as liable to
lead to veneration of 'stocks and stones'. One of the questions to be
asked of Lollard suspects in a later list is 'an genuflexiones, inclinaciones, thurificaciones, deosculaciones necnon luminarium accenciones
et aque benedicte asperciones in ecclesia fieri consuete sint licite et
meritorie'.[3] This inclusion suggests that, although direct reference to
such practices is rare in Lollard abjurations, disapproval amongst the
sect was commonplace. It is clear, however, that the established form
of service still exercised an overwhelmingly strong influence on Ramsbury: he might leave out prayers, but as yet there is no indication of
the insertion of new material. It is unlikely that the two inversions
mentioned above have doctrinal motivation. Furthermore, the traditional
actions appear to have been retained, even though there was no longer
any reason for them: thus after the Lavandum, Ramsbury returned to
the altar, 'iterum reuertebatur ad populum, nichil dicendo, deinde
reuertebatur ad altare'. The omission of the prayer *Orate fratres et
sorores* . . . makes these actions meaningless. It is in the form of consecration that the influence of the orthodox service is most clearly seen:
the prayer is not said, but the elevation is made. Despite the stress placed
by Wyclif and the Lollards on the words of institution,[4] the normal
prayer would imply to Ramsbury an unacceptable interpretation of those
words; yet no substitution of another prayer was made. The retention
of the elevation, with its traditional association of adoration, is perhaps
more surprising: the typical Lollard view is expressed in a later abjuration 'the sacramente of the awter lyfte vp ouer the priestis hed is not to be
wurshipped more than materyall brede lifte vp ouer myn hede'.[5] It may

---

[1] I have used the Sarum Missal in the editions of F. H. Dickinson (Burnt-
island, 1861–83) and J. W. Legg (Oxford, 1916). Dr. C. Hohler, for whose advice
on liturgical aspects of this account I am most grateful, suggests that these
apparent displacements may be due to the correction of the original deposition
by Ramsbury, and subsequent scribal insertion of the material at the wrong
places; there are no indications of intended transposition in the Register trans-
script. For the position of the *Agnus Dei* cf. J. A. Jungmann, *Missarum Sollemnia*
(Freiburg, 1958), ii, pp. 413–22.   [2] Dickinson, cols. 3, 15; Legg, pp. 46, 15.
[3] Polton register (Worcester), p. 113; Harley MS. 2179, f. 157ᵛ.
[4] For Lollard views, see the vernacular texts in Trinity College, Dublin, MS.
C. 5. 6, ff. 145–146ᵛ and Cambridge University Library MS. Ff. 6. 31 (2),
ff. 27ᵛ–35ᵛ, and the Latin text in Trinity College, Cambridge, MS. B. 14. 50,
ff. 56–8.   [5] Stillington register (Bath and Wells), opening 52 for 1475.

have been Ramsbury's method of demonstrating to the congregation his view that 'in altari post consecracionem non est corpus Christi set panis'. Equally, and more simply, the retention may be due to Ramsbury's efforts to avoid detection, a supposition that may also explain the earlier phrase 'nichil dicendo set labia mouendo ac si diceret'. Certainly, the four years during which it was alleged that Ramsbury had celebrated this form of mass would suggest, not merely that Waltham and his predecessor Ralph Erghum had been inactive in their pursuit of Lollards, but also that its unorthodox implications may not have been entirely obvious. It is worth noting also that, though Ramsbury disapproved of the payment of money for the celebration of masses (accusation 5), the inclusion of the *Fidelium* shows that he did not reject masses for the dead entirely.[1] Similarly, the retention of the *Benedictio panis* reveals the ambiguous position of this early Lollard: the ceremony and distribution are retained, but the words of blessing are omitted, as open to false interpretation.[2]

The use of the established liturgy, albeit abbreviated, for this mass goes some way to explain how Lollards could often survive for a long time unsuspected by their orthodox fellows. As modern critics have inferred, their beliefs were not always incompatible with regular attendance at mass, though they might have mental reservations about the declared interpretation of the ceremony they witnessed. As the bishops discovered to their cost, Lollard beliefs about the Eucharist were not confined to a simple denial of transubstantiation outright; the varieties of remanence, impanation, and consubstantiation that are. found in Lollard opinions required very careful questioning to elicit; equivocation was simple. An unusually explicit statement emerges from a later trial in the same Salisbury diocese: in 1498 Thomas Boughton of Hungerford, a shoemaker and woolwinder, stated that 'I haue euery yere receyved the said holy sacrament, not for that I had any stedfast byleve therin, but that I shuld not be noted and knowen of the people. And, beyng in the church or ellyswher whan the said holy sacrament was present, I feyned with myn hondys to honoure it as Cristen men vse to doo, but my mynd and entent was nothyng therto but to God almyghty above in heven, thinkyng that he was not ther present in the blessyd sacrament.'[3] Such an attitude continues the tradition that was expressed

---

[1] For such rejection see the texts printed by T. Arnold, *Select English Works of John Wyclif* (Oxford, 1869–71), iii. 208/3 ff., 337/1 ff.

[2] The form is printed by Dickinson, cols. 849*–850*, and by Legg, p. 455. For Lollard rejection of the ceremony see the East Anglian group (Westminster Cathedral MS. B. 2. 8, pp. 235, 246, etc), and Fisher register (Rochester), ff. 47, 127.

[3] Blythe register, f. 74.

by William Thorpe in his account of his trial before Arundel in 1407, where he explained that he stopped the men of Shrewsbury from leaving his sermon to go to hear mass because 'þe vertu and þe mede of þe moost holi sacrament of þe auter stondiþ myche moore in þe bileue þereof þat ȝe owen to haue in ȝoure soulis þan it doiþ in þe outward siȝt þerof'.[1]

The most remarkable feature of Ramsbury's case, however, remains the length of time 'per quadriennium proximum preteritum' that he had taught, apparently without hindrance. Though it is not explicitly stated, the implication of the commission given to Ramsbury by Fishbourn is plainly that he had celebrated these unorthodox masses for the same length of time. Though it is possible to parallel Ramsbury's preaching,[2] there appears to be no comparable case of the celebration of services in church. An interesting contrast is between Ramsbury's activities and the situation at Northampton in 1392–3: in the latter town, despite the favour of the mayor and of many citizens, the Lollards only preached, interrupting the masses of orthodox priests but not substituting their own.[3] Whilst, particularly in the period up to the Oldcastle rising, a number of the lower clergy appear as Lollard sympathizers,[4] no account survives of the services they conducted; nor is there another instance of their abrogation of their rights to celebrate mass in favour of a layman. Clearly, to some extent this absence of evidence is due to incomplete documentation: Fishbourn must obviously have been a second, and earlier, instance. But, though Ramsbury's case cannot have been peculiar, it seems, to judge from Walsingham's reference, to have gained unusual notoriety.

NOTE ON THE TEXT

Because of the repetitive nature of the formal parts of the *Processus*, a summary only is given of those sections not directly concerned with

[1] Bodl., MS. Rawlinson c. 208, f. 40; the MS. of the fifteenth century, is the full account of Thorpe's trial. For many years it has been stated that no English manuscript was extant, the trial only being recorded in two Latin Hussite manuscripts (Vienna Nationalbibliotck 3936 and Prague Metropolitan Chapter O. xxix) and in an early print of the vernacular ([Antwerp? 1530?]).

[2] Many instances could be given from the early period; for a close parallel see the account of the Leicester group given by Crompton, 'Leicestershire Lollards'.

[3] See the document printed by E. Powell and G. M. Trevelyan, *The Peasants' Rising and the Lollards* (London, 1899), pp. 45–50.

[4] The returns of the commission of inquiry following the Oldcastle rising preserved in P.R.O., K.B. 9, 204/1 show a number of *capellani* both as adherents of Wyclif and as supporters of Oldcastle.

Ramsbury's views and activities. Modern punctuation and capitalization have been supplied; contractions are expanded without notice; marks of suspension on place-names are ignored. The accusations have been numbered for convenience of reference.

(f. 222)   Processus contra Willielmum Remmesbury

[Proceedings in the chapel of the manor of Sonning, 3 July 1389, before John Waltham, bishop of Salisbury, concerning William Ramsbury of the same diocese, accused of heresy and divers errors. The bishop's advisers were Robert Ragenhill, archdeacon of Dorset,[1] Ralph Selby, chancellor of the diocese,[2] doctor of civil and canon law,[3] John Stachdene O.F.M., warden of the Reading convent, John Poul O.F.M., lector from the same house.]

Comparuit personaliter dictus Willielmus Rammesbury, cui dictus reuerendus pater ex officio suo mero ad anime sue correccionem proposuit et obiecit quod ipse idem Willielmus quasdam opiniones et conclusiones abhominabiles, hereses et errores in se continentes, fidei catholice euangelice et apostolice doctrine sacris canonibus et tocius ecclesie sancte determinacioni contrarias, repugnantes et dissonas, procurante omnium malorum satore, pertinaciter tenuit, asseruit et affirmauit. Ac officium predicandi, cum quasi laicus existebat, modicam habens litteraturam, presumptuosa temeritate sibi vsurpans, easdem plebi et populo diuersorum locorum dicte Sarum diocesis coram eo congregatis palam et publice, ac eciam clanculo in confabulacionibus et potacionibus, tam in ecclesiis, cimiterijs quam eciam tabernis et alijs locis, predicauit, sermocinauit et docuit; et eos ad sic tenendum et credendum prout in eis continetur suis sacrilegis falsis et confictis doctrinis et exhortacionibus sub cuiusdam similate sanctitatis vmbraculo allic[i]ebat, et induxit in Dei et ecclesie sue contemptum [et] fidei catholice euersionem, ac anime sue et aliarum animarum simplicium ad nouitates modernis temporibus se faciliter inclinancium graue periculum ac decepcionem multiplicem et illusionem. Quas quidem opiniones et conclusiones eidem Willielmo dictus reuerendus pater tunc legi fecit et exposuit, que tales sunt:

1 In primis tenuit, asseruit et predicauit quod nec papa habet potestatem creandi episcopos, nec episcopus sacerdotes.

2 Item quod nec papa nec episcopus neque sacerdos potuit vel potest conficere corpus Christi.

---

[1] A. B. Emden, *A Biographical Register of the University of Cambridge to 1500* (Cambridge, 1963), p. 470; J. Le Neve, revd. J. M. Horn, *Fasti Ecclesiae Anglicanae, 1300–1541*. III Salisbury Diocese (London, 1962), p. 7.

[2] Le Neve states that John Norton was chancellor from 1361 till 1402 (p. 17).

[3] Emden, *Cambridge*, p. 517.

3 Item quod in altari post consecracionem non est corpus Christi set panis.

4 Item quod nullus debet offerre in ecclesia in exequijs mortuorum, purificacionibus mulierum, solempnitatibus nubencium; et si qui hoc fecerint, sunt excommunicati a Deo.

5 Item quod si quis dederit sacerdoti pro missis celebrandis denarios vel aliquam pecuniam, sunt excommunicati a Deo.

6 Item quod nullus, nec papa nec episcopus nec aliquis sub eis, habet potestatem excommunicandi, et quod sunt apostate omnes eo quod omnes predicti postponunt fidem Christi, vt dixit.[1]

7 Item quod dictus Willielmus et sequaces sui fuerunt et sunt in vera fide et nulli alij.

8 Item quod non tenebatur confiteri se sacerdoti, nec sacerdos habet potestatem se absoluendi, set sufficiebat confiteri Deo.

9 Item quod melius et maius meritorium esset sacerdotibus et religiosis quibuscumque accipere sibi vxores et apostotare quam viuere religiose siue in castitate; et idem tenuit et predicauit de monialibus.

10 Item quod si quis coniugatus haberet vxorem de qua non posset procreare prolem, quod meritorium ei esset ipsam dimittere et capere aliam de qua posset prolem procreare.

11 Item quod maius meritorium esset sacerdotibus transire per patriam cum biblia sub brachio et predicare populo quam dicere matutinas vel celebrare missas vel alia diuina officia exercere.

12 Item quod nullus debet venerari aliquas ymagines in ecclesia, et si quis fecerit est excommunicatus.

13 Item quod non fuit peccatum cognoscere monialem carnaliter.

14 Item quod licitum est cuicumque (f. 222v) sacerdoti et alij cognoscere carnaliter quascumque mulieres eciam moniales, virgines et vxores, et hoc propter multiplicacionem generis humani; et ita fecit dictus Willielmus cognoscendo virgines, vxores et alias mulieres solutas a tempore quo dictas opiniones tenuit.

15 Item quod prefatus Willielmus, tonsuratus vt asser[u]it per quemdam dominum Thomam Fishburn, ipsum de erroribus et heresibus predictis informantem, tonsura sacerdotali et quodam habitu, videlicet tunica de russet cum mantello de eadem secta, per eundem indutus, data sibi potestate per ipsum dominum Thomam publice predicandi et missas sub forma infrascripta celebrandi, diuersas missas sancteque beate Marie et de sancta Trinitate in diuersis locis, secundum informacionem eiusdem domini Thome, prophanauit sub hac videlicet forma:

[1] Cf. Matt. v. 44, xiii. 28–30.

Primo induebat se vestimentis sacerdotalibus, et ad gradum altaris dixit *Adiutorium* etc., *Confiteor* et *Misereatur*, *Absolucionem* et sic, absque oracionibus alijs, processit ad Officium cum oracionibus, videlicet prima *Concede*,[1] vel *Omnipotens* quando celebrauit de Trinitate,[2] *Deus qui corda*,[3] *Deus qui vnigeniti*[4] et *Fidelium*.[5] Quibus dictis, legeret Epistolam, Gradalem, postea Euangelium. Et tunc vertebat ad populum et dixit *Dominus vobiscum*; deinde Offertorium. Et fecit signa crucis super hostiam et calicem, nichil dicendo set labia mouendo ac si diceret, et sic processit ad Lauandum. Postea redijt ad altare et iterum reuertebatur ad populum nichil dicendo. Deinde reuertebatur ad altare et ibidem fecit moram nichil dicendo vsque ad Prefacionem. Et Prefacione publice lecta, nichil dixit set signa fecit vsque ad Leuacionem nichil dicendo, et sic leuauit panem et calicem. Post Leuacionem nichil dixit vsque ad *Pater Noster*; quo dicto, nichil dixit vsque ad *Agnus Dei*; et dicto *Agnus Dei*, siluit vsque ad fraccionem panis. Factaque fraccione, recepit panem more presbiterorum, et alia fecit ad modum presbiterorum. Et missas sic finiuit cum duobus Euangelijs, videlicet *Missus est* et *In principio*.[6]

Et diebus diuersis quando solebat distribuere panem benedictum post missam, mouebat labia super panem et fecit signum crucis, nichil dicendo.

Et missas sic prophanauit apud Sherston iuxta Malmesbury, Aldeburn, Wermynstre, Brighteston, Slaaghtonford, in ecclesia beate Marie de Marleburgh; item apud Calne, Bradestok, Cristmalford, Remmesbury.[7]

Quibus quidem conclusionibus et opinionibus alijsque supradictis erroribus sibi propositis lectis, expositis et per eum intellectis, idem Willielmus Remmesbury humiliter fatebatur coram nobis se premissos hereses et errores omnes et singulos quasi per quadriennium proximum preteritum tenuisse, affirmasse et palam ac publice in quam pluribus locis nostre diocesis, videlicet apud Sutton, Westkyngton, Ӡatton, Box,

---

[1] *Missa de sancta Maria*, Dickinson, col. 779*; Legg, p. 390.
[2] *Missa de sancta trinitate*, Dickinson, col. 735*; Legg, p. 384.
[3] *Missa de sancto spiritu*, Dickinson, col. 743*; Legg, p. 385.
[4] *Missa de sancta cruce*, Dickinson, col. 748*; Legg, p. 386.
[5] *Missa pro omnibus fidelibus defunctis*, Dickinson, col. 879*; Legg, p. 442.
[6] The first is Luke i. 26 ff., though its liturgical justification in this position is unclear if it was used, as the wording seems to imply, on all occasions. The second is John i. 1 ff., regularly included in the medieval Sarum Use at the end of mass, see W. H. Frere, *The Use of Sarum* (Cambridge, 1898–1901), i, p. 89.
[7] Now Sherston, Aldbourne, Warminster, Brixton Deverill, Slaughterford, Marlborough, Calne, Bradenstoke-cum-Clack, Christian Malford, Ramsbury; all are in Wiltshire.

Aldeborne, Hungerford, Remmesbury, Brynkeworth, Chippenham, Stepil Ashton, Melkysham, Westbury, Wermynstre, Deuerellangbrigg, Brighteston, Kyngeston Deuerel, Boyton, Blaneford, Sturmynster Marchal et Swanewych,[1] clero et populo in eis congregatis, in ecclesiis et cimeterijs locorum predictorum, ac clanculo in confabulacionibus et potacionibus, in tabernis et alijs locis; in quibusdam locis ex hijs omnes hereses et errores predictos et in alijs quosdam ex eis predicasse et docuisse ac omnia alia et singula que de prophanacionibus missarum et cognicione mulierum suprascribuntur modo et forma premissis dampnabiliter commisisse et perpetrasse.

[Since it appeared that Ramsbury was contrite and prepared to accept correction, together with whatever penance the bishop might impose, it was agreed that his abjuration should be accepted and that he should be released from excommunication. As part of his penance, he was to appear in Salisbury cathedral the following Whitsunday, and in a clear and audible voice renounce all his heresies and errors before the whole clergy and people; at the high mass the same day he was to prostrate himself on the ground beside the altar from the Elevation to the Communion. This was to be repeated on the following three days. He was then to go to all the monastic, collegial, and greater churches of the diocese, and particularly to all the churches in which he had preached his errors, and there make public renunciation of his heresy. He was to pay special respect to all clergy he met. When this was accomplished, he was to report back to the bishop. To this the bishop added:]

(f. 223v) quod toto tempore vite sue abstineret se ab omnimoda arte mimorum gestis et cantilonis, exceptis hijs que in ecclesijs ad honorem Dei vel alicuius sancti fiunt; omni die toto tempore vite sue diceret genuflectendo quinque *Pater noster* et *Aue* cum primo *Miserere*; et quod per septennium ieiunaret sextis ferijs in pane et aqua. Et, si sue ad hoc sufficere possent facultates, quod hoc anno Jubileo nouiter instituto[2] adire pergere[t] Romam, visitare limina[3] apostolorum et recepturus remissiones in eodem concessas.

[The abjuration and penance were duly confirmed.]

[1] Sutton cannot be certainly identified: it could be Sutton Veny (Warminster hundred), Sutton Benger (Startley hundred), or less probably, Sutton Mandeville (Cadworth hundred). The others are now West Kington, Yatton Keynell, Box, Aldbourne, Hungerford (Berks.), Ramsbury, Brinkworth, Chippenham, Steeple Ashton, Melksham, Westbury, Warminster, Longbridge Deverill, Brixton Deverill, Kingston Deverill, Boyton, Blandford, Sturminster Marshall, and Swanage. The last three are in Dorset and are the only places south of Salisbury that Ramsbury visited.

[2] The Jubilee of 1390, and its indulgences, was proclaimed by Urban VI on 8 April 1389 in the bull *Salvator noster*: N. Paulus, *Geschichte des Ablasses im Mittelalter* (Paderborn, 1922–3), iii, p. 181.   [3] *Ms.* lumina.

discrecōn to knowe þe good from þe

Noon may distrye yuel / Cap. ix.

þise twoo parties : þcan iche þo of /
wandiryng i þis secoūde chirche : for licnes
lis þt þei vsen / and also þei han i comūe : wiþ
þe nēþe pigis // ffor oure lord haþ i his chirche /
laburers aboute his virtue / þo þe prostars
þiars : ⁊ also walkars / Almicdars be in
þis chirche : þt þchowrs ⁊ vedars of lessoūs
⁊ singars þerlen here also : þt ministraws
of sacmentis / þt studiars i goodis lawe :
⁊ me þt make lonedues // And like seruaūts
haþ þe fende : i þe pridde chirche / but þei
don þer seruyse : ⁊ a strange maue / þepe
les þei be hard to knowe : þ fore we schal
marke hē / hou woundirfulli þei variē : in
þise forseide condicōus / Tertia ffastars i
ctis chirche : Abstynen hē fro lustis / for to
tempir þe coragenes : of þe reble fleische
⁊ kepe her bodi clene chast : ⁊ suget to her
soule / for semt austin i his book : techiþ
þis lore // Caro tua vnut de aīa tua . aīa

8

THE EXAMINATION OF LOLLARDS

THE WIDE DIVERSITY of beliefs held in the fifteenth century by men who were described as Lollards has become a commonplace of historical criticism.[1] Equally recognized is the fact that many of the beliefs, characterized as unorthodox by ecclesiastical authorities in the century and a half after Wyclif's death, did not originate with Wyclif; in particular, the criticism of clerical government, culminating in the designation of the pope as Antichrist, can be found in writings, clerical and lay, Latin and vernacular, before Wyclif, which writings, even if not welcomed by the hierarchy, were not the object of heretical inquisition.[2] It is, consequently, not always easy to determine the orthodoxy or otherwise of certain texts written in the fifteenth century: whilst episcopal registers regularly state that a case under review is one of heresy, and often designate it specifically as Lollardy, original writings do not so openly admit their affiliations. The difficulty has been particularly acute in regard to vernacular texts, where Lollardy, because of its adherents' convictions about the use of the native language, must often come in question. A good instance is the text known as 'The Pore Caitif', a series of tracts found in a number of fifteenth-century manuscripts; earlier critics assumed that it was Lollard, but this has recently, and correctly, been called in question.[3] Similarly, the dialogue 'Dives and Pauper' was said by Bishop Alnwick in a heresy trial of 1429–30 to contain 'multi errores et hereses quamplures', yet its orthodoxy would seem assured by the fact that Abbot Whethamstede paid for the making of a copy of it for St. Albans.[4] As a result of these and similar difficulties, there has developed a scepticism about the Lollard movement as a whole, concerning its reliance upon Wyclif, its prevalence and its coherence.[5] It is therefore instructive to discover the matters on which contemporaries thought that unorthodox opinion might be revealed. Even if all the views might not be

[1] See J. A. F. Thomson, *The Later Lollards 1414–1520* (2nd edn., Oxford, 1967), pp. 239–50 and references there given.

[2] For some aspects of Wyclif's debt to earlier writers in his criticism and speculation, compare A. Gwynn, *The English Austin Friars in the Time of Wyclif* (1940), pp. 80–9, 249–69, and M. Wilks, 'Predestination, Property and Power: Wyclif's Theory of Dominion and Grace', *Studies in Church History*, ii (1965), 220–36; anticlerical satire is surveyed by J. A. Yunck, *The Lineage of Lady Meed* (Notre Dame, 1963).

[3] The critical views about this text are described by M. T. Brady, '*The Pore Caitif*', *Traditio*, x (1954), 542–8.

[4] Westminster Cathedral MS. B. 2.8, pp. 289, 291; *Annales Mon. S. Albani*, ed. H. T. Riley (Rolls Ser., 1870–1), ii. 269.

[5] K. B. McFarlane, *John Wycliffe and the Beginnings of English Nonconformity* (1952), pp. 121–88; G. Leff, *Heresy in the Later Middle Ages* (Manchester, 1967), ii. 574 ff.

held by any one heretic, and even if some of the tenets can be paralleled earlier than Wyclif, what were regarded as the salient questions to be asked of a suspect?

Material most fully preserved in the register of Bishop Thomas Polton of Worcester (1426–33)[1] provides useful evidence on this matter. Two lists of questions from the register are printed below, one 'concepti per iuristam', the other 'concepti per theologos', together with procedural material concerning the methods of examination and judgment. The first list is much the more extensive; despite some minor alterations of wording, there is nothing in the second list that is not represented in the first. The omissions in the second, if the title correctly represents its origin, are more surprising: some of the questions left out might be regarded as covered by the remaining material, but, in view of the frequency with which pilgrimages appear as a matter of enquiry in ecclesiastical investigations of Lollardy, it is odd to find the topic ignored by the theologians.[2] The jurist's list is, on the other hand, a searching enquiry. The first four questions should reveal any belief in remanence, as well as simple denial of transubstantiation, and detect any Donatist leanings;[3] the following three, as well as investigating views on the sacraments of confession and baptism, imply scrutiny of the Wycliffite tenets about the predestinate and the *praesciti*, a topic more explicitly opened in the final question. The later questions on private religion, worship of images, pilgrimages, the legality of oaths, the status of tithes, the validity of excommunication, are all to be expected from the accounts of Lollard beliefs found in episcopal registers. Questions 13 and 14 raise the problems of dominion and the rights of the secular lord over clerical subjects, problems that are less frequently reflected in accounts of actual cases.[4] It is interesting that both lists contain the question 'an omnia debent esse communia'.[5] The communistic beliefs of continental sects, including certain branches of the Hussite movement, are well known; Wyclif himself put forward the idea, but never made it one of his chief tenets, and it does not seem to have become part of the mainstream of Lollard opinion.[6]

The jurist's list of questions appears twice again outside the Polton

[1] Worcester, St. Helen's Record Office, Reg. Thomas Polton.

[2] Pilgrimages and images are probably the two topics on which most frequently unorthodox opinions were expressed by Lollard suspects; see, for instance, the series of abjurations from 1428 to 1431 recorded in Westminster Cath. MS. B. 2.8, pp. 205 ff., and those from 1498 in Salisbury Diocesan Registry, Reg. John Blythe fos. 70–79v.

[3] For questioning by suspects of the validity of sacraments administered by those in deadly sin see Salisbury Diocesan Registry, Reg. Thomas Langton pt. ii fo. 25v and Guildhall, London, MS. 9531/9, Reg. Richard Fitzjames fo. 7.

[4] For instances, however, see Westminster Cath. MS. B. 2.8, pp. 319, 354.

[5] Appendix, I(37), II(9).

[6] Leff, ii. 693; Wilks, *ubi supra*, p. 232; Robert Hoke in 1425 confessed to believe that 'lordes temporell' been holden by the lawe of god to have all'thinges in commun' (*Reg. Henry Chichele*, ed. E. F. Jacob (Canterbury and York Soc., 1943–7), iii. 111).

register, first as an introduction to the same procedural material in Harley MS. 2179, and secondly in use in an actual enquiry in the register of Thomas Bekynton of Bath and Wells in 1449.[1] The first, like the entry in the Polton register, is a memorandum of theoretical nature; the second shows that the theory was put into practice at least once. The procedural material that accompanies the list in the Polton register and the Harley manuscript is in itself of less interest, since, as the references to canon law show, there is little in it that was peculiar to investigations of Lollardy. To ecclesiastical authorities, however, that had not in the two centuries preceding Wyclif been much troubled by serious popular heresy, the instructions must have been useful. Two notes, parallel to parts of these instructions, appearing in the register of Richard Clifford of London (1407–21), bear this out.[2] The influence of the procedural material can, furthermore, be seen in the fifteenth century. Whilst only the trial of 1449 in the Bekynton register shows the use of the full set of questions (though the custom of recording only the heretical views of suspects probably disguises its use elsewhere), the form of abjuration can be traced in a number of cases. The register of Bishop Boulers at Lichfield in recording a trial in 1454 gives the Latin abjuration, omitting the sentences on books and substituting the beliefs relevant to the suspect, and the form of absolution as recorded here.[3] The Bekynton register in the trial of 1449 records an English translation of the abjuration; an independent vernacular translation is also recorded in the Salisbury register of Bishop Aiscough in 1443. Many of the later abjurations from the Salisbury diocese are still recognizably in the same pattern, though some abbreviation was made in the course of time.[4] That the pattern was not universal can be seen, for instance, from the abjuration of John Whitehorne in 1499 recorded in Morton's register at Lambeth.[5] The appearance of the Polton type of abjuration outside the three main texts printed here suggests that the questions also are likely to have been widely available. That there was a need for such an ingeniously contrived list is clear from the inept questioning of Lollard suspects from Bristol in 1417: a group of men were asked about the articles of the faith, the ten commandments, the seven sacraments, the seven works of mercy and the seven cardinal virtues. Hardly surprisingly, their answers were orthodox, though it remains plain from the

[1] British Museum, Harley MS. 2179 fos. 157–9; *Reg. Thomas Bekynton, bishop of Bath and Wells, 1443–65*, ed. H. C. Maxwell-Lyte and M. C. B. Dawes (Somerset Record Soc., xlix–l, 1934–5), i. 120–7; Taunton, Somerset Record Office, D/D/Ba6 (Bekynton), openings 94b–96b.

[2] Guildhall, London, MS. 9531/4, fo. 188v; see further below pp. 129-30.

[3] Lichfield Diocesan Registry, Reg. Reginald Boulers fos. 50v–51: see Appendix VII below.

[4] Salisbury Diocesan Registry, Reg. William Aiscough pt. ii fos. 53–4; also Reg. Langton pt. ii fos. 35v–42 (1485) and Reg. Blythe fos. 70–79v (1498). The abjuration in the earlier Salisbury register, Reg. Robert Nevill pt. ii fo. 57v (1434), seems to use extracts from an English translation.

[5] Lambeth Palace Libr., Reg. Morton pt. i fo. 194v; cf. also the abjuration of Elisabeth Sampson of Aldermanbury parish in 1509 (Reg. Fitzjames fo. 71r–v).

account that there could be little doubt of their implication in the Lollard heresy.[1]

The date and origin of the lists and procedural material printed below can be traced with some confidence. In the Polton register the name *Brouns* appears at the end of the procedural material.[2] This led Dr. Thomson to suggest that parts of the material, at any rate, were drawn up by Thomas Brouns, Chichele's chancellor from 1426 to 1433, and that a date towards the end of 1428 would be suitable.[3] Study of the text reinforces the suggestion that it derives from discussions and actions in the Canterbury convocation of 1428. Chichele's concern to improve the methods of dealing with heresy, and particularly Lollardy, reached its culmination in the July and November meetings of that convocation.[4] On July 14 before the assembled clergy Brouns

produxit ... in publicum et legit quemdam tractatum de modo procedendi contra hereticos ac eciam quandem formam abjuracionis errorum et heresum. Videbanturque modus procedendi et forma abjuracionis hujusmodi prelatis et clero paucis additis sive mutatis satis sufficientes et validi.[5]

Following this, further discussion of the matter took place in the ensuing meetings. After the prorogation, on 15 November, it was decided to set up a committee consisting of 'certi episcopi prelatique alii et clerici tam in theologia quam jure civili et canonico doctores' to consider provisions for the better pursuit of heresy, necessary because of the daily increase ('de die in diem excrevit') of it in the Canterbury province.[6] Brouns is not named as a member of the committee, but Polton is, together with Stafford, bishop of Bath and Wells, Morgan, bishop of Ely, and Langdon, bishop of Rochester. Lyndwood produced a report, which was discussed at some length in the following sessions.[7] A number of pieces of evidence combine to suggest that the material below emanated from this convocation. Polton's register preserves a list of questions 'concepti per iuristam' and another 'concepti per theologos', a single lawyer but several theologians: this would obviously fit with Brouns' prior action followed by the deliberations of a committee that included theologians. It would seem unlikely that the agreement between the two lists can be accidental: much more likely is it that one represents a modification of the other. Furthermore, many of the people with whom this procedural material is associated were present at the 1428 convocations, and at the relevant sessions. Brouns has already been mentioned; Polton was a member of the committee. The bishop of Bath and Wells was also a

---

[1] *Reg. Nicholas Bubwith, bishop of Bath and Wells, 1407–24,* ed. T. S. Holmes (Somerset Record Soc., xxix–xxx, 1913–14), i. 283–90; see also the case of Christina More in 1418 in the same register, *ibid.,* p. 298.

[2] Reg. T. Polton p. 115; the name is in the hand of the preceding material.

[3] Thomson, p. 225.

[4] *Reg. Chichele,* i, pp. cxxix–cxliv.

[5] *Ibid.,* iii. 187.

[6] *Ibid.,* p. 191.

[7] *Ibid.,* p. 192.

member, and it may be noted that Thomas Bekynton, in whose Bath and Wells register the questions were later used, was the archbishop's commissary at the convocation from 19 November.[1] Harley MS. 2179 appears to be a collection of material from Lichfield, mainly consisting of precedents for various ecclesiastical writs. The questions and the procedural texts printed below form part of the last quire of the volume; they are succeeded by a denunciation of one Thomas Stevens for heresy by Robert, bishop of London, and by various earlier statutes against heresy.[2] The earlier writs are predominantly in the title of the bishop of Lichfield, though a number are in that of the bishop of London; the majority of the dated texts seem to be between 1427 and 1442.[3] The Lichfield connection, however, seems assured in the light of a note dated 1473 in favour of Thomas Heywood, dean of Lichfield, and of his name on the final flyleaf 'Thomas Heyuod in vtroque iure Bacallarius';[4] it would seem likely that the volume belonged to Heywood. William Heyworth, bishop of Lichfield from 1420 to 1447, was also present at the session of 15 November 1428 when the committee was set up, though he is not himself named as a member. Heyworth's own register records no proceedings for heresy, though, as has been mentioned, Boulers at Lichfield used the abjuration and absolution here printed in 1454. Unfortunately, neither the Rochester nor the Norwich registers of Brouns himself record any heresy trials. Brouns' continued concern can, however, be seen from three items in his Rochester register: an order to seek out 'nonnulli . . . diuersi et perfidi noue secte' and a second to enquire into those preaching without licence, and thirdly a command to arrest two suspects from Strood and Rochester and to investigate the contents of their homes.[5]

The only evidence that might seem to gainsay this dating is the appearance of the two procedural notes in the London register of Bishop Clifford. Two points should, however, be borne in mind. In the first place, the notes are written into a leaf that was largely blank, by a hand other than that of the preceding or following items; their date is therefore uncertain. Secondly, the procedural material in the Polton form is, on internal evidence, declaredly not original but based on the precedents of established canonistic

[1] *Ibid.*, p. 193.

[2] The case of Stevens cannot, unfortunately, be dated since it is only recorded here. The bishop 'Robert' could be Braybrooke (1382–1404), whose name appears in another document on fo. 41, Fitzhugh (1431–6) or Gilbert (1436–48). Following this case are a copy of parts VIII–XII of Arundel's 1408 constitutions, and the 1409 statute of Henry IV, printed by D. Wilkins, *Concilia Magnae Britanniae* (1737), iii. 317–19, 328–9.

[3] The Lichfield documents are in the name of 'William', which in the cases that are also dated must always be Bishop Heyworth (1420–47), rather than Booth (1447–52). The London documents are in the name of 'Robert', like the Stevens case.

[4] Brit. Mus., Harl. MS. 2179 fos. 162, 163.

[5] Maidstone, Kent County Record Office, DRc/R6 fos. 112v–113, 114v and 116v. It is particularly tantalising that in the third instance the arrest of the two suspects is not followed by a record of their trial.

practice. It is therefore quite likely that Brouns, or the committee of convocation, would have taken over material that might earlier have been found to be satisfactory. On internal evidence the reference in the Clifford notes to 'sentencia interlocutoria' envisages the situation after Chichele's enactments of 1416, when a convicted suspect might be referred to the Provincial Council.[1]

Although Brouns and the convocation committee, if they are the originators of this material, took over earlier procedural instructions, they do not seem to have been much influenced by earlier lists of questions. The Council of Constance in 1417 set out a 'Modus interrogandi aliquem suspectum de heresi', of which a copy is found in Bodleian MS. e Musaeo 86, the only manuscript of the 'Fasciculi Zizaniorum'.[2] Similarly, continental manuscripts preserve lists of questions designed to detect Hussites or *Wycliffistes*.[3] But, although some of the questions of necessity concern the same matters as the lists here printed, there is sufficient discrepancy between them for complete certainty about their independence.

Further evidence for the examination of Lollards at the same time as the Polton material is found in the courtbook of William Alnwick, bishop of Norwich, dating from the autumn of 1428 to the spring of 1431, now surviving as Westminster Cathedral MS. B.2.8.[4] The abjurations there, both in Latin and English, are in a form very similar to that printed here, but in wording there are slight differences. This form of abjuration also seems to have had currency wider than a single diocese, since an English instance in identical form is found in a case of 1431 in the Rochester register of Bishop Langdon.[5] It is possible that this type also goes back to the same convocation, since on 6 December 1428 the second abjuration, that of Richard Monk of Melton Mowbray, made before the high cross at St. Paul's was in this form.[6] The Alnwick courtbook also reveals that the examination of suspects involved the use of a set of questions, though these were different from the Polton list; only in this way can the identity of views, even from men from different ends of the diocese, be explained and the similarity in parts of the ordering of those views.[7] It seems quite clear that this Norwich list began with a

[1] Guildhall, London, MS. 9531/4, fo. 188v; *Reg. Chichele*, iii. 18–19.

[2] Bodl. Libr., MS. e Musaeo 86 fos. 142v–143v (original foliation, fos. 134v–135v); this part was not printed in *Fasciculi Zizaniorum*, ed. W. W. Shirley (Rolls Ser., 1858).

[3] For instance Prague Univ. Libr., MS. I.F. 18, fos. 25–9, and a different set in Prague National Museum, MS. XVI E 16, fos. 263–267v. A very much more elaborate set seems to have been used in the cases discussed by H. Heimpel, *Drei Inquisitions-Verfahren aus dem Jahre 1425* (Göttingen, 1969).

[4] Some account of the MS. is given by E. Welch, 'Some Suffolk Lollards', *Suffolk Institute of Archaeology*, xxix (1962), 154–65.

[5] Maidstone, Kent County Record Office, DRc/R6 fo. 94r–v.

[6] *Reg. Chichele*, iii. 207–8.

[7] Although the largest number of cases derive from the neighbourhood of Beccles and Bungay and from the village of Martham, one heretic came from South Creake in the north of Norfolk and another from Nayland on the southern border of Suffolk (Westminster Cath. MS. B. 2.8, pp. 293–4, 209–13).

series of questions on the sacraments: regularly the first five views concern the validity of clerical baptism and of episcopal confirmation, the necessity of oral confession to a priest, the Eucharist, and the obligation of ecclesiastical ceremony in matrimony.[1] Less invariably follow views on the priesthood and on unction. The order of the rest of the inquisition can only be guessed, but its content is clear: it had the expected questions on oaths, pilgrimages, images and tithes, on the legitimacy and validity of excommunication, on the nature of the church and the position of the pope, on the obligation to fast and the legitimacy of work on feast. days. It also contained some questions not covered by Brouns' list: whether prayer was necessarily more meritorious in church than in the open field, on pacifism and legal execution, on church bells and on the value of blessed bread. Very few of the abjurations cover views other than those mentioned.[2] This fact also reveals how much the form of questions asked determined the amount and content of the information given: obviously, it is quite likely that, for example, these East Anglian heretics held unorthodox views about the validity of private religion (Brouns' list questions 16–18, 23), but they never seem to have been asked about this. Only one of them reported any belief related to this matter, and this merely the idea that friars were destroying the world.[3] Equally, and more surprisingly, they seem not to have been asked about the legitimacy of unauthorized preaching, a topic not properly covered by the question on the priesthood. Conversely, one can see in the light of this Norwich list the defects of Brouns'; in particular, it allowed little room for the eliciting of a suspect's views on the question of the 'priesthood of all believers', a view held by the majority of the East Anglian Lollards.[4]

The comparison of these two lists, that of Brouns and that which can be deduced from Alnwick's courtbook, suggests a more general point that should be borne in mind in the consideration of Lollard confessions and abjurations. This is that, here even more than usual, use cannot be made of negative evidence. Obviously, the views confessed or abjured were held in some form by the suspect; conversely, however, it should not be assumed that a Lollard view omitted from a particular confession or abjuration was not held by the suspect. The omission may be simply the result of a failure to ask the necessary eliciting question. In a series of abjurations from one diocese in a small period of time finer analysis is, of course, possible: if one of a series admits heretical views about, for instance, unlicensed preaching, it is perhaps unlikely that a second in the same series would not have been asked the same question. But if a whole series contains no mention of a Lollard belief of some frequency elsewhere, one is probably correct in

[1] The list of errors printed by Welch, *ubi supra*, pp. 159–60, that were abjured by Robert Cavell, priest of Bungay, provides a typical instance of these first five views.
[2] The statements of Margaret Baxter of Martham (Westminster Cath. MS. B. 2.8, pp. 273–7) include some other views, many of them extreme; but this case is something of an oddity in the MS. since it includes accusations of others against Margaret.
[3] John Burell, reporting the view of another, *ibid.*, p. 286.
[4] Thus Richard Fleccher of Beccles 'þat every cristen man is a prest' (*ibid.*, p. 330).

assuming that this is only because the examining authority did not question on that topic. It is also perhaps to be suspected that in some cases omissions may be due either to the difficulty of eliciting a clearly heretical or, conversely, orthodox response, or to unwillingness on the part of the examiners to become embroiled in dubious questions. The first may explain the absence of the Eucharist from some abjurations and the presence of only one, apparently rather unsatisfactory, question on the topic in the Norwich list.[1] The second may account for Brouns' inclusion of only one, fairly simple question on the subject of the Lollard belief in the church as 'congregatio omnium predestinatorum'.[2]

The interest of the first list of questions below remains, however, considerable. Unlike lists that derive from actual examinations, even in such a series as that in Alnwick's courtbook, its contents are not determined by the peculiarities of individual circumstances but are the best that a skilled contemporary could produce to elicit Wycliffite leanings. Even in the most favourable circumstances, the answers to these questions would only produce bare and negative statements; such is the disadvantage of the study of the Lollard movement made exclusively from documentary sources. For the reasons that lie behind the bald heretical views expressed in the bishops' registers, one must go to the English writings produced by the Lollards. But as a brief survey of the topics of Lollard belief it would be hard to parallel this jurist's list.

Notes on the edition

The edition below is taken from the Polton register since this is the fullest and, so far as is possible to assess, also the earliest version. The order of the sections, numbered I–IX for ease of reference, is that of Harley MS. 2179; in the Polton register sections I–II are set between section VIII and section IX, thus separating material that clearly belongs together.

In the footnotes are recorded the variants from the other available manuscripts, though alternation of *vel/seu* and *si/an* has not been noted. In section I three witnesses are available, Harley MS. 2179 (H) and the Bekynton register (B) as well as the Polton register (P). In item II only the Polton register has the text. For items III–IX Polton is compared with Harley MS. 2179. The Bekynton register has a text of item III, but, as this is in the vernacular, collation is impossible; since an accurate print is available[3] a separate edition is not here included. The earlier version of sections VI and VIII in the Clifford register is printed separately at the end, since the number of variants from Polton makes normal collation unsatisfactory.

[1] The difficulties of examination on the Eucharist can be seen from the early trials of Aston and Oldcastle recorded in the *Fasciculi Zizaniorum*, pp. 329–33, 438–44, and of William Thorpe (printed A. W. Pollard, *An English Garner* (1903), pp. 129–32).

[2] Leff, ii. 516 ff.; for Lollard confessions dealing with the question see Salisbury, Reg. Nevill pt. ii fo. 52v, Reg. Aiscough pt. ii fo. 53v and *Reg. J. Stafford, bishop of Bath and Wells*, ed. T. S. Holmes (Somerset Record Soc., xxxi–xxxii, 1915–16), i. 78.

[3] See p. 127, n. 1 above.

In the second bank of footnotes to sections IV–IX, a–q, are given the modern forms of the references in the text to canon and civil law and the commentators.

Abbreviations are expanded without notice and modern punctuation and capitalization have been supplied. The figures in brackets in section II refer to the equivalent questions in section I.

APPENDIX

Worcester, St. Helen's Record Office, Register of Thomas Polton, pp. 111–15.

I [p. 113] Articuli super quibus heretici vel Lollardi debent examinari concepti per iuristam.[1]

1. In primis an post consecracionem sit in altari verum corpus Christi et non substancia panis materialis[2] neque vini.

2. Item si sacerdos habeat potestatem conficiendi corpus Christi.[3]

3. Item an episcopus vel sacerdos, existens in mortali peccato, ordinat, consecrat, conficit vel baptizat.

4. Item [si][4] sit fundatum in euangelio quod Christus missam ordinauerit.

5. Item in casu quod homo fuerit contritus, si tunc confessio exterior sit sibi vtilis.

6. Item an sit necessarium ad salutem[5] anime confiteri sacerdoti.

7. Item an puer natus de muliere christiana indigeat baptizari in aqua, vel si baptismum in aqua factum secundum consuetudinem ecclesie sit necessarium ad salutcm anime.[6]

8. Item an post Vrbanum sextum sit aliquis recipiendus in papam et si papa sit verus Christi vicarius in terris.

9. Item an sit contra scripturam sacram quod viri ecclesiastici habeant possessiones.

10. Item an aliquis prelatus debeat aliquem excommunicare nisi prius sciat ipsum[7] excommunicatum a Deo.

11. Item an aliquis debeat dimittere predicare vel verbum Dei audire propter excommunicacionem homini.[8]

12. Item si liceat alicui diacono vel presbitero predicare verbum Dei absque auctoritate sedis apostolice siue episcopi catholici, et an liceat vnicuique indifferenter predicare verbum Dei.

13. Item an domini temporales possunt[9] ad arbitrium suum auferre bona temporalia ab ecclesia et[10] a viris ecclesiasticis.

14. Item an populares possint, siue licitum sit eis, dominos delinquentes ad suum arbitrium corrigere.

15. Item an decime debent dari personis ecclesie, vel si sint pure elemosine et si parochiani possint propter peccata suorum prelatorum ad libitum suum eas auferre.[11]

[1] concepti per iuristam *om.*H; title *om.*B.
[2] materialis] panis materialis H.   [3] *question after 19* B.
[4] si *om.*P.   [5] ad salutem *om.*B.
[6] *Question after 19 following 2* B.   [7] sciat ipsum] sciat eum H, scit ipsum B.
[8] homini] hominum B.   [9] possunt] possint B.
[10] ab ecclesia et *om.*B.   [11] *Set out as three questions* B.

16. Item an aliquis qui ingreditur religionem priuatam qualemcumque, tam possessionatorum quam mendicancium, reddatur habilior et apcior ad obseruanciam mandatorum Dei.[1]

17. Item si fratres teneantur per labores manuum victum acquirere et non per mendicitatem.

18. Item si religiosi viuentes in religionibus priuatis sint de religione[2] christiana.

19. Item an licitum sit alicui accipere salarium de bonis temporalibus ad orandum pro defunctis.

20. Item si excommunicacio pape vel cuiuscumque prelati sit timenda.

21. Item an necessarium sit[3] credere Romanam ecclesiam esse supremam inter alias ecclesias.

22. Item an confirmaciones iuuenum, ordinaciones clericorum, locorumque consecraciones sint necessarie vel licite.

23. Item an Augustinus, Benedictus et Bernardus bene fecerunt in eo quod habuerunt possessiones et instituerunt religiones priuatas.

24. Item an quadragesima fuerat ordinata per Deum, et si sit necessarium ieiunare in eadem et abstinere a carnibus et a lacticinis.

25. Item si ieiunia instituta ab ecclesia prosint[4] ad salutem anime vel si[5] sint obseruanda a Christi fidelibus.

26. Item an veneraciones crucis et ymaginum sint faciende.

27. Item an oblaciones facte ad ymagines in ecclesijs in honore sanctorum illorum quos ipse ymagines representant sint meritorie.

28. Item an peregrinaciones ad loca sancta sint necessarie siue meritorie ad salutem animarum.[6]

29. Item an oraciones sint fiende ad aliquos sanctos.

30. Item si dirigi deberent oraciones tantummodo ad Deum.

31. Item si sit licitum alicui seipsum crucis signaculo benedicere.

32. Item si papa vel episcopi possint facere constituciones.

33. Item an decreta, decretales siue constituciones papalia,[7] sinodalia seu prouincialia sunt seruanda.[8]

34. Item an iurare super librum sit licitum.

35. Item an iuramenta in vtroque foro, videlicet ecclesiastico et temporali, in casibus consuetis et more solito prestanda sint licita.[9]

36. Item an genuflexiones, inclinaciones, thurificaciones[10] deosculaciones necnon luminarium accensiones et aque benedicte asperciones in ecclesia fieri consueta sint licite et meritorie.

37. Item an omnia[11] debent esse communia.

38. Item an sabbatum et festa principalia sint necessarie obseruanda et sanctificanda vel ad libitum.

39. [p. 114] Item an licitum sit sacerdoti habere vxorem.

40. Item an mali sint pars ecclesie catholice.

[1] et . . . obseruancium] et cercior ad conseruancium B.
[2] religione] regione B.   [3] necessarium sit] est necessarium H.
[4] prosint] prosunt B.   [5] si *om.*B.
[6] animarum] anime B.   [7] papalia] statuta papalia B.
[8] sunt seruanda] sint seruanda H, sint obseruanda B.
[9] *Questions 35, 37 and 38 added after original writing in P, marked for insertion but order unclear; order here follows that of B and H.*
[10] thurificaciones] purificaciones P.
[11] omnia] bona H.

II Articuli concepti per theologos super quibus Lollardi debent examinari.

1. An sacerdos rite consecrans conficit corpus Christi. (2)
2. An corpus sic confectum sit in altare terrestri corpus Christi naturale et non panis naturalis neque vinum. (1)
3. An episcopus vel sacerdos, existens in mortali, pretendens facere in forma ecclesie, ordinat, consecrat, conficit vel baptizat. (3)
4. An missa secundum formam modernam ecclesie habeat fundamentum in euangelio Iesu Christi. (4)
5. An sit necessarium ad salutem peccatori adulto habenti facultatem confitendi ecclesiastice quod ecclesiastice confiteatur. (6)
6. An ex fidelibus procreato sit baptismus aque necessarius ad salutem. (7)
7. An post Vrbanum sextum sit aliquis per eleccionem taxatam sancte Romane ecclesie recipiendus in papam, qui sit verus Christi vicarius in terris et capud ecclesie. (8)
8. An sit contra scripturam sacram quod clerici et viri ecclesiastici habeant possessiones rerum temporalium. (9)
9. An omnia debent esse communia. (37)
10. An aliquis prelatus debet aut potest aliquem excommunicare nisi prius ipsum sciat excommunicatum a Deo. (10)
11. An aliquis debeat dimittere predicare vel verbum Dei audire propter excommunicacionem homini. (11)
12. An liceat vnicuique predicare verbum Dei absque auctoritate sedis apostolice siue episcopi catholici. (12)
13. An reges et domini temporales existentes in peccato mortali eo ipso cadunt ab omni iure et titulo ad illa regna vel dominia. (13)
14. An populares possint libere ad suum arbitrium dominos delinquentes corrigere vel iudicare. (14)
15. An decime dande personis ecclesie sint pure elemosine, et si parochiani possint propter peccata suorum prelatorum ad suum iudicium eas subtrahere vel auferre. (15)
16. An aliquis ingrediens religionem priuatam, possessionatorum vel mendicancium, redditur eo ipso habilior et apcior ad obseruanciam mandatorum. (16)
17. Si religiosi viuentes claustraliter sint de religione Christiana. (18)
18. An sancti sint orandi et oraciones dirigende ad eos. (29)
19. An sancta crux sit adoranda et ymagines Christi, beate virginis et sanctorum sint cultu aliquo catholice venerande. (26)
20. Si sanctum sit et sanum menti et corporis quod vir Christianus se muniat signo crucis. (31)
21. An Augustinus, Benedictus et Bernardus bene fecerint in eo quod habuerunt possessiones et instituerunt religiones priuatas.[1] (23)

III [Abiuracio super predictis][2]
[p. 111] In Dei nomine Amen. Coram vobis etc. ego N.B. etc. parochianus

---

[1] Following the end of this list in the Polton register appear two notes in the same hand. The first, concerning the honour due to the shrines of saints, is said to be from the *De Ecclesiasticis Dogmatibus*, ascribed here to Augustine; it corresponds to Migne, *Patrologia Latina*, XLII, col. 1219, cap. xl. The second, on the veneration of the cross, is again ascribed to Augustine, *De Visitatione Infirmorum*; it is found in *P.L.*, XL, col. 1154, bk. II, cap. iii to 'tibi reducens'.

[2] *Heading from* H; *not in* P.

ecclesie N. etc. senciens et[1] intelligens et perpendens quod ante hanc horam nonnullos articulos et opiniones fidei catholice et determinacioni sancte Romane ecclesie repugnantes ten[u]i, docui et affirmaui, videlicet quod venerabiles ymagines non sunt venerande seu adorande, ac eciam quod peregrinaciones ad gloriosum Thomam martirem et alia loca pia non sunt licite etc., quodque eciam libros, hereses et errores continentes, temere scripsi, compilaui et penes me retinui, et scripta in eisdem approbaui et affirmaui, ac ea occasione fuissem[2] coram vobis reuerendissimo patre etc. iudicialiter constitutus;[3] per vosque qui curam anime mee geritis satis sufficienter sum informatus et veraciter sciam articulos supradictos ac libros fuisse et esse hereticos, falsos et erroneos[4] et aduersus doctrinam sancte Romane ecclesie temere procedentes, volens catholicam sequi doctrinam et ab omni heretica recedere prauitate ac ad vnitatem ecclesie spontanea et proua voluntate redire, attendens quod ecclesia nulli claudit gremium redire volenti, et quod Deus non vult mortem peccatoris sed pocius vt conuertatur et viuat, puro corde profiteor et detestor meos heresim et errorem in premissis, ac articulos et opiniones supradictos fateor esse hereticos, peruersos, falsos, erroneos ac determinacioni sancte Romane ecclesie repugnantes. Et quia per predictam que tenui, docui, approbaui et affirmaui, exhibui me corruptum et infidelem, vt de cetero incorruptum et fidelem me ostendam ac ne similate reuersus existimere, catholicam fidem et doctrinam me obseruaturum fideliter promitto; omnemque heresim et errorem ac hereticam prauitatem, doctrinam et opinionem quamcumque aduersus catholicam fidem et determinacionem sancte Romane ecclesie se extollentem et presertim articulos supradictos abiuro. Et iuro [su]per[5] hunc librum quod de cetero non tenebo, predicabo, dogmatizabo nec docebo hereses seu heresim, errores aut errorem, seu doctrinam peruersam contra fidem catholicam et sancte Romane ecclesie determinacionem, nec quouis alia[6] aliquo modo pertinaciter defendam, nec docentem seu dogmatizantem per me vel[7] interpositam personam tubeor publice vel occulte. Non ero hereticorum aut de heresi suspectorum receptor, fautor, consiliarius aut defensor; nec eis credam aut scienter associabor, nec familiaritatem aut consilium impendam, seu fauorem, dona seu munera eis non mittam, nec eos[8] quouis modo consolabor. Libros siue quaternos ac rotulos, hereses, errores siue erronea continentes, quos me scripsisse noui et quos penes me habeo, vel in aliorum manibus esse scio, ipsosque libros huiusmodi quos me recipere seu quos ab alijs recipi,[9] scribi seu dictari scire me continget, vobis reuerendissimo patri seu deputatis vestris cum ad vestri seu depu[ta]torum[10] virorum presenciam cicius peruenire possem, absque dolo, fraude vel malo ingenio quocumque, liberabo. Et sic ab alijs receptos seu scriptos aut penes eos reconditos intimabo, necnon quoscumque hereticos de heresi, vel suspectos eorum fautores, consolatores, consiliarios et defensores, seu occulta conuenticula celebrantes a communi doctrina ecclesie presertim Romane et a communi conuersacione fidelium discrepantes, seu bonis moribus aduersantes, vobis reuerendissimo patri, seu loci eorem diocesano, celeriter nunciabo. Sicut Deus me adiuuet et hec sancta Dei Euangelia per me [corporaliter][11] tacta.

Informacio ad procedendum contra hereticos.

[1]senciens et] sciens H.   [2]fuissem *om*.H.
[3]constitutus] constituta H.   [4]erroneos] errores H.
[5]super] per P.   [6]alia] talia H.
[7]vel] vel per H.   [8]eos] eis H.
[9]recipi] recepi H.   [10]deputatorum] deputorum P.   [11]corporaliter *om*.P.

IV In primis, postquam hereticus est detectus vel denunciatus seu delatus episcopo vel eius vicemgerenti, scribatur denunciacio per notarium publicum. Quo facto, si poterit sciri[1] vbi hereticus moratur, arrestetur vigore statuti regij editi apud Leycestr' anno primo regis Henrici quinti,[a] et scrutetur domus eiusdem incontinenter an possint reperiri libri in Anglico reprobate[2] leccionis.

V [p. 112] Si vero hereticus non potest personaliter apprehendi, tunc discernat episcopus, vel ipse cui commisit vices suas, ipsum personaliter citandum ad comperendum coram ipso certis die et loco, personaliter responsurum super fide. Et, si certificetur quod non potest personali citacione apprehendi quia subterfugit, discernat episcopus etc. ipsum fore citandum personaliter, si poterit apprehendi alioquin per publicum edictum in locis vbi morari consueuit et in ecclesia cathedrali diocesis. Et si non compareat, pronunciet ipsum contimacem et in penam[3] contimacie sue. Si habeat testes ad probandum articulos detectos, vel[4] ad conuincendum ipsum super heresi, recipiat eosdem. Et si sit probatum crimen heresis, condempnet ipsum hereticum eciam abcentem per sentenciam suam diffinitiuam. Si vero non habeat probaciones vnde posset condempnare hereticum abcentem, in penam[3] contimacie reputet eum, vehementer suspectum, et excommunicet eum. Et si steterit per annum in excommunicacione animo indurato, potest vt hereticus condempnari, quia vehemens suspicio propter contimaciam suam transit in violentam.[5] Prima pars istius probatur 'De dolo et contimacia', capitulo *Veritatis*;[b] secunda pars patet 'De Hereticis', capitulo *Cum contimacia* de hereticis, Libro Sexto.[c] Et iste est modus procedendi contra hereticum abcentem quem approbat Archidiaconus 'De hereticis',[6] capitulo *Vt commisi*, Libro Sexto, super verbo *procedendi*.[d]

VI In comperentia modus procedendi est talis:
Nam si compereat hereticus et errorem suum vel heresim sibi impositum[7] fateatur, vel quod habuit familiaritatem cum hereticis vel habuit libros reprobate leccionis vel libros in Anglico erronea continentes et non intimauit ordinario loci, si vult petere misericordiam et redire ad vnitatem ecclesie, tunc abiuret omnes articulos et conclusiones quos tenuit et affirmauit et[8] generaliter omnem errorem et heresim vt supra in forma iuramenti.[e] Et tunc episcopus, recepta caucione, in forma ecclesie consueta absoluat ipsum a sentencia excommunicacionis in quam incidebat ea occasione tenendo conclusiones peruersas; et tunc per modum sentencie interlocutorie non diffinitiue iniungat penitenciam. Et ferat sentenciam in hunc modum:

---

[1]sciri] scribi P.   [2]reprobate] et reprobate P.
[3]penam] plenam P.   [4]vel] valeat H.
[5]violentam] violenciam H.   [6]De hereticis *om*.H.
[7]impositum] imponitum P.   [8]et *om*.H.

[a] *Rotuli Parliamentorum*, iv. 24–5.
[b] *Decretales*, II. xiv. 8; *Corpus Iuris Canonici*, ed. E. Friedberg (Leipzig, 1879–81), ii, cols. 296–7 (hereafter referred to as Friedberg).
[c] *Sextus*, v. ii. 7; Friedberg, ii, col. 1071.
[d] Guido de Baysio, *Super Sexto* (Milan, 1490), fo. Pi^r, cols. 1–2.
[e] See above pp. 135–6.

VII [Absolucio ab excommunicacione et carceribus adiudicacio vsque etc.][1]
In Dei nomine Amen. Nos etc. contra te legitime procedentes quia inuenimus te
heretica dixisse et tenuisse, vel cum hereticis conuersasse vel libros reprobate
leccionis scienter habuisse; vis vt asseris ex corde puro et non ficto ad sanam
doctrinam et vnitatem ecclesie redire. Ideo, abiurata[2] per te primitus omnia
heretica prauitate, ac[3] prestita caucione de parendo iuri ab excommunicacionis
sentencia in qua ea occasione prestitisti, te absoluimus et sacramentis ecclesie
restituimus. Et quia in Deum et sanctam matrem ecclesiam Romanam in ea
parte temere deliquisti, te carceribus mancipandum in partem penitencie tue
et saluo custodiendum vsque ad proximam prelatorum et cleri conuocacionem
discreuimus in hijs scriptis. Ista probantur 'De hereticis', capitulo *Vt
commissi* Libro Sexto,[f] in verbo *obedientes* et in verbo *carceri* per Archidi-
aconum;[g] et per constitucionem prouincialem que incipit *Cum inter ceteras*,[h]
et 'De penis', capitulo *Quamuis* Libro Sexto.[i] Et si[4] ipse cui carceri iniun-
gitur pro penitencia efugerit[5] carceres vt[6] noluerit peragere penitenciam, potest
dampnari vt hereticus, vt notatur 'De presumpcionibus', capitulo *Literas*.[j] Et si
talis confitens errorem siue heresim recusauerit abiurare errorem siue heresim, vel
si interrogatus an vult abiurare tacet, moueatur tunc sub pena iuris vt respondeat;
et si non vult respondere, pronuncietur contimax et in penam contimacie condemp-
netur vt hereticus, probatur argumento legis Digesti 'De Interrogatoriis accioni-
bus', libro *De etate*, paragrafo *Qui tacet*.[k]

VIII Si vero comparet et negat articulos sibi obiectos, tunc recipiantur testes
super articulis negatis. Et si ipse petat copiam inquisicionis et testium, si iudex
videat quod[7] non iminiat periculum, discernat sibi copiam; si tum[8] viderit quod
ex donacione copie muneret periculum propter personas testium, tunc non dabit
copiam; quod totum relinquitur discrecioni iudicis. Vbi tum vult ipse hereticus
exprimere nomina testium quos credit productos contra eum suspectos, tunc[9]
specificet nomina testium et causam quare habet eos suspectos[9] puta municicie.
Et si iudex videat causam legitimam et probatam, detrahat iudex testimonio
eorum alias ex dictis testium condempnet hereticum; probatur hec 'De hereticis',
capitulo finali Libro Sexto.[l] Et sic seruat consuetudo generalis.

IX [p. 115] Si vero crimen non est plene probatum sed semiplene, tunc potest
torqueri inquisitus si negauerit; vt notatur 'De hereticis', capitulo primo in
Clementinis,[m] et II.q.i 'Inprimis'.[n]

[1]*Heading from* H; *not in* P.   [2]abiurata] abiurato H.
[3]ac] et H.   [4]si *om*.H.
[5]efugerit] offregerit H.   [6]vt] vel H.
[7]quod] et P.   [8]tum *om*.H.
[9]tunc . . . suspectos *om*.H.

[f] *Sextus*, v. ii. 12; Friedberg, ii, col. 1075.
[g] Guido de Baysio, fo. Pi[r], col. 2.
[h] *Reg. Chichele*, iii. 18–19.
[i] *Sextus*, v. ix. 3; Friedberg, ii, col. 1091.
[j] *Decretales*, ii. xxiii. 14; Friedberg, ii, col. 357.
[k] *Digestum*, xi. i. 11, 4; *Corpus Iuris Civilis* (Berlin, 1954), i. 182.
[l] *Sextus*, v. ii. 20; Friedberg, ii, col. 1078.
[m] *Clementines*, v. iii. 1; Friedberg, ii, cols. 1181–2.
[n] Gratian C. 2 q. 1 c. 7; Friedberg, i, cols. 439–42.

Vnde notandum est quod nunquam procedendum ad recipiendum purgacionem heretici nisi formis istis precedentibus, vbi crimen est negatum et deficientibus probacionibus; 'De purgacione canonica', capitulo *Inter solicitudines*.[1,o]

Nota eciam quod vehementer suspectus contra quem crimen non est probatum quia forte communicauit cum hereticis vel habuit libros in Anglico suspectos; debet abiurare omnem heresim et errorem: 'De hereticis', *Accusatus* Libro Sexto;[p] et in dicto[2] capitulo *Inter solicitudines*,[1] et ibi Bernardus.[q]

Register of Richard Clifford, Guildhall, London, MS. 9531/4, fo. 188v.

Modus procedendi contra Lollardum comparentem.

VI   Si compareat et heresym vel errorem suum fateatur, vel quod habuit familiaritatem cum hereticis, vel habuit libros reprobate leccionis vel libros in Anglico erronia continentes et non intimauit ordinario loci, si voluerit petere misericordiam et redire ad vnitatem ecclesie, tunc abiuret omnes articulos et oppiniones quos tenuit et affirmauit, et generaliter omnem errorem et heresym sub forma etc. Et tunc episcopus, recepta caucione, in forma ecclesie absoluat ipsum a sentencia excommunicacionis in quam incidebat ea occasione, et tunc per modum sentencie interlocutorie et non diffinitiue iniungat penitenciam.

VIII   Si non compereat et negat articulos, tunc recipiantur testes; et si petat copiam inquisicionis et testium, si non imineat periculum animarum, iudex decernet sibi copiam, nisi propter hoc esset periculum circa personas testiùm, tunc non dabit copiam; quod totum relinquitur discrecioni iudicis. Vbi tum vult ipse hereticus dicere testes suo inimicos, et sic suscriptos tunc specificat nomina testium et causam allegatam, et si iudex videat causam legitimam, retrahat testimonium eorum, alias ex dictis testium condempnat hereticum probatum. Hec 'De hereticis', capitulo finali Libro Sexto.

---

[1] solicitudines] solitudines H.
[2] et in dicto *om.*H.

[o] *Decretales*, v. xxxiv. 10; Friedberg, ii, cols. 872–4.
[p] *Sextus*, v. ii. 8; Friedberg, ii, cols. 1071–2.
[q] Bernard of Parma, *Summa Decretalium*, ed. E. A. T. Laspeyres (Ratisbon, 1860), pp. 258–60.

Appendix

Since the paper above appeared in 1973, it has come to my attention that there is another copy of the material in Balliol College Oxford MS 158, ff. 190v-192v. The manuscript falls into three sections: the first contains (ff. 2-135) a copy of *Constitutiones Othonis et Ottoboni*, the second (ff. 136-192v) a collection of English provincial constitutions, and the third (ff. 193-248) a copy of the *Consolacio Peccatorum* of Jacobus de Theramo.[1] All of the material printed in the article as sections I-IX from the Polton register is found in the Balliol manuscript; the two paragraphs from the Clifford register are not paralleled. The copy in the Balliol manuscript is very close to that found in the Polton register, including the presence of the two notes (see p. 135 n. 1) after the lists of questions; the order of the sections is, however, that of MS Harley 2179 (see p. 132). The questions in the jurist's list numbered here 35-38 appear in the Balliol copy in the sequence 38, 35, 37, 36; this would seem to be the order envisaged by the correction marks in the Polton register. The Balliol copy adds nothing to the evidence for the origins of the questions and procedural material. The second section of the manuscript was written by various scribes over a period of time from the late fourteenth to early fifteenth centuries. The latest dateable legislation in it comes from archbishop Chichele in 1414. But, as Mynors points out in his *Catalogue*, ff. 190v-192v is written in another hand and one much less formal than the rest of the section, apparently, since the final leaf of the quire was evidently blank and has been cut out, using up a gap left some time earlier. At the end of the material is written *Suppleant defectus discreciones intuencium* together with the name, presumably that of the scribe, *M. Mannyng*.

1.   R.A.B. Mynors, *Catalogue of the Manuscripts of Balliol College Oxford*, (Oxford, 1963), pp. 142-4. The similarity of the second section to the collection of material in Cambridge University Library MS Ii.3.14, noted by Mynors, does not extend to the last two folios.

9

LOLLARDY: THE ENGLISH HERESY?

SYTHEN witte stondis not in langage but in groundynge of treuthe, for tho same witte is in Laten that is in Grew or Ebrew, and trouthe schuld be openly knowen to alle manere of folke, trowthe moueth mony men to speke sentencis in Yngelysche that thai han gedired in Latyne, and herfore bene men holden heretikis.

Such is the opening sentence of the tract known in the only surviving manuscript as *Tractatus de Regibus.*[1] The text owes much of its material to Wyclif's *De Officio Regis*, though the prologue does not derive from this source, and is undoubtedly of lollard origin; its date cannot be later than the early fifteenth century.[2] The sentiments of the first part of the sentence are typically Wycliffite, though not exclusively so.[3] The interesting part of it is the last clause, and particularly the word *herfore*. I want in this paper to investigate the implications and validity of this word. The meaning of the word is superficially clear: 'for this reason are men considered heretics'—most modern writers would use 'therefore'. But can the anonymous author of this tract really be accurate in seeing a causal connection between the use of English and the detection of heresy? At a time when Chaucer, Gower and the *Gawain* poet were using the vernacular for poetry that is at the least orthodox, in the

[1] The complete tract is edited, with some unfortunate misinterpretations of the medieval English, in *Four English Political Tracts of the Later Middle Ages*, ed J.-P. Genet, *CSer*, 4 series 18 (1977) pp 5–19. The passage here quoted is also printed in [A. Hudson,] *Selections [from English Wycliffite Writings]* (Cambridge 1978) no 25/1–5. (In ensuing references to texts, line numbers, where given, follow an oblique stroke; unless the extent of the passage is open to doubt, only the opening line number will be given. In quotations from manuscripts, and from older editions, modern punctuation has been introduced; all abbreviations are expanded without notice.)

[2] See *Selections* pp 200–1; the only contemporary allusions point towards the end of the fourteenth century as the date of composition, though the sole surviving manuscript, Oxford Bodleian MS Douce 273, is paleographically of the early fifteenth century.

[3] For lollard instances see below; for an apparently orthodox statement compare the English version of Robert of Greatham's *Miroir*, Oxford Bodleian MS Holkham Misc. 40 fol 1ᵛ 'and so hit is ful gret foli to speke Latyn to lewd folk, and he entermeteth hym of a fol mister that telleth to hym Latyne. For eche man schal be undurnome and aresound aftur the langage that he hath lered.'

case of Gower declaredly anti-lollard, such a view would seem very
unlikely to be right.[4] Admittedly, we may recall the case in the later
fifteenth century when a copy of *The Canterbury Tales* was produced for the prosecution in a case of heresy;[5] but the instance is
isolated, and is usually dismissed as an instance of neurotic
officiousness on the part of the bishop's minions.[6] Yet I think that
the quotation needs a little more thought before it is likewise
dismissed as an expression of 'persecution mania'. After all,
modern scholars have succeeded in demonstrating that almost all
the elements of Wyclif's heresy are traceable to earlier thinkers, to
Marsilius of Padua, to Bradwardine, to FitzRalph, to Berengar
amongst others, and yet none of these aroused the 'witch hunt' that
followed the condemnation of Wyclif in 1382.[7] Why did these old
ideas suddenly become dangerous? Was it just the combination of
so many distasteful notions in the thought of one man? Or was
there a new ingredient? One new ingredient was, of course, the fac
that these distasteful notions were no longer confined within the
precincts of a university debating hall; that, whether with his
encouragement or not, Wyclif's followers spread his views not
only in writing but also on preaching tours of the countryside.[8]

[4] *The Complete Works of John Gower*, ed G. C. Macaulay, 4 vols (Oxford 1899–1902),
Confessio Amantis, Prol. 346 *seq*, bk 5. 1803 *seq*; *Carmen super multiplici viciorum
pestilencia*, 13 *seq*.

[5] Lincoln register Chedworth fol 62ᵛ, concerning John Baron of Amersham in 1464.
The group of lollards in the Chilterns investigated by Chedworth seems to have
been well provided with books (see C. Cross, *Church and People 1450–1660*
(Edinburgh 1976) pp 32–5 for a brief account of the group), and the authorities
particularly undiscriminating in their suspicion. As well as the Chaucer volume, a
second containing 'a play of seint Dionise' and a third containing the 'Myrrour of
Synners'—for the usual tract that went under this name see C. Horstman,
Yorkshire Writers, 2 vols (London 1895–6) 2, pp 436–40, manuscripts listed by P. S.
Jolliffe, *A Check-List of Middle English Prose Writings of Spiritual Guidance* (Toronto
1974) p 81—the 'Myrrour of Matrimony', the 'lyff of oure Lady, Adam and Eve'
and 'other sermones' were confiscated from Baron. The group owned several
copies of biblical translations and other religious works.

[6] For instance J. A. F. Thomson, *The Later Lollards 1414–1520* (Oxford 2nd ed 1967)
p 243.

[7] See, for example, G. Leff, *Heresy in the Later Middle Ages*, 2 vols (Manchester/
New York 1967) 2, pp 494–558; J. A. Robson, *Wyclif and the Oxford Schools*
(Cambridge 1966); M. J. Wilks, 'The *Apostolicus* and the Bishop of Rome', *JTS* ns
14 (1963) pp 338–54. For Wyclif's own references to Berengar see my note
appended to 'The Expurgation of a Lollard Sermon-Cycle', *JTS* ns 22 (1971)
pp 464–5; here, pp 214–15.

[8] For a reassessment of the evidence that Wyclif initiated the preaching see M. Wilks,
'"Reformatio Regni": Wyclif and Hus as leaders of religious protest movements',
SCH 9 (1972) pp 109–30 especially pp 119–21.

This brings me back to my opening quotation: was the crucial new ingredient the use of the vernacular? and the use of that vernacular for the discussion of matters that had hitherto been obscured from the view of most of the populace under the thick veil of Latin? After all, the anonymous author does not assert that the use of English, plain and simple, is the ground of suspicion, but that the trouble is the use of English for the expression of ideas that have been gathered from Latin writings. Was lollardy, then, the *English* heresy?

To attempt to show that the single major heresy known in medieval England arose from a concatenation of peculiarly insular factors would be, I think, a forlorn enterprise. Nor does it seem right to discern nationalism as a major force in the origin of lollardy or in its continuance. Certainly, there were peculiar elements in the heresy of lollardy: almost alone amongst the heresies of the high middle ages, lollardy and its relation Hussitism derive from academic controversies but came to be popular movements. But whilst Hussitism did become identified with the incipient movement towards a recognition of national identity, Lollardy did not.[9] Certainly, Wyclif used arguments that might be described as nationalistic to further his case: one such was his objection to the drain on the resources of the country that resulted from payments to the pope or through religious orders.[10] But this was not a new argument: earlier suppressions of alien priories had partly occurred from the same objection.[11] Equally, as Edith Tatnall has urged, Wyclif did speak often of an *Ecclesia Anglicana*; but frequently this phrase seems merely a useful weapon with which to beat the temporal pretensions of the clergy, and especially the claims of the papacy to jurisdiction in any realm.[12] Whether, as Tatnall

[9] For this aspect of the Hussite movement see especially F. Šmahel, 'Le mouvement des étudiants à Prague dans les années 1408–1412', *Historica* 14 (Prague 1967) pp 33–75, and the same author's 'The Idea of the "Nation" in Hussite Bohemia', *Historica* 16 (1969) pp 143–247 and 17 (1969) pp 93–197; a revised form of these last two was published as *Idea národa v husitských Čechách* (České Budějovice 1971).

[10] All quotations from Wyclif are from the editions of the Wyclif Society (1883–1921). See here, for instance, Wyclif's insistence on the various aspects of the 'dead hand' of clerical possession on property in England, *De Veritate Sacre Scripture*, 3 p 20, *De Ecclesia* p 338, *Dialogus* p 70/23, *De fundatione sectarum, Polemical Works* I p 28/14.

[11] See Knowles, *RO* 2 pp 161–5: more generally compare *Rotuli Parliamentorum* ([London 1767–77]) 46 Edward III item 27, 47 Edward III item 30, 50 Edward III items 95 and 124.

[12] [E. C.] Tatnall, ['John Wyclif and *Ecclesia Anglicana*'], *JEH* 20 (1969) pp 19–43; the

maintains, Wyclif shows himself conscious of a 'distinctly English ecclesiastical tradition' seems to me less than proven. Grosseteste is often quoted with strong approbation, Becket's example is, in contrast to Wyclif's followers, cautiously commended and Pecham once quoted as an example of episcopal good sense; but the references are far from constant, and the nationalistic stress missing.[13] One area which would repay further investigation is that of Wyclif's references to English law: there are a number of occasions when Wyclif sets canon law against civil law, often specifying English law and mentioning Magna Carta as evidence that certain papal claims some of them embodied in canon law, cannot legally be maintained in England.[14] This is a train of thought that was pursued by one of Wyclif's disciples in an unpublished tract in which the assertion that the king and the temporal rulers are entitled to deprive erring clerics is demonstrated by an analysis of the clauses of the king's coronation oath; the date of this tract is likely to be early since the oath used is distinctively that of Richard II.[15] But this is an area where more expertise in law and legal history is needed than I possess.

Two matters relevant to my purpose have been investigated in the recent past and may be summarised first. Wilks incidentally examined the evidence for Wyclif's own views about the use of English, and in particular about the translation of the bible into the vernacular.[16] He concluded that not until the last two years of his

---

earlier discussion in L. J. Daly, *The Political Theory of John Wyclif* (Chicago 1962) pp 132–51 hardly tackles the issue. For cases where 'English' customs or law are merely ancillary references see, for example, *De Civili Dominio* 2 p 134, *De Veritate Sacre Scripture* I p 354 and 3 pp 18, 55.

[13] See Tatnall pp 34–43 where the references to Wyclif's works are given. For lollard views about Becket see J. F. Davis, 'Lollards, Reformers and St. Thomas of Canterbury', *University of Birmingham Historical Journal* 9 (Birmingham 1963) pp 1–15.

[14] Some of these passages are briefly mentioned in Tatnall pp 24–31. See also F. W. Maitland, 'Wyclif on English and Roman Law', *Collected Papers*, ed H. A. L. Fisher (Cambridge 1911) 3 pp 50–3. Despite its title, W. Farr's *John Wyclif as Legal Reformer* (Leiden 1974) does not fully discuss this question.

[15] In Prague University Library MS X.E.9 fols 206–7ᵛ, Vienna Nationalbibliothek MS 3928 fols 189–90 and 3932 fols 155ᵛ–6; for the distinctive character see P. E. Schramm, trans L. G. Wickham Legg, *A History of the English Coronation* (Oxford 1937) p 236.

[16] [M.] Wilks, ['Misleading manuscripts: Wyclif and the non-wycliffite bible'], *SCH* 11 (1975) pp 147–61, especially pp 154–5 and notes. I find it hard to accept the main thesis of Wilks's paper, that there existed a pre- or non-Wycliffite vernacular

life did Wyclif show any interest in the vernacular, or in the need for the laity to be able to study the scriptures in a language that they understood. A couple of incidental references that are probably earlier, one from the *De Veritate Sacre Scripture* and one from the *De Eucharistia*, can be added to Wilks's analysis, but these do not change the basic truth of his assertion.[17] There seems very little evidence that Wyclif himself thought the vernacular important before the last years of his life, or at least explicitly so.[18] But if we are prepared to accept the view, so cogently revived by Wilks himself, that Wyclif did envisage a band of poor preachers touring the country with the message of the *Doctor Evangelicus*, then we are forced to acknowledge that Wyclif must have confronted the vital question of the medium through which that message was to be conveyed.[19] As I shall argue, it was only very slowly that the authorities of the established church came to see that the vernacular lay at the root of the trouble, and that the use of it was more significant than just the substitution of a despised barbaric tongue for the tradition of Latin—that the substitution threw open to all the possibility of discussing the subtleties of the Eucharist, of clerical claims, of civil dominion and so on, and that this possibility was being seized not only by men such as Walter Brut, *laycus litteratus*, or Sir John Oldcastle whom Hoccleve reproached with 'climbing too high' by meddling with scripture,[20] but also by the artisans of Wiltshire or Norfolk. The readiness with which lollards seized upon the vernacular texts produced has been fully demonstrated by Margaret Aston in her paper 'Lollardy and Literacy' in

---

bible which the lollards took over and modified. My main objection is that when the lollards came to justify their demand for such a bible they cited many precedents, but never alluded to the existence of such a complete translation of scripture; since such a pre-existing, orthodox version would have immensely helped their case, it seems inconceivable that they should have omitted to mention it. This disagreement does not, however, affect the point at issue here.

[17] *De Veritate Sacre Scripture* 2 p 243 urges the necessity of preaching in the vernacular, *De Eucharistia* p 90/13, whilst it states that it is preferable to use Latin rather than English for the consecration of the mass because of custom, implicitly acknowledges the possibility of using the vernacular even whilst denying the desirability.

[18] The constant repetition of the need for preaching to the laity means that Wyclif must have envisaged the use of the vernacular, see *Sermones* 2 p 448/16; 3 pp 75/20, 341/13.

[19] See his paper n 8 above; compare also my paper 'A Lollard Compilation and the Dissemination of Wycliffite Thought', *JTS* ns 23 (1972) pp 65–81; Above 13–29.

[20] See *Registrum Johannis Trefnant*, ed W. W. Capes, *CYS* (1916) pp 278–365. The

History 1977.[21] As well as collecting together a large number of references to the ownership of books by lollards, she has exemplified the trouble to which lollards would go to obtain the literacy to read English books, or to find someone who would read to them, and to borrow or purchase such volumes. From the end of the fourteenth century to the Reformation there is no shortage of detail to prove the value that lollards set upon literacy and the possibilities that literacy opened up to them.

My own aim here is to fill the gap between the evidence of Wilks and that of Aston. When is it possible to discern a realisation that the matter of language was a crucial one, and not just an incidental detail? When, in fact, did either the heretics or their opponents realise that in many ways the medium was a significant part of the message? It seems to me that the terminal date for the search can be definitely fixed. By 1407 when the terms of Arundel's Constitutions were drafted the authorities had perceived the danger of English.[22] The details of the Constitutions are worth looking at again, for, though their general import is well enough known, their precise implications are much less so, and are indeed much less clear. The first two Constitutions are fairly straightforward reiterations of previous legislation: that no-one should preach in the vernacular or in Latin without a proper licence, such licences should only be given to those whose orthodoxy had been assured by examination, and that anyone admitting an unlicensed preacher should be excommunicated. The third is more significant: the preacher should regulate his observations according to his congregation, specifically that clerical vices should only be castigated to a congregation of

---

learning of Brut is evident from the length of his written replies to the charges made against him; since there is no indication to the contrary, and elsewhere Trefnant's register records in English replies given in that language, the Latin in which these replies are couched must be Brut's own. For the taunt of Hoccleve see *Hoccleve's Works: The Minor Poems*, ed F. J. Furnivall and I. Gollancz, revised J. Mitchell and A. I. Doyle, *EETS* extra series 61 and 73 (1970) no II/194, with which compare II/137–60.

[21] *History* 62 (1977) pp 347–71.

[22] I have used the text in Wilkins 3 pp 314–19; Arundel appears to have drafted the Constitutions in 1407 and issued them in 1409 (see E. F. Jacob, *The Register of Henry Chichele, archbishop of Canterbury 1414–1443*, 4 vols (Oxford 1938–47) I pp cxxx–cxxxi). For lollard references to the Constitutions see *The Lantern of Lizt*, ed L. M. Swinburn, *EETS* 151 (1917) pp 17/17, 100/1; BL MS Egerton 2820 fols 48ᵛ–9, BL MS Cotton Titus D V fols 46, 57.

clergy and not before one in which the laity were present.[23] The fourth forbade the discussion by any preacher of any of the sacraments of the church: the determinations of the church might be set out, but no doubt cast on any part of these. The next went beyond the preacher to forbid anyone teaching others from concerning himself in his instruction with any matter of theology. The sixth and seventh are those that mainly concern the present issue, and I will return to them more fully in a moment. The eighth and ninth dealt in more detail with the discussion or disputation of theological or ecclesiastical questions in the universities; the tenth goes back to the matter of licenses, this time specifying the need for a chaplain to have one before celebrating mass in the province of Canterbury. The eleventh contains the provision for enquiry about the views of every student in an Oxford hall once a month; this was the final defeat in Oxford's longstanding dispute over the right of the metropolitan to interfere in the university's affairs.[24] The two final sections dealt with the penalties for infringing the Constitutions and the method of procedure against such infringements. The central sixth section made the precise target of Arundel's legislation plain: no book or tract by John Wyclif or by any other written at his time or since should be read in the schools or anywhere else unless it had been examined and found orthodox; such an examination must be carried out by a minimum of twelve members of the university who had been approved by the archbishop or his successors, and the judgment of orthodoxy must be by unanimous vote.[25] The seventh went on to forbid the translation of any text of sacred scripture into English, and the ownership of any translation of the bible made in the time of Wyclif or later without the express

[23] Wilkins III p 316 'Praedicator . . . in praedicando clero sive populo, secundum materiam subjectam se honeste habeat, spargendo semen secundum convenientiam subjecti auditorii; clero praesertim praedicans de vitiis pullulantibus inter eos, et laicis de peccatis inter eos communiter usitatis, et non e contra'.

[24] For the earlier stages see K. B. McFarlane, *John Wycliffe and the Beginnings of English Nonconformity* (London 1952) pp 108–16, 156–7; also M. Aston, *Thomas Arundel* (Oxford 1967) pp 329–34.

[25] Wilkins 3 p 317 'nisi per universitatem Oxonii aut Cantabrigiae, seu saltem duodecim personas ex eisdem, quas eaedem universitates aut altera earundem, sub nostra, successorumve nostrorum discretione laudabili duxerint eligendas, primitus examinetur, et examinatus unanimiter per eosdem, deinde per nos seu successores nostros expresse approbetur, et universitatis nomine ac auctoritate stationariis tradatur, ut copietur; et facta collatione fideli, petentibus vendatur justo pretio sive detur, originali in cista aliqua universitatis extunc perpetuo remanente'.

permission of the diocesan, and this permission was only to be
given after the translation had been inspected. This restriction upon
the date of translation led to the alteration of the date 1408 at the
end of one manuscript of the Wycliffite bible to 1308, a date that
would have escaped the censure.[26]

The wording of this seventh constitution is, to my mind,
obscure. The vital section is this:

> statuimus igitur et ordinamus, ut nemo deinceps aliquem
> textum sacrae scripturae auctoritate sua in linguam Ang-
> licanam, vel aliam transferat, per viam libri, libelli, aut trac-
> tatus, nec legatur aliquis hujusmodi liber, libellus, aut tractatus
> jam noviter tempore dicti Johannis Wycliff, sive citra, com-
> positus, aut in posterum componendus, in parte vel in toto,
> publice, vel occulte . . .

The obscurity lies in the force of *per viam*, 'by way of': does this
imply that the clause applies whether the translation is of the whole
bible, or only of a part of that vast book? or does it mean that any
work that involves, even as only a part of a larger whole, the
rendering of biblical quotations into English falls under the same
condemnation as a complete English bible? That this second
interpretation is not over fanciful is surely suggested in the
Constitution itself by the word *tractatus*, a term that could hardly be
applied to any section of the bible straightforwardly rendered.
Lyndwood's annotations to this part of the text in his *Provinciale*
confirm the suspicion that this second meaning is relevant: the
words *aut tractatus* are glossed

> sic videlicet, quod de dictis doctorum, vel propriis, aliquem
> tractatum componat applicando textum sacræ scripturæ, et
> illius sensum transferendo in Anglicum, vel aliud idioma. Et
> eodem modo potest intelligi, quod dicit de libro sive libello, ut
> scilicet textum sacræ scripturæ in tali libro vel libello applicet,
> et textum ipsum transferat in aliud idioma.[27]

---

[26] Oxford Bodleian MS Fairfax 2 fol 385; see H. Hargreaves in *CHB* 2 p 394.

[27] I have used the 1968 Gregg reprint of the *Provinciale* (Oxford 1679) p 286; see C.
R. Cheney, 'William Lyndwood's *Provinciale*', reprinted in *Medieval Texts and
Studies* (Oxford 1973) pp 158–84. I have checked the gloss in the following
manuscripts: Oxford Bodleian MSS Bodley 248 fol 278[v], Laud Misc 608 fol 176,
Oxford Corpus Christi College MS B.71 fol 240, BL MS Royal 11 C.viii fol 200,
BL MS Royal 11 E.i fol 229[v], Cambridge Peterhouse MS 53 quire 28 leaf 8,
Cambridge Peterhouse MS 54 fol 166[v], in all of which the gloss appears as printed;
the gloss is abridged in Oxford Magdalen College MS 143 fol 217[v] and Cambridge

This gloss, of course, extends the scope of the Constitution vastly. But it does bring the seventh into line with the sixth: any book, in Latin or in English, that deals with matters of theology or church affairs, may only be used after the archbishop or his appointed surrogates have approved it.

A glance at any lollard text makes it plain why such a ruling could have given rise to the view with which I began this paper: that the expression of ideas gained from Latin books and expressed in English was *ipso facto* evidence of heresy. To Wyclif and his followers the bible was the main, if not the only, source of authority; therefore any view is always supported by the citation of biblical justification. This is true of the Latin *Opus Arduum* or *Floretum*, just as it is of the vernacular writings; but, after the first few years, the latter were much more important to the movement.[28] Indeed, if the confiscated copy of *The Canterbury Tales* had included, for instance, the Pardoner's Tale or, even more, the Parson's Tale, it could on a rigorous interpretation of this Constitution rightly have been regarded as indicative of heresy. Ensuing legislation and proceedings did little to allay the fear that use of the vernacular in itself was dangerous. The address by abbot Whethamsted in 1426/7 to suspected heretics, and the confession of one of them that follows, may detail the errors in the books that the lollard possessed, but the ordinance that precedes these baldly states that the cause of heresy is *librorum possessio et lectura, qui scribuntur in vulgari idiomate nostro*. It orders the investigation of all such books and those who own them, only *præcipue qui aut materiam aut occasionem ministrare poterunt erroneæ opinionis et malignæ*.[29]

By 1407 suspicion of lollardy had embraced the fact of the importance of the vernacular. This seems certain. What is rather more difficult is to establish the date at which this notion first becomes perceptible, and to trace the stages by which it achieved

---

Pembroke College MS 309 fol 316, and does not appear at all in the more heavily abridged glosses in BL MS Royal 9 A.v, BL MS Royal 9 A.xiii and Cambridge University Library MS Ee.6.32.

[28] For the first see my paper 'A Neglected Wycliffite Text', *JEH* 29 (1978) pp 257–79, for the second most recently *The Middle English Translation of the 'Rosarium Theologie'*, ed C. von Nolcken, *Middle English Texts* 10 (Heidelberg 1979); for the vernacular texts compare the footnote biblical references to texts nos 20–6 in *Selections*. See above pp 43–65.

[29] *Annales Monasterii S. Albani a Johanne Amundesham*, ed H. T. Riley, 2 vols, *RS* (London 1870–1) I pp 222–8.

sufficient importance to be formalized in legislation. I have argued elsewhere that in Oxford in 1401 it was still possible for men to urge the desirability of vernacular translations of the bible without being suspected as heretics.[30] Richard Ullerston, a man otherwise known as a pillar of orthodoxy and apparently not one who had sown wild-oats of Wycliffism in his youth, and William Butler, a Franciscan friar, both spoke on the matter at length, though on opposite sides of the debate, without mentioning that the lollards notably supported translation. The case is, of course, stronger for Butler: it would have helped his opposition had he been able to cite the danger of the spread of lollardy as one of the undesirable outcomes of vernacular versions. But to think that the switch of views amongst the orthodox came between 1401 and 1407 is unconvincing, and there is evidence that this debate did not reveal the whole picture. I should like now to look further at the evidence for the period between 1382, when Wyclif mentions the use of the vernacular in enthusiastic terms, and 1407 when Arundel's legislation condemned it outright.

The earliest edicts against Wyclif and his followers do not appear to mention books or pamphlets of any kind, Latin or English.[31] The first statement that I have found comes from 1388 when a series of mandates was sent out by the king to various authorities, secular and ecclesiastical, requiring them to search out the books, booklets or quires written by Wyclif, Hereford, Aston or Purvey. Some of these specify that the books might be written in English or in Latin.[32] Earlier than this there is implicit recognition of the use of English, since we find mention as early as 1382 of the preaching of

[30] ['The Debate on Bible Translation, Oxford 1401',] *EHR* (1975); above pp 67–84.
[31] For the stages of early legislation see H. G. Richardson, 'Heresy and the Lay Power under Richard II', *EHR* 51 (1936) pp 1–28. The edicts in *Calendar of Patent Rolls 1381–1385* (London 1897) pp 150, 487 do not mention any heretic by name; Courtenay's letter used by various bishops in 1387 (see Wilkins 3 pp 202–3 for the copy in Wakefield's Worcester register) mentions various heretics by name but not books. Compare A. K. McHardy, 'Bishop Buckingham and the Lollards of Lincoln Diocese', *SCH* 9 (1972) pp 131–5.
[32] *Calendar of Patent Rolls 1385–1389* (London 1900) pp 448, 468, 536; *Calendar of Close Rolls 1385–1389* (London 1921) p 519. [Henry] Knighton, [*Chronicon*], ed J. R. Lumby, 2 vols, RS (London 1889–95) 2 pp 260–5 gives an account of new measures taken in 1388, mentioning (p 263) 'librosque eorum Anglicos plenius examinarent', and giving a specimen royal commission which orders the inspection and confiscation of books 'tam in Anglico quam in Latino' (pp 264–5). Compare the later material exemplified in A. Hudson, 'The Examination of Lollards', *BIHR* 46 (1973) p 156. See above p 136.

Wyclif's views to lay people *utriusque sexus.*[33] But it would appear that the language did not merit mention. The references to preaching to the laity are both early and frequent. The chroniclers, even though the dates they assign cannot be regarded as firm, provide a chorus of testimony on this score. Walsingham under 1382 records that Wyclif himself preached *in vulgari plebe*, and connects Wyclif's escape from censure in 1378 to the way in which he had charmed the ears of the Londoners with his perverse doctrines.[34] Knighton, who notes Wyclif's own part in biblical translation, describes in some detail the preaching of Aston, Purvey and another (who, we might suspect, may have been Knighton's fellow canon, Philip Repingdon); the fact that the chronicler twice mentions vernacular phrases in these accounts makes it clear that the sermons were often, if not always, in English.[35] The continuator of the *Eulogium Historiarum* describes under 1381 how Wyclif's *discipuli . . . hanc doctrinam predicabant et divulgabant per totam Angliam multo laicos seducentes etiam nobiles et magnos dominos qui defendebant tales falsos prædicatores*, and again, under the following year, how these disciples taught the heretical view of the Eucharist *non solum in multis popularibus et laicis, sed etiam in nobilibus et literatis.*[36] More specifically, the notarial account of Nicholas Hereford's Ascension day sermon in Oxford in 1382 particularly states that this highly controversial discourse was *in vulgari ydeomate anglicano;* Hereford might have been chosen to give the sermon by the chancellor, Robert Rigg, an action which led many to think that Rigg had Wycliffite leanings, but his congregation was plainly not limited to an academic group.[37]

But I do not want to multiply evidence of lollard preaching. That is easy to do, but it only implicitly advances my investigation—that the Wycliffites saw the need to use the vernacular if the mass of people was to be convinced of the rightness of their views, and that the opposing authorities equally tried to prevent such unorthodox preaching in whatever language it might be delivered. What is

[33] Winchester, reg. Wykeham, ed T. F. Kirby, *Hampshire Record Society* (1896–9) 2 pp 337–8.
[34] [Thomas Walsingham,] *Historia Anglicana*, ed H. T. Riley, 2 vols, RS (London 1863–4) II p 51 and I p 363; compare *Chronicon Angliæ*, ed E. M. Thompson, RS (London 1874) p 335.
[35] Knighton II pp 151–2; p 176 Aston, p 179 Purvey, p 174 unnamed Wycliffite.
[36] *Continuatio Eulogii Historiarum*, ed F. S. Haydon, RS (London 1863) pp 351–5.
[37] For the sermon see Oxford Bodleian MS Bodley 240, p 848; for the assumption see *Fasciculi Zizaniorum*, ed W. W. Shirley, RS (London 1858) pp 298–9.

more relevant is the evidence that specifies English, and that which
defines more closely the dangers of using the vernacular. Here
material is rather less easy to discover, at least in any direct form.[38]
Much of the evidence comes from tracts or debates that are overtly
on other subjects. It seems clear from a number of sources that
objections to the use of the vernacular had been raised, and that
defenders of English felt it necessary to answer the points made.
The fact that the same arguments are advanced both by those
defending the vernacular and by those opposed to its use points to
the existence of a widespread debate, even though the two sets of
texts do not formally answer each other. It is also noteworthy that
defenders of the vernacular reveal the same points, whether or not
they are otherwise sympathetic to lollard causes. As I shall show,
the orthodox Ullerston uses some of the same contentions as the
writers of lollard sermons. As usual, there is difficulty with many
of the lollard texts in determining precisely their date of composition. In each case I shall endeavour to provide one example from a
dated text, to show that the idea was current before 1407, even if
some of the evidence comes from works that are later in date than
Arundel's Constitutions.

The first group of arguments focus on the matter of language
itself. Wyclif in his *De nova prevaricancia mandatorum*, dated as late
1382 or 1383, already refers to those who argued that vernacular
scriptures were legitimate since Christ and his apostles had used
various languages in their preaching.[39] This idea was taken up by an
additional prologue to Saint John's gospel found in one manuscript
of the Wycliffite bible and in other anonymous lollard texts.[40] The
Opus Arduum, written between Christmas 1389 and Easter 1390
reiterates this, and reinforces the argument by the observation that
Jerome had written many of his letters to women to whom he must
originally have used the vernacular.[41] In the late *De contrarietate
duorum dominorum* Wyclif had argued that language, whether

---

[38] There is apparently little in the Latin tracts written against Wyclif by men such as
Woodford, Rymington or Netter.

[39] *Polemical Works* I p 116/6; for the date see Wilks p 155. Compare [T.] Arnold,
[*Select English Works of John Wyclif*], 3 vols (Oxford 1869–71) 3 p 100/20; [F. D.]
Matthew, [*The English Works of Wyclif hitherto unprinted*], EETS 74 (1880) p
429/11.

[40] Printed in [*The Holy Bible . . . made from the Latin Vulgate by John Wycliffe and his
Followers*], ed [J.] Forshall and [F.] Madden, 4 vols (Oxford 1850) 4 p 685b.

[41] Brno University Library MS Mk 28 fols 136ᵛ–7; for the text see my paper 'A
Neglected Wycliffite Text', *JEH* 29 (1978) pp 257–79. See above pp 43–65.

Hebrew, Greek, Latin or English was *quasi habitus legis domini*, that the teaching of Christ was not affected by language and that therefore the most familiar should be used.[42] This was taken up by the anonymous Latin sermons found in three Oxford manuscripts:

> Quamuis enim ydiomata sint diuersa, tamen idem articuli fidei et eorum veritates euangelice sunt eedem in numero vtrobique quia quamuis lingue sint diuerse, tamen veritates euangelice non variantur. Ideo idem euangelium potest scribi et pronunciari in Latinis et Grecis, in Gallicis, in Anglicis et in omni lingua articulata. Et euangelium scriptum in Anglicis quia bonitas euangelii non habet attendi penes bonitatem ydiomatis sed penes perfeccionem veritatis credite et Dei approbantis eandem.[43]

Others, however, had doubts about this equivalence of languages. Ullerston in his 1401 paper refers to the view that English is a barbarous language, lacking a grammatical structure and also deficient in a number of the terms that would be necessary for a rendering of scripture. He himself dismisses these difficulties, arguing that English can find the necessary terms, and observing that even the Vulgate made use of some non-Latin terms such as *hosanna, racha, alleluia* from Hebrew to remedy Latin inadequacies.[44] The insufficiency of English was taken up much more fully by Thomas Palmer in a determination which, from its failure to mention recent legislation effecting the prohibition on vernacular scriptures that its author so much desired, must probably be dated from before 1407. Palmer spends a lot of time labouring the point which had been taken in the prologue to the Wycliffite bible, that languages are not symmetrical—that English, for instance, lacks the fully inflected definite article or relative pronoun of Latin. He also produces a number of Latin words for which he urges English has no equivalent; but the examples hardly forward his argument, since they are mostly cases relevant not to biblical

[42] *Polemical Works* 2 p 700/27; compare *De Amore, (Opera Minora)* p 9/20, *Speculum Secularium Dominorum (Opera Minora)* p 74/6, *Opus Evangelicum* 2 p 115/4. With Arnold 3 p 98/4 'the treuthe of God stondeth nou3t in one langage more than in another' compare the Waldensian text cited by [J. Gonnet and A. Molnar,] *Les Vaudois [au moyen âge]* (Turin 1974) p 394 note 120 'sacra scriptura eundem effectum habet in vulgari, quem habet in Latino'.

[43] Quoted from Oxford Bodleian MS Laud Misc 200 fol 201; the other two manuscripts do not extend so far. I owe knowledge of this group to Dr Christina von Nolcken, who is investigating the material.

[44] Vienna Nationalbibliothek MS 4133, fols 195ᵛ, 202.

translation but to theological discussion, and some at that reveal only Palmer's ignorance of contemporary vernacular writing.[45]

Related to this linguistic argument is the citation of precedent for translation. Ullerston produced a long list of earlier English versions, from Bede and Alfred to Richard Rolle. These English models are found also in numerous lollard texts, and are referred to by Palmer.[46] A comparable argument is that other nations have the scriptures in their own tongue. Wyclif in *De triplici vinculo amoris* referred to queen Anne's possession of the gospels in three languages, Czech, German and Latin, and this royal example was taken up by the English tract derived from Ullerston's discussion. The same point in more general terms was made in the *Opus Arduum* and is mentioned, though not discussed, by Palmer.[47]

Coming closer to the heart of the matter is the argument that urges the necessity of communicating essential commands in a language intelligible in those who should obey them. If the English king sent out letters patent in Latin or French 'to do crie his lawis, his statutes and his wille to the peple, and it were cried oonly on Latyn or Frensche and not on Englisch, it were no worschip to the kynge ne warnynge to the peple'. Similarly, what good would it be if a watchman warned of impending danger only in an unknown tongue? To teach Christ's law in Latin is an equally, indeed more, dangerous and foolish enterprise.[48]

An argument that could more easily be disposed of was that if it were legitimate to teach the scriptures in the vernacular through sermons, it must be allowed to write it in the vernacular. This is

[45] Palmer's determination was printed from the sole manuscript, Trinity College Cambridge MS B.15. 11 fols 42^v–7^v, by [M.] Deanesly in [*The Lollard Bible*] (Cambridge 1920) pp 418–37, but Deanesly's views about the nature and position of the determination need modification; see here pp 421–2, 425–8, 436–7. The form of Palmer's text is, as it stands, a muddle; it would seem that it may be notes taken from a whole series of debates.

[46] Vienna Nationalbibliothek MS 4133 fol 198$^{r/v}$; Palmer, ed Deanesly p 435. For other lollard instances see Matthew p 429/22, Forshall and Madden 1 p 59, and the so-called 'Lollard Chronicle of the Papacy', ed E. W. Talbert, *Journal of English and Germanic Philology* 41 (Urbana 1942) pp 163–93, lines 99 *seq*, 136 *seq*.

[47] Polemical Works I p 168/9; the English text printed by Deanesly p 445 (the conjecture about authorship is unwarranted), where the vernacular in which Anne's books were written has become English; *Opus Arduum*, Brno University Library Mk 28 fol 174^v; Palmer, ed Deanesly pp 419–20.

[48] Cambridge University Library MS Ii.6.26 fols 5^v–6; compare fol 11 where the story of the Ethiopian eunuch in Acts 8:26–38 is told in favour of even partial understanding since this will incite the ignorant to search for more.

alleged in the *Opus Arduum* and in various English tracts.[49] But, as opposition to vernacular scriptures grew, it became obvious that this parallel was far from exact. Sermons could select uncontroversial passages of the bible, the passage could then be explained by the preacher, and, furthermore, the preacher himself would have to be licensed by the bishop if he were to operate legally. The naked text in the ploughman's hand was a much more dangerous and much more readily available weapon, as both sides realised right down to the reformation period.[50] The prefatory epistle to Nicholas Love's translation of the pseudo-Bonaventuran *Meditations on the Life and Passion of Christ* is relevant here. This text is presented as an alternative to the Wycliffite scriptures, by the time of the translation banned, and Love observes that the text offers a commentary on the harmony of the gospels, explaining the significance of the stories retold. The preface also records Arundel's authorization of the text.[51]

The issues here, however, lead on to the central point in this debate on translation: the prerogative of the clergy in scriptural, theological and ecclesiastical matters. Both sides in the debate perceived that the availability of vernacular scriptures would make possible the participation of the laity in questions of such a kind. To William Butler in 1401 this was the chief objection to translation. At one point he cited Aristotle's *Rhetoric* to the effect that 'quanto maior est populus, tanto minor vel remotior est intellectum'. Butler had a strictly hierarchical view of society: the lower ranks

[49] Brno University Library MS Mk 28, fol 137; compare Oxford Bodleian MS Bodley 288 fol 133ᵛ (one of the lollard versions of Rolle's Psalter commentary), Cambridge University Library MS Ii.6.26 fol 42, Arnold 3 p 98/10.

[50] See for instance More's *Dialogue concerning Tyndale*, ed W. C. Campbell (London/New York 1931) bk I caps 22–3, bk III caps 14–16, and compare the account in *The Confutation of Tyndale's Answer*, ed L. A. Schuster et al., 3 vols (New Haven/London 1973) 3 p 1155, and|the text *Rede me and be nott wrothe* (STC 21427, [1528]) sig. c ii, where the anonymous reforming author narrates how Tunstall 'at Poulis crosse ernestly

> Denounced it to be heresy
> That the gospell shuld come to lyght,
> Callynge theym heretikes excecrable
> Whiche caused the gospell venerable
> To come vnto laye mens syght!

[51] For the text see *The Mirrour of the Blessed Lyf of Jesu Christ A Translation . . . by Nicholas Love*, ed L. F. Powell (London 1908) pp 7–13, 300–1; but the manuscript that Powell printed, Oxford Brasenose College MS e.9 does not contain the whole Latin preface, for which see E. Salter, 'Nicholas Love's "Mirrour of the Blessed Lyf of Jesu Christ"', *Analecta Cartusiana* 10 (Salzburg 1974) pp 1–2.

are to be entirely dependent upon the higher for their instruction and since, in his opinion, to read the scriptures is an activity suitable only to the higher ranks, nothing should be done that would foster wider consultation of the bible.[52] The lollard texts are, we may think, more realistic about society at this stage of the medieval period. They point out that, between the clergy and illiterate labourer there is a large group of laymen who are relatively well educated, who can read their native language and who have wealth to purchase books. Teaching of a more sophisticated kind is needed for them. And it is surely better that such literate men should 'ocupie hem and othere in redeynge of Goddis lawe and deuocioun than in redeynge of lesyng, rebaudie and vanite'.[53]

However, as the authorities perceived, the reading of scripture would lead inevitably to the teaching of scripture. Though Ullerston might attempt to answer this by asserting the right, indeed the duty, of a parent to instruct his children, of a master to instruct his servants, or even in the case of a mother with her child or an abbess with her nuns for a woman to teach, this did not really answer the charge.[54] The problem is brought out in numerous heresy cases in the fifteenth century. That of John Edward, priest of Brington in the Lincoln diocese in 1405, epitomises all: Edward's writings were in Latin and in English, and two of his opinions were that any layman can preach the gospel of God anywhere, and that any good man, even if he were not lettered, was a priest.[55] Here the dilemma was pushed one stage further: if any good man, by which Edward would have meant any predestined man, teaching the gospel freely, were a priest, then the rights of the clergy were seriously infringed—it is a short step from there to an assertion of the redundancy of the clergy. This danger was one that is continually stressed by the macaronic sermons that have been described by Roy Haines. They date from after Arundel's Constitutions, but their sentiments echo ideas that are traceable much earlier: 'every lewde man is becomen a

[52] Butler's determination, found in Oxford Merton College MS 68 fols 202–4^v, was also printed by Deanesly pp 401–18, here pp 405–7. The text is dated 1401, but, whilst it uses some of the same points as Ullerston's of the same year, neither can be taken as a direct answer to the other. Butler was a Franciscan friar.

[53] Cambridge University Library MS Ii.6.26 fol 3; compare also fols 6^v, 7–8^v, 21, and Oxford Bodleian MS Laud misc.200 fols 32, 128, 146^v, 147^v, 198^v, Bodley 288 fol 96, BL MS Additional 41321 fols 14^v, 30, Arnold 3 p 184/22, Matthew p 159/4.

[54] Vienna Nationalbibliothek MS 4133 fols 202^v–3.

[55] The case is printed from the Arundel register in Wilkins 3 pp 282–4.

clerke and talkys in his termys', the layman now *vult smater se de summa diuinitate, mouebit dubia de venerabili sacramento altaris et intromittet se boldliche de eterna sapiencia Dei, . . . isti laici nimis vadant in clerimonia scripturis et consuetudinibus ecclesie.*[56] Ullerston in his determination to some extent anticipated this objection, but did not fully answer it. The various replies of the lollards were even more unacceptable. Hardly likely to find favour was the view that 'Crist seyde that stonys schulde cry, and secler lordys schuld, in defawte of prelatys, lerne and preche the law of God in here modyr tonge'. More outspoken was the retort that, in objecting to the use of the native language, the clergy wanted to make the laity as ignorant as themselves. Equally unpopular was the taunt that the chief cause of the friars' dislike of vernacular scriptures was that 'ȝef the truthe of Goddes lawe were knowen to the peple, thei schulden lacke miche of her worldely worschepe and of her lucre bothe'.[57]

As time went on a more substantial objection to English scriptures was the danger that such would arouse or further heresy. As I have mentioned, neither Ullerston nor Butler associate support for the vernacular with lollardy, but in Palmer's paper this point is made.[58] But the charge was familiar before the turn of the century. The *Opus Arduum*, written between Christmas 1389 and Easter 1390, refers to the persecution of those *qui scripta ewangelica in Anglicis penes se detinent et legunt . . . qui ut lolardi deffamantur.*[59] It is clear also that Ullerston knew of the objection that translation would foster heresy, even if he did not specify heresy as lollardly.

---

[56] '"Wilde wittes and wilfulnes": John Swetstock's attack on those "poyswunmongeres" the Lollards', *SCH* 8 (1972) pp 143–53, and 'Church, society and politics in the early fifteenth century as viewed from an English pulpit', *SCH* 12 (1975) pp 143–57; the attribution to Swetstock is unlikely, see the latter n 95. I have worked from the manuscripts, here Oxford Bodleian MS Laud Misc 706 fol 160ᵛ, Bodley 649 fol 14ᵛ, and compare the latter fols 38ᵛ, 70ᵛ, 80, 98, 125ᵛ and the charge repeated in Matthew p 159/1 and in the citation from Cambridge University Library MS Ii.3.8 fol 149 quoted in [G. R.] Owst, *Preaching [in Medieval England]* (Cambridge 1926) p 135.

[57] See respectively Arnold 3 p 114/10, Cambridge University Library MS Ii.6.26 fol 13 and BL MS Additional 41321 fol 38ᵛ; compare Arnold 3 p 393/22, 405/37 and Matthew p 428/14 and the anti-fraternal poem printed by R. H. Robbins, *Historical Poems of the XIVth and XV Centuries* (New York 1959) no 69 especially lines 1–12.

[58] See *EHR* 90 (1975) p 16; Palmer, ed Deanesly p 425 'Quomodo igitur non errarent simplices, idiote circa scripturam, si eam haberent in vulgari idiomate modo, propter malum intellectum Lollardorum et simplicium grammaticam solum intelligentes.' See above p 82.

[59] Brno University Library MS Mk 28 fol 161ᵛ.

He attemp.ed to answer this charge by alleging that a careful study of scripture, in whatever language, is a useful antidote to heresy. Perhaps more cogently, he later added that heresy may be found in Latin as in English—heresy is not the prerogative of one language.[60] An English lollard tract takes up the same point, and urges it more strongly:

> many men wolen seie that ther is moche eresie in Englische bookis, and therfore no man schulde haue Goddis lawe in Englische. And I seie be the same skile ther schulde no man haue Goddis lawe in bookis of Latyn, for ther is moche heresie in bookis of Latyn, more than in Englische bookis.[61]

The argument that English scriptures lead to heresy was extended into the secular field by the contention that they also led to rebellion. The preaching of Wyclif and his followers was seen in retrospect by Walsingham and the compiler of the *Fasciculi Zizaniorum* as instrumental in the Peasants' Revolt.[62] The accuracy of this hindsight is debated amongst modern historians,[63] but it is obvious that the reproach was a familiar one to the lollards, and that their support for English scriptures was seen as tending towards another rebellion. One lollard answered this charge directly: 'ignoraunce of Goddis lawe is cause of alle meuynge and vnstabilite in the comoun pepel . . . redi to rebelle a3ens her souereyns'.[64]

But was the question of the vernacular really as important as these writers seem to suggest? To us, with our more sophisticated views about language and with our familiarity with translations of

[60] Vienna Nationalbibliothek MS 4133 fols 195ᵛ, 196, 199 'nam si propterea non permitteretur ewangelium scribi in Anglico, quia sunt multi tractatus Anglicani continentes hereses et errores, a pari siue a fortiori prohiberent scripturam in Latino que per totam Christianitatem posset disseminari', and fol 205 urges care over Latin 'ex vi lingue incomparabiliter lacius diffundi posset quam in nostro Anglico exaratus qui ultra terminos maris Britannici non posset facilius se diffundere'.

[61] Cambridge University Library MS Ii.6.26 fol 4ᵛ; compare Forshall and Madden I pp 57–8 'no doute he shal fynde ful manye biblis in Latyn ful false if he loke manie, nameli newe; and the comune Latyn biblis han more nede to be correctid . . . than hath the English bible late translatid.'

[62] *Historia Anglicana* 2 pp 32–3, *Fasciculus Zizaniorum* pp 273–4; compare also Knighton 2 p 170.

[63] See the discussion by R. B. Dobson, *The Peasants' Revolt of 1381* (London 1970) pp 5, 373, and M. Aston, 'Lollardy and Sedition', *PP* 17 (1960) pp 1–44, expecially pp 3–5; for another view see J. H. Dahmus, *The Prosecution of John Wyclyf* (New Haven/London 1952) pp 82–5.

[64] Cambridge University Library MS Ii.6.26 fol 19ᵛ.

all kinds, the debate seems merely peripheral. There were surely more important matters in lollard teaching, matters that might more reasonably have led to persecution. It is here perhaps worth while looking at the later case of Reginald Pecock. Pecock was, of course, an outspoken opponent of lollardy; yet he too was convicted of heresy. But in one regard he shared the view of his opponents: that the vernacular must be used. If lollardy were to be refuted, then Pecock conceived that it could only be refuted by means of the medium the heretics themselves used, the English language.[65] V. H. H. Green, who in 1944 wrote the only full-length biography of Pecock, claimed 'the fact that [Pecock] wrote in English was probably even more irritating to his accusers than the views which his books contained.'[66] If this opinion is tenable, then it would suggest that the question of the vernacular was in the late fourteenth and fifteenth centuries more central than we can readily perceive. Certainly, in the records of the investigations into Pecock there is mention of the fact that Pecock's writings were in English as well as in Latin, that the books Pecock had to consign to the fire were English tomes and Latin, that the subsequent pursuit of his disciples was directed against owners of his books in either language.[67] But the lists of tenets that Pecock was forced to abjure do not contain any mention of the vernacular.[68] Nor, perhaps more surprisingly, is there any allusion to Pecock's contravention of the terms of Arundel's Constitutions by his publication of books that discussed the sacraments and doctrines of the church, and that cast

---

[65] *Repressor* [*of Overmuch Blaming of the Clergy*], ed C. Babington, 2 vols RS (London 1860) I pp 1–2; *The Folewer to the Donet*, ed E. V. Hitchcock, EETS 164 (1924) pp 7/1–8/21; *The Reule of Crysten Religioun*, ed W. C. Greet, EETS 171 (1927) pp 21, 93–4; *The Book of Faith*, ed J. L. Morison (Glasgow 1909) p 116.

[66] [V. H. H.] Green, [*Bishop Reginald Pecock*] (Cambridge 1945) p 188. In addition see [E. F.] Jacob, ['Reynold Pecock, bishop of Chichester'], *PBA* 37 (1951) pp 121–53, especially here pp 141–3.

[67] See *Registrum Abbatiæ Johannis Whethamstede*, ed H. T. Riley, 2 vols RS (London 1872–3) I p 280; *Calendar of Entries in the Papal Registers relating to Great Britain and Ireland: Papal Letters II 1455–64*, ed J. A. Twemlow (London 1921) pp 77, 529; *An English Chronicle of the Reigns of Richard II, Henry IV, Henry V and Henry VI*, ed J. S. Davies, CSer 64 (1856) p 75 states that Pecock 'had labored meny yeres for to translate holy scripture into Englysshe'. The abjuration recorded in Oxford Bodleian MS Ashmole 789 fols 303ᵛ–4 is in English but the list of articles abjured is in Latin; the same manuscript, fol 324, has a copy of a letter objecting to the graduation of J. Harlowe because of his favour for, and ownership of books by, Pecock.

[68] According to Jacob p 138 n4, the most authentic version of the abjuration is that in Oxford Bodleian MS Ashmole 789 fols 303ᵛ–4.

doubt on tne accepted teachings. Interestingly, it is Gascoigne who provides the best evidence in support of Green's contention. Gascoigne records his disapproval of Pecock under many headings.[69] His most extended account starts by narrating how in 1467 the realm of England was much disturbed by the English books that Pecock had written. He then explains that all the lords of the temporal realm agreed that Pecock should be expelled from the Council.[70] The reasons he gives probably omit one of the most important, that Pecock had been backed by political lords who by that time had lost power.[71] But the first reason that Gascoigne produces, however incredible politically it may seem to us, is 'because he wrote such profound matters in English, matters more likely to harm those who read or heard them than to benefit them . . . and also he composed a new creed, large and long, in English words'. The same point is repeated later: Pecock 'wrote high matters and profound in English, which lead the layfolk from good rather than to it'.[72]

The Austin friar John Bury, the first part of whose answer to Pecock's *Repressor* entitled *Gladius Salomonis* survives in MS Bodley 108, takes up Pecock's argument that the laity should be grateful for the availability of books such as his own in their vernacular, since this allows them to learn the rudiments of natural and moral philosophy.[73] Bury quotes from Malachi *labia sacerdotis custodiunt scienciam* and other biblical and patristic passages in his outraged polemic against Pecock. Pecock's books, he laments, are worse than those of Mahomet, Sabelius, Arius and Wyclif. The use of the vernacular passes almost unnoticed in Bury's anger that the laity should dare to meddle in such topics. Bury is outspoken, but his view echoes that of many other clerics of the century.[74]

[69] Thomas Gascoigne, *Loci e Libro Veritatum*, ed J. E. Thorold Rogers (Oxford 1881) pp 15, 26–7, 35, 40, 44.

[70] pp 208–18.

[71] See Jacob pp 130–2, Green pp 28–30, 39–40, 46.

[72] p 213 'una fuit, quia scripsit tales profundas materias in Anglicis, quæ magis aptæ erant lædere legentes et audientes quam illis proficere . . . et ideo novum cimbolum magnum et longum in Anglicis verbis composuit'; p 214 'et magnæ causæ movebant clericos et dominos temporales multum contra eum, scilicet quod scripsit altas materias id est profundas in Anglicis, quæ pocius abducerunt laicos a bono quam ex vero simili plures ducerent ad bonum.'

[73] For Bury see Emden (O) I p 323; extracts from the *Gladius Salomonis* are printed at the end of *Repressor* 2 pp 567–613.

[74] *Repressor* 2 pp 600, 602; Oxford Bodleian MS Bodley 108 fols 51, 53ᵛ. The entire section covers fols 53ᵛ–7ᵛ, but the extracts given pp 600–7 give a reasonable idea of

It is interesting to compare the position at the end of the fifteenth century with that in the first half of the thirteenth. In 1238 Grosseteste had set out his ideas for the reform of his clergy: each parish priest should teach the laity concerning the decalogue, the seven deadly sins, the sacraments of the church and those matters necessary to a true confession; these should be taught *in idiomate communi*; the boys of the parish were to be taught the Lord's prayer, the creed and the Ave Maria; since, Grosseteste has heard, many adults are ignorant of these matters, enquiry should be made of all coming to confession and instruction given as necessary.[75] Grosseteste was, of course, taking up the terms of the 1215 Lateran Council, as many others at that time had done.[76] The ninth canon of that Council, it is often forgotten, had allowed the use of different languages, even in the services of the church *pontifices . . . provideant viros idoneos, qui secundum diversitates rituum et linguarum divina officia illis celebrent*; this section was incorporated into the Decretals.[77] In 1281 Pecham in the Lambeth constitutions ordered the preaching of the basic elements of religion *vulgariter*.[78] But by 1485 John Smith of Coventry was dilated for heresy because he stated *quod quilibet tenetur scire dominicam orationem, salutacionem angelicam et simbolum in Anglicis*; his neighbour Richard Gilmyn was similarly apprehended because *habuit orationem dominicam et salutacionem angelicam et simbolum in Anglicis*.[79] Even earlier than this, in the Norwich diocese it was felt significant when John Burell stated that his brother had in 1426 taught him the Pater, Ave and Credo in English.[80] In some instances, certainly, it is possible to see

---

Bury's argument. For a lollard interpretation of the same passage of Malachi see BL MS Egerton 2820, fols 5[r/v].

[75] *Roberti Grosseteste . . . Epistolæ*, ed H. R. Luard RS (London 1861) pp 155–7; compare J. H. Srawley, 'Grosseteste's Administration of the Diocese of Lincoln', *Robert Grosseteste Scholar and Bishop*, ed D. A. Callus (Oxford 1955) pp 168–9.

[76] See E. J. Arnould, *Le Manuel des Péchés* (Paris 1940) pp 1–59.

[77] See HL V.ii (1913) p 1339; *Corpus Iuris Canonici*, ed E. Friedberg 2 vols (Leipzig 1879–81) 2 Decretals lib. i tit. xxxi cap. xiv.

[78] Wilkins 2 p 54.

[79] Lichfield reg Hales fol 166[v]; compare the much earlier text described in *Selections* pp 185–6, BL MS Egerton 2820 fol 52 'thei grucchen if ony nedi man haue so moche of this breed that he undirstonde his *pater noster* in his modir tunge'.

[80] *Heresy Trials in the Diocese of Norwich, 1428–31*, ed N. P. Tanner CSer, 4 series 20 (1977) p 73; compare p 69 where John Baker of Tunstall 'recognovit iudicialiter se habuisse unum librum de Johanne Burge de Beghton dicte diocesis, qui quidem liber continebat in se Pater Noster et Ave Maria et Credo in lingua Anglicana scripta'.

why the bishops were concerned: the 'one suspecte boke of commaundementis' produced before bishop Langton of Salisbury in 1490 may well have been one of the lollard commentaries on the decalogue, where the command against graven images was predictably seized upon by the heretics for a recitation of their views.[81] Even the apparently innocent words of the Lord's prayer could form the starting point for unorthodox opinions, as they do in two lollard commentaries.[82] But in many cases there is no evidence that a commentary was in question. Though the group of heretics investigated by bishop Longland of Lincoln in the Chilterns between 1518 and 1521 owned a wide selection of books, the terms of the investigation suggest that mere knowledge of the elements of the faith in English was evidence of heresy.[83] Marian Morden had been taught these by her brother; William Littlepage had been taught the creed in English by his grandmother, the Pater Noster and Ave Maria by a brother. Most interestingly, James Morden had used the Pater Noster and creed so often in English that he had forgotten many of the words of these in Latin.[84] Here any question of commentary is ruled out. Also here the matter of language is pin-pointed: knowledge in Latin is acceptable, knowledge in English is not.

Enquiries such as these are, obviously, an extreme. Others in the

[81] Salisbury reg Langton 2 fol 35; the version printed in Arnold 3 pp 82–92 is not outspoken, but more distinctively lollard are those found in BL MS Harley 2398, Trinity College Dublin MS 245, York Minster Library MS XVI.L.12 and Harvard University MS Eng.738. Miss Rachel Pyper is at present engaged in sorting out the various versions of the Decalogue commentaries, an enterprise that will correct and enlarge the scope of A. L. Kellogg and E. W. Talbert, 'The Wycliffite *Pater Noster* and *Ten Commandments* . . .', *BJRL* 42 (1960) pp 345–77. Compare Matthew p 429/30 'and herfore freris han tau3t in Englond the paternoster ‌in Engli3ch tunge, as men seyen in the pley of 3ork, and in many othere cuntreys', though Cambridge University Library MS Ii.6.26 fol 13ʳ notes the efforts of clerks to prevent people knowing this in English.

[82] See Arnold 3 pp 98–110 and its version in *Selections* no 20, also Matthew pp 198–202. Compare the reason assigned to Arundel for his refusal to return Thorpe's psalter in Thorpe's own account of his trial, Oxford Bodleian MS Rawlinson c.208 fol 38 'forthi that thou woldist gadere out thereof and recorde scharpe verses a3ens vs'; such, according to this account, 'is the bisinesse and the maner of this losel and siche other, to pike out scharpe sentencis of holy writ and of doctours, for to maynteyne her sect and her loore a3ens the ordenaunce of holi chirche'.

[83] The investigations are summarized by Foxe in his *Actes and Monuments*, ed S. R. Cattley, 8 vols (London 1837–41) 4 pp 221–41; compare the comments of M. Aston, *History* 62 (1977) p 355.

[84] Foxe 4 p 225, 227–8, and for James Morden p 225.

fifteenth century were, we may think, more subtle and more enlightened: English sermons are found in that period that show a declared hostility to lollardy, thus revealing that the use of the vernacular was not necessarily a sign of heresy.[85] Nonetheless, the association of the vernacular with clerical suspicion was not new in lollardy. The Waldensians much earlier on the continent had fallen under suspicion for exactly the same matter: an insistence upon the native language, a preoccupation with vernacular scriptures and, the apparently inevitable consequence, lay preaching.[86] Even the anti-lollard sermons indirectly reflect the importance the Wycliffite movement attached to language: the enemy must be confronted on his own ground. There is then a sense in which it may not be unreasonable to claim lollardy as the heresy of the vernacular, the English heresy.

[85] See, for instance, the material cited by Owst, *Preaching* pp 135–40 and in *Literature and Pulpit in Medieval England* (2 ed Oxford 1966) p 374, to which may be added *Mirk's Festial*, ed T. Erbe, *EETS* extra series 96 (1905) p 171/18, *Jacob's Well*, ed A. Brandeis, *EETS* 115 (1900) pp 19/1, 59/26, Durham University Library MS Cosin V.iv.2 fol 130ᵛ, Lincoln Cathedral MS 66 fols 25 ʳ/ᵛ.
[86] See *Les Vaudois* pp 319–404.

ordeyne ȝe þo contemptible men opir
of litil reputacioñ þ ben among ȝou for
to deme / þat is ordeyne ȝe seculer mē
þat han litil of goſtli knolbinge to de
me seculer doms . ꝗ þ clerkis be ocupi
ed aboute goſtly offias in helpe of mē
nis soulis / þe sentence of þis article is
opinli tauȝt bi þe rule of apoſtlis set
in decrees in þe . lxxxvni . diſtincciou .
c̄ . Eps . ꝗ c̄ . neȝ / ꝗ i . xxi . cauſe . iii .
queſtioñ . c̄ . Cipanus . ꝗ manie mo . ꝗ
opinli bi þe piſtil of ſeynt petir ſent
to clement i þe . vi . cauſe . i . queſtioñ
c̄ . De quidē . ꝗ bi ſeynt gḡ i his mo
rals ꝗ in his paſtoralis ꝗ regiſtre . ꝗ
bi ſeynt jerom in hiſe piſtlis as de
crees witneſſen . ꝗ bi crisoſtom on þe . b .

Prelatis ꝗ pſtis ꝗ c̄ . of mathu
as curatis owen to ſheelbe to
þe puple ensaumple of holi lyuyge
ꝗ to prche truli þe goſpel bi werk ꝗ
word / þis sentence is open bi holi
writ i þe . i . c̄ . of dedis . ſhū bigan

10

A LOLLARD SECT VOCABULARY?

A recurrent feature of the accounts given by hostile critics of the Lollard movement in the period between 1384 and 1525 is the use by the heretics of a distinctive language.[1] The fullest description appears in one of the most perceptive of the first generation of opponents, Henry Knighton, the fellow canon of Philip Repingdon at the Augustine house in Leicester; Knighton's chronology can sometimes be faulted, and his tendency to associate recurrent ideas with a single person may mislead, but his apprehension of the important aspects of Lollardy is hard to parallel. Knighton makes several comments about the mode of speech and style of argument favoured by the heretics. The most detailed is this:

> Et licet de novo conversi, vel subito et recenter hanc sectam imitantes, unum modum statim loquelae et formam concordem suae doctrinae mirabiliter habuerunt; et doctores Evangelicae doctrinae tam viri quam mulieres materno idiomate subito mutato effecti sunt. Et hoc acsi essent de uno gignasio educati et doctrinati ac etiam de unius magistri schola simul referti et nutriti. Quod credibile haberi potest, nam credi absque ambiguitate potest, quod qui eos sibi in servos et malorum dolorum initiatores et invidiarum inter Christicolas propinatores adoptavit, idem ipse eos eadem identitate spiritus sui simul aptavit, et conformitate unius loquelae cum fervore desiderii in suum obsequium inspiravit.[2]

Knighton goes on, in case the identity of this teacher should be in doubt, to attribute this to Wyclif, and to comment on the Lollards' style of teaching 'eloquentes, in omnibus versutiis atque verbosis colluctationibus caeteris prae- valentes; validi in verbis; in garulis fortes; in sermocinationibus praepotentes, in litigiosis deceptationibus omnes superclamantes'. Knighton's comments mingle the linguistic with the stylistic in these passages, matters of composi- tion with the words in which these were expressed. But so detailed is Knigh- ton's description that it seems worth examining whether there is any substance in his claims.

The purpose of this paper is to look at only one part of Knighton's analysis: his assertion that all Wycliffites used 'one mode of speech'. It is important to define first what is here meant. The identification of a 'Wycliffitte dialect', in the traditional sense of that word involving orthography, phonology and mor- phology, is not here in question; any attempt to demonstrate this, or to disprove its existence, must wait for further editions of Wycliffite manuscripts and for the publication of the Edinburgh Dialect Survey's material; claims that have been made hitherto seem premature.[3] At the other extreme I do not want here to discuss the stylistic implications of Knighton's argument: in many ways this aspect is much simpler to demonstrate, particularly from the more defensive Lollard texts such as the *Thirty-Seven Conclusions*, the *Apology for Lollard Doctrines* or the *Lanterne of Liʒt*.[4] Equally I do not wish to deal with perhaps the most obvious reason for the similarity of many Lollard writings, their repeated use of identical quotations; this aspect may well have been in Knighton's mind, but the methods by which it was achieved have been described by Dr von Nolcken in her edition of part of one of the source books, the *Rosarium Theologie*.[5] What I wish to investigate is whether there was a particular Lollard sect vocabulary, and to consider the problems that must be faced in discerning such a language.

A little earlier than the general description which I have quoted, Knighton provides a specific example. Like the previous instance, the passage occurs under 1382; but, though this must imply an early recognition of an identifiable vocabulary, other material covered under that year shows that the date cannot be a precise one. This example occurs in the account of John Purvey, but the plural pronouns of the passage make clear that the observation is a general one concerning Lollard preachers:

> Similiter et cæteri de secta illa frequenter et absque taciturnitate in
> suis sermonibus et sermocinationibus inexquisite clamitaverunt, *Trewe
> Prechoures, False Prechoures,* opinionesque mutuas et communes
> sicut unus ita et omnes. Et ita connexae erant atque concatenatae
> opiniones eorum, quod qui istas habuit, habuit et alterius; et qui alter-
> ius opiniones habuit, habuit et opiniones istius.[6]

Again Knighton passes from vocabulary to style and to belief, apparently seeing all as interconnected; again only the first point concerns us here. Knighton provides no explanation of his two examples, presumably because he expected his reader to be able to understand their force without his aid. It is not difficult to guess their import: *trewe prechoures* are those who propound Wycliffite doctrine, *false prechoures* those who controvert this, or who preach orthodox beliefs rejected by the Lollards. Many texts could be adduced to support this interpretation, as for instance *oure Helye now, bi whom I vndirstonde* þe <u>trewe prechours</u> *of* þe *gospel, hewiþ upon* þis *roote* [sc. clerical possessions] . . . *wiþ* þe *swerd of* þe *gospel, or for* þouʒ *per be manye precheours,* þer ben fewe <u>trewe prechours.</u>[7] Knighton's example is in fact an illustration of a very common opposition between *trewe* and *false* in these texts. The most usual is the use of *trewe men: liʒtli miʒten* <u>trewe men</u> *discomfite* þese *freris . . . and here moun men liʒtli se wheþer seculers ben* <u>trewe men.</u> One of the sermons traces this to II Corinthians 6.8: *as disseyveres and trewe men, for Goddis servauntis shulen have a name of þe world þat þei disseyven men, and ʒit þei shulen holde treuly þe sentence of Goddis lawe.*[8] The term could be used as a shorthand expression *And þus men of þes newe sectis, fro þe first to þe last, procuren deþ of trewe men þat tellen hem even Goddis lawe.*[9] After the listing of the sixteen points *putte be bischoppis ordinaris vpon men whiche þei clepen Lollardis,* the reply opens *trewe cristen men schulden answere here aviseliche,* where clearly *trewe cristen men* is the term preferred by the sect who, at that early date, still regarded *Lollard* as the abusive term that it was in origin intended to be.[10] Later Thomas Netter referred to this usage: 'omnes, quos appellant *fideles,* ad praedicandum habilitent in Ecclesia verbum Dei'.[11] Netter plainly abhorred the claim to sole righteousness implicit in this term.

Lollard usage here can be traced back to Wyclif himself. Many times Wyclif referred to himself as *quidam fidelis,* and to his followers as *fideles.* The 'fidelis . . . predicator* debet notare evangelium et ipsum cum dictis appendiciis predicare'; conversely *pseudopredicatores* may be described by the injuries enumerated by Paul in II Corinthians 11.19-21. Wyclif is often more specific than the vernacular writers about the precise nature of the opposition: the *novi predicatores sophistici* have been introduced by the ecclesiastical hierarchy to the confounding of the gospel message.[12] Knighton in the passage quoted at the start is, of course, referring to another usage that may be traced back to Wyclif, even if it cannot be shown to have been used by him: just as Wyclif's Latin by-name was *Doctor Evangelicus,* so his doctrine could be called *doctrina evangelica,* a suggestive ambiguity pointing forward to the Hussite denomination of Wyclif as the 'fifth Evangelist', and his followers equally *doctores evangelicæ doctrinæ.*[13]

These most obvious examples raise, I think, two questions. First, have we anything more here than the usual sectarian tendency to use words of approbation for themselves and for the views they approve, whilst using terms of reproach for their opponents and views of which they themselves were critical? As with John Faldo's glossary of Quaker terms produced in 1673 *'Pollutions of the world . . .* whatever customs they dislike',[14] is this language in any way denotative, or was it intended only as emotive, at most as discriminatory shorthand? Secondly, is the vocabulary limited to sect naming? A second example mentioned by an opponent of Lollardy is here interesting. Reginald Pecock in the *Repressor of Over Much Blaming of the Clergy*, a text written about 1450, observed that the Lollards

> ʒeuen a name propre to hemsilf and clepen hemsilf <u>knowun men,</u> as
> thouʒ alle othere than hem ben vnknowun; and whanne oon of hem
> talkith with another of hem of sum other thridde man, the heerer wole
> aske thus: 'Is he a knowen man?', and if it [be] answerid to him thus

> *'He is no knowen man' thanne perel is castid forto miche homeli dele
> with him.*[15]

Pecock suggests that the origin of this term was I Corinthians 14.38 'Si quis
autem ignorat, ignorabitur'; but the more likely source is II Corinthians 6.8
'sicut qui ignoti, et cogniti', a phrase translated and explained in the sermon-
cycle *as unknowun and knowun men to God and seintis, for þei shulen not
accepte persones, but telle treuly Goddis word, as þei weren not knowun of
men, but as aungels þat camen fro hevene*, from the same chapter as produced
trewe men.[16] Here the naming intention is supreme. In the early texts *known
men* does not appear to be common, though the sermon just quoted might
suggest that the application of the biblical words to the sect had already been
made. But in the later period the words were very commonly used as a name;
as Foxe observed, in the persecutions of Lollardy in the Lincoln diocese
during the episcopacy of Longland in 1521 Lollards repeatedly referred to them
selves and their associates as *known men*, and the bishop's questions take up
this appellation.[17] The same usage is found in London during the investigations by Tunstall in 1527.[18] In the Lincoln trials the suspects were less frequently described as *justfast men*, apparently a near synonym of the earlier
trewe men.[19] But whilst *known men* is plainly an identificatory term, it is
less obviously an emotive term, at least without the explanation given by the
sermon. It is also more opaque than the other name which Pecock implies the
Lollards gave themselves: *Bible men.*[20] After the Arundel Constitutions in
1407 such a title could in the popular mind be readily associated with the
sect that insisted that the bare word of scripture should be available to all in
the vernacular.[21] How accurate Pecock is in his implication seems unclear,
since the name does not appear to be readily discoverable in Wycliffite writings or in investigations by the authorities.

These elements of Lollard vocabulary are those that it is simplest to deal
with: all are mentioned by opponents and all, with the exception of the last,
can readily be exemplified from the surviving evidence about the sect. But
they advance the enquiry very little. For a sect to name itself is not remarkable; for a sect persecuted as was Lollardy to adopt titles that would not immediately be identifiable by its opponents, as would *Wyclifistes* or *Lollardi*,
is only common prudence; that these names, albeit opaque in origin, became
familiar to the sect's opponents is the inevitable consequence of human vari-
ability. Is this all there is to Knighton's case? It is hard to think so from the
general terms in which it is couched, and from the fact that other critics,
though in less suggestive terms, seem to echo his view. To go further, however, requires considerable circumspection. One problem, that most of the
texts from which illustration must be drawn do not proclaim themselves of
Lollard authorship, must here be sidestepped: it must be taken on trust that

the views expressed in all the texts used make the Wycliffism of their writers beyond reasonable doubt. To what extent all Lollard texts utilized the elements to be discussed must await critical editions of more of the material; so far it would appear, as might be expected from a scattered sect, that whilst some terms were widespread and longlasting, others might be the property of only a limited community.

This raises the first problem: were the terms genuinely common property, or were they the idiosyncracies of an individual writer? The anonymity of much of the surviving material makes it sometimes hard to answer this question. Indeed, a simplistic answer to just this question underlies many of the early critics' attempts to ascribe many Lollard works to a single author, often John Purvey: similarity of terminology and identity of quotation are the commonest props to such arguments.[22] I hope to examine elsewhere the fallacy of this kind of reasoning with regard to Purvey. But the existence of this possibility makes it important to use only elements of vocabulary that can be found in a wide variety of texts. In some instances, as has already been seen in the case of *known men*, record evidence makes it plain that elements found a currency beyond the writing of one individual. Even if a single Lollard originated a usage, it would be hard to argue that the instances distributed over a period of some seventy years and geographically separated are all conscious quotations from this one source. Certainly Lollard communities were tightly knit and inward looking enclaves in a hostile world, with a learning that depended greatly upon memorizing by rote.[23] But whilst this could explain the rapid dissemination of sect language, it would hardly allow for awareness of individuality of vocabulary as the peculiar property of a single preacher. A study of the standard Lollard sermon-cycle produces a number of recurrent words, but very few of them are not traceable in other Lollard works. One of the most characteristic words is also one of the few grammatical items to be mentioned, the conjunction *alȝif*, used in the sense of 'even if' or 'although', and used to the exclusion of all forms of *pouȝ* or *alpouȝ*.[24] But, though this is found on average once per sermon or more, it is not unknown in other texts; in some cases an isolated example, alongside predominant *alpouȝ*, leads to the suspicion that, whilst the original used *alȝif*, this has been modified through scribal interference with the uncommon word.[26] Here a further factor, that of dialectal restriction, may be in question; most of the instances outside Wycliffite texts cited by *M.E.D.* are from northern areas. Similarly, a group of words such as *autentik, mawmetrer, mawmetrie,* the prefix *pseudo-* also used independently as a noun, *purvyaunce, quilage* (or *quilet, colect*), *renegate,* are very common in the two tracts written by a single Lollard preacher; the earlier is a sermon found in four manuscripts, the later a tract composed between the death of Henry IV in March 1413 and that of Arundel in February

1414, and found in one manuscript. Again, however, most can be paralleled in other texts unlikely to be by the same author.[26] But the necessity of proving community of usage remains a requirement to be remembered.

The examples just given raise a further problem. Most, if not all, of the words can be found in texts either clearly orthodox or where there is no reason to suspect Lollardy. The same is even more plain if other examples of possible Lollard sect vocabulary are given: words such as *blabber, cautel, chaffare* sb. and vb., *chargeous, clowtyd, colour* sb. and vb., *contrary*, vb., *covent, customable begging* or *beggar, gab* and *gabbyng, glose* sb. and vb., *ground* sb. and vb. *impugn, jape* sb. and vb., to limit the list to common words from the first half of the alphabet.[27] For all of these the *Middle English Dictionary* provides citation from texts of orthodox or neutral kinds, even for the specialized senses that the context of words such as *glose* require. Does this invalidate any claim for a 'sect usage'? It seems that a distinction needs here to be made. The appearance of these words in writers such as Chaucer and Gower (not to enter upon the more dubious ground of Langland) makes it plain that no exclusive claim can be made for this language. Usage of these words, or of any others so far discerned, cannot be claimed as the sole prerogative of Lollard writers. Consequently, vocabulary alone can never be used (as it sometimes has been in the past) as a test of a text's Wycliffism.[28] But conversely Knighton did not claim that the identity of language that he discerned made that language unintelligible to those who were not members of the sect; since, after all, the sect aimed to convert the unreformed, an exclusive or entirely private vocabulary would be self-defeating. The elements of the ordinary vocabulary must be used for communication, and any slanting of the usual meaning of that vocabulary must in most instances be clarified by the context in which the individual word appears. Only with a few names or phrases can complete opacity be tolerated. Apart from the terms such as *known men* already described, an instance of this is recorded in the Lichfield courtbook of 1511-12 where mention was made 'de secreto vocabulo inter eos dicit quod *may we all drinke of a cuppe*' and at the departing '*God kepe you and God blesse you*'.[29] Here the vocabulary is entirely commonplace, and one would guess that the force of these phrases as secret 'pass-words' must have been very short-lived.

Nonetheless, despite the lexical normality of much of the vocabulary, there are instances where the semantic force of the words appears to be, if not peculiar to Lollard texts, at least characteristic of them. Even clearer than the slanting of *trewe men* already discussed is the loading given to the terms *pore men* and *pore prest.* These terms are lexically commonplace, occurring frequently in neutral contexts. But the force is often particularized: *and herfore þei pursuen wiþoute merci pore prestis þat in lyuyng and word techen þe pouert of pore Crist and hise apostlis to be kept in al þe staat of þe clergie*, or *and what <u>trewe prest</u> or <u>pore man</u> spekiþ openly aȝenst þis cursed marchaundise, he shal be sumoned, suspendid fro prechyng and treuþe-seyng, or cursed, prisoned, or exilid.*[30] As well as the strongly approbatory sense given to the words, it is plain that the persecution described is that which the Lollards are suffering; the terms are often obliquely self-naming. Similar instances of commonplace terms that occur frequently with loaded senses are *God's Law*, opposed to *man's law* or to the *traditions* of the *new sects*, the *new orders* of the *four sects* that *reverse Christ's order*, the *new religious* who are the *pharisees*, the *prelates* who are the *scribes.*[31] Early in the sermon already mentioned a definition is given *I calle alle þo <u>newe sectis, be þei neuere so old in tyme, þat ben brouȝt into þe chirche and not expresli foundid of Crist,*</u> and thereafter this interpretation is assumed; in many other works the force is the same but no explanation was apparently felt necessary.[32] Such words and phrases are used as a form of shorthand: they carry with them implications that the listener is expected to deduce without the waste of words of explication, and they bear strong emotional loading. At times the shorthand could also usefully conceal. As well as the opaque *trewe men*, the introductory words *many men think/say/feel* or *it seems to many men* regularly introduce an expression of Lollard belief. Thus *it semeþ <u>to many men</u> þat if a prest presume for pride þat he haþ passyngly þis power* [to absolve sin], *in þat he shewiþ þat he wantiþ it,* or *and þus þenken <u>many men</u> þat þis was a fendis dede for to slee so many men for a synful and a roten office þat þe pope chalengiþ so folili*, referring to the Despenser Crusade and incidentally showing how *many men* without the ensuing verb has its usual general meaning.[33] That these introductory words could indeed conceal heresy is shown by the expurgation of the standard sermon-cycle effected in MS. Bodley Don.c.13, where the expurgator appears occasionally to have failed to recognize the force of this introduction.[34] In many instances the same force seems to be true of *some men think/say* etc.: thus *and so as <u>sum men þynke</u> þese popys ne þese prelatys ar nat part of holy chirche, but of synagoge*, or *and so it semeþ <u>to sum men</u> þat monkis or false cardinals may bygile þe litil flook now lefte of cristen men.*[35]

It is worth looking at another example in a little more detail. An interesting case is *ground*, which may be used as noun or verb, and its derivatives. The commonest sense of the noun in these texts is that given in *M.E.D.* as sense 5(a) 'the basis for a doctrine, dogma or opinion; the authority for knowledge of information'; so *þei shulden teche men bileve þe which is <u>ground</u> of Cristis ordre.*[36] Similarly, the verb normally has the sense recorded in *M.E.D.* as 4 'to base, to derive' or 5 'to prove something, to establish a fact, to justify something'. Sense 5 *M.E.D.* exemplifies from Arnold iii.353/15 *Aftir þis myȝte a man axe . . . how <u>groundiþ</u> þis frere his ordre, and in what tyme it bigan . . .*

*But noon groundiþ here his word, as noon of þes new ordris groundiþ þat
he cam in bi Crist.* Here the first instance is presumably thought to mean 'justify', the last 'establish as a fact'; but the second remains by *M.E.D.*'s definition
obscure. The explanation for this second, and for many similar instances in
these texts, lies in the Lollard belief that the only true *ground* is scripture, and
particularly the example of Christ as revealed in scripture. Thus friars *shulden
faile, as þei began wiþouten ground.*[37] The second instance of the verb in
M.E.D.'s citation has the force 'find a justification in scripture', The same is
the case with many similar uses: *ordeyned pope Innocent a lawe of confes-
sioun . . . and addede myche to þis lawe þat he kowde noȝt grounde* means
not the bland *M.E.D.* sense 'justify', but the more precise 'establish as deriving
from the Bible'.[38] Absolute senses of the verb such as these clearly derive
from a translation into the vernacular of the Latin *fundatus*, commonly found
in mediaeval theological writers, but with the very particular sense familiar in
Wyclif.[39] This basic force of noun and verb is even clearer in their derivatives.
The very common participial adjective *vngroundid* has the meaning 'not justifiable from scripture'; hence the friars' mendicancy is *vngroundid beggerie*,
the clergy's response to oral confessions *vngrounded absoluciouns*, the assertions of the papacy *vngrounded fantesies of antecrist.*[40] Equally the adverb
groundli has a more precise sense than *M.E.D.* allows: it is not merely an
intensifying adverb as 'strongly, vehemently, thoroughly' suggest. Clauses
such as *her fadir Lucifer bi enpungnyng of truþe of Goddis word brouȝte yn
al þe errour groundli þat is in mankynde*, or *þis sacrefice was groundli sac-
rificed to þe Fadur in Crist vpon þe cros* are meaningless if these are the senses
of the word.[41] The force is surely 'as is shown in holy scripture'. Similarly
the example quoted by *M.E.D.* from *37 Concs. 'To ordeine vnworthi men to
the gouernaunce of soulis is to haue come to the hiest poynt of greete synnis.'
Grosted seith groundli al this* has not their general sense but the meaning 'with
evidence drawn from scripture', a meaning amply justified by a glance at the
Grosseteste sermon in question.[42] Finally, the adjective *vngroundable* found
in the same text has the force 'not possible to justify from scripture': *feiþful
men forsaken þe noueltees of þis Innocent wiþ opere lik him þat ben vngroundable . . . and cleeue þei feiþfulli to þe wordis and lif and ordenaunce of Iesu
Crist where noon errour mai be founde.*[43]

　　　Another interesting case concerns the words *bishop* and *prelate*. The two
were not used in Middle English entirely synonymously: *prelate* could cover
the holder of any high office in the church, and hence could be used for an
abbot or prior of a religious house or the superior of an order as well as for a
bishop. Occasionally Lollard usage conforms to this, and *prelate* is purely
denotative: *siþ a prelate shulde more ordeyne for goostli fode þan an house-
bonde shulde ordeyne for bodili fode to his folk.*[44] Much more frequently,

however, in Lollard texts *bishop* and *prelate* are denotatively equivalent, but
the first is approbatory, the second condemnatory. Thus *Crist was bishop . . .
oure bishop Crist in al þes þingis mut nedis passe al oþer bishopis,* but with the
contrast implicitly made *and here þenken many men þat, fro þis state was
turned to pryde, þei ben clepid prelatis.* [45] The abstract term *prelacie* also
regularly carries a strongly derogatory force. [46] But the force of the two words
is in one instance equally regularly broken: the term *bishop of Rome* is always
in Lollard texts reserved for contexts where the pretensions of the papacy are
particularly under attack. [47]

A further question that must be considered if Knighton's assertion of a
peculiar Wycliffite vocabulary is to be accepted is the extent to which that
vocabulary may be the outcome not of a conscious or unconscious choice by
the sect, but as a necessary concomitant of the type of subject its members
wished to discuss. At a time when theological debate and any extended discussion of the ecclesiastical establishment was most frequently conducted in
Latin, was it inevitable that a group of people who wished to argue about these
questions in the vernacular should use a vocabulary either invented for the
purpose or drawn from normal words but with abnormal meanings? An
obvious case where this question is involved are the terms *latria, dulia* and
yperdulia sometimes incorporated into English Lollard treatises. In some the
unfamiliarity of the terms is evident from the explanations given, but in
others the writer seems to be able to expect the comprehension of his audience.
These are academic terms, familiar from Latin discussion of the differing
degrees of honour allowable or due to God, to Christ, to the saints and to the
images of saints or to holy places. [48] Other similar terms are *accidents, subiect*
and *substaunce*, particularly in the phrases *accidentis wiþoute subiect* or *accidentis wiþoute substaunce.* Here it could be argued that the beliefs of the
Lollards made essential the translation of the Latin *accidentes sine subiecto* or
accidentes sine substancio. [49] Equally *attricioun* and *determinacioun,* the
latter in the sense of 'papal decree or pronouncement', are technical terms. [50]
Ideally, it might seem that before a word could be claimed as an element of a
'sect' vocabulary, it must be shown that a synonym has been rejected. But this
requires the identification of a text that discusses the same subject matter in
different terms and from an orthodox standpoint, hardly an easy demand.
Further, it requires that that text should not be attempting to refute Lollardy,
since the language of the refutation may adopt the colours of the opponent to
gain its end. [51] Given the paucity of theological discussion in English before
the rise of the Lollard movement, this seems an impossible condition.

Nonetheless, before any claims for a Lollard sect vocabulary can be firmly
sustained, an analysis must be made of other works dealing with similar subject
matter. An interesting case in this regard is *Dives and Pauper,* a text once con-

fiscated from an East Anglian suspect as evidence of heresy, but whose orthodoxy is vouched for by the fact that abbot Whethamsted of St Alban's paid for
a copy to be made for the library of his house.[52] Many matters that were
discussed by the Lollards are raised, and the verdicts of Pauper, whilst theo-
logically orthodox, are critical of the contemporary state of the church and
never polemically directed against the Lollards. The text seems to date from
between 1405 and 1410, a time towards the end of the period between
Wyclif's death and the Oldcastle revolt during which most of the Lollard texts
here under discussion were written.[53] A systematic study of the vocabulary of
this text would be illuminating. My impression is that, though some of the
typically 'Lollard' words here described occur, they do not bear the associations regularly involved when they are found in Wycliffite texts and, more
importantly, they do not occur in the clusters so characteristic of these. Yet,
even within material apparently heretical, use of the vocabulary seems not to
have been universal. In British Library MS. Additional 41321 and Bodleian
MS. Rawlinson C 751 appear a group of sermons whose author seems plainly
of Lollard sympathies; yet many of the words here discussed are not found
within them.[54]

What then of Knighton's allegations? Can a case be made out for a distinctive Lollard vocabulary or idiom? Anyone who has worked for a long time on
the vernacular Lollard texts, particularly amongst the 'central' texts from
which I have here drawn my examples, will probably answer firmly that there
is; but can this be objectively established, and can its components be defined?
To do so would be a long and difficult task, not possible until more texts have
been critically edited. The texts that are important for this purpose are not
only those whose Lollardy is guaranteed by their content, but also orthodox
religious works; such must be available to provide a control against which the
asserted Lollard terminology can be checked. It will be important to exclude
words whose presence or absence may be determined by dialectal factors; for
this the completed *M.E.D.* will be invaluable. Computer-generated concor-
dances would obviously be essential to make information accessible: the significance of certain words may emerge only after half the corpus of material
has been studied. But much depends on human judgment about semantic
force, as the example of *ground* above shows, and about the impact of a word
or phrase within the complete work. Here, however, it is hard to avoid the
dangers of tautology. A statement such as '*many men think* that confession to
God is sufficient without confession to a priest' reveals from its content that
the *many men* are Lollard; one could therefore argue that *many men* is not
itself semantically loaded. Yet any neutral statement, such as '*many men
think* that the first apostles of Christ were poor men' does not establish any
limitation on *many men*: no doubt the Lollards did believe this, but so did

most other Christians. In a few instances this vicious circle can be broken by the comments of their opponents upon Wycliffite terminology, or by the failure of an expurgator to appreciate the force of an expression. But these are likely to remain unhappily few. Anyone attempting to take the question further would be well advised to look more widely at Lollard vocabulary, for there are implications that lead out from the movement as well as those considered here within it. One of the effects of the teaching of Wyclif and his followers was a broadening of the circles in which theological, ecclesiastical and even political issues might be discussed, and discussed not only in satirical but also in theoretical terms. The results of this in the vernacular vocabulary remain to be examined.

NOTES

1 Texts are referred to by abbreviated title as explained below. Reference to modern editions are by page and line number, the first line of the quotation or the line of the word in question being given; where the edition does not print line numbers, these have been provided ignoring all headings. References to manuscripts are by folio number. Punctuation has been modernized, and in some printed editions has been altered Unprinted episcopal registers are cited by diocese, bishop's name, volum number where appropriate, and folio. Some details about the unprinted texts are given in my *Selections from English Wycliffite Writings* (Cambridge, 1978), abbreviated hereafter *Sel.*

Arnold: *Select English Works of John Wyclif*, ed. T. Arnold (Oxford, 1869-71), 3 vols.

Apol.: An Apology for Lollard Doctrines, ed. J.H. Todd (Camden Society, London, 1842).

LL: The Lanterne of Liȝt, ed. L.M. Swinburn (E.E.T.S. o.s. 151, 1917).

Matthew: *The English Works of Wyclif hitherto unprinted*, ed. F.D. Matthew (E.E.T.S. o.s. 74, 1880)

Upland: Jack Upland, Friar Daw's Reply and Upland's Rejoinder, ed. P.L. Heyworth (London, 1968).

WB: The Holy Bible . . . made from the Latin Vulgate by John Wycliffe and his Followers, ed. J. Forshall and F. Madden (Oxford, 1850), 4 vols.

Add.: British Library MS. Additional 24202 (see *Sel.* pp. 179, 187).

Eg.: British Library MS. Egerton 2820 (see *Sel.* pp. 185-86).

Harl.: British Library MS. Harley 1203.

Taylor: Bodleian Library MS. Douce 53, ff. 1-30.

Tit.: British Library MS. Cotton Titus D.v (see *Sel.* p. 186).

37 Concs.: British Library MS. Cotton Titus D.i (see *Sel.* pp. 198-99; quotations have been given from the manuscript rather than from the inaccessible edition by J. Forshall under the title *Remonstrance against Romish Corruptions* (London, 1851).

2 *Chronicon Henrici Knighton*, ed. J.R. Lumby (Rolls Series, London, 1889-95), ii. 186-87; for the date at which Knighton was writing see V.H. Galbraith, 'The Chronicle of Henry Knighton', *Fritz Saxl . . . A Volume of Memorial Essays*, ed. D.J. Gordon (London, 1957), pp. 136-48.

3 See M.L. Samuels, 'Some applications of Middle English dialectology', *English Studies* 44 (1963), pp. 4-7. For a more recent analysis of the language of one Wycliffite manuscript, MS. Bodley 959 of the Early Version of the Bible translation, see M.L. Samuels's survey in C. Lindberg, *Stockholm Studies in English* 20 (1969), pp. 329-39.

4 There is room for study beyond the two so far published, H. Hargreaves, 'Wyclif's prose', *Essays and Studies* (1966), pp. 1-17, and P.A. Knapp, *The Style of John Wyclif's English Sermons* (The Hague & Paris, 1977).

5 C. von Nolcken, *The Middle English Translation of the Rosarium Theologie* Heidelberg, 1979).

6 Knighton p. 179.

7 *Eg.* f. 119v, *LL* 101/2; cf. *Tit.* f. 29, *Harl.* f. 65v.

8 Arnold i.212/17, ii.271/19; for the biblical phrase WB has the same as the sermon (the translation printed by M.J. Powell (E.E.T.S. E.S. 116, 1916), p. 114 has *as dysseyuars and trewe*, but that printed by A.C. Paues (Cambridge, 1904), pp. 68-69 *as gylores bote as men þat beþ trewe*).

9 Arnold ii.352/19; cf. Arnold i.172/24, 180/29, 195/9, 208/10 etc., Taylor ff. 11v, 21v, *Tit.* f. 79v, *Harl.* f. 67, *LL* 20/8, 54/18. Compare the declaration of faith recorded in 1443 in Salisbury reg. Ayscough ii, f. 53v *holi chirche catholike is congregacioun of trewe men wiche only schul be saued.*

10. *Sel.* no. 2/50. For the term Lollard see *Sel.* p. 8, and see my paper 'A neglected Wycliffite text', *Journal of Ecclesiastical History* 29 (1978), pp. 257-79, esp. p. 259. See above pp. 43-65, esp. 45.

11 Edited F.B Blanciotti (Venice, 1757-59), iii, cols. 232-33.

12 *Sermones*, ed. J. Loserth (Wyclif Society, London, 1887-90), i.359/16, iii.129/36; *Polemical Works*, ed. R. Buddensieg (Wyclif Society, London, 1883), i.263/21; cf. *Sel.* p. 146.

13 See F. Smahel, ' "Doctor evangelicus super omnes evangelistas": Wyclif's fortune in Hussite Bohemia', *Bulletin of the Institute of Historical Research* 43 (1970), p. 25 and n. 3; cf. for earlier insular usage my paper cited in n. 10, pp. 265-67. See above pp. 51-3.

14   John Faldo, *Quakerism no Christianity* . . . (London, 1673), pt. iii
      pp. 61-90; cf. *'Natural man.* Every man that is not a Quaker', *'The
      Priests.* A word of scorn put on all indifferently, who are separated to
      the work of the Gospel-Ministry by men, or that receive maintenance
      for their work'. For material on later sectarian usage see G. Lawton,
      John Wesley's English (London, 1962), pp. 15-58, and K. Watson, *The
      Use of Religious Diction in the Nineteenth-Century Novel* (Oxford
      unpubd. M. Litt. thesis, 1970), pp. 233-99.

15   Ed. C. Babington (Rolls Series, London, 1860), i.53/15.

16   Arnold ii.271/22; WB for the first passage has *if ony man vnknowith, he
      schal be vnknowen,* for the second *as thei that ben vnknowen, and
      knowun* (one manuscript of EV has added the glosses *vnknowen of God
      . . . of hym known and prouyd*).

17   *The Acts and Monuments of John Foxe*, ed. S.R. Cattley (London, 1837-
      41), iv.218-27, 241.

18   J. Strype, *Ecclesiastical Memorials under King Henry VIII* (Oxford,
      1772), iv.123, 127-31.

19   Foxe pp. 218-19; cf. *feiþful men* in *37 Concs.* ff. 40v & 47.

20   *Repressor* i.36/24.

21   For references see *Sel.* pp. 162-64.

22   See E.D. Jones, 'The authenticity of some English works ascribed to
      Wycliffe', *Anglia* 30 (1907), pp. 261-68; H.B. Workman, *John Wyclif*
      (Oxford, 1926), i.329-32.

23   See M. Aston, 'Lollardy and literacy', *History* 62 (1977), pp. 347-71.

24   See Arnold, i.2/31, 7/2, 9/2, etc. From collation of all the available
      manuscripts of these sermons it emerges with as near certainty as is
      attainable that *alȝif* was the form of the author(s); the vast majority
      retain this, though the isolated, and otherwise inferior, manuscript may
      substitute *þouȝ* or *alþouȝ*.

25   For frequent use see the text called by Arnold *De Pontificum Roman-
      orum Schismate*, Arnold iii.244/3, 245/3, 248/3, 254/6, 255/24; also
      Matthew 293/31, *Tit.* ff. 13v, 51, 71 and *Eg.* f. 76 but *alþouȝ* more
      frequently. From the wordlists provided by Lindberg (*Stockholm
      Studies in English* 6 (1959), 8 (1961), 10 (1963), 13 (1965), 20 (1969),
      29 (1973),) it appears what WB did not use the conjunction, at any rate
      in the Old Testament EV.

26   The texts are those here cited as *Eg.* and *Tit.*; for the manuscripts see
      Sel. pp. 185-86; I am preparing an edition of these texts, along with
      Taylor and Thorpe. The details are: *autentik Eg.* ff. 14v, 29, 46v, 111v,
      Tit. ff. 25, 41, 69v, 85, 88, 89v, cf. *Apol.* 6/15 and *M.E.D.*; *mawmetrer*
      and *mawmetrie Eg.* ff. 37v, 42, 49, 50v, *Tit.* ff. 37, 52v, 79v, cf. *LL* 18/8,

101/10, 132/19, Arnold iii. 293/37, Taylor ff. 5v, 29 and *M.E.D.*; *pseudo* as prefix *Tit.* ff. 21v, 38, 46, cf. Arnold i.176/31, 200/23, 228/ 18; as noun *Eg.* ff. 102 twice, 112 twice, *Tit.* ff. 44, 74, cf. Matthew 296/1 etc., 479/23 and *O.E.D.* (the usage probably derives, directly or indirectly, from William of St. Amour); *purvyaunce Eg.* ff. 85, 86, 108, *Tit.* ff. 67, 87v, cf. Taylor ff. 19, 21, *Harl.* f. 78 and *O.E.D.* senses 5 and 6; *quilage* see *Sel.* p. 187 and add *Harl.* f. 79v; *renegate Eg.* ff. 106v, 115v, *Tit.* ff. 13, 15, 18, 20v, 25, 29, 34, cf. *LL* 79/21 and *O.E.D.*

27   For selective instances of these common words: *blabber* Arnold i.376/ 16, ii.8/34, iii.217/20, *Eg.* ff. 27, 62, 115, *Tit.* f. 98v; *cautel* Arnold i.192/26, 198/7, 200/29, 206/10, ii.16/6, 27/4, iii. 242/6, 247/4, *LL* 45/2, 80/27, 108/10, 112/21; *chaffare* Arnold i.184/20, 212/32, 252/ 25, 381/26, iii.211/6, *LL* 14/8, *Harl.* f. 64; *chargeous Eg.* f. 9v, *Harl.* ff. 64, 68v, Arnold i.305/5, Taylor f. 24, *LL* 26/31; *clowtyd* Arnold i.4/35, 73/24, 84/27ff, 353/5, *LL* 2/24, 16/14, 55/28 *Eg.* f. 19v; *colour* Arnold i.168/10, 193/7, iii.227/11, 296/34, 305/28, Taylor ff. 17v, 24v *Tit.* ff. 15v, 35v, 37v, *Harl.* ff. 70v, 89v, *37 Concs.* f. 51; *contrary* vb. Arnold i.220/17, 302/4, ii.260/1, iii.231/23, Matthew 56/18, 409/33; *customable begging* and *beggar Eg.* ff. 31v, 105v, 111, 113v, *Tit.* ff. 46v, 58v, Taylor f. 27v; *gab* and *gabbyng* Arnold i.169/29, 196/13, 202/19, 212/29, 258/17, 358/12, 361/21, iii.252/9, 266/21, 292/28; *glose* Arnold i.128/24, iii.227/6, 248/20, *Tit.* ff.7, 8, 18v, 20v, *Harl.* ff. 69v, 71v, 90, *LL* 52/7, 58/18, 131/11, *Apol.* 31/28, 105/2; *ground* will be examined below and examples there given; *impugn Apol.* 73/32, Taylor f. 27, *Eg.* ff. 47, 48v, 91v, 96v, *Tit.* ff. 15v, 24v, 79v; *jape* Arnold i.227/ 23, ii.256/27, 301/12, *Tit.* f. 95, *LL* 37/7, *Apol.* 8/25.

28   See, for instance, the type of evidence used by the critics cited above n. 22 and A.L. Kellogg and E.W. Talbert, 'The Wyclifite *Pater Noster* and *Ten Commandments . . .*', *Bulletin of the John Rylands Library* 42 (1960), pp. 360, 370.

29   Lichfield B/C/13 ff. 5v and 7; the first is quoted by J. Fines, 'Heresy trials in the diocese of Coventry and Lichfield, 1511-12', *Journal of Ecclesiastical History* 14 (1963), p. 166.

30   *Eg.* f. 47, Arnold iii.332/1; cf. Arnold ii.411/20, iii.231/20, 309/4, 341/ 27, Matthew 23/32, 71/27, 229/2, *Add.* f. 4, *Sel.* no. 3/1.

31   See for example Arnold i.96/18 *For many wete someres ben comen to þe chirche, and so* mannis lawe *growiþ and* Goddis lawe *is lettid and speciali bi lawes of þes* newe ordres; Matthew 38/11 *Certis þe [i] chargen men ouer myȝt and maken hem bysy to kunne wrongful* trad- iciouns *of synful folis makynge and to leue holy writt vnstudied, vnknoud and vnkept; and þis is a sotil cautel of þe fend to fordo* Goddis

lawe; Arnold ii.267/37 *Lord, whi wolen not þes four sectis suffre þat Goddis worde renne, and þat Cristis ordenaunce stood hool? . . . But certis þanne alle þes four sectis shulden leve þer patrouns and þer reulis, and come clenly to Cristis sect*; *Tit.* f. 13 [*a man*] *most graunt Cristis wordis and his apostlis and so reuerse þe determynacioun of þis renegat* [sc. the pope] *and diȝe bodili for Crist and his lawe, or ellis reuerse Crist and his lawe.*

32   *Eg.* f. 10; cf. Arnold i.7/8, 209/10, 223/21, 224/7; *LL* 38/15, 41/16, *Tit.* ff. 48v, 49, 52v, 69, 74v, 91v, etc.

33   Matthew 342/19, Arnold ii.316/16; cf. *Add.* f. 52, Arnold i.178/12, 303/13, 331/2, 399/32, 400/9, iii.243/28, 244/21, 245/29, 258/29 etc.

34   See my paper 'The expurgation of a Lollard sermon-cycle' *Journal of Theological Studies* N.S. 22 (1971), 455-58. See above pp. 205-8.

35   Arnold iii.116/26, 245/23; cf. Arnold iii.175/31, 236/32, 505/23, Matthew 337/3, 421/1, 449/33, 482/26 etc.

36   Arnold i.248/2.

37   Arnold i.212/20; this belief, of course, underlies Pecock's naming of the Lollards as *Bible-men.*

38   Arnold iii.255/24; cf. Arnold i.191/16, 202/14, 206/9, iii.244/13, 248/16, *LL* 59/8, 65/11. *Apol,* 20/9, 29/11, 35/28, *37 Concs.* ff. 43, 46v etc.

39   See the discussion in P. de Vooght, *Les sources de la doctrine chretienne* . . . , (Bruges, 1954), pp. 168-200 and M. Hurley, ' "Scriptura Sola": Wyclif and his critics', *Traditio* 16 (1960), pp. 275-352.

40   *Eg.* ff. 106, 111v, 115, *Tit.* ff. 41, 58v, *Tit.* f. 92; cf. Arnold i.202/15, *LL* 13/3, 39/1, 48/37, 55/29, *Apol.* 8/21.

41   *Eg.* f. 21, *Tit.* f. 41v; cf. *Eg.* f. 44v, *Tit.* f. 64, 74.

42   *37 Concs.* f. 77; the source, referred to by incipit, is the sermon numbered 19 in S. Harrison Thomson, *The Writings of Robert Grosseteste* (Cambridge, 1940), p. 173-74; see MS. Bodley 830, ff. 175v-185, especially ff. 178-178v.

43   *37 Concs.* f. 47.

44   Arnold i.288/30; cf. 81/23, 100/26, 132/31, 261/22, *37 Concs.* f. 4v.

45   Arnold ii. 280/22, 247/27; cf. Arnold i.220/34, 270/3, 286/1, iii. 248/26, 251/30, 272/15, *LL* 105/20, *Apol.* 56/9, 90/5, *Harl.* f. 70.

46   Arnold i. 305/9, 378/15, iii.281/28, 289/34, *Tit.* ff. 4, 5, 26v, 80v, *37 Concs.* f. 77v; that adversaries recognized this is shown by Dymmock's objection to the term, see *Liber contra duodecim errores Lollardorum,* ed. H.S. Cronin (Wyclif Society, London, 1922), pp. 29-30.

47   Arnold iii.281/17, 306/28, 427/25, Matthew 84/7, 89/27 etc.

48   See the English version of the *Rosarium Theologie* (above n. 5) p. 124,

Tit. f. 75, *Sel.* no. 3/102. *M.E.D.* record the first and last from non-Wycliffite texts, but always with an explanation provided.

49   See, for instance, Arnold i.92/2, 133/16, 181/7, 213/9, 247/24, 361/4, ii.82/6, 91/17, 358/32, iii.403/21, 407/36, 485/5, Matthew 19/15, 357/28, *Upland* 393, *37 Concs.* ff. 25v-26, 43v, *Sel.* no. 1/36, 21A/89.

50   Arnold iii.254/35, *37 Concs.* ff. 41, 43, 43v, *LL* 31/28.

51   Pecock's awareness of the need to refute Lollardy in its own usual language is obvious in many of his writings; see, for instance, his *Reule of Crysten Religioun,* ed. W.C. Greet, (E.E.T.S. o.s. 171, 1927), 21/6, 94/16.

52   See *Heresy Trials in the Diocese of Norwich, 1428-31*, ed. N.P. Tanner (Camden Society London, Fourth Series 20, 1977), pp. 99, 102, and *Annales Monasterii S. Albani*, ed. H.T. Riley (Rolls Series, London, 1870-71), ii.269.

53   The first half of the text is now available ed. P.H. Barnum (E.E.T.S. o.s. 275, 1976); the remainder will appear as E.E.T.S. o.s. 280 (1980); for the date see the references given in the first p. ix. See for instance the discussion of images and the honour due to them in the first commandment (pp. 81-117); here the terms *dulia* and *yperdulia* are used (p. 108/39, 49), and many of the same arguments found as in Lollard texts (cf. *Sel.* pp. 153, 179-82), but the vocabulary in general is markedly different.

54   These sermons are being edited by Gloria Cigman, to whom I am indebted for the loan of the printout of her computer concordance. Instances of words discussed above that do not appear in these sermons are *alʒif, autentik, blabber, cautel, chaffare, clowtyd, colect* etc., *contrary* vb., *customable begging/beggar, jape, pseudo, reverse, traditions.* Words or phrases that do occur are *chargeous, gabbyng, glose, Goddis lawe, ground* sb. and vb., *many men think, mawmetrie, trewe men* and *trewe prestis. Sects* is only applied to biblical *pharisees* and *scribes,* and these words are themselves not used with regard to contemporary figures.

11

SOME ASPECTS OF LOLLARD BOOK PRODUCTION

IT has recently been observed that 'the corpus of surviving lollard literature is regrettably small, and it is to be found in the volumes of Wyclif's so-called English writings and a few other printed and manuscript works'.[1] To one concerned to re-edit the vernacular lollard literature the position seems otherwise: the corpus is formidably large, the printed material inadequately represents the state of the texts so edited, and there are a large number of other works still in manuscript. The printed material, if grouped together, would extend to perhaps five bulky volumes, in all about 2400 pages; a rough estimate of the vernacular texts now known suggests that this is perhaps only a fifth of the evidence available.[2] Moreover, the editors were ignorant of a large number of the manuscripts of the works they printed, and hence could not assess the circulation of the texts: to give an example, Arnold used only one manuscript of what I shall call the standard lollard sermon-cycle, with fitful reference to three others, whereas now thirty manuscripts are known, together with a further three containing a modified series based on the original set.[3] It is also impossible from the existing printed editions to gain any picture of the views of the lollard authors: only extensive

---

[1] [J.] Crompton, ['Leicestershire Lollards'], *Transactions of the Leicestershire Archaeological and Historical Society*, XLIV (Leicester 1968–9) pp 14–15.

[2] The main printed material is contained in [T.] Arnold, [*Select English Works of John Wyclif*], 3 vols (Oxford 1869–71) and [F. D.] Matthew, [*The English Works of Wyclif hitherto unprinted*], Early English Text Society Original Series 74 (London 1880). For a survey of the other published writings see the bibliography by E. W. Talbert and S. Harrison Thomson in *A Manual of the Writings in Middle English 1050–1500*, II, ed J. Burke Severs (Hamden Conn. 1970) pp 521–33; the list of manuscripts, and of works unprinted, there given requires considerable amplification. For continued help with the paleography, and for knowledge of some of the manuscripts here considered, I am indebted to the great kindness of Dr Ian Doyle.

[3] The sermon-cycle was printed by Arnold in vols I–II of his edition; for full consideration of the nature of this cycle see my article in *Medium Ævum*, XL (Oxford 1971) pp 142–56. The modified series is found most completely in Trinity College Dublin MS C.1.22 and in part in St John's College Cambridge MS G.22 (fols 1–78v) and Cambridge University Library MS Add. 5338; isolated phrases from the cycle version are incorporated into new and longer sermons.

commentary will reveal the implications of remarks made and vocabulary used.

It is, of course, a regular feature of investigation of suspected Lollardy that English books are mentioned; regularly the commission requires that the contents of a suspect's house be examined for ownership of books, and the abjuration commonly includes the forfeiture of such books and the promise that, if books, or information about them, subsequently come to the notice of the penitent, they will be passed on to the diocesan authorities.[1] It is clear, furthermore, that the market for lollard books was good and was also well supplied. Amongst the early suspects of Lollardy are a number of *parchemyners* and scribes, and the quality of the early manuscripts, in particular, attests to their excellence.[2] Even in the later period, whilst it is true that the adherents of Lollardy were mostly of low social status, literacy was obviously important and widespread: the situation mentioned in bishop Blythe's register at Salisbury in 1498 can be frequently paralleled 'we and eyther of vs hath holden company beyng present with them sundry tymes at the techyng and redyng of their erroneous opinions and bokys'.[3] The tradition had persisted since 1414, when *plures libros Anglicos* had been seized in Colchester, where they had been read *infra mansiones*, 'tam per diem quam per [noctem] secrete et aperte, aliquando ad invicem et aliquando per se'.[4] Whilst it is true that ownership of the Wycliffite Bible was not confined to lollard sympathisers but extended to people of such unimpeachable orthodoxy as Henry VI, and whilst it is possible that the Bible translations may also have been copied by orthodox scribes (a possibility quite credible for the vast majority that lack the

---

[1] References are too numerous to be given in full; for the early period see *Calendar of Patent Rolls 1385-9* (London 1900) pp 427, 430, 448, 468 etc.; for a later form, including the terms of abjuration, the procedural material recorded in Worcester, *Register Polton* pp 111-12 and in BM MS Harley 2179 fols 157v-159 is typical. Suspicion of all English books is not uncommon: see, for instance, Wells, *Register Stafford* for 1441, ed T. S. Holmes, *Somerset Record Society*, XXXI-XXXII (London 1915-16) II, p 267.

[2] For instance William Perchemener and Michael Scryvener, both of Leicester, mentioned in Courtenay's register in 1389, J. H. Dahmus, *The Metropolitan Visitations of William Courtenay Archbishop of Canterbury 1381-1396* (Urbana 1950) pp 164-7; for further early copying in Leicester see further below. For lollard manuscripts of fine quality see, for instance, BM MS Egerton 617-18, Cambridge University Library MSS Dd.1.27 and Mm.2.15 of the Wycliffite Bible, BM MSS Royal 18 B. ix and Additional 40672 and Christ's College Cambridge MS 7 of the sermon-cycle, or Bodleian MS Bodley 143 of the Glossed Gospels; the list could be considerably extended.

[3] Salisbury, *Register Blythe* fol 71, the abjuration of two women from the parish of St Giles in Reading. For the later period see J. A. F. Thomson, *The Later Lollards 1414-1520* (2 ed Oxford 1967).

[4] PRO K.B.9. 204/1 nos 10-11.

distinctively Wycliffite prologue), the number of surviving manuscripts remains astonishing: over 235 are now known.[1] Even when one comes to the sermon-cycle, a work that cannot have been unwittingly copied by orthodox scribes, the thirty manuscripts that survive would be hard to equal from other middle English prose works of comparable length. It is, moreover, clear from the textual relations of the manuscripts that this can be only a small proportion of the original number.

The nature of lollard books can only be roughly assessed from episcopal and chancery records. Three types are regularly mentioned: *schedulae*, *quaterni* and *libri*, clearly in ascending order of size; in English the equivalents appear as *rollis*, *quairis* and *bookis*.[2] So far as I am aware, no example of a *schedula* survives in its original form, though documentary evidence of some is available, and it is possible to suggest that some surviving texts originated in this form. Of the first, the so-called 'Twelve Conclusions of the Lollards', or the lists of anti-mendicant complaints scattered round London by Patteshull, an apostate friar, in 1387 are more obvious examples.[3] The second is possible with the vernacular version of Wyclif's confession, with the short text 'Answeris to hem þat seien we schulden not speke of Holy Writte', and may account for some of the shorter items found in lollard anthologies such as Trinity College Dublin MSS C.3.12 and C.5.6.[4] The *schedulae* were obviously ephemeral documents, of the same kind as the *bills* copied by Thomas Ile of Braybrooke in 1414 and distributed round Leicester by William Smith.[5] One use for them is

---

1 Ownership of Bible manuscripts is dealt with by M. Deanesly, *The Lollard Bible* (Cambridge 1920) pp 319–50. The most recent list of manuscripts is by C. Lindberg, 'The Manuscripts and Versions of the Wycliffite Bible; a preliminary survey', *Studia Neophilologica*, XLII (Uppsala 1970) pp 333–47.

2 See the commission and abjuration mentioned above, p182 n 1, also Lincoln, *Register Repingdon* 15, fol 152v and Chichele's *Register*, ed E. F. Jacob, Canterbury and York Society (London/Oxford 1943–7) III, p 198; for the English form see Chichele's *Register* III, p 207 and Ely, *Register Grey*, fol 133.

3 H. S. Cronin, 'The Twelve Conclusions of the Lollards', *EHR* XXII (1907) pp 292–304; for Patteshull see Walsingham, *Historia Anglicana*, ed H. T. Riley, RS 28 (1863–4) II, pp 158–9; the documents nailed to the door of St Paul's by Hereford and Repingdon in 1382 – D. Wilkins, *Concilia Magnae Britanniae et Hiberniae* (London 1737) III, p 165 – and Aston's schedule of the same year – *Fasciculi Zizaniorum*, ed W. W. Shirley, RS 5 (1858) p 329 – must also have been of this form. Compare also Lincoln, *Register Repingdon* 15, fol 173.

4 The appearance, out of context, of Wyclif's shorter confession in Bodleian MS Bodley 647, fols 63v–64v, suggests such circulation; the short text, in all about 24 lines, appears in BM MS Harley 2322, fols 87–8, and Bodleian MS Add.B.66, fols 90–90v; many of the texts from the Trinity College Dublin MSS were printed by Arnold, III, and by Matthew but a number of short items from the end of each were unaccountably omitted.   5 PRO K.B.9.204/1 nos 130 and 141.

shown by an episode in the career of William Taylor when, before
Chichele's convocation in 1421, he 'extraxit de sinu suo quasdam
auctoritates et dicta in quadam papiri cedula scripta'.¹ Of the *quaterni*
a single example has survived, and is now preserved in Durham
University as MS Cosin V.iii.6; it is a quire of eight leaves, the hand
dating from before or about the year 1400, containing a dialogue
between a knight and a clerk on the subject of civil and ecclesiastical
jurisdiction. Its survival intact, with only interleaving to distort the
original format, makes it possible to appreciate episcopal concern about
these apparently trivial documents.² Again it seems likely that works
now surviving only in composite manuscripts may originally
have circulated as *quaterni*: some of the many tracts that provide
lists of biblical and patristic texts on such lollard subjects as images,
pilgrimages and the eucharist may well have started life in this
form.³ It seems likely that such compilations were intended for use
in the centres of lollard instruction of which the documents provide
evidence.⁴

The books are, of course, both the most frequent survivals and the
most interesting, not merely from their content but also from the
implications of their relationship and appearance. They can, I think,
be divided into two groups that I shall call 'official' and 'peripheral', a
tendentious division that I shall hope to justify. The 'official' group is
the easier to characterise: the texts that fall into it are preserved in a
relatively large number of manuscripts of expensive type, are often set
out for reading aloud, and are usually corrected, even in the most
minute and immaterial detail. The most obvious member of this group
is the Wycliffite Bible, with its ramifications of version and revision;
but this is a separate topic which I do not wish to deal with here.⁵

¹ Chichele, *Register* III, p 67.
² For discussion of this manuscript, its form and content, see my article 'A Lollard
  Quaternion', *Review of English Studies*, xxii (1971). See below pp 193-200.
³ For instance texts on images in Bodleian MS Eng.th.f.39, fols 1-8, 37-8, Trinity College
  Cambridge MS B.14.50, fols 34-5, BM MS Additional 24202, fols 24r/v, 26-8v; on
  pilgrimages in Eng.th.f.39, fols 12v-14v; on the eucharist in Trinity College Dublin
  MS C.5.6, fols 145-6v and Cambridge University Library MS Ff.6.31(3), fols 27v-35v.
  The material on the necessity of preaching found in Bodleian MS Laud Misc. 210,
  fols 168-74v, and in Durham University MS Cosin V.v.1. fols 175v-9v, may well be
  of the same type.
⁴ For instance a letter of Alexander [Tottington], bishop of Norwich 1407-13, written
  into a precedent roll, BM MS Additional 35205, m.xivᵈ; compare also the material
  cited by Crompton p 19. I have deliberately excluded from consideration here the
  question of Latin writings produced by lollard centres.
⁵ Most recent discussion, and bibliography, is to be found in S. L. Fristedt, *The Wycliffe
  Bible Part II*, Stockholm Studies in English, xxi (1969).

The others in this category are the Gospel commentaries, extensive and not yet edited,[1] the sermon-cycle to which I shall return, and a small group of shorter tracts including *Vae Octuplex* and *Of Ministers in the Church*.[2] Paleographically many of the manuscripts of these works date from the end of the fourteenth or early years of the fifteenth century, and the richness of their production and the organisation that must lie behind their corrected texts suggest composition before the Oldcastle rebellion. To these points I will return. The 'peripheral' group is more amorphous, but the texts that belong here share certain features: they are preserved in only a small number of manuscripts, less than six, those manuscripts are usually of poorer quality, with little sign that they were intended for public reading, and with scant trace of systematic correction. Their content is extremely varied, from material based on, though not straightforwardly translated from, Wyclif's Latin works, such as the *Tractatus de Regibus* in Bodleian MS Douce 273 (fols 37v–53), dependent upon the *De Officio Regis*, or the dialogue between *Reson* and *Gabbyng* in Trinity College Dublin MS C.5.6 (fols 154v–61), drawn from the first part of the *Dialogus*, to more extreme diatribes against ecclesiastical abuses, such as the long text, purporting to be a report of a sermon against the mendicants, preserved in Cambridge University Library MS Dd.14.30(2).[3] In date these texts are more difficult to assess: there is rarely internal evidence for composition and equally rare is external dating, such as is available for *The Lanterne of Liȝt*;[4] the actual surviving manuscripts range in

---

[1] The nature of these has been surveyed by H. Hargreaves, 'The Marginal Glosses to the Wycliffite New Testament', *Studia Neophilologica*, XXIII (1961) pp 285–300.

[2] These two were printed by Arnold II, pp 379–423; of the first fourteen manuscripts are now known, of the second seventeen. The two are related to, though not translations of, Wyclif's expositions of Matt. 23 and 24, *Opera Minora*, ed J. Loserth, Wyclif Society (London 1913) pp 313–82. Apart from these, and leaving aside commentaries on certain canticles, prayers and creeds printed by Arnold III, pp 5–116, almost none of the works printed so far is known to survive in more than six manuscripts (the one exception is Arnold III, pp 188–201 found in seven).

[3] Unfortunately, the manuscript is defective at both ends; but sufficient of the conclusion remains for an assessment of the work's nature to be made. The relevant material is (fol 100v) 'Now sires, þe dai is al ydo and I mai tarie ȝou no lenger, and I haue no tyme to make now a recapitulacioun of my sermoun. Neþeles I purpose to leue it writun among ȝou, and whoso likiþ mai ouerse it...And certis if I haue seid ony þing amys, and I mai now haue redi knowleche þerof, I shal amende it er I go; and if I haue such knouleche herafter, I shal wiþ beter will come and amende my fautis'.

[4] Edited L. M. Swinburn, EETS, OS 151 (1917); a second manuscript, BM MS Harley 6613, and the print of [1530?] by Redman should be added. The evidence for dating, between 1409 and 1415, is summarised on pp viii–xiii. The dating of most vernacular lollard works from internal evidence is very difficult, because the abuses mentioned are normally persistent and not isolated ones.

date through the fifteenth century. Obviously, when so many manuscripts were destroyed by ecclesiastical authorities, it would be unwise
to argue simply from the chance survival of manuscripts, but the
nature as well as the number of them distinguishes the two groups:
whereas the first group is the result of organised production, the
second seems the chance outcome of individual, and often idiosyncratic, interest.[1]

From the viewpoint of the movement's history as a whole, the
'official' group of texts is the more important; to illustrate its interest
I should like to deal more extensively with the standard sermon-cycle.
This has been available to critics for the last hundred years in the
edition of Arnold, but the deficiencies of that edition have hidden its
importance. In the first place it was presented as part of the 'English
Works' of Wyclif himself, and has, therefore, been treated as if
belonging to the heresiarch's thought, a part that can safely be ignored
as a pale reflection of views expressed with more sublety and cogency in
Latin. The evidence in favour of Wyclif's authorship of the cycle, or
indeed of any English works, is very poor: in only one manuscript of
the cycle is Wyclif's name attached by the medieval scribe, and the
manuscript is textually not a good one.[2] The evidence against
Wyclif's authorship is much more convincing: references are found to
events after Wyclif's death which, since the cycle is quite certainly to
be regarded as a single unit and not as the chance outcome of the
assembly of a number of texts, must settle the issue.[3] This is not to say
that the cycle has nothing to do with Wyclif: a number of the sermons
draw on ideas found in the Latin sermon for the corresponding occasion
and are, therefore, clearly the work of someone acquainted with

---

[1] A case in point would be BM MS Additional 24202, containing, amongst other items,
tracts against miracle plays, printed in *Reliquiæ Antiquæ* ed T. Wright and J. O. Halliwell
(London 1841–3) II, pp 42–57, against dicing, on tithes, on the duties of priests, and a
section of a longer treatise against the religious orders.

[2] In Bodleian MS Douce 321, fol 65v, appears the rubric 'Expliciunt tam epistole quam
Euangelia Dominicalia secundum exposicionem Doctoris euangelij'; this manuscript,
probably of the early fifteenth century, was in quality over-estimated by Arnold
(I, pp xiii, xviii–xix) as a full collation reveals. Wyclif's name appears also in New
College Oxford MS 95, but not attached to these sermons. In Corpus Christi College
Cambridge MS 336, p 475, the Ferial set ends with the enigmatic note 'Expliciunt
euangelia ferialia secundum M.J.' by the original scribe. The evidence of Netter (cited
by Arnold, II, p v) is probably to be ascribed to his knowledge of some relationship
between the vernacular sermons and Wyclif's own, but cannot on its own account be
regarded as decisive.

[3] For evidence that the cycle must be considered as a unit see the article mentioned
above, p 181 n 3; these arguments must be taken to modify the discussion of

Wyclif's own work.[1] The second, and more serious, deficiency of the old edition is Arnold's lack of interest in anything beyond the provision of a bare text: to this end he printed, without emendation even when manifestly corrupt, a single manuscript, giving only the sketchiest list of some other manuscripts and adding virtually no commentary to his text.[2] As a result, amongst other things, he missed certain clear implications of the manuscripts. The sermon-cycle as Arnold printed it falls into five sets: sermons, 294 in all, for the Sunday Gospels, the *Commune* and *Proprium Sanctorum*, Ferial Gospels and the Sunday Epistles, in that order. Only one other surviving manuscript preserves that precise order, though two others, lacking one or more sets, agree as far as their limited material allows.[3] A wide number of permutations is found amongst the other manuscripts. More far-reaching are two re-organisations, one intercalating the sermons on the Sunday Epistle and Sunday Gospel to form a complete dominical cycle, found in five manuscripts,[4] and a second intercalating Sunday Epistle, Sunday Gospel and Ferial Gospel for the ensuing week to form a single sermon-cycle for the liturgical year, an arrangement found in three extant manuscripts.[5] The fact that each of these re-organisations occurs more than once suggests a clear motivation in the use to which the sermons were to be put. This is borne out by the fact that the groups of five and three manuscripts involved in these particular arrangements are not textually closely related; they are not, in other words, copies made

E.W. Talbert, 'The Date of the Composition of the English Wyclifite Collection of Sermons', *Speculum*, XII (1937) pp 464–74, and M. W. Ransom, 'The Chronology of Wyclif's English Sermons', *Washington State College Research Studies*, XVI (1948) pp 67–114.

[1] *Sermones* I–III, ed J. Loserth, Wyclif Society (London 1887–9) contain Wyclif's Latin sermons on the Sunday Gospels, *Commune* and *Proprium Sanctorum* and Sunday Epistles; it should be noted that no Latin source is available for the lengthy vernacular Ferial set and that many of the English Sunday Epistle sermons bear no relation to the Latin work for the equivalent occasion.

[2] Arnold printed MS Bodley 788; in his list of other manuscripts known to him (1, pp xvii–xx) he admitted that he had not seen all, and had only examined most cursorily. Somewhat fitfully, he records identification of patristic references in the text, but many allusions pass unremarked.

[3] The single manuscript in complete agreement is Leicester Wyggeston Hospital 10.D.34/6, unknown to Arnold; Trinity College Cambridge MS B.2.17 agrees in the order of the first four sets but lacks the last, whilst Corpus Christi College Cambridge MS 336, wanting sets 1 and 5, contains sets 2, 3 and 4 in that order.

[4] Namely Bodleian MS Douce 321, BM MS Cotton Claudius D.viii, Robert Taylor MS Princeton (once Wrest Park 32), Lambeth MS 1149 and Bodleian MS Don.c.13.

[5] The arrangement is found complete in BM MS Royal 18 B.ix and, though now mutilated by later loss of leaves, St John's College Cambridge MS C.8; BM MS Harley 2396 contains this arrangement for the period between Advent and the fourth Sunday after the octave of Epiphany.

from a single exemplar in each case.[1] It seems likely that a patron, or group of sympathisers, seeking a copy of the cycle, would be given the option of three basic 'patterns' for the manuscript to be made. Liturgically, of course, each pattern is quite comprehensible.

In the production of the manuscripts, once the basic pattern was selected, considerable care was taken. Of the thirty surviving manuscripts, no two are in the same hand. Yet twenty-seven share certain common features: they are most scrupulously rubricated and a rigid division is observed between the underlining in red of the gospel or epistle text that forms the basis of the sermon and the absence of such underlining for other biblical texts incidentally quoted; they are corrected, by the original scribe or another, even in matters of quite insubstantial kind, such as the omission or inclusion of the definite article.[2] It is noticeable, also, that such correction is systematic and not random: when a correction appears at a certain place in one manuscript, it is very unusual for that correction not to appear at the same place in others. One manuscript contains the note 'Ista euangelia dominicalia corriguntur per primum originalem'.[3] The three exceptional manuscripts reinforce the case: one appears to be an unfinished product, incompletely rubricated and not yet fully corrected, a second is an idiosyncratic attempt to incorporate the Sunday Gospel sermons into larger tracts, and the third is a late copy, plainly from its size and hand designed for private use only.[4] The large majority of manuscripts, however, appears to be the product of an organised attempt to supply books of lollard instruction, a supply that must have been closely

[1] This is particularly obvious in the case of the first arrangement: discrepancy in ordering, resulting from two faulty but independent attempts at alternation, are found in the Taylor manuscript and in Bodleian MS Don.c.13; similarly, the text of Lambeth MS 1149 is very closely related to that of BM MS Additional 40672, itself having the five sets separate.

[2] Vernacular manuscripts of this period rarely show this combination of care for the accuracy of the text together with attention to its appearance. The quality of lollard manuscripts even aroused comment from an investigating authority in the case of John Galle, priest of London, in 1428, found to possess 'quidam liber in vulgari de evangeliis bene scriptus' (Chichele, *Register* III, p 190); compare also the Pauline epistles 'in amplo volumine' recorded in J. Fines, 'Heresy Trials in the Diocese of Coventry and Lichfield 1511–12', *JEH*, XIV (1963) p 165.

[3] Leicester Old Town Hall MS 3, fol 216v; the claim cannot fully be justified until further work has been done on the text, but the correction has certainly been carefully done.

[4] The first is Trinity College Cambridge MS B.14.38, the second Sidney Sussex College Cambridge MS 74; for its text see E. W. Talbert, 'A Fifteenth-Century Lollard Sermon Cycle', *University of Texas Studies in English* (1939) pp 5–30, the third New College Oxford MS 95.

supervised. Amongst the scribes involved, one at least can be found at work on another lollard manuscript, a copy of the later Wycliffite version of the Gospels translation.[1] It is likely that, as work on the bulk of manuscripts proceeds, more such overlapping will be found. The question, of course, immediately arises of the whereabouts of the places in which this supervised copying took place. Linguistically, the scribes show considerable variation: phonology and morphology obviously did not come under the close scrutiny to which matter and even syntax were subjected. Most scribes can, however, be localised by their language as coming from the East Midlands, in its widest sense.[2] Oxford is an obvious suggestion, but is both linguistically improbable and inherently unlikely since the Wycliffite ideas, before they left Oxford, were almost exclusively the property of men whose written language was Latin.[3] Much more probable, both linguistically and historically, is the area between Northampton and Leicester, an area which includes Braybrooke and in which a number of copyists are known to have worked, men such as Thomas Ile, William Smith, Michael Scryvener and Thomas Scot.[4] It is perhaps not insignificant that two of the manuscripts of this sermon-cycle are now at Leicester.[5] Documentary evidence for such a centre, as opposed to evidence for individual scribes, is lacking at present, but this may well be attributable to the skill of the lollards in covering their tracks rather than to the

[1] The hand of BM MS Harley 2396 appears in part of Gonville and Caius College Cambridge MS 179/212, containing a fragment of the Gospels in the later Wycliffite version.

[2] Exceptions are the scribe of Bodleian MS Don.c.13, clearly a northerner, and that of Trinity College Cambridge MS B.14.38, who must have come from the south-west. I am grateful to professor McIntosh for discussing linguistic questions about these manuscripts with me.

[3] The English dialect of Oxford can be roughly gauged from the evidence presented by S. B. Meech, 'Nicholas Bishop, an exemplar of the Oxford dialect of the fifteenth century', *Publications of the Modern Language Association*, XLIX (Menasha 1934) pp 443–59. The evidence concerning the preaching expedition of Hereford, Aston and others in the Winchester diocese in 1382 makes no mention of written material: see *Wykeham's Register*, ed T. F. Kirby, *Hampshire Record Society* (London 1896–9) II, pp 337–8.

[4] For the relevant period the persistence of Lollardy in Northampton and Leicester is well established: for Northampton in 1389 by the Courtenay register (above, p 148 n 2) p 169, for 1392–3 by Lincoln, *Register Buckingham* 12, fols 398, 406, and the document printed by E. Powell and G. M. Trevelyan, *The Peasants' Rising and the Lollards* (London 1899) pp 45–50, and for 1416 by Lincoln, *Register Repingdon* 15, fol 176v; for the Leicester material see the article by Crompton. For Braybrooke, and its lord Sir Thomas Latimer, see K. B. McFarlane, *John Wycliffe and the Beginnings of English Nonconformity* (London 1952) pp 146, 173 and 178. Note also the mention of Thomas Scot of Braybrooke, *scriveyn*, in the 1414 return, PRO K.B.9.204/1 no 111.

[5] Namely Leicester Old Town Hall MS 3 and Leicester Wyggeston Hospital MS 10.D.34/6.

fact that none existed. It will be remembered that Nicholas Faulfiš and his friends obtained copies of some of Wyclif's Latin works on a visit to Braybrooke in 1407.[1]

The numbers of vernacular lollard manuscripts surviving do much to explain the constant concern of the bishops about the *schedulae*, *quaterni* and *libri*, whilst the wide distribution that the sermon-cycle must have achieved may also explain the recurrence of certain specific ideas in different areas of the country. In the Salisbury diocese there seems to have been a particularly good supply of lollard writings, to judge by the series of references running throughout the fifteenth century. In 1416 is recorded a mandate to seek out 'libros suspectos in lingua vulgari Anglicana conscriptos', in 1418 John of Bath was interrogated before the next bishop, John Chaundler, 'super certis articulis in quibusdam libris Anglicis secum inuentis' and quotations from his books are given; in 1428 it is reported that William Fuller, *alias* Heede, kept 'libros tractatus articulos et opuscula' containing heresies and errors.[2] Under Aiscough, bishop from 1438 to 1450, a number of heretics were apprehended; almost all of them admitted to possessing forbidden books, whilst one of them, John Piers, *alias* John Fyncaisshe, of Netheravon used one of his *quaterni* to refresh his memory in the course of interrogation 'Also y haue bileued diuers other articles and opynyons conteyned in a quaier in English writen to the whiche y refferre me'.[3] In 1478 brief reference to books is again found, but the importance of them reappears in the series of investigations under bishops Langton and Blythe from 1490 to 1498. 'One suspecte boke of commaundementis' contained material against the worship of images, a claim that can certainly be borne out from extant lollard literature; 'a suspecte boke conteynyng errours and heresies' included the claim that laymen could preach.[4] The importance of written material in the persistence of Lollardy is seen in the story of the 'redyng of...erroneous opinions and bokys' mentioned earlier; it also explains the claim of Thomas Boughton of Hungerford that 'sith the tyme of my first acqueyntaunce with the said heretikes, I haue had

---

[1] See A. B. Emden, *A Biographical Register of the University of Oxford to A.D. 1500*, II (Oxford 1958) p 670.

[2] Hallum, *Register*, fol 127; Chaundler, *Register* pt II, fols 17v–18; Nevill, *Register* pt II, fol 77v, with which compare the acknowledgement of a man from Devizes, fol 57v, that he 'was woned an vsed to here in secret place, yn holkys and hyrnes, the redyng of the byble yn Englyssh'.

[3] Ayscough, *Register* pt II, fol 52v; further confessions appear on fols 52v–54v.

[4] Beauchamp, *Register* pt II, fol 17v for 1478; Langton, *Register* pt II, fols 35 and 38v, compare also fols 36 and 40v.

a great mynde to here sermouns and prechynges'.[1] The contents of the lollard books that survive give some colour too to the assertion of Joan Baker, this time from the London diocese, a woman probably associated with a group having a considerable library of heretical tracts, that 'she cold here a better sermond at home in hur howse than any doctor or prist colde make at Poulis crosse or any other place'.[2]

[1] Above, p 182 n 3. Blythe, *Register*, fol 74v.
[2] Guildhall, London, *Register Fitzjames*, fol 27; for the group see Trinity College Dublin MS D.3.4, fols 122v–124v.

kniȝt of þe kinges of yngeland & a clerk of
yngland þt was like comen fro þe counte were
to gid in a place. So þt þe clerk bigan to speke
of þe pope & in man repned þe kniȝt & said. In þe
grete wond he said þat þe kinge & som of his counseil
& of his kniȝtes & of men of þe temralte þat schuld be
gouned bi holichirche. as bi þe pope & bi bisshopes &
bi þe clergy. melley þam of men of holichirch & of þair
godes. in þing mislykes goddes lawe & agaynes holy
chirch. for þai ne schuld noman mell oyer pope ne oyer clergy
for þai bene abouen all men. bi power 3euen to þam
bi god him self als holy writt bere þ witnes & þe lawe
canone also.
¶ Der sir said þe kniȝt þou spekes of a matr, þt clerkes
han oft moued amonge þe comone pupel. & þe pepel
þai oft bene & es in a were & in dont þof. And I my
self haue oft wondrid þt þe pope & þe clergi haue
taken vpon þem. to þis land þe kinge þt es lorde
of his land & alto þai bene about more & more to ab
ege & lessen his power & his lordschip. which as me þink
schuld noman on is half god haue to done wiþ ne
mell þam þof. Aþeles bicause þt i am a litil lered
& vnderstonde conncele holy writt. I drede me þat i
miȝt trist to mich to myne oun witt in þis matere.
& so offend & gilt to god. And þou ert a man of holy
chirch a preste & semes a clerk cominge of clergi
I wold gladlich lerne of þe. for it es oft sene þt
mom prestes & clerkes. þat beth gretelich auanncid
gone wele arraied. & wele toward as þou tos þt beng
no cominge men of clergie ne of redoune. And þ
for þ i þi þe tell me what degre of scole þou has.
þt i may knowe wheþer þou be abil of cominge
to teche me in þis matr. þt i am in dont.
Sir said þe clerk bi cause þat it þon has desire to
lere i am riȝt glad to tell þe þt þou as it. & as all
be i vnworþi i am a doctor of decreec. & haue duel
no longe tyme in þe counté of rome. & bene i office
wiþ þe pope.
In gode faiþ said þe kniȝt i am wele paied. for i
hope to be wele tauȝt bi þe of þat matere þt we haue

12

A LOLLARD QUATERNION

AMONGST the manuscripts in the Cosin Library at Durham University is a slim volume,[1] entitled on its first leaf 'A Memorable Monument of Antiquitye provinge the lawfull soveraigntye & supremacye of Christian kings & defendinge it against yᵉ vnlawfull & tirannicall Primacye of the Pope'. The rest of the title-page and the ensuing dedicatory epistle make clearer the nature of the tract and the reason for the manuscript's present appearance. The compiler was William Crashawe, father of the poet Richard, and an ardent Puritan; his purpose was to bring to the notice of King James I a text in English, dating, he erroneously thought, from 'above 300 yeares agoe' (f. 3), which argued strongly in favour of the superior power of the king over the pope. Crashawe was an antiquarian and book-collector of considerable note: some of his books form the core of the present collection of manuscripts in St. John's College, Cambridge.[2] He followed in the tradition of men such as Parker, who thought that the assembly and printing of texts written in England in earlier centuries could furnish antecedents for the tenets of the reformed church.[3] Despite this interest in the earlier English church, there is no indication in the dedicatory epistle that Crashawe connected the text with Wyclif or the Lollards; had he done so, he could have dated the manuscript more accurately. Crashawe plainly hoped, by presenting the volume to James, to gain support for the publication of such texts. Whether James took any interest in the book is unknown, though its present position in Cosin's library suggests that he did not.[4] The date of Crashawe's compilation

[1] Press-mark V. iii. 6. I owe knowledge of this manuscript to the unfailingly generous help of Dr. Ian Doyle; the dating of the hand of the medieval section (see below) is Dr. Doyle's.

[2] Earlier accounts of Crashawe have been superseded by P. J. Wallis, *William Crashawe, the Sheffield Puritan* (1963; reprinted with addenda and index from *Transactions of the Hunter Archaeological Society*, viii, pts. 2–5 (1960–3)). See also the same author's article 'The Library of William Crashawe', *Transactions of the Cambridge Bibliographical Society*, II. iii (1956), 213–28. Of Lollard manuscripts now in St. John's Library, one, C. 8, came from Crashawe's collection (see M. R. James, *A Descriptive Catalogue of the Manuscripts in the Library of St. John's College, Cambridge* (Cambridge, 1913), p. 75) but it contains no annotation by him.

[3] See the articles in note 2; Wallis (1963), p. 33, mentions Crashawe's preface to a text preserved in MS. Royal 17 B. ix: 'Let yoʳ Ma. vouchsafe to take order to gather up & preserve yᵉ antient Manuscripts, & to procure the universityes furnished wᵗʰ such as be wantinge, little cost will do it.'

[4] See Wallis (1963), p.34, n. 28 for suggestions as to how Cosin may have come by the manuscript.

cannot be exactly determined: he describes himself as 'preacher at ye Temple', a position which he held from 1605 to 1613.

The material that follows the dedicatory epistle consists of a quire of eight parchment leaves, the last blank, interleaved and surrounded by paper leaves.[1] On the paper leaves is written a modernized paraphrase of the text on the parchment; this modernization is not in Crashawe's hand but in another of the same period. Crashawe himself annotated the margins of the parchment with side-notes drawing attention to the most important material and commenting on the enormity of the papal pretensions. The modernization is only a partial translation, the orthography of the medieval text being altered, but little of the vocabulary; from various deletions it is clear that the transcriber did not always immediately understand the words he was copying, but this, in the case of some unusual words, is hardly surprising.[2] As has been said, Crashawe's dating of the original hand was incorrect: the contents confirm the evidence of the handwriting that the manuscript was written about or slightly before the year 1400.

The contents of the medieval quire are unusual and interesting. They form a dialogue between a knight and a clerk, the latter, by his own confession, a doctor of canon law who had spent some time in office at the court of Rome: 'I am a doctor of decreeze and haue dwellid longe tyme in þe courte of Rome and bene in office wiþ þe pope.'[3] No indication of the knight's identity is given, nor of his office beyond the fact that he is 'a kniȝt of þe kinges of Yngeland'. The subject of discussion, as Crashawe noted, is that of dominion: what are the bounds of secular lordship and what is the province of papal authority? where the two interests clash, which should be regarded as paramount? how far should the temporalities of the church come under royal command? The opinions voiced by the disputants are those that would be expected from their professions, and it is clear throughout that the author's sympathy is with the knight. The impartiality of the clerk is impugned from the start, as the knight complains that he would rather have a master of theology than of canon law as opponent:

I had hopid þat þou haddest bene a maistere o diuinite, connynge of Goddes

---

[1] The manuscript is bound in parchment; the quiring is as follows: i paper flyleaf (conjugate with pastedown), 1⁴ paper, 2¹⁸, 3² paper, i paper flyleaf (conjugate with pastedown). In the large central quire, leaves 1, 3, 5, 7, 9, 10, 12, 14, 16, and 18 are paper, leaves 2, 4, 6, 8, 11, 13, 15, and 17 parchment.

[2] He had difficulty with *benym* f. 10, *vndernymmynge* f. 17, and, more understandably, with *auentisid* f. 10ᵛ.

[3] F. 6. Modern punctuation and capitalization have been added to all Middle English quotations; abbreviations have been expanded without notice. Despite the similarity of title, the work owes nothing to the *Disputatio inter clericum et militem super potestate prelatis ecclesiæ atque principibus terrarum* attributed to Occam (London, ?1531).

lawe, for þan þou woldist haue said þe soþe and bene noȝt so fauorabil to þe pope as I suppose þou wolt be now, for þou art a doctor of his lawe.[1]

At the end the clerk loses his temper and the knight concludes with biblical evidence in favour of the purely spiritual authority of the pope: the clerk quotes the passage from Luke 22: 38 concerning Peter's two swords, interpreted as 'þe swerde of temperalte and þe swerde of spiritu-alte'; the knight retorts with Christ's order to Peter to sheathe his sword (Matthew 26: 52) 'in token þat þe temperale swerde langid noȝt to him'.[2] From the opinions expressed by the knight, it is clear that the author of the dialogue was a Wycliffite, though no mention is made of some of the more extreme views of Wyclif himself (such as those on the Eucharist or on the church as 'congregatio omnium predestinatorum') or of his later followers. The date of composition is difficult to establish in view of the absence of clear contemporary reference; the argument is on the level of political theory and the social criticism is general rather than specific. The pope is always spoken of in the singular, but it is difficult to suppose that the dialogue can have been written before the Schism began in 1378. The papal court is always described as *þe courte of Rome*, but this, like the last point, is probably only indication of the theoretical nature of the argument rather than of a precise location. This is borne out by the fact that these two points, a single pope and the court at Rome, are contradictory: the return of the papal court from exile in Avignon was followed almost immediately by the death of Gregory XI and the outbreak of the Schism. It seems fairly clear, however, that the debate was written before the prohibition of vernacular Bibles in 1408. The knight reproaches his opponent for clerical ignorance of biblical teaching 'moni of ȝow con litel of Goddes lawe ne of þe popes lawe neiþer; and þerfor ȝe wold þat borell clerkes couþ no more þan ȝe' (f. 17). The clerk, like the knight, quotes scripture to his own advantage, but he neither shows surprise at the knight's knowledge of the Bible nor expresses any doubts about the knight's orthodoxy such as might have been expected had the latter's extensive quotation laid him open of itself to the charge of heresy.

The form of the tract, a debate in dialogue, is not unusual in Lollard literature. None of the texts printed so far are in this form, though some,

---

[1] For Wyclif's own views of canon law see, for instance, *De Officio Regis* (ed. A. W. Pollard and C. Sayle, Wyclif Society, 1887), p. 222, and *De Veritate Sacrae Scripturae* (ed. R. Buddensieg, Wyclif Society, 1905–7), i. 383, 400 ff. Criticism by his followers may be found frequently in the sermons printed by T. Arnold, *Select English Works of John Wyclif* (Oxford, 1869–71), for instance, ii. 71/22, 172/18; iii. 327/26.

[2] The biblical quotations are not in the translation of either Early or Late Version of the Wycliffite Bible. This is not to be interpreted as evidence against Lollard authorship, since the undoubtedly Wycliffite sermons printed by Arnold equally do not use either version in their scriptural quotations.

with their regular alternation of the views of the orthodox church followed
by the objections of 'true men', resemble the type.[1] But at least three
other dialogues survive in manuscript, one between a secular priest and
a friar in Trinity College Dublin C. 3. 12 (ff. 212ᵛ–219), a second between
Reson and *Gabbyng* in Trinity College Dublin C. 5. 6 (ff. 154ᵛ–161), and
a third between *Jon* and *Richerd* in Trinity College Cambridge B. 14. 50
(ff. 35–55ᵛ). The first two manuscripts are undoubtedly Lollard compilations, most of whose contents were printed by Arnold or Matthew;[2] the
third contains a Lollard tract on Bible translation, a text against images
and the work that has been called 'Purvey's Sixteen Points'.[3] None of
these three, however, gives the impression of a real argument that is conveyed by the Durham debate. In the *Reson and Gabbyng* dialogue, a free
translation of chapters 1–12 of Wyclif's *Dialogus*, even the elementary
alternation of the two characters often breaks down: *Reson* discourses on
a topic and, though the repetition of his initial with a gap left for the
rubricator to fill in his name confirms the break that the change of subject
indicates, no answer from *Gabbyng* is heard.[4] Further, the translator,
following Wyclif, announces the identity of *Reson* with Christ and *Gabbyng* with the devil at the beginning, but then puts into the former's
mouth statements concerning Christ in the third person. The whole could
easily be rewritten in the form of a tract without dialogue. The central
subject of the dialogue is clerical poverty, but various other topics, such
as resistance to evil prelates and objections to automatic acceptance of
papal bulls, are mentioned. In the dialogue between the priest and the
friar there is a more equal division between the two roles, but again little
interplay between them: the friar sets forward a doctrinal issue, which is
then disputed by the secular, who propounds the Lollard view. Two subjects form the basis of the material: the nature and extent of sin, and,
secondly, the question of begging. The introduction to this debate is
interesting, since it would appear to give evidence that it actually occurred:

Moost worschipfulleste and gentilleste lord duke of Glowcestre, ȝoure seruaunt
sendiþ ȝou disputusun writen þat was bifore ȝow bytwixe a frere and a seculer
ȝoure clerk, preiynge of boþe sidis to chese and apreue þe trewþe (f. 212ᵛ).

---

[1] See, for instance, Arnold, iii. 366–401 [Fifty Heresies and Errors of Friars] and iii.
454–96 [on the Twenty-Five Articles].
[2] See Arnold, III. xiv and, more extensively, F. D. Matthew, *The English Works of
Wyclif Hitherto Unprinted* (E.E.T.S. 74, 1880), pp. vii–viii. For no clear reason, ff. 211–19
of C. 3. 12 and ff. 126–7, 145–64, 218–19 of C. 5. 6 have not been printed; these omissions
do not correspond to any division in the manuscripts' composition nor is there a change
of orthodoxy at these points.
[3] For the manuscript, see M. Deanesly, *The Lollard Bible* (Cambridge, 1920), pp. 284–5,
437–45, 461–7.
[4] For Wyclif's original text see the edition by A. W. Pollard (Wyclif Society, 1886),
pp. 1–25; it was probably written in 1379.

It seems that the Duke of Gloucester in question must be Thomas of Woodstock, younger brother of John of Gaunt, and that the date of composition must therefore be before 1397, the year of his death.[1] *Jon and Richerd* is more unified in its subject than the last two debates, being concerned only with the legitimacy and practice of the mendicants' orders, but the defendant Richerd, obviously a friar, is allowed little speech.[2] Here there is little indication of date within the work, save for a reference to the existence of two popes, necessitating (as one would anyway suppose) a date after 1378. In the Cosin dialogue the clerk's position is fairly fully set out: his position may be easily assailable, but the papal argument is heard and answered. It is perhaps possible that the author had learnt something from the tradition of secular debate literature, which provided him with the idea of an opening passage to set the scene. Here conversation describes the setting, but the argument gains much from the fact that the clerk is allowed to establish his credentials first.

The debate covers the usual arguments advanced by Wyclif and the Lollards against the contemporary power and aspirations of the pope.[3] Many of the points made go back to debate prior to Wyclif but, by the date of the writing of this tract, would be identified by English readers as distinctively Wycliffite: by association and development, many views previously only anti-clerical became outright heresy.[4] The origins of papal authority are discussed, the donation of Constantine and its implications for England reviewed.[5] The clerk advances the opinion that temporalities

---

[1] For strong evidence that British Museum MS. Egerton 617–618, a copy of the Early Version of the Wycliffite Bible, was made for Thomas of Woodstock, see S. L. Fristedt, 'A Weird Manuscript Enigma in the British Museum', *Stockholm Studies in Modern Philology*, N.S. ii (1964), 116–21.

[2] Many of the questions raised are those also objected against the friars in *Jack Upland* (ed. P. L. Heyworth (Oxford, 1968), pp. 54–72); in *Friar Daw's Reply* (same edition, pp. 73–101) are found some of the defences raised by Richerd in this dialogue. The two halves of the dialogue are here separated into independent works.

[3] For a summary of Wyclif's views, of which the Lollard account was a popularization and extension, see G. Leff, *Heresy in the Later Middle Ages* (Manchester, 1967), ii. 516–49. Of the twenty-four propositions of Wyclif condemned at the London Council in 1382 (see *Fasciculi Zizaniorum*, ed. W. W. Shirley (Rolls Series, London, 1858), pp. 277–82), three are expressly concerned with temporalities; all three, and others on the subject of evil-living priests, are reflected in the present dialogue.

[4] For early medieval discussion, see especially W. Ullmann, *Medieval Papalism* (London, 1949), pp. 76–198, and E. H. Kantorowicz, *The King's Two Bodies* (Princeton, 1957), *passim*. The heretical nature of such views in the early fifteenth century is shown by a list of 'Articuli super quibus heretici vel Lollardi debent examinari' found in the Worcester Register of Bishop Thomas Polton (1426–33), pp. 113–15, and partially in MS. Harley 2179, ff. 157^{r-v}.

[5] It was a mark of Wyclif's thought that many of his arguments, both on the papacy and topics such as the Eucharist, were based on historical considerations; for the papacy in connection with England see *De Officio Regis*, pp. 249 ff. Lollard objections to papal pretensions are seen throughout the works printed by Arnold and Matthew (e.g. Arnold iii. 298/17 ff., Matthew 292/3 ff.).

given to the church are inalienable, which the knight counters with the usual Lollard rider that this would mean eventually that the king must become the vassal of the clergy, and with the less common inquiry that, if this is really so, how do clerks buy food?—logically merchants cannot take their money, since this is inalienable, and all money must in the end become holy. The clerk is unwise enough to admit that he is the king's vassal and this opens the way for the knight to demonstrate the duties that follow.[1] Several specifically Lollard views are expressed: the knight defends the deprivation of evil-living clergy, the laity being the judge of the clerk's morality;[2] he likewise implies that the priesthood is dispensable, with his argument that the faith survived in Mary alone between the crucifixion and the resurrection 'and 3it was scho no preste'.[3] There is, however, no indication that the knight wished to press this point to the more extreme Lollard position of desiring the abolition of the clergy. Some parallels are found between the dialogue and another Lollard work of political theory, the *Tractatus de Regibus* preserved in Bodleian MS. Douce 273, which itself has affinities with Wyclif's own *De Officio Regis*.[4] Both texts deal with the question of clerical exemption, and particularly with the problem of foreign priests who hold positions in the English church; both also consider the authority of the king if the clergy should gain control over the greater part of the land in the realm.[5] But the parallels are not extensive or significant. What emerges from a comparison is the skill of the dialogue writer: all the polemical points are made, the authorities cited and interpretations disputed, with a colloquial liveliness. A king subject to the pope 'were . . . no kinge, bot as kinge in a somer game or elles as a kinge paintid on a wall'; the clerk is ignorant of the Bible 'and þerfor 3e wold þat borell clerkes couþ no more þan 3e, for þan mi3t blynde Baiard be þe boldest hors in þe cart'.[6] Such colloquialism is not common in Lollard literature. The fact, furthermore, that the positions of the opponents have not hardened into the acrimonious dialectic of many

---

[1] Cf. Arnold, ii. 88/20 ff., iii. 391/14 ff., 516/2 ff.

[2] For Wyclif's view see, for instance, *De Veritate Sacrae Scripturae*, ii. 247/29 ff.; cf. Arnold iii. 315/8 ff.

[3] The maintenance of belief by the Virgin alone is a commonly mentioned argument; see, for instance, Occam's *Dialogus*, pt. i, bk. ii. 25 (ed. M. Goldast; *Monarchiæ S. Romani Imperii* (Frankfurt, 1612–14), ii. 429). It is not, however, usually employed as here to argue against the necessity of a priesthood.

[4] The text, ff. 37ᵛ–53, follows that printed in Arnold, iii. 455–96 and precedes Arnold, iii. 119–67. MS. Douce 274 was probably originally part of the same manuscript. The *Tractatus* remains to be studied in detail; it is not a straight translation of the *De Officio Regis*, or of parts of that work, but it follows at times the argument of it and the citation of biblical and patristic authorities.

[5] MS. Douce 273, f. 43 and ff. 44–5 respectively. The citations from Cyprian, Augustine, and Gregory in the latter passage are found in *De Officio Regis*, pp. 134–5.

[6] Ff. 17ᵛ and 17 respectively.

Lollard texts is additional evidence for an early date. There are some obvious points of contact between this dialogue and Trevisa's *Dialogus inter militem et clericum*;[1] the same stress is laid on the supremacy of the king in temporal matters, a similar emphasis on the purely spiritual sphere of the church. But the implications are not, in Trevisa's dialogue, carried nearly so far: for instance, the clerk asks (p. 29/14) whether goods once given to the church can ever be alienated, but the knight does not press the eventual ownership of all by the clergy; instead he turns the point to refer to the spiritual gifts of the priesthood conferred by God. Trevisa's dialogue remains within the bounds of orthodoxy, the Cosin debate does not.

The format of the dialogue is as interesting as its form. As has been said, it covers seven leaves of an eight-leaf quire, the last leaf being present but blank. As such it is the sole survivor as yet known of a type of Lollard document that must have been very common: the quaternion. It is regular in episcopal registers to find that, when Lollards were being sought or examined, their books came under scrutiny.[2] Literacy was commoner in the sect than might be thought and books were very highly valued by them, even apparently among the illiterate members. Bishops regularly ordered the searching of a suspect's possessions, and conversely it is clear that the mere ownership of unorthodox writings might be sufficient to bring a person to a charge of heresy.[3] Indeed the author of the *Tractatus de Regibus* goes even further 'trowthe moueþ mony men to speke sentencis in Yngelysche þat þai han gedirid in Latyne, and herfore bene men holden heretikis' (f. 37ᵛ). Many of the Lollard texts formed large volumes, but the episcopal records also mention two other types of document: *quaterni* and *schedulae*. Clearly, as less substantial and less permanent in form, the vast majority of these have by now been lost; many were burnt by the clerical authorities.[4] But we know of a few *schedulae*: the documents nailed

[1] Edited by A. J. Perry (E.E.T.S. 167, 1925); for the possibility of Trevisa's implication in the first stages of the Wycliffite Bible translation see D. C. Fowler, 'John Trevisa and the English Bible', *Modern Philology*, lviii (1960), 81–98, and id., 'New Light on John Trevisa', *Traditio*, xviii (1962), 289–317.

[2] For the period after the Oldcastle rising, see J. A. F. Thomson, *The Later Lollards 1414–1520* (Oxford, 2nd edn. 1967), *passim*. The scrutiny of Wyclif's own writings formed the basis of attacks against him, as is seen from the *Fasciculi Zizaniorum*. Documents from 1388 onwards show the hunt for Lollard books: see *Calendar of Patent Rolls 1385–9* (London, 1900), pp. 427, 430, 448, 468, etc.

[3] See, for instance, the commission recorded in Lincoln Register 15 of Repingdon's Memoranda, dated 5 August 1416 (f. 152ᵛ), to examine 'libros et quaternos omnes et singulos' in the possession of John Bagworth, vicar of Wilsford.

[4] The commission noted above includes the instruction to burn all condemned books and quaternions. A form of abjuration found in Worcester Register Polton, p. 111 and MS. Harley 2179, ff. 157ᵛ–158 includes the guarantee that the suspect has given up 'libros siue quaternos ac rotulos hereses errores siue erronea continentes quos me scripsisse noui et quos penes me habeo'; the penitent also had to promise to reveal any other such books that should subsequently come to his notice.

to the door of St. Paul's by Hereford and Repingdon in 1382 and by Patteshull in 1387 could have been described in this way,[1] and the vernacular version of Wyclif's own confession seems to have circulated in this form.[2] Aston in 1382 refused to accept his condemnation: 'talem scripsit confessionem in Anglico et Latino, et eam in plurimis schedulis fecit distribui per vicos Londoniarum et plateas.'[3] Thomas Ile of Braybrook was said in 1414 to be a common *factor billarum*:[4] the documents he made and distributed were probably *schedulae*. But of the nature of the *quaterni* we are more ignorant. Like the *schedulae*, their contents may have been copied into larger volumes, and equally they may have been bound up with other material of the same format, and so now be unrecognizable from other composite manuscripts. There are cases where the sermons *Vae Octuplex* and *Of Mynystris in the Chirche* form separate quires within larger manuscripts, and the possibility of independent circulation may have dictated this arrangement.[5] But the interest of Crashawe has preserved a single quaternion intact in its original form. Certainly, to judge from this example, the bishops were right to be concerned about these apparently trivial and insubstantial documents: their contents were as dangerous as longer writings and, being cheaper to reproduce, were capable of wider circulation.

[1] See D. Wilkins, *Concilia Magnae Britanniae et Hiberniae* (London, 1737), iii. 165 from the Register of Archbishop Courtenay. For Patteshull see Thomas Walsingham, *Historia Anglicana* (ed. H. T. Riley, Rolls Series, 1863–4), ii. 158–9.

[2] For the text see Henry Knighton, *Chronicon* (ed. J. R. Lumby, Rolls Series, 1889–95), ii. 157–8, 161–2; that the second circulated separately is suggested by its presence out of context in MS. Bodley 647, ff. 63ᵛ–64ᵛ. The manuscript also contains (ff. 70–70ᵛ) the confessions of Hereford, Repingdon, and Aston of 19 June 1382.

[3] *Fasciculi Zizaniorum*, p. 329.

[4] P.R.O. KB 9. 204/1, nos. 130 and 141; the document is a return to the commission of inquiry set up in 1414 after the Oldcastle rising.

[5] The most noticeable case of this is in MS. Pembroke College Cambridge 237 where *Of Mynystris in the Chirche* on ff. 145–153ᵛ forms a separate quire of eight leaves plus an extra leaf added to take in the end.

13

THE EXPURGATION OF A LOLLARD SERMON-CYCLE

AMONGST the thirty manuscripts of the standard Lollard sermon-cycle is one oddity, a handsome manuscript now Bodleian Don. c. 13.[1] The manuscript stands out because it is the only surviving text systematically to remove material from the sermons; at first inspection, it would appear that the expurgation was designed to remove statements offensive to orthodox believers. The Bodleian *Summary Catalogue* describes the sermons as shortened, but does not explain how, or with what purpose, they were so abbreviated; it is the purpose of the present paper to attempt an explanation.

The Lollard sermon-cycle in question, that printed by Arnold in volumes I–II of his *Select English Works of John Wyclif*,[2] consists of 294 sermons, apparently intended for use during a single liturgical year. One sermon is provided for the Epistle and one for the Gospel for each Sunday, 31 for the Commune Sanctorum, 37 for the Proprium Sanctorum (a limited set in accordance with Lollard views on the honour due to saints), and a large set of over a hundred for ferial days. Each sermon is closely attached to the text, the usual method being the exposition of a part of the passage at a time; the texts chosen are in accordance with the Sarum Use. That all were to be used during a single year seems likely from two facts: first, that no two sermons are found on a single text nor, conversely, is any occasion (save for doctrinal reasons in the Proprium Sanctorum) omitted; secondly, the varying arrangement of the sermons in different manuscripts seems to be determined by differing conditions of their use, so that, for instance, the arrangement in three manuscripts where a complete ferial cycle is

[1] See the typescript description in *A Summary Catalogue of Western Manuscripts in the Bodleian Library at Oxford*; also *Friends of the Bodleian Sixth Annual Report 1930–31* (Oxford), pp. 15–16 and plates I and IV. Following the sermons described below, the manuscript contains six poems described by B. D. Brown, 'Religious Lyrics in MS. Don. c. 13', *Bodleian Quarterly Record*, vii (1935), pp. 1–7 and plate 1, and Rolle's *Super Orationem Dominicam*; H. E. Allen, *Writings ascribed to Richard Rolle* (New York and London, 1927) deals with this work pp. 155–7, but, though she knew of the present manuscript (pp. 361–2), she did not realize it contained this work.

[2] Published Oxford, 1869–71; Arnold's list of manuscripts, pp. xvii–xx, can now be amplified by the addition of eleven more. Quotations, unless otherwise stated, are from Arnold's edition; line references (not provided by Arnold) ignore all headings. In quotations from manuscripts, modern punctuation and capitalization are supplied; abbreviations are expanded without notice.

obtained by intercalating Sunday Epistle, Sunday Gospel, and weekday sermons into a single set suggests that the preacher would proceed straight through this set, only having to turn to another part of the manuscript for the Commune and Proprium Sanctorum. The sermons in their normal form are undoubtedly Lollard; their frequent denomination as 'Wyclif's English sermons' is less certainly correct.[1]

The sermon-cycle presented by MS. Don. c. 13, which will be called hereafter Z (its scribe Z), is complete: that is, despite the very considerable cutting of material from individual sermons, no item is entirely omitted. The arrangement of the sermons is basically one paralleled in four other manuscripts: a dominical group, formed by setting the Gospel sermon immediately after the Epistle sermon for each Sunday, then, separately, sermons for the Proprium Sanctorum, the weekday ferial cycle, and, finally, the Commune Sanctorum. The precise arrangement of Z is not found in any other manuscript, the order of the last three sets being different in the four others that have the Sunday Epistle and Gospel sermons mixed. It seems likely that Z may have made his copy from an exemplar in which the five sets were kept separate: this emerges from a peculiar error, subsequently corrected, in the order of sermons following Christmas. Z also includes copies of two sermons so frequently found with this cycle that they seem to be an authorized appendage to it, *Vae Octuplex* and *Of Mynystris in the Chirche*.[2] Palaeographically the manuscript appears to be of the very late fourteenth, or early fifteenth, century; linguistically the dialect shows it to come from the north, more specifically probably from north Yorkshire.[3] It is the only one of the surviving manuscripts of these sermons to show such a northerly dialect.

The interest of Z lies in the fact that the scribe edited his text very severely. Despite the controversial nature of these Lollard sermons, expurgation seems to have occurred only in this case; the omission of ten Commune Sanctorum sermons from Magdalene College Cambridge MS. Pepys 2616, and of short passages from five ferial gospel sermons in Bodleian MS. Douce 321, cannot be regarded as coherent attempts to expurgate the material. From the tradition of the manuscripts as a whole it is clear that the copying was elsewhere scrupulously accurate, care being taken over immaterial wording as well as over the preservation of

[1] For the evidence concerning these statements see my article 'A Lollard Sermon-cycle and its Implications' in *Medium Aevum*, xl (1971), pp. 142-56.

[2] Printed by Arnold ii. 379–89, 393–423; in Z, ff. 68ᵛ–69, 91–3.

[3] Differences in certain letter-forms can be seen between ff. 1–26ᵛᵃ, 68ᵛ–69ᵛ, 162ᵛ–167 on the one hand, and ff. 26ᵛᵃ–68ᵛ, 70–162ᵛ on the other, but it is not certain whether these indicate that two scribes wrote these sections. The dialect, and the treatment of the text, are the same in both.

the writer's intention. It is well known that Lollard 'farcing' of orthodox writings was carried out fairly frequently: Lollard versions of the *Ancrene Riwle*, of Thoresby's *Lay Folks' Catechism*, and of Rolle's English Psalter survive to reveal this process.[1] Less common was the attempt to render Lollard writings innocuous. Partly this was due to an orthodox abhorrence of all things Lollard, which led to the indiscriminate burning of their books and papers rather than to any attempt to make use of what might be advantageous; even more it seems likely to have been the result of a perception that the process was almost impossible, that Lollard writings were so trenchantly and uncompromisingly filled with Wycliffite polemic that expurgation would leave almost nothing. This latter difficulty became very evident to *Z* in his version of *Vae Octuplex*. The sermon in its original form, running to ten printed pages, is a highly detailed indictment of all the faults of late-fourteenth-century prelates and friars. Following the eight denunciations of Matt. xxiii. 13–33, all the traditional anti-mendicant arguments are heard, together with more specifically Wycliffite objections to the friars' teaching on the Eucharist and to the asserted infallibility of the pope. *Z* seems to have started on his copy without realizing its content: he began by simply removing the necessary explanation that Christ's words concerning 'scribes and pharisees' are to be referred to contemporary friars and prelates, but before he had progressed far he seems to have perceived that the only part of the sermon acceptable to him was the biblical text. From the third *vae* on, therefore, he transcribed the text alone, with only the slightest sentence of introduction to each imprecation left from the intervening material.[2]

The nature of this sermon alone is sufficient to show that it is *Z* who is expurgating and not, a theoretically possible hypothesis, that *Z*'s version represents the original into which a Lollard interpolator has added the inflammatory material found in the other manuscripts. The same point emerges from various cases where *Z*'s efforts to avoid statements he did not like have resulted in the production of a nonsensical sentence.[3] This

---

[1] For the first, preserved in Magdalene College Cambridge MS. Pepys 2498, see E. Colledge, '*The Recluse*, A Lollard Interpolated Version of the *Ancren Riwle*', *R.E.S.* xv (1939), pp. 1–15, 129–45; for the second see the edition by T. F. Simmons and H. E. Nolloth (E.E.T.S. 118, 1901), pp. xx–xxvii; for the third D. Everett, 'The Middle English Prose Psalter of Richard Rolle of Hampole', *M.L.R.* xvii (1922), pp. 217–27, 337–50, xviii (1923), pp. 381–93.

[2] Omitted are Arnold ii. 379/2–4, 380/25–381/8, 381/22–383/7, 383/19–384/6, 384/13–18, 384/25–385/5, 385/16–389/11. The text is related to, but not a straight translation of, Wyclif's *Exposicio textus Matthei XXIII* (*Opera Minora*, ed. J. Loserth, Wyclif Society, 1913), pp. 313–53.

[3] To take a single example: Arnold i. 115/24 ff., *Z* includes the matter printed by Arnold 'And riȝt as in Cristis tyme, and after bi hise apostlis, he turnede

occasional failure of sense, which is due not to the usual hazards of scribal copying (dittography, haplography, etc.) but to the process of expurgation itself, suggests that it is the scribe of Z himself who is the expurgator. Were Z merely a copy of an already expurgated text, one would expect the scribe to 'iron out' these infelicities; many are very simple and could have been eradicated without difficulty. They are the sort of infelicities very easy to miss when altering at the same time as copying. There is one further piece of evidence of a more satisfactory kind that establishes the same point. On f. 78ᵛ, referring to sermon 101 for St. Matthias's Day, appears in the scribe's hand a note at the head of the column *de electione pontificis*. The text that follows in Z has nothing that could explain this note. But in the unexpurgated version, the election by lot of Matthias is used as a basis for a condemnation of the contemporary methods of papal election. The note could, therefore, only have been made if Z had in front of him an unexpurgated text.[1]

The interest of the expurgation lies not merely in its occurrence but also in its purpose: what did Z feel to be offensive? This is a complicated question, and it must be admitted that he does not seem to have been wholly consistent. The chief method of expurgation is omission, an omission very carefully done so that only once is a part of the biblical text left out. The loss is inevitable, given Z's views, since in this instance the text is inextricably involved in the exegesis: Z omits the sentence, including paraphrase of 1 Cor. i. 4, 'And þus newe prelatis ȝyven þer þankyngis to men for love of Anticrist, where *apostlis þankiden God in Jesus Crist*, bi whom þei profitiden'.[2] Z was normally very ingenious in eliminating the comment whilst retaining the text; in this he would have been helped by the format of these sermon manuscripts, in which the biblical text of the sermon (but not of other scriptural texts incidentally quoted) is regularly underlined in red. Only rarely did Z alter a sentence or lengthy phrase, though he occasionally substituted one

---

many heþene men to Cristis religioun, so now', then omits 'in tyme of Antecrist', adds 'ben Cristene men maad heþene', leaves out the diatribe against the warring popes, but adds on his own initiative 'as syn of ire and slayng of Cristen men'. The conclusion does not fit the sentence but has plainly been suggested by the original, to Z unacceptable.

[1] Arnold i. 351/28–33; that the note might have been made by Z after scrutiny of an exemplar other than that from which his copy was made seems an unnecessarily complicated hypothesis. Support for the view advanced is found in the marginal addition on f. 108ᵛ: Arnold ii. 74/27–75/2 was first omitted, then realized to be harmless and added.

[2] Arnold ii. 359/21–3 'And thus contemporary prelates render thanks to men because of love for Antichrist, where the apostles thanked God in Jesus Christ, by whom they had profit'.

word for another. One such unusual alteration is the following: the original text read 'And þus þre ordris in Cristis tyme unabliden hem to be of þis rewme, for bi keping of þer ordris þei leften keping of Goddis heestis. And so my3ten boolde men seie to þes ordris þat ben today, for as þer weren in Cristis tyme Essey, Saducey and Pharisey, so þer ben now in oure tyme, freris, chanons and monkis', from which Z removed all contemporary reference 'and þus thre ordres in Cristis tyme vnablid þaim to be of þis reume, Essees, Saducees and Pharisees, for þir thre bi kepyng of þaire ordris lefte kepynge of Goddis biddynges'.[1] The main subject on which Z found his exemplar unacceptable was the whole spectrum of ecclesiastical government and hierarchy, criticism of which fills a very large part of these sermons. Omission in Z is constant, but a fair example might be taken to be his complete excision of the sections concerning the 'four sects' in five successive Sunday Epistle sermons. The Epistle sermons for the fourth and fifth Sundays after Epiphany, for Septuagesima and for Sexagesima contain in their original form detailed indictments of, in order, the pope and his court (the first sect), the monastic orders, the canons, and, as the fourth sect, the mendicants; the sermon for Quinquagesima uses the qualities of charity enumerated by Paul in 1 Cor. xiii as a means of drawing together condemnation of all four. The indictment has no parallel in Wyclif's Latin sermons for these Sundays, though the points made are found elsewhere in his writings. All of these passages in the vernacular sermons Z completely omitted; in the first four cases the omission was simple, entailing the truncation of the conclusion, but in the last, where a detail about the sects follows the citation of each quality, the omission was slighter but none the less comprehensive.[2]

These five sermons sum up in little Z's objections. The original criticism of the papacy, both in theory and in practice, is entirely removed; only a single reference to 'anticristis lawe', that is canon law,

---

[1] Arnold ii. 36/3–8 'And thus in Christ's time three orders cut themselves out of this realm, for, through keeping their own orders, they left the observance of God's commands. And bold men might say the same to these orders that exist today, for as in Christ's time there were Essenes, Saducees and Pharisees, so in our time there are friars, canons and monks'; altered by Z to 'And thus in Christ's time three orders cut themselves out of this realm, Essenes, Saducees and Pharisees, for these three, through keeping their own orders, left the observance of God's commands'. There are a few instances where Z's reading differs from Arnold's print of MS. Bodley 788 because of the inferiority of the latter; see, for instance Arnold, i. 219/1, Z, f. 147ᵛ.

[2] Omissions are in Arnold ii. 253/33–254/31, 257/9–27, 259/29–260/18, 264/10–33; in the last 266/27–30, 36–267/5, 8–11, 15–17, 19–21, 26–9, 32–5, 37–268/5, 9–11, 14–17, 20–1, 269/16–32. For Wyclif's sermons see edition by J. Loserth (Wyclif Society, 1889), pp. 105–44.

remains, presumably by oversight.[1] One of Z's rare alterations involves
the change of a reproach to the popes for pretending 'þat þei ben Cristis
vikers in erþe, and siþ þei ben proud blasfèmes, no man is ferþer fro
þis state' into a warning that 'na man suld feyne þat he war euen to
Cristis manhede'.[2] The condemnation of the prelacy is likewise largely
eliminated, though in a few cases the criticism is allowed to stand with
the minor alteration of *prelates* to *men* or *hie men of haly kirke*.[3] The
rejection of endowment in the original sermons, rejection both of its
abuse, of its historical justification, and of its theory, again largely
disappears; the single passage left is a relatively mild objection to the
dangers inherent in possessions.[4] Criticisms of the clergy are treated
rather more sparingly. The need for reformation amongst the priesthood
remains, together with some attacks on clerical avarice, self-seeking,
worldliness, and lack of adherence to Christ's rule.[5] Z seems to have
sympathized with the Lollard desire for more preaching, though he
carefully eliminated all allusion to the persecution of 'true men' preaching without licence.[6] More surprising is Z's ambiguous position concerning absolution and confession. An early conviction of Wyclif was
that, since God alone could forgive sin, absolution by a priest was valid
only if in agreement with God's prior forgiveness; the view was part
of his wider tenet that 'nullus præscitus est pars ecclesia', a tenet which
was one of Wyclif's earliest questionable propositions. From this
theoretical position, as well as from an abhorrence of the abuses,
indulgences were rejected.[7] Again, the rejection of oral confession was

[1] References are too numerous to be given complete; see, for typical examples,
Arnold i. 225/4 ff., 232/9–14, 247/18 ff.; ii. 60/15 ff.; the single instance left is
Arnold i. 4/35–5/1, Z, f. 42ᵛ.
[2] Arnold ii. 284/34–6 'that they are vicars of Christ on earth, and, since they
are proud blasphemers, no man is further from this position'; Z, f. 28 'no man
should pretend that he might be equal to Christ's humanity'.
[3] For the omissions see, for instance, Arnold i. 220/34–222/13; ii. 89/8–11,
109/14–16; for the alterations ii. 23/5, 105/9. Sometimes the alteration is less
successful, the indefinite *þa* 'those' being substituted for *prelatis* as ii. 159/2,
163/12.
[4] Examples of omission are Arnold i. 199/19–28, 308/10–311/13; the remaining passage is i. 96/16–18.
[5] Retained are Arnold i. 25/31–26/1 on the purging of the temple, but the
end of the sermon, which is concerned with contemporary detail rather than
generality, is omitted; 95/9–11 concerning the preoccupation of the clergy with
benefices, 119/26–34, 387/8–11, ii. 28/29–33, this last claiming the current moral
superiority of laity over clergy.
[6] Arnold ii. 368/20–4 is retained, though with alteration of *prelatis* to *many*;
omitted are i. 139/8–11, 176/5–177/4, 209/5–17, ii. 11/13–16, 166/17–167/9,
172/26–173/1, 18–174/8.
[7] See *Fasciculi Zizaniorum* (ed. W. W. Shirley, Rolls Series, 1858), p. 2; for
Wyclif's own views see his *De Ecclesia* (ed. J. Loserth, Wyclif Society, 1886),

both theoretical, that God alone could know the penitence of the sinner, and practical, that the confessional was used by priests, and especially by the mendicants, for the exercise of undesirable influence.[1] All these points, theoretical and practical, are found in the vernacular sermons. Lollard maintenance of these positions in the fifteenth century is shown from the list of questions to be asked of a suspect, found most fully in the Worcester Register of Bishop Polton (pp. 113–14), where the fourth and fifth matters for inquiry are 'in casu quod homo fuerit contritus si tunc confessio exterior sit sibi vtilis' and 'an sit necessarium ad salutem anime confiteri sacerdoti'. One might expect that, if Z had any sympathy for the Lollard views, he might support the criticism of the abuses whilst disagreeing with the opposition to confessional theory. In fact the position is not so simple as this. He retains a statement that the absolution of a priest without prior absolution by God is invalid, copies some doubts about the value of indulgences and letters of fraternity, and reproduces a rejection of the need for shrift by mouth.[2] On the other hand, some passages concerning these matters are removed. The only difference would appear to lie in the proximity of the objections made to reference to the ecclesiastical hierarchy: if the attack on traditional teaching concerning absolution, indulgences, and confession is not closely associated with a reproach to their instigators, the attack is left; if it is so related, it is removed.[3]

The same principle may lie behind the acceptance of one affirmation of the superior value attached to the Pater Noster as compared with other prayers, but the rejection of other statements concerning the new prayers ordered by the pope. It is possible, however, that the retention of one passage is the result of Z's failure to understand Lollard jargon: he retained a derogatory allusion to the papal indulgence granted for the recital of a prayer between consecration and Agnus Dei in the mass, an allusion that follows the authority of *many men*.[4] The introduction of an

---

pp. 2–6, 12–13, a work dating from 1378, or his later *Trialogus* (ed. G. Lechler, Oxford, 1869), pp. 356–60.

[1] *Trialogus*, p. 372; *De Ordinatione Fratrum* (*Polemical Works*, ed. R. Buddensieg, Wyclif Society, 1883), i. 94; *Cruciata* (*Polemical Works*), ii. 622–5.

[2] His retained statements are Arnold i. 35/2–9; 60/14–19 and ii. 77/4–21, 89/14–17; ii. 87/29–36 and 303/25–6; the last is perhaps the most surprising 'ful charite dose away synnes, al if man schrife him neuer bi mouth': 'complete charity removes sin, even if a man never confess orally'.

[3] See, for instance, the omission of Arnold i. 136/4–18 where the question of absolution is closely interlocked with the conflicting claims of the two popes to this faculty, or i. 380/28–381/34 where letters of fraternity inevitably involve the claims of 'the orders'.

[4] Arnold i. 354/19–25; omitted are ii. 213/9–22, 24–37, 301/4–15, 302/8–19, 303/1–13.

opinion by the subject *many men* or *true men* is a regular indication in these sermons that a Lollard view is in question. *Z* occasionally seems to have taken such an introduction at its face value. Similarly, though the usage is less regular, *prelates* is generally a term of abuse, the neutral word being *bishops*. The two can be seen together in one sentence that *Z* omitted 'And here þenken many men, þat fro þis state was turned to pryde, þei ben clepid prelatis, and born above by wynde of pryde'.[1]

The matter which most seems to have concerned the expurgator was the question of the new orders. The term is used somewhat loosely by the original writer: it can cover monastic, mendicant, and canonical orders, though predominately the second alone is meant.[2] A contrast is regularly made between Christ's order and new orders, between Christ's sect and new sects. The unexpurgated sermons contain unbridled condemnation of every aspect of the friars: their claims for their orders, their asserted biblical justification for begging, their exemption from diocesan jurisdiction, their privileges in preaching and confession, as well as the abuses of their position. The Wycliffite stress on the Bible here emerges, both in the criticism of the mendicants' claim that Christ sanctioned begging, and in the wider objection to orders 'ungrounded' (to use a favourite Lollard term) in scripture.[3] Almost all of these strictures are eliminated by *Z*, or are so altered as to remove their force; in particular, all save one of the objections to the original founding ideas of the friars have disappeared. Even the one remaining passage is so altered as to become innocuous: the original read 'and þus þes newe ordris ech on, which ben so lef to lye, muten nedis be groundid in þe fend, þe which is fadir of lesingis', but *Z* has altered the subject to *þa* 'those men'.[4] A very few of the reproaches to the current abuses of mendicancy remain. The most interesting are the minor alterations: *freris* is altered to the vaguer *brither*, *ordris* to *ydil men*, objections to *coventis* 'convents' to the same objections to *couetise* 'avarice'; the phrase

---

[1] Arnold ii. 247/27–9 'And on this matter many men think that, since this rank was turned to pride, they have been called prelates and have become inflated by the wind of pride'.

[2] Arnold ii. 52/19–25 (omitted by Z) must, from its reference to enclosing 'men quyk in stoones', be taken to mean the monastic orders; ii. 260/3–4 is declaredly the canons.

[3] Arnold i. 20/22, 178/19–28, 223/30–2, all omitted by Z. Mendicancy is the commonest subject in many Lollard writings: as well as the material printed by Arnold in volume III (1871) and F. D. Matthew, *The English Works of Wyclif hitherto unprinted* (E.E.T.S. 74, 1880), there are unprinted tracts in C.U.L. Dd. 14. 30 (pt. II), Trinity College Cambridge B. 14. 50, ff. 35–55ᵛ, and B.M. Add. 24202, ff. 37–60ᵛ.

[4] Arnold ii. 298/22–4 'And thus each of these new orders, which so delight in lies, must of necessity be founded in the devil, who is the father of lies'.

dowing aȝens his lawe 'endowing against Christ's law' is robbed of its sting by the alteration of the first word to *doynge* 'doing'. The Vulgate *sectae* of Gal. v. 20, translated *sectis* in the original sermons and referred to 'the four sects', becomes *newe maner of doyngis* and the comment is omitted.[1]

The most interesting matter, and the one which affords some insight into *Z*'s own views, is the Eucharist. Wyclif's assertions on the Eucharist were the turning-point in his career, assertions which pushed the growing opposition into public condemnation. Wyclif was here challenging doctrine, as opposed to criticizing the actuality of church government or questioning received theory; he also in this challenge pushed further his earlier claim 'quod nullus existens in peccato mortali est dominus, sacerdos, vel episcopus' to undermine the one undisputed clerical faculty.[2] The Lollards went further than Wyclif ever finally committed himself: some denied the Real Presence, some explicitly denied the need of a priesthood.[3] The unexpurgated sermons of the present cycle do not reflect these more extreme views. They assert Wyclif's opinion that material bread remains after the consecration, and that Christ's words of institution are to be understood figurally only; they repeatedly attack the Occamist opinion that the accidents of bread remain, whilst its substance is annihilated. The usual proof-texts, from the Bible, Ambrose, Augustine, and Jerome, are adduced.[4] But there is no denial of the Real Presence nor, more surprisingly in view of the attack on the entire clergy and clerical hierarchy, is any doubt expressed about the necessity of the priest for the celebration of the Eucharist. Wyclif's views on the Eucharist were opposed almost immediately, and in the succeeding persecution of the Lollards this matter remained the central question.[5] The first inquiry in the Worcester list mentioned above (p. 457) is 'an post consecracionem sit in altari verum corpus Christi et non substancia panis materialis neque vini'; the second

[1] See Arnold i. 57/23–9, ii. 47/24–8 for the retentions; for the mentioned alterations ii. 43/24–6, 80/4, i. 347/10, ii. 36/32; for the changed translation of the biblical text ii. 349/35–350/3.

[2] For the progress of the opposition to Wyclif see particularly *Fasciculi Zizaniorum*, pp. 104–317; see also G. Leff, *Heresy in the Later Middle Ages* (Manchester, 1967), ii, pp. 549–57 and references there given.

[3] See J. A. F. Thomson, *The Later Lollards 1414–1520* (Oxford, 2nd ed., 1967), pp. 246–7; for Wyclif's views see *De Eucharistia* (ed. J. Loserth, Wyclif Society, 1892), pp. 112–15.

[4] See Arnold i. 133/3–134/12, ii. 82/1–25, 112/5–31, 169/11–170/19; for citation of Ambrose i. 125/12, 379/1, ii. 91/14, 386/30, of Augustine i. 125/14, 133/13, ii. 82/17, 135/4, 386/27, of Jerome ii. 386/24.

[5] For evidence of some delay in opposition to Wyclif see G. A. Benrath, *Wyclifs Bibelkommentar* (Berlin, 1966), pp. 266–71.

bears this out 'si sacerdos habeat potestatem conficiendi corpus Christi'. The accounts of the examinations of Hereford, Repingdon, and Aston, and later of the trials of Richard Wyche, William Thorpe, and Oldcastle himself, show the care with which the authorities endeavoured to obtain an unequivocal confession from the suspects.[1] Many statements were orthodox so far as they went, but were not accepted because they made no explicit denial of the existence of material bread after consecration. On the Lollard side, the collection of proof-texts continued: lists of passages asserted to be favourable to their views are found in several Lollard manuscripts.[2]

Here then is a matter on which the authorities and the sermons under discussion are perfectly clear and categorically opposed. If Z's aim was orthodoxy, all references to the Eucharist should have been expunged or altered to the received view. It is clear, however, that Z did nothing of the sort. The Wycliffite view is several times asserted: for instance 'þe bred of þe sacrid hooste is verre bred in his kynde and is eten bodily, bot it is Goddis body in figure', or again 'þis ooste is bred in his kinde, as er oþer oostis vnsacrid, and sacramentaly Goddis body, for Crist sais sa þat may not lie'.[3] Some statements of the Lollard opinion have been removed, but in every case this is because they occur in close juxtaposition to a criticism of the friars. Inevitably, it is usually the mendicant view of the Eucharist that is in question, but it seems clear that this is incidental to Z's omission. He included condemnation of the view that the bread after the consecration is accident without subject; only where this is explicitly associated with a reference to the erroneous views of the friars was it removed. Thus an unequivocal denial of the Occamist view is included 'And þus þe hooste of þe auter is verra bred to many wittis; it is bred made of whete and als it is Goddis body; and sa it groundis bileue and is an obiect of vertues. Bot fle we to calle þis bred accident

---

[1] For the first three see *Fasciculi Zizaniorum*, pp. 289–333, and the entries in A. B. Emden, *A Biographical Register of the University of Oxford to A.D. 1500* (Oxford, 1957–9); for Wyche *FZ*, pp. 501–5 and F. D. Matthew, 'The Trial of Richard Wyche', *E.H.R.* v (1890), pp. 530–44; for Thorpe the account in Vienna Nationalbibliothek MS. 3936, ff. 1–22ᵛ; for Oldcastle *FZ*, pp. 433–50.

[2] For instance C.U.L., Ff. 6. 31, ff. 27ᵛ–35ᵛ, Trinity College Dublin C. 5. 6, ff. 145–6ᵛ; also *An Apology for Lollard Doctrines* (ed. J. H. Todd, Camden Society, 1842), pp. 45–8. Many are quoted by Wyclif in *De Eucharistia* and *De Apostasia* (ed. M. H. Dziewicki, Wyclif Society, 1889), and were derived from the list in canon law: see E. Friedberg, *Corpus Iuris Canonici* (Leipzig, 1879–81), i, cols. 1325–51.

[3] Arnold ii. 112/17–18 (Z, f. 116ᵛ) 'the bread of the consecrated host is true bread in its nature and it is eaten physically, but in symbol it is God's body'; ii. 169/28–170/2 (Z, f. 129) 'this host is bread in its nature, as are other unconsecrated hosts, and sacramentally it is God's body, for Christ, who cannot lie, says so'.

wiþouten suget'.¹ On the other hand, in another sermon, having quoted, with the usual Wycliffite gloss, Ambrose 'shewand comune speche of Crist, þat þe sacrid ooste is not brede for it is not principaly brede', Z then omitted the ensuing comment 'And such error blindiþ many, in þe sacrament of þe auter, to seie þat it is an accident wiþouten suget, and no breed, as Ambrose seiþ . . . But þis is ful of eresie, as falshede in which it is groundid. And defaute of undirstonding þat shulde be of Goddis lawe and of þis doctour, Ambrose, blyndiþ here þes eretikis'.² The only possible explanation of this difference of treatment would seem to lie in the implicit reference to the friars as heretics in the second but not in the first. In one case Z's retention cannot, however, be explained in this way, since open condemnation of the friars is found 'for it was noȝt trowid bifore þe fende was losid, þat þis worthi sacrament was accident wiþouten subiecte. And ȝit dwellis trew men in þe alde bileue, and latis freris foule þaym self in þair newe herisie';³ even if Z did not understand the reference to *trew men*, the final clause is explicit enough.

What then was the standpoint of the expurgator? Clearly he was heretical and not merely radical: his views on the Eucharist, frequently stated, are sufficient to establish that. The contrast between Z's expurgated sermons and the Middle English text known as *Dives and Pauper* is instructive here: *Dives and Pauper* is a dialogue, the opponents declaredly taking their names but not their opinions from the parable. The questions of Dives are designed to investigate every aspect of ecclesiastical and liturgical practice; the answers of Pauper show astringent criticism of many abuses, clerical and popular. But, whilst the condemnation of practice is almost as far-reaching as that in the unexpurgated sermons, there is no challenge to received doctrine; the teaching on the mass is entirely orthodox.⁴ It is practice not theory that is

¹ Arnold ii. 82/3-6 (Z, ff. 109ᵛ-110) 'And thus the host of the altar is true bread to many senses; it is bread made of wheat and also it is God's body; and so it establishes faith and is an object of virtues. But we must avoid calling this bread accident without subject'.

² Arnold i. 379/1-10 (Z, f. 84) 'showing forth the common speech of Christ that the sacred host is not bread because it is not principally bread . . . and such error concerning the sacrament of the altar misleads many into saying that it is an accident without subject, and not bread as Ambrose says . . . But this is completely heretical, as is the falsehood in which it is based. And the lack of due comprehension of God's law and of this doctor Ambrose blinds these heretics in this matter'. For the Wycliffite gloss, see the appendix below.

³ Arnold i. 133/15-18 (Z, f. 30) 'For it was not believed before the devil was let loose that this worthy sacrament was accident without subject. And yet true men (i.e. Lollards) keep to the old faith, and leave friars to foul themselves in their new heresy'.

⁴ The text exists in several manuscripts, whose relations have not yet been studied, and seems from internal evidence to date from between 1405 and 1410.

under attack; in the former the author is radical, and probably learned some of his arguments from the Lollards, but in the latter he is utterly traditional. Indeed, like the writings of Pecock, but without running into that author's own heterodoxy, the tract was probably designed as an anti-Lollard work. Also heretical in *Z*'s versions of the sermons is the teaching about confession and absolution. Complete consistency of treatment is not found, but sufficient remains to show that *Z* sympathized with Lollard opinions. As a rider to these views is found also condemnation of the sale of indulgences and of the papal use of excommunication. On the other hand, *Z* plainly did not agree with the original wholesale condemnation of the clergy, including the papacy, and was particularly anxious to expunge most criticism of the mendicant orders. Was *Z* then a friar? There seems little in the text itself to make this unlikely. The relatively small amount of anti-mendicant material that remains is not incompatible with such an explanation: *Z* gives away his own position when he adds the words *il leuand* 'ill-living' before *freris* in a stricture on begging.[1]

Historically there are more difficulties in this view. Originally the mendicants, or some of their members, sympathized with Wyclif's views; as late as the *De Apostasia* Wyclif still wrote of the friars 'confido de bonis sociis, qui michi confidenter in causa dei astiterant'.[2] But the preaching of his views on transubstantiation seems to have alienated the friars to such an extent that it was they who took the lead in the condemnation that followed: Tissyngton, Stokes, Wynterton, Woodford, and later Netter were all friars.[3] Wyclif's own last writings increasingly identified the forces of Antichrist with the mendicant orders; in these there is no exception made to the condemnation of the 'private sects' in theory as well as practice.[4] A few later mendicant adherents are known. Peter Patteshull, an Augustinian friar, preached in 1387 against the evils of the mendicant orders and, with the aid of a crowd

I have used MS. Douce 295; the mass is dealt with ff. 118ᵛ–119, 172ᵛ–173. That the text was orthodox (despite an accusation recorded against its possession in Westminster Cathedral MS. B. 2. 8, an audience court-book of 1429/30 for the Norwich diocese) is seen from its printing by Pynson in 1493 and de Worde in 1496.　　　　　　　　　　　　　　　　[1] Arnold ii. 47/26 (Z, f. 102ᵛ).

[2] *De Apostasia*, p. 42. For Wyclif's relations with the friars see particularly A. Gwynn, *The English Austin Friars in the Time of Wyclif* (London, 1940), pp. 211–79.

[3] Accepting Wyclif's own statement that he was condemned by seven votes to five on Chancellor Barton's inquiry (*De Blasphemia* (ed. M. H. Dziewicki, Wyclif Society, 1893), p. 89), it is usually assumed that six of the seven were the mendicants on the commission (*FZ*, pp. 112–13).

[4] *De Blasphemia*, pp. 201–71; *Opus Evangelicum* (ed. J. Loserth, Wyclif Society, 1895–6), ii. 36–9; *Trialogus*, pp. 433–47.

described by Thomas Walsingham as Lollards, affixed a schedule of their crimes to the door of St. Paul's cathedral.[1] An apostate Carmelite, Nicholas Weston, was involved in the Lollard group at Northampton in 1393, but nothing is known of his views apart from that of the group.[2] In 1426 Thomas Richmond, a Franciscan of York, was examined by Archbishop Kempe on certain errors; some show Lollard ancestry.[3] But it is noteworthy that in none of these cases is the Eucharist mentioned, whilst the first two cases do involve anti-mendicant arguments. One manuscript of the unexpurgated sermons, British Museum Royal 18 B. ix, belonged in the fifteenth century to a Dominican friar, Thomas Dekyn, from Dunstable. This, however, is almost certainly an irrelevant coincidence. Since Dekyn copied his preaching licence into the volume, it is very unlikely that he had sympathy with Lollard views, which included outspoken opposition to such licences and the need of obtaining them.

Finally, then, the expurgation remains something of an enigma. It must have been done after 1383, since the unaltered sermons contain references to Spencer's crusade of that year; allusions to persecutions of heretics make a date after 1390 more probable.[4] On palaeographic and historical grounds a date before Oldcastle's rising in 1414 is likely. The chief heresy is the eucharistic one; the anti-clerical material is reduced and, in any case, less exclusively Wycliffite. The main problem remains the purpose of the expurgation. Concealment cannot be in question, as the later annotator who added *caue* in many margins perceived. That there were Lollards who denied transubstantiation whilst tolerating the private sects is difficult to establish from the records: certainly, trials of Lollards sometimes only mention the eucharistic heresy, but this is probably because this single error was sufficient for condemnation and implied the holding of other Lollard tenets. Nor can the motive have been a desire to render useful in the orthodox church the wheat of the vernacular sermons, whilst discarding the heterodox chaff (a motive similar to that which led to the Lollard version of the *Ancrene Riwle*, in its original form so alien to Lollard views about private religion); not only does heterodox chaff remain, but in some cases the elimination of anti-clerical material leaves little beyond

[1] Thomas Walsingham, *Historia Anglicana* (ed. H. T. Riley, Rolls Series, 1863–4), ii. 157–9.

[2] See Register Buckingham (Lincoln) 12, ff. 398, 406 and the text printed by E. Powell and G. M. Trevelyan, *The Peasqnts' Rising and the Lollards* (London, 1899), pp. 45–50; also K. B. McFarlane, *John Wycliffe and the Beginnings of English Nonconformity* (London, 1952), pp. 141–4.

[3] Register Kempe (York), ff. 314ᵛ–319ᵛ.

[4] Arnold i. 115/28, 136/20, ii. 314/6–8; i. 209/5–9.

a simple translation of the biblical text.[1] It seems that the existence of yet another eclectic variant in the broad spectrum of Lollard opinion must be admitted.

APPENDIX

Wyclif's gloss on Ambrose

The vernacular gloss on Ambrose, quoted above, p. 211, is an often repeated one in Wycliffite writings and one which goes back to Wyclif himself. The fullest treatment is in the late *Opus Evangelicum*, ii. 163/21 ff.

> Et quantum ad obiectus doctorum, patet quod oportet catholicos secundum quod docet fides scripture et racio glosas suis sermonibus applicare, ut Ambrosius videtur dicere quod non manet panis post consecracionem sed solummodo corpus Christi. Cuius verba sic sane possunt intelligi quod illa hostia non manet principaliter panis post consecracionem sed sic solummodo corpus Christi; et sic potest iste sanctus sane intelligi et cum hoc salvari fides scripture Apostoli et dictum Augustini dicentis quod ille panis cotidianus est hostia consecrata.

The passage in question from Ambrose is *De Sacramentis*, IV. iv. 14 (ed. O. Faller, *Sancti Ambrosii Opera, VII* (*C.S.E.L.*, 1955), pp. 51–2) 'Tu forte dicis: "Meus panis est usitatus." Sed panis iste panis est ante verba sacramentorum; ubi accesserit consecratio, de pane fit caro Christi'; it is cited by Gratian, Pt. iii; Dist. II. c. 55 and by Peter Lombard in book IV of the *Sentences* (*P.L.* 192. 861) and, therefore, regularly appears in discussions of the Eucharist. Wyclif's gloss on the passage, implied in his *Confessio* (*FZ*, p. 127) and used in *De Eucharistia* (pp. 151–2, 154, 226) and *De Apostasia* (pp. 53, 64, 160, etc.), seems, however, without antecedent. His opponent Thomas Wynterton attacked the interpretation (*FZ*, p. 220); later Netter criticized Wyclif's reading of Ambrose more fully in his *Doctrinale* (ed. Venice, 1571), ii, f. 82ᵛ. Netter regarded Wyclif's chief teacher, as far as his Eucharistic errors were concerned, to have been Berengar: 'Berengarius, magnus magister' (f. 9ᵛ); Woodford in his *Quæstiones LXXII de Sacramento Altaris* (MS. Bodley 703, ff. 128, 140) lends support to this idea. But this charge cannot be accepted without two reservations: first, that Wyclif stated himself to be in agreement with the condemnation embodied in the confession *Ego Berengarius* of 1059 (*De Apostasia*, p. 68/4; *Trialogus*, p. 249/26), even if his interpretation of that condemnation departed

---

[1] Within the main liturgical set, almost nothing remains, for example, of the sermon for the fourth Friday in Advent by the excision of Arnold ii. 14/10–24, 15/4–6, 9, 13 to end.

from its intention; second, that there seems no evidence that Wyclif
had access to any of Berengar's writings at first hand. He knew the
confession from Gratian (Pt. iii, Dist. II. c. 42), and glosses on it (*De
Eucharistia*, p. 225/9 ff.), which he regarded as sophistical. He also had
seen the account of Berengar's career in Higden's *Polychronicon* (*De
Eucharistia*, p. 107/5 ff.). More importantly, he refers to Lanfranc's
Liber de Corpore et Sanguine Domini (*De Eucharistia*, p. 283/19 ff.), in
which are included long quotations from Berengar's lost first work on
the subject (*P.L.* 150. 407–42). But it is unlikely that Wyclif knew
Berengar's second work, *De Sacra Coena*; only a single manuscript is
now known, and it must have been rare even in the fourteenth century.
Berengar in this work deals at length with Ambrose's *De Sacramentis*
(ed. W. H. Beekenkamp (The Hague, 1941), pp. 68–73, 97–8, 114–15,
etc.), but, though using Ambrose for a similar purpose, namely to urge
the remanence of bread after the words of consecration, Berengar's
arguments are rather different from those of Wyclif. Berengar's analysis
might be described as 'grammatical' (see p. 114 for instance), whereas
Wyclif was more concerned with Ambrose's intention in the whole of
book IV (see *Opus Evangelicum*, i. 290/14 ff.). Whether or not Wyclif
learnt any of his Eucharistic thought from Berengar, he certainly did not
acquire this gloss from that source. The gloss continues to appear in the
vernacular writings, in the sermons dealt with in the foregoing article,
in tracts that include a discussion of the Eucharist, and in the lists of
Eucharistic proof-texts. These last draw much of their material from
canon law, as is shown from the marginal references, but add material
such as this which derives from Wyclif's Latin writings: examples are
found in Trinity College Dublin C. 5. 6, ff. 145–6ᵛ, and Cambridge
Univ. Libr. Ff. 6.31, ff. 27ᵛ–35ᵛ.

Attendite
a falsis pro-
phetis qui
venuit ad uos in vesti-
mentis ouiū: intrinse-
cus aūt sūt lupi rapaces
Crist in mathewes
gospel spekiþ þese wor-
dis mathew þe seuēþe
chaptur and beþ þus
myche to seie bey war
of false profetis þat co-
men to ȝou in cloþiṅg of
scheep...þynne forsoþe
þei ben rauysschiṅge wol-
ues for many false pro-
fetis schullē rise seiþ crist
in þe gospel · and many þer
schullen disceyue, and
poul seiþ þ þei schullen
be in multitude þat
greuose to þe peple, and

petur in his pistil seiþ on
þis wise sovely þer werē
false profetis in þe pe-
ple : as ī þer schullen be
in ȝou maistris heritis þe
whiche schullen lede in
sectis of perdiciou · bi þe
whiche þe were of trewþe
schal be blasfemed be seiþ
and in auarice wiþ fey-
ned wordis þei schul chaffare of ȝou · bi þe fruytis
of hem crist seiþ þ men
schul knowe hem · up on
þe texte of þis gospel of
matheu seiþ þe gret clerk
origene, þei þat were false profetis first in fude·
þe trewe profetis of cri...
to ... þei pursuetē· as
ierome ... myþee ... ma-
ny mo oþir, þus þese
false profetis now we seiþ
and false cristen mē pur

London, British Library MS Harley 1203, f. 64r. Lollard tract on Matthew 7. 15.

14

OBSERVATIONS ON A NORTHERNER'S VOCABULARY

In the investigation of Middle English dialects the field of vocabulary has been a neglected area. Whilst much has been done on phonology and morphology and, more recently, on orthography, relatively little has been published on dialect lexicography. The basic study, to which reference is always made, is still that published in 1937 by Rolf Kaiser.[1] It is clear that in the course of the dialect survey that has been under way in Edinburgh for the last twenty-five years a lot of material on vocabulary must have been assembled, but it has not yet been published; indeed, it is easy to see that the presentation of lexical material will be difficult to present in survey form.[2] The slow publication of the *Middle English Dictionary* has provided potentially a lot of evidence, but, as will emerge from the comments that follow, a dictionary is only a rough tool for the purposes of dialect lexis.[3]

Kaiser took as his starting point the manuscripts of the *Cursor Mundi* which Morris had printed in the Early English Text Society edition.[4] It is difficult to challenge the theory that led to this decision: if a true comparison between dialects is to be made, there must be no chance that the discrepancies in vocabulary between two texts could be explicable on the basis of their differing interests. The easiest way to exclude factors of subject matter, register or audience is to use a single text, whose original provenance is known, and a derivative copy in another dialect. But, as Kaiser recognized,[5] and as is evident to anyone who checks

[1] R. Kaiser, *Zur Geographie des mittelenglischen Wortschatzes*, Palaestra 205 (Leipzig, 1937).
[2] I am indebted for information to Professor Angus McIntosh and, particularly in recent years, to Dr Michael Benskin. Some comments on dialect lexicography may be found in the publications of the Edinburgh group, such as A. McIntosh, 'A New Approach to Middle English Dialectology', *English Studies* xliv (1963), 1-11; 'Some Words in the *Northern Homily Collection*', *Neophilologische Mitteilungen* lxxiii (1972), 196-208; 'Word Geography in the lexicography of medieval English', *Annals of the New York Academy of Sciences* ccxi (1973), 55-66; 'Middle English Word-Geography: its Potential Role in the Study of the Long-Term Impact of the Scandinavian Settlements upon English', *Acta Universitatis Upsaliensis* (Symposium Universitatis Upsaliensis annum quingentesimum celebrantis) 8 *The Vikings*, ed. T. Andersson and K. I. Sandred (1977), 124-30; M. L. Samuels, 'Some Applications of Middle English Dialectology', *English Studies* xliv (1963), 81-94; *Linguistic Evolution* (Cambridge, 1972).
[3] The last fascicule of *MED* to be available to me in writing this paper was 0.1.
[4] *Cursor Mundi*, ed. R. Morris (EETS O.S. 57, 59, 62, 66, 68, 99, 101, 1874-93); the glossary was made by Max Kaluza. The manuscripts chiefly in question are BL Cotton Vespasian A. iii (C), Göttingen theol. 107 (G), Bodleian Fairfax 14 (F), and Trinity College Cambridge R. 3.8 (T).
[5] Kaiser 14-16.

up from Morris's glossary a dozen relevant words in the Vespasian and Göttingen texts, the main 'northern' manuscripts, and the Trinity text, the main 'Midland' manuscript, there is a dilemma concerning the use of verse for this purpose. The advantage of verse is that the original dialect can the more readily be established by rhyme and metre; but there is the compensating disadvantage that a scribe may retain forms, phonological, morphological or lexical, in rhyme that he would naturally himself replace. It may be true that these retained forms reveal the extent of his tolerance, that they imply that the scribe understood them and thought his readers would do the same; but this is to assume that a scribe is never lazy, never takes the easiest way out.[6] There are a number of cases where Trinity retains in rhyme words that he elsewhere replaces: thus 7556 and 12086 *flite* : *despite*, 15804 *flite* : *wite* in agreement with the northern texts, but 6681 Trinity *chide* but northern manuscripts *flites* within the line.[7]

Translation from northern dialects into southern or Midland versions is a familiar phenomenon in Middle English, found in the *Cursor Mundi*, in the *Pricke of Conscience* and in versions of Rolle's writings, to name only the best known.[8] The reverse situation, the translation of southern or Midland texts into northern English, is much less common. Presumably the spread of the standard language in the fifteenth century made northerners more tolerant of a written form of English discrepant from their own, whilst southerners shared Higden's objection to the rude sounds of the northern dialect.[9] However, amongst the manuscripts of the standard Lollard sermon-cycle is one text, now Bodleian MS Don. c. 13 (Z), which presents a rare case of such translation as the text moved northwards.[10]

6 For some discussion of the problems of translation see my own paper 'Tradition and Innovation in some Middle English Manuscripts', *RES* n.s. xvii (1966), 359-72; P. J. Lucas, 'A Fifteenth-Century Copyist at Work under Authorial Scrutiny: An Incident from John Capgrave's Scriptorium', *Studies in Bibliography* xxxiv (1981), 66-95 and, most importantly, M. Benskin and M. Laing, 'Translations and *Mischsprachen* in Middle English manuscripts', in *So meny people longages and tonges: Philological Essays . . . presented to Angus McIntosh*, ed. M. Benskin and M. L. Samuels (Edinburgh, 1981), 55-106, in which on lexical translation see especially pp.93-8 and notes.
7 Compare *dede* 'death' in all printed manuscripts in rhyme at lines 905, 1619, 3994 but rewording to *depes* in FT 7592 within the line; *ill* 46 all manuscripts in rhyme, but within the line 4422 CFG *ill* but T *euel*.
8 Familiar though the idea is, however, the evidence for the study of such translations is in most cases difficult of access: only the *Cursor Mundi* has been edited in a form which makes the material readily available, a fact which has led to the excessive reliance upon this text here as in other studies. *The Pricke of Conscience* has so far been printed only from British Library MS Cotton Galba E. ix by R. Morris (Berlin, 1863). I am indebted to Mrs S. J. Ogilvie-Thomson for the loan of a copy of her thesis *An Edition of the English Works in MS Longleat 29 excluding 'The Parson's Tale'* (Oxford D. Phil., 1980); I had hoped to use her edition of the Rolle items in this manuscript for comparison with the northern Cambridge University Library Dd. 5.64, but for reasons of time and space have been unable to do so.
9 For one instance, however, see M. Görlach, *An East Midland Revision of the South English Legendary* (Heidelberg Middle English Texts 4, 1976), especially pp.24-8.
10 The cycle is being reedited by Pamela Gradon and myself under the title *English Wycliffite Sermons* (Oxford, 1983-). However, since only one of the eventual three text volumes has yet appeared, references will here be made to the old edition by T. Arnold in *Select English Works of John Wyclif* (Oxford, 1869-71), vols i-ii, by page and line number (ignoring all headings). Arnold used MS Bodley 788 as his base text; the new edition will use British Library MS

It is, since the sermons are prose, in the last resort impossible to prove that the original cycle was written in a south Midlands dialect. But the predominance of this type in the majority of the thirty-one manuscripts makes it in the highest degree improbable that the translation was from north to south Midlands rather than the reverse.[11] Z is, in addition to its linguistic irregularity, textually aberrant: its version of the 298 sermons is drastically abbreviated by the expurgation of many Lollard opinions, most notably those concerning the friars. I have elsewhere examined this expurgation, and suggested on textual grounds that it was the scribe of the manuscript Z himself who was responsible for the expurgation.[12] Both these points, the originality of the more southerly language and the responsibility of the scribe of Z, can be reinforced from the evidence of vocabulary. There are two cases, in the first matter, where the majority of manuscripts present forms of the verb *clip* (Arnold ii. 26/21 and ii. 30/12); in both Z substitutes forms of the verb *call*, from a confusion of *clip* with *clepe*. That *clip*, not *clepe*, is correct is shown from the fact that both cases translate passages from the Vulgate where the Latin has forms of *complexo*.[13] There is another similar case (Arnold i. 343/2) where Z misread *serve* as *sewe*, and substituted *folowe*.[14] That it was the scribe of Z himself and not an ancestor who was engaged in the translation is suggested by a correction he made: at Arnold i. 353/24 most manuscripts read *siþ* or *siþen*, whilst Z first wrote *siþen* but then altered it by the subpunting and crossing through of *i* and *þ* to give his regular spelling *sen*.

There is one minor hazard in the use of Z for lexical purposes: the fact that the text is an expurgation means that there are a few cases where doubt arises concerning the cause of alteration. Is the change made because of lexical divergence or because of a dislike of the matter involved in the original text? The substitution of *doynge* for *dowing* in the phrase *dowing aȝens [Goddis] lawe* reveals nothing about Z's vocabulary but only about Z's reaction to the sermons' original attitude towards the temporalities of the church. But, though this is a theoretical hazard, in actuality very few doubts arise. Z's expurgation was a skilful but fairly simple one: what he did not like he omitted, with only the most minimal changes in the surrounding words to link up the remaining material. There are few changes in individual words for ideological reasons.[15] Leaving aside the omissions, Z is

Add. 40672 and give full material, but not linguistic, variants from the other thirty manuscripts now known.

[11] This is reinforced by the textual contiguity of at least twenty-five of the remaining manuscripts; see the introduction to the new edition. The linguistic diversity is greater than is suggested by Samuels in *English Studies* xliv, 84-7 or by Benskin and Laing (1981), 90, but the general type is south central Midlands.

[12] 'The expurgation of a Lollard Sermon-Cycle', *Journal of Theological Studies* (1971); above .201-15; for an account of the physical features of the manuscript see the new edition i. 87-8. The final items in the manuscript, ff.162v-7, including a good copy of *The Lay Folks' Catechism*, are in different hands; slight changes of appearance in the script of the sermons more probably reflect change of pens than of scribes, and certainly do not affect language.

[13] Mark 10.16 *complexans* and Mark 9.35 *complexus*; in the second instance one other manuscript has a similar error.

[14] The other manuscripts available at this point do not share Z's mistake.

[15] See the paper mentioned in n.12, pp. 208-9 for other examples.

otherwise an accurate text though, like almost all the manuscripts of the cycle, it is impossible to trace precisely its affiliations.

That Z's dialect was a northern one can readily be demonstrated from the phonology and morphology, in all features of which Z's orthography is remarkably consistent. Thus OE *ā* and the group *ald* are regularly spelt with <*a*> (*haly*, *ald* etc.), initial OE *sc* appears as <*s*> in *sal* and *suld*, unpalatalized forms such as *kirk*, *mykil* and all parts of *give* are invariable; verbal inflections are 3sg. and the plural pres. ind. -(*i*)*s*, pres. part. -*and*; pronominal 3pl. *þai, þaim* (less frequently *þam*), *þair(e)* and demonstrative *þir* 'these'. I am indebted to Dr Michael Benskin for the information that other features of Z's orthography, particularly the use of *efter*, *es* and *er* for 'is' and 'are', but *gode* for 'good', along with *alif, þof, thorow* and *hie*, limit the likely provenance to a small area on the borders of county Durham and the North Riding of Yorkshire bounded by Richmond at the south, Bishop Auckland in the north west and Darlington in the east.[16]

The following analysis of the vocabulary changes made by Z is a strictly limited and preliminary one. Ideally, the study should have been made with the assistance of a computer-generated concordance, but this is not yet available; my own collection of Z's alterations, whilst intended to be complete, has doubtless missed instances where Z has *not* changed some instances of words he normally altered. It is, of course, impossible to deal with all items or to record all the evidence here. A comparison was made with the *Cursor Mundi*, using primarily the references in the glossary to Morris's edition (followed through to the texts), supplemented where available with the Middle English Dictionary. The *Cursor Mundi* manuscripts are not ideal for comparison: the text dates from earlier than the Lollard sermon-cycle, even if the dates of some of the manuscripts are not dissimilar.[17] But it is one of the few texts for which the available edition is adequate for these purposes, and which is long enough to provide a reasonable amount of material. Beyond this my investigations have been cursory, because of the limitations of time and space. As will appear, however, there may be an interest in a strictly synchronic investigation of one 'translator's' modifications. In this case we have a substantial body of material, some 800 pages in Arnold's edition of which about two-thirds remain in Z's expurgation. Though the date of the original is not firm, it is likely to be between 1384 and 1401; Z is dated palaeo-

16 In correspondence of February 1982. The fact that this small area includes the villages to which Wyclif's birth is conjecturally assigned (see H. B. Workman, *John Wyclif* (Oxford, 1926), i. 22-8) is intriguing; but, though an interest, albeit unrecorded in heresy investigations, in ideas inspired by a local man may be reflected here, the coincidence should not be held to indicate anything about the origin, or original language, of the sermons. All the textual evidence points to the secondary, derivative nature of Z's version of the sermons.
17 The most recent datings of the main manuscripts are those in the unpublished thesis by C. Ross, *An Edition of Part of the Edinburgh Fragment of the Cursor Mundi* (Oxford B. Litt., 1971), 5-43: C and G are dated late fourteenth to early fifteenth-century, F about 1400 and T about 1400-1425. Professor McIntosh (*English Studies* xliv, 7) attributes one of the hands in Bodleian MS Rawlinson A. 389 and British Library MS Harley 1205 to the same scribe as T, and locates the scribe's place of work (*Acta* 128 n.11) to Lichfield; F he places in or near Lancaster.

graphically by Dr Doyle as end of the fourteenth century. If the arguments above are accepted, the northern version is largely uncontaminated by scribal interference.

There are first a large number of words where Z's evidence confirms the distribution that emerges from the *Cursor Mundi* manuscripts. Thus Z agrees with manuscripts C and G of that text in preferring *rais* to *arere*, *hight* to *bihest*, *lathe* to *berne*, *bank* to *brynke*, *flite* to *chide*, *clething* to *cloþ*, *crib* to *cratche*, *myrk* to *derke*, *deed* to *deþ* in the sense 'death', *ilkane* to *ech*, *ille* to *yvel*, *leuenyng* to *liȝtyng*, *ger* to *make* in the sense 'cause', *slek*, *sloken* or *fordo* to *quenche*, *tytter* to *raþer*, *gedir* or *schere* to *repe*, *sper* to *shitte*, *swethlyng* to *swaþing*, 'swaddling', *wranguisly* to *wrongli*.[18] In many cases the preferred word is of Scandinavian origin or form, and is hardly surprising in the north.[19] In several instances Z's word is found in the northern manuscripts of the *Cursor Mundi*, but the Midland Trinity manuscript either omits the word or alters the line. Thus Z's *gyldre* vb. is found in the northern texts and is accepted by Kaiser as a distinctively northern word, but the majority manuscripts' *gnare* or *grane* is not witnessed in *Cursor Mundi*.[20] Similarly, it would seem that Z would not tolerate the word *anon*, substituting regularly a number of synonyms, *swiftly*, *hastily*, *sone* or *swithe*. *Cursor Mundi* has the full range of Z's alternatives, but only a few instances of *anon*.[21]

This leads on to perhaps the most interesting aspect of the evidence of Z. Because most studies of regional vocabulary have involved texts originally written in the north and translated into a more southerly dialect, it has been possible to see which words the more southerly version rejects, but not which words are avoided by a northern scribe. It is plain from the comparison of any two languages, and of two periods of the same language separated in time, that the vocabulary of the two is not symmetrical: one language will represent by two words what the other expresses by only one. That the same is true for regional dialects of the same chronological state of the language can only be discerned from translation in both directions. The last example is a rich case: all of the

---

18 To give full references would be impossibly bulky. For the *Cursor Mundi* evidence, see the glossary to that text. For the sermons I give a single reference only, here with the Z form but Arnold's page and line number; *rais* i.191/30, *hightis* ii.227/26, *lathes* i.408/9, *bank* ii.39/10, *flite* i.17/9, *clething* ii.252/4, *crib* ii.208/22, *myrk* i.2/30, *deed* ii.90/26, *ilkane* i.92/3, *ille* i.90/31, *leuenyngis* ii.310/2, *ger* i.60/9, *slek* ii.202/17, *sloken* ii.232/19, *fordone* i.195/20, *tytter* ii.346/10, *gedir* ii.353/34, *scheris* i.37/24, *spere* ii.43/8, *swethlyng* ii.99/20, *wranguisly* ii.348/25.
19 See A. Rynell, 'The Rivalry of Scandinavian and Native Synonyms in Middle English especially *taken* and *nimen*', *Lund Studies in English* xiii (1948), *passim*; amongst those here *raise*, *lathe*, *ill* and *leuening* are discussed by Rynell.
20 Kaiser 44, 209; Arnold ii.186/17. Compare the substantive Arnold ii.186/5 and ii.363/4, in both of which cases Z has *gyldre* for other manuscripts' *gnare*. There is one case where the verb *gilder* may have been original: Arnold ii.322/25 where the majority of manuscripts have *gildrid*, though Z appears to have misunderstood the passage and has *gedrid*.
21 The commonest substitution is of *sone* (e.g. Arnold i.53/21), less frequently *hastily* (Arnold i.90/2); *swithe* or *swithly* is used twice (i.46/24 and ii.70/1) and *swiftly* once (ii.309/7). See all of these in the glossary to *Cursor Mundi*, together with *onan*.

variants *swiftly*, *hastily*, *sone*, *swithe* and *anon* would have been available to a southern or Midland speaker, but only apparently the first four were in common use for a northern one.[22] A more striking case is to be seen in the regular substitution by Z of *trowe* and *trowth* for *bileve* verb and noun.[23] *Cursor Mundi* gives evidence of *trowe* and *trowth* in its northerly manuscripts, but because these existed in the dialect of the Midland T (as they did in the dialects of the majority of the Wycliffite sermon manuscripts), there was no reason why *bileve* should be substituted.[24] In many cases such a substitution would have resulted in a distortion of the metre, and would therefore have involved a more drastic re-writing of the line to be accommodated. It is only, therefore, through a translation from a southerly to a more northerly dialect of English that the absence of *bileve* from northern dialects can be perceived. Comparable instances where Z had only one word for more southerly areas' two are *doufe* for *culver/doue*, *suppose* for *gesse/suppose*, *corn* for *greyn/corn*, *couer* for *hile/cover*, *rof* for *hiling/rof*, *sla* for *kill/slee*, *morn* for *morewe/morn*, *clymbe* for *scale/clymbe*, *pappis* for *tetis/ pappis*.[25] One of Z's most regular substitutions is of *folow* for *sue*, but *folow* exists also in the language of the original version of these sermons. *Cursor Mundi* does not appear to contain the verb *sue*; all manuscripts have *folow* frequently. *OED* records the French loan word from the thirteenth century onwards, but it would appear not to have been tolerated by Z's language; even the adverb *suyngli* is replaced by *folowandly*.[26]

There is one example in this category which merits further investigation. Z does not seem to have been willing to use the verb *mot* or *moste* in the sense 'must' or 'had to'. For these he invariably substituted *bihoues* or *bihoued*. These forms were known to the original writer of the sermons, but were rarely used by him (for one case see Arnold ii.134/23). Because of the exhortatory nature of the homilies, cases of *mot* and *moste* are extremely frequent. One might expect that the substitution of *bihove* would require the alteration of the subject pronoun. This is sometimes the case: for instance Arnold i.23/12 *þei mut* becomes *þaim bihoues*, i.84/6 *Y moste* becomes *me bihoued*, ii.290/8 *þou most* becomes *þe bihoues*. But with surprising frequency no change is made: i.118/12 *ȝe mut graunt* is changed to *ȝe bihoues graunte*, ii.148/4 *he mut wex and Y mut wanese* is partially modified to *he bihoues waxe and me bihoues wane*. Where the subject pronoun was the propword *it*, it is not surprising that the old inanimate *him* was rejected in favour of the less ambiguous *it* in the new construction. The usage is

---

22 See the relevant words in *MED* and *OED*; that *swith* was known in the south in the sense 'swiftly' is shown by *OED*'s citation (*swith* adv. sense 3) of Hoccleve's *Regement of Princes* 744.

23 Because of the subject matter of the sermons, the substitutions are very common; for the verb see, for instance, Arnold ii.222/17, for the noun ii.222/29.

24 Judging by the glossary, *Cursor Mundi* uses *tru* vb., *truth* sb.; *beleue* 'faith' sb. is recorded once in British Library MS Add. 10036, line 675 which Morris did not print in full.

25 See *doufe* i.78/5 (all manuscripts have *dove* at ii.49/17), *supposid* ii.263/29, *corn* ii.35/18, *couer* i.99/36, *rofes* i.194/20, *slayne* i.49/3, *morn* ii.115/5, *clymbe* ii.6/18, *pappis* i.120/5.

26 Parts of *sue* are very common; for Z's substitution of *folow* see i.6/3, 15 etc.; all manuscripts have *folowe* at i.169/26, ii.98/35; for the adverb see i.180/18, ii.15/3, ii.106/21.

thus similar to that claimed by *MED*, though few of the examples there cited have a nominative pronoun subject in such close juxtaposition to the verb as in *ʒe/he bihoues* here.[27] There is no sign in Z of the characteristic northern form *bus*, as an abbreviation of *bihoues*. The *Cursor Mundi* apparently used *most* and the verb *behoue*.[28] It would appear, therefore, that *mot* and *most* may have disappeared from later northern dialects, or at least from the particular northern speech used by Z.[29]

Comparison of Z with the *Cursor Mundi* makes it possible to illustrate the opposite position, where the northern dialect had two words whilst the south had only one. In most instances, however, the north appears to have had a strong preference amongst the two. Thus *Cursor* has both *gang* and *ga*, Z regularly *gang* and other manuscripts *go*; *hyng* is the verb preferred in Cursor northern manuscripts and Z, *hang* is, however, found in all and is the regular form in the other manuscripts of the sermon cycle; *Cursor* has both *to* and *ouer* in the sense 'too', Z *ouer* and other sermon manuscripts *to*; *Cursor* has both *wepe* and *grete* evidenced in rhyme, Z prefers *grete* and the other sermon manuscripts conversely *wepe*; *Cursor* uses both *wand* and *yerd*, Z prefers *wand* and the other manuscripts *ʒerde*.[30] The verb *picche* is common in the majority of sermon manuscripts, varied in some by *prick*; Z usually substitutes *fitche* but once *nail*, the only form apparently in *Cursor Mundi*.[31]

So much for the similarities between Z and northern manuscripts of the *Cursor Mundi*. There are, however, a number of discrepancies. Since the starting point for this investigation was Z, it is not surprising that the most noticeable differences are cases where Z's usage is more restrictive than that of the *Cursor Mundi* — in other words, where Z suppresses a word found in other sermon manuscripts which is also exemplified in C and G texts of the poem. If the comparison had started from the other end, it is likely that the converse would have emerged, of Z tolerating forms which C and G did not use. The most striking instance is Z's regular replacement of *clepe* by *call*, though the northern manuscripts of *Cursor Mundi* used both verbs.[32] Similar cases are Z's suppression of *lake* in

[27] *MED* s.v. *bihoven* v.; similar examples with no change of pronoun are in Z at ii.33/6, 106/18, 110/13, 257/3, 272/17, 292/18, 313/1.
[28] In *Cursor Mundi most* is used as a present tense (as lines 916 CGF, T *mot*, 1243 CFT, G *bus*), as well as preterite (2400 all manuscripts); forms of *behoue* are found in all manuscripts at 422, 5512, 6455. Z seems to have regarded *mut* as variably present or preterite tense (e.g. ii.324/26, 28 *he mut* is replaced by *him bihoued*).
[29] At Arnold ii.230/13 Z substituted *mon* for *mut* in the sense 'must'; cf *MED* s.v. *monen* v. (2) and Kaiser 49.
[30] For the *Cursor Mundi* forms see the glossary to that text; Z's *gang* for instance i.93/32 (cf Kaiser 206-7); *hyngand* ii.128/20 but *hange* ii.128/30; *ouer* i.38/22; *grete* i.25/1 (cf Kaiser 27, 211); *wand* ii.321/10, 19.
[31] The verb is inevitably common in the Good Friday sermon, Arnold ii.125/12, 22, 127/4, 16, 130/13, and 127/27 which is the only instance of *nail*.
[32] There must be over five hundred examples of Z's replacement of *clepe* by *call* (e.g. i.1/10, 2/26, 4/5), in almost all of which Leicester Old Town Hall MS 3 likewise uses *call*; for *Cursor Mundi* note 1118 *clepe ne cale* in all manuscripts. Rynell summarises his findings on *call* 317-18.

favour of *dike*, of *greting* in favour of *hailsyng*, of *snybbe* in favour of *snaip*, in all of which the northern manuscripts C and G knew both words; Z also suppresses *eke* in favour of *als(e)*, though *eke* is amply recorded in *Cursor* even in rhyme, and *kyn* in favour of *kynreden*, though *Cursor* attests both as original by the metre.[33] There are a few instances where Z is in direct contradiction to the evidence of *Cursor Mundi*: Z replaces *cheping* by *market*, *plat* by *flat* where the poem only records the first word of each pair; Z rejects *terre* in favour of *stirre*, but *terre* is found twice in C.[34]

This leads, of course, to the question of the representative nature of Z's usage. How many of the substitutions can be interpreted as indicating the preference of the dialect? How many are purely ideolect choices? Where Z agrees with the northern manuscripts of the *Cursor Mundi* it seems reasonable to assume the first explanation. But in some instances purely personal preference seems to be in question. Z seems to have a dislike of compound adverbs whose first element is *her*, regularly substituting *þer* in cases such as *herof*, *herto*, *herwiþ* and, most frequently, *herfore*. It is difficult to suppose from the evidence presented by dictionaries and glossaries that this was anything more than an individual whim.[35] A similar minor alteration that is very common in Z is the replacement of the suffix *-ever* with *-saeuer* in compounds such as *however*, *whanever*, *whatever*, *wherever*, *whiderever* or *whoever*.[36] Though forms with instrusive *-sa-* are frequent in northern texts, the virtually entire exclusion of the other forms may be an idiosyncrasy of this one scribe.

A stranger case, and one where the question of textual history reappears, concerns the conjunction *alȝif* 'even if', a word characteristic of the sermon cycle and of a number of other Wycliffite texts. In the sermons of the Commune Sanctorum and the Proprium Sanctorum Z regularly replaces this by *alþof*; but in the three sets of Sunday gospel, Sunday epistle and weekday gospel sermons the form *alif* is invariable where other manuscripts have *alȝif*.[37] This situation is

---

[33] Z uses *dike* at i.73/29, 31 (though cf Z *lake* at ii.22/19); CM has *lake* in all four main MSS at 11943, 12018 and *dikes* in rhyme with *likes* at 10063. Z *hailsyngis* at ii.62/15; CM *greting* 5158 CGF, *hailsing* 5318, 11045 all MSS. Z *snaip* ii.75/14 and many times in the same homily; CM *snibbed* all MSS at 18228 and *snaip* in CF 13027, 22103, 18853. Z *als* repeatedly, e.g. i.81/34, 89/20; CM *eke* in rhyme 6331, 18055, 18981 (cf Rynell 329 on rivalry of *ok* and *ek(e)*). Z *kynreden* i.240/8; CM *kyn* in rhyme 113 etc., *kinrede* 6967 all MSS.

[34] Z *market* i.99/3, ii.62/15; CM *cheping* 15419 all MSS. Z *flat* i.194/16 but CM *plat* 17709 all MSS in rhyme. Z *stirre* ii.44/14 but CM 26787 CF and 28153 C have forms of *tar*; *terre* or its variant *tarre* is a characteristic Wycliffite word, common in the Bible translation and in other texts (cf *OED* s.v. *tar*, *tarre*, v.2., for some exemplification).

[35] Z *þerof* for *hereof* i.79/22, 93/1 etc., *þerto* for *herto* i.108/11, 20, *þerwiþ* for *herwiþ* i.80/27, 97/35, *þerfor* for *herfore* i.41/30, 44/30 etc. Forms with *þer-* are, of course, also found alongside those in *her-* in other manuscripts with the usual semantic differentiations.

[36] Z *housaeuer* for *however* ii.18/7, 19/6 etc., *whensaeuer* for *whanneever* ii.28/10, *whatsaeuer* for *whatevere* ii.98/20, *wharesaeuer* for *whereevere* ii.204/3, *whidirsaeuer* for *whidirever* ii.17/19, *whasaeuer* for *whoever* ii.26/20. CM exemplifies many of these compounds in *-ever* as well as in *-saever*, but generalization about northern usage is difficult because of the variable treatment by editors of these forms as one, two or three words.

[37] Z uses *alþof* in some forty instances in the Sanctorale sermons (e.g. Arnold i.166/9, 273/28), but *alif* frequently in the other sets (e.g. i.2/31, ii.65/3, 138/32).

particularly odd in that Z did not copy these sets of sermons in two coherent sequences: the weekday gospel sermons were inserted between the Proprium and Commune Sanctorum groups (which occur in that order in Z). The only credible explanation must lie in the textual history of the Sanctorale, as opposed to the Temporale, sermons as they came down to Z. Z's exemplar of the Sanctorale sermons must already have suppressed the conjunction with some form of ȝif/if as its second element, in favour of that with some form of þouȝ/þeiȝ; on the other hand Z's exemplar of the Temporale sermons retained alȝif or alif. It is clear that Z would tolerate some form of the latter conjunction, since he used it so often. Concomitant with the replacement of al(ȝ)if with alþof, and found in almost exactly the same places, is a replacement of ȝif with þof.[38] Suppression of alȝif is not wholly unexpected: the form is not particularly common in Middle English, and the fact that it was normally followed by a subjunctive made alþeiȝ/ alþouȝ (or their variants) a natural substitute.[39]

These last points reveal with nice precision the problems of disentangling the usage of the scribe of the extant manuscript from the usage of another scribe somewhere back in the textual tradition. Evidence was presented earlier to suggest that Z was working from a manuscript whose linguistic characteristics were significantly different from his normal usage, and that that exemplar was linguistically similar to the majority of other manuscripts of the sermons. This conclusion remains, I think, valid. But what is concealed behind that general statement is considerable uncertainty about the details of the exemplar's language, or about the homogeneity of that language, or, indeed, about the homogeneity of that exemplar – was it the same throughout or variable? and had it throughout the same history? Despite the considerable length of the material here analysed, it is only in the treatment of alȝif and ȝif that significant variation in Z's usage emerged. That in itself suggests an inherited difference, and the division between exemplars for different sets of sermons is provable textually elsewhere in the tradition. If then any conclusion is possible from this investigation, it must, I think, be a cautionary one: that notions of dialect vocabulary are difficult to assemble, and that only the full study of a text's history, as well as of the language of its manuscripts, is necessary before the information offered by any single version can be assessed. The simple term 'translation' may cover a variety of complex and

---

38 There are two instances in the Sunday gospel sermons, i.127/24, 143/3 and ten in sets of the Sanctorale. The replacement of ȝif is by no means invariable, however, even in the latter sets; the cases of replacement are all where the dependent verb is distinctively, or possibly, subjunctive.

39 In the Sunday gospel set MS Add. 40672 reads alþow in a half dozen instances near the beginning (Arnold i.9/2, 10/2, 35, 15/5, 16/2, 9), many of them subsequently corrected; after this point the scribe appears to have grasped that alȝif was the required form. I am much indebted to Dr Michael Benskin for sending me a preliminary map of the location of alȝif and associated forms; it appears from this that alȝif is most frequently found in the area of Huntingdonshire, the Isle of Ely and the Holland section of Lincolnshire, whilst alif is of somewhat commoner occurrence, on the western borders of Kesteven, Lindsey and northern Nottinghamshire as well as in scattered parts of the West Riding of Yorkshire and further north (including that area indicated by other features to be the home of Z).

differing operations, as the work of recent scholars has made clear; the operations may change within the course of a single scribe's stint. That single scribe may be working on exemplar(s) of similarly varied form and history. Until the resources of modern technology (machine reading and computer indexing in particular) are fully developed and fully utilized on all the surviving evidence for a medieval text (in other words, on all manuscripts and not just on an edited text), it seems unlikely that any satisfactory conclusions can be drawn about dialect vocabulary.

15

'NO NEWE THYNG': THE PRINTING

OF MEDIEVAL TEXTS IN THE

EARLY REFORMATION PERIOD

IT is well known that there are a number of English Wycliffite texts that were printed in the early Reformation period during the reigns of Henry VIII and Edward VI. Equally familiar is the fact that a group of texts found their way into print then that claim or imply Lollard origins, but which are untraceable in manuscripts of the early Lollard period.[1] Best known of these are *Wycklyffes Wycket* and the *Ploughman's Tale*, the latter foisted upon Chaucer; less notorious is the *Praier and Complaynte of the ploweman*. These works, attested and unattested in the medieval period, raise a number of interesting questions. Why did the sixteenth-century reformers resort to these old texts? How did they regard the ideas of an earlier reforming movement? How did they treat the texts—respectfully, or in cavalier fashion, interpolating their own preoccupations and altering the medieval terms to accord with sixteenth-century ideas? Most importantly for a literary critic, can the claims of the unattested works to be medieval compositions be sustained, or are they forgeries? There is not space here to answer fully the

---

[1] Many of these texts were described by Margaret Aston in her two papers, 'Lollardy and the Reformation: Survival or Revival?', *History*, xlix (1964), 149–70 and 'John Wycliffe's Reformation Reputation', *Past and Present*, xxx (1965), 23–51. It should be noted that Wyclif's *Trialogus* was printed in Basel in 1525, and that a version of the Wycliffite *Opus Arduum* appeared with a preface by Luther on Wittenberg in 1528; I have discussed the latter in 'A Neglected Wycliffite Text', *Journal of Ecclesiastical History*, xxix (1978), 257–79. See above pp. 43–65.

first two questions; what I hope to do is to answer the third, and
by so doing to throw some light on the last.

The texts with which I shall be dealing were printed within
the period 1525 to 1550. Many of them were reprinted during
the following sixty or seventy years, a time which saw also the
issue of other Lollard texts. But the motives of the later editors
were more complicated by antiquarianism, an interest in history
as apart from theology.[2] The earlier prints, as the prefatory
epistles to many make clear, were direct contributions to an
ongoing, contemporary debate; they were directly polemical in
the intent of their printers, just as they had been polemical in the
purpose of their original authors. This contemporary relevance
is demonstrated by the fact that many of them were printed
abroad on the same presses that issued the texts of Tyndale,
William Roye, Simon Fish, and George Joye.[3] Several of them
appeared on the various lists of proscribed books that were
issued before 1560;[4] the names of George Constantine and
William Tyndale were associated with the editorship of one of
them.[5] These books, like the works of contemporary reformers,
were confiscated and held as evidence of heresy. Because of their
dangerous nature, many of the bibliographical details about
them are obscure: the printers concealed their own names and
the place of publication, and many carry no date of imprint. Few
survive in more than five copies, many in only one or two. It is
quite possible that other Lollard texts were printed, but have not

[2] See, for instance, Thomas James's edition of *Two Short Treatises, against
the Orders of the Begging Friars* (Oxford, 1608; STC 25589). It is, of course,
impossible to make a firm distinction between antiquarian and theological
interest, as the works of Bale and Foxe make very clear.

[3] See Anthea Hume's 'English Protestant Books Printed Abroad, 1525–1535:
An Annotated Bibliography', in L. A. Schuster *et al.* (edd.) *The Confutation of
Tyndale's Answer*, (New Haven and London, 1973), ii. 1065–91. There is an
illuminating account of the context of these editions in W. A. Clebsch, *England's Earliest Protestants 1520–1535* (New Haven, 1964).

[4] See *Concilia Magnae Britanniae et Hiberniae*, ed. D. Wilkins (London,
1737), iii. 707, 719–20, 739 and John Foxe, *Actes and Monuments* (London,
1563), 573–4; also Clebsch, pp. 262–9.

[5] See Hume, pp. 1077–8, but cf. Clebsch, pp. 265–7.

survived; the titles under which the existing editions are found do not always correspond to their medieval titles, and many Lollard texts are in any form without title. My concern here is not bibliographical, and I have accepted the views of others on details of date and place of publication. For ease of reference, however, I give here a list of the texts with which I shall be dealing and the basic bibliographical details about them.[6]

A. The editions for which medieval manuscripts survive fall into two subgroups, the first published abroad, the second in England:

A proper dyaloge, betwene a gentillman and an husbandman ... ([Antwerp, 1530?]; STC 1462. 3); this contains part of the Lollard treatise entitled in its modern edition The Clergy may not hold Property.[7]

A compendious olde treatyse, shewynge, howe that we ought to haue ye scripture in Englysshe (Hans Luft, Marburg [i.e. Johannes Hoochstraten, Antwerp] 1530; STC 3021); another edition appeared under the same title printed by Richarde Banckes in London [c. 1538?], STC 3022; both include a version of a short Lollard text defending biblical translation.[8]

The two treatises above were issued together, in an extended frame of the first (for which see below), with the title of the second (Hans Luft, Marburg [i.e. Hoochstraten, Antwerp], 1530; STC 1462. 5, formerly 6813).[9] In the following discussion I have used the earliest, separate versions.

[6] I have used, save in individual cases noted below, Hume's list together with STC. I am grateful to Miss Pantzer for providing me with a xerox of the revised entries for the first two texts described below.

[7] See The English Works of Wyclif hitherto unprinted, ed. F. D. Matthew (EETS 74, 1880; 2nd revd. edn. 1902), 362–404.

[8] The text has been printed twice, by M. Deanesly, The Lollard Bible (Cambridge, 1920), 437–45 and by C. Bühler, 'A Lollard Tract: on Translating the Bible into English', MÆ vii (1938), 167–83; I have used the latter. The comments of both editors on authorship should be ignored. Foxe printed it Actes (1563), 452–5.

[9] It was this version that was reproduced in facsimile by F. Fry (London, 1863) and appeared in the Arber Reprints (London, 1871).

The examinacion of Master William Thorpe ... [with] *The examinacion of ... syr Jhon Oldcastell* ... ([Antwerp, 1530]); STC 24045); the first part of this survives in a fifteenth-century manuscript, Bodleian Rawlinson c.208, and the second part will be discussed below.[10]

The Lanterne of Lyght (Robert Redman, [London, 1535?]; STC 15225); the medieval text survives in two manuscripts.[11]

Jack vp Lande (John Gough, [London, 1536?] STC 5098); this is found in two medieval forms, Latin and English.[12]

The dore of holy scripture (John Gowgh, London, 1540; STC 25587. 5, formerly 3033); an edition of the text now known as the General Prologue to the Wycliffite Bible translation.[13]

The true copye of a prolog wrytten ... by J. Wycklife ... (Robert Crowley, London, 1550; STC 25588); the text is the same as the last, but the print was an entirely new one from a different manuscript.

B. The texts for which no medieval evidence survives are the following:

The praier and complaynte of the ploweman vnto Christe ([Antwerp, 1531?]; STC 20036); this was reprinted in London and issued [*c.* 1532?], STC 20036. 5.[14]

[10] Foxe, *Actes* (1563), 143–72 reprinted the 1530 edition; a modern reprint appeared in *Fifteenth Century Prose and Verse*, ed. A. W. Pollard (Westminster, 1903), 97–189; a facsimile of the British Library copy was produced recently (Amsterdam and Norwood, N. J., 1975).

[11] It was edited by L. M. Swinburn (EETS 151, 1917); Swinburn did not use the print.

[12] See the edition of *Jack Upland, Friar Daw's Reply and Upland's Rejoinder* by P. L. Heyworth (London, 1968); Heyworth did not know of the Latin form, whose significance will be discussed below. For the date of the edition, and the possibility that there was another separate printing, see the same author's paper 'The Earliest Black-letter Editions of *Jack Upland*', *Huntington Library Quarterly*, xxx (1967), 307–14. Foxe reprinted Upland in *Actes*[2] (1570), i. 341–5.

[13] See *The Holy Bible* .... *made from the Latin Vulgate by John Wycliffe and his Followers*, edd. J. Forshall and F. Madden (Oxford, 1850), i. 1–60.

[14] The earlier version was reprinted in *Harleian Miscellany* (London, 1744–6), vi. 84–106. The later altered the preface heading from 'To the christen reader' to 'W.T. to the reader', which may be why both Bale, *Illustrium Maioris Britanniae scriptorum summarium* (Ipswich, 1548), f. 221, and Foxe, *Actes*[2] (1570), 494–501 ascribed the edition to Tyndale.

The examinacion of . . . syr Jhon Oldcastell; see above.

[*The ploughman's tale*] (Thomas Godfrey, London, [1536?]; STC 5099. 5); the tale was also incorporated into the reprint of William Thynne's edition of Chaucer's work issued in 1542, and subsequently appeared in all sixteenth-century editions of Chaucer.[15] Another separate edition was produced by William Hyll ([1548?]; STC 5100), and an edition with a commentary was issued in 1606 (STC 5101).

Wycklyffes wycket . . . (Norenburch, [i.e. London, John Day?], 1546; STC 25590); there is a variant version apparently issued the same year and place (STC 25590. 5), two editions probably published two years later (STC 25591 and 25591a), and a much later edition (London, 1612; STC 25592) declaredly based on an earlier printed copy.[16]

With two exceptions, one of which may be the result of accidental loss of the title page in the single surviving copy, all these texts acknowledge their early origins. Some are specific about their date: Thorpe's trial is dated 1407 (sig. A1), the *Proper Dyaloge* is said to have been written in the 'tyme of kinge Rycharde the secounde' (sig. B4) and the *Compendious treatyse* about 1400 (sig. A1ᵛ). The antiquity of the *Praier and complaynte*, alleged to derive from 'not longe after . . .' 1300 (sig. A1), and of the Prologue to the Wycliffite Bible, in both editions stated to

[15] See A. N. Wawn, 'The Genesis of *The Plowman's Tale*', *Yearbook of English Studies*, ii (1972), 21–40 and 'Chaucer, *The Plowman's Tale* and Reformation Propaganda: the Testimonies of Thomas Godfray and *I Playne Piers*', *Bulletin of the John Rylands Library*, lvi (1973), 174–92. A modern print of Thynne's text appears in W. W. Skeat, *Chaucerian and other Pieces* (Oxford, 1897), 147–90. There is a copy of Thynne's 1532 edition of Chaucer (STC 5068) now in the University of Texas library in which appears inserted a sixteenth-century manuscript copy of the *Ploughman's Tale*; see A. S. Irvine, 'A Manuscript Copy of *The Plowman's Tale*', *Texas Studies in English*, xii (1932), 27–56. Irvine did not know of STC 5099. 5, but suggested that the manuscript did not derive directly from either STC 5100 or Thynne's 1542 edition.

[16] Appended to the *Wycket* in the early editions was *The testament of maister Wylliam Tracie esquier, expounded by Wylliam Tyndall* (STC 25590, sigs. B3ᵛ–C3ᵛ). There have been various modernizations of the *Wycket*, for which see E. W. Talbert in *A Manual of the Writings in Middle English 1050–1500*, ii, revd. J. Burke Severs (Hamden, Conn., 1970), 523.

have been written 'two hondred yeares past' (1540, sig. A3; 1550, sig. A1), is overstated—in the 1550 edition of the latter despite the attribution to Wyclif himself. The title of the *Wycket* indicates Wyclif's authorship and alleges the date, impossible for the ascription, of 1395 (sig. A1); the print of *Jack vp Lande* claims Chaucer's paternity (sig. A1), though, perhaps surprisingly, this was not taken up by editors of Chaucer until Speght's second edition of 1602.[17] The surviving copy of the *Ploughman's Tale* lacks an original title page, but the implied authorship of the text, which may originally have been explicit, was accepted by 1542.[18] The only text which is completely opaque about its origins is the *Lanterne of Lyght*, a work which in many ways presents the fullest picture of Lollard beliefs. This opacity is interesting: presumably it implies that those responsible for issuing the edition thought that it could stand without apology or explanation, as a statement of opinions that would appeal to men of a reforming cast of mind in the 1530s without the excuse of antiquity. As such it is to be compared with those trial documents of the 1520s and 1530s where it is now unclear, and plainly was in some instances to the enquiring authorities, whether the suspect was old Lollard or new Lutheran.[19]

Turning to the way in which the sixteenth-century editors treated their medieval texts, the simplest cases are very easy to state. The latest edition, the second printing of the General Prologue, claimed to derive from 'an olde English Bible bitwixt the olde Testament and the Newe. Whych Bible remaynith now in yᵉ Kyng hys maiesties Chamber' (sig. A1). Forshall and Mad-

---

[17] *STC* 5080 and 5081, ff. 348-50ᵛ; Speght's head-note to the text makes the unfortunate suggestion 'This is thought to bee that Crede which the Pellican speaketh of in the Plowmans tale', confusing Upland with *Pierce the Ploughmans Crede* (ed. W. W. Skeat, EETS 30, 1867).

[18] In William Thynne's second edition of Chaucer's. works, *STC* 5069 and 5070, ff. 119-126ᵛ at the end of the *Canterbury Tales*; in the third edition, *STC* 5071-4 ([1550?]), it was moved to a position before the Parson's Tale (ff. 93-100), a position it retained in all subsequent sixteenth-century editions.

[19] See A. G. Dickens, *Lollards and Protestants in the Diocese of York 1509-1558* (London, 1959), *passim*, and C. Cross, *Church and People 1450-1660* (Edinburgh, 1976), 31-80.

den in their edition of the Wycliffite Bible identified this manuscript as that now classified as Mm.2.15 in the Cambridge University Library, in which the Prologue stands between the testaments.[20] Collation of six chapters confirms this view, and reveals that Crowley's print is an extremely accurate version, preserving even some of the linguistic eccentricities of its exemplar. Somewhat more interesting because the precise exemplar has disappeared is the case of the *Proper Dyaloge* in both its separate and combined forms. The frame, the dialogue of the title, is a wholly sixteenth-century device, though many of the complaints voiced, against clerical interference in secular life and the temporal claims of the clergy, are, as the speakers acknowledge, of long standing. The Husbandman produces the medieval text, 'aboue an houndred yere olde', in the following words (sig. B4):

> halfe the boke we want
> Hauynge no more left than a remenant
> From the begynnynge of the .vi. chapter verely

This accuracy is roughly confirmed by the one surviving manuscript of this version of the text, now Lambeth 551, in which the opening words of the print are found near the beginning of chapter VII.[21] In fact, were Lambeth the only medieval version of this text to survive, it might be difficult to establish that the print did not derive straight from Lambeth—so close is the agreement between the two. But another longer version is found in three medieval manuscripts (CUL Dd.14.30(2), BL Egerton 2820, and Huntington Library HM 503) and one sixteenth-century manuscript (CUL Ff.6.2). Though the precise relation between the two medieval versions is hard to ascertain, there are a handful of agreements between the *Proper Dyaloge* and this better attested medieval version and against Lambeth 551, agreements which can only be explained on the assumption that the print

[20] Forshall and Madden, i, pp. liv–lv.

[21] In Matthew's edition, p. 382/25. The print continues to Matthew 396/10 including what Matthew regarded, without justification in the Lambeth manuscript, as an appendix but omitting the Latin authorities.

derives from a manuscript very close to Lambeth but not identical with it.[22] Such a conclusion also, of course, accounts for the
alleged incompleteness of the Husbandman's exemplar and for
the apparent discrepancy in chapter numbering.[23] Apart from
these few agreements against Lambeth, the print is entirely faithful to the text as attested in Lambeth. The reason for the fidelity
may perhaps be inferred from the Gentleman's response to the
text (sig. C6ᵛ):

> Nowe I promyse the after my iugement
> I haue not hard of soche an olde fragment
>   Better groundyd on reason with scrypture.
> Yf soche auncyent thynges myght come to lyght
> That noble men hadde ones of theym a syght
>   The world yet wolde chaunge perauenture.
> For here agaynst the clergye can not bercke
> Sayenge as they do/ thys is a newe wercke
>   Of heretykes contryued lately.
> And by thys treatyse it apperyth playne
> That before oure dayes men dyd compleyne
>   Agaynst clerckes ambycyon so stately.[24]

The third instance of almost complete faithfulness to a medieval exemplar is, however, the text which nowhere proclaims its
antiquity: the *Lanterne of Lyght*. Two medieval copies survive,
Harley 2324, used by Swinburn, the editor of the EETS text, and
Harley 6613, not known to Swinburn and defective because of
loss of leaves. A third copy is known to have existed in the
possession of John Claydon in 1415; the second folio incipit is

[22] The full evidence will be set out in the edition of the longer version I am
preparing for EETS; the best evidence is the print's inclusion of three lines after
Matthew 386/26 (sig. B7ᵛ) and of two after Matthew 387/12 (sig. B8), in both
cases supported by the longer version.

[23] The chapter numbering is quite clear in Lambeth, and the edition's numbering is not a simple omission of a minim since it is given both as a numeral
and as a word. It seems likely that the edition's exemplar had a different
chapter division.

[24] The search for precedent, for evidence that the reformers were in a tradition of thought, is obvious in many of these texts and was taken up by Bale; see
especially L. P. Fairfield, *John Bale, Mythmaker for the English Reformation*
(West Lafayette, 1976).

given in the trial proceedings in Chichele's register, an incipit
that does not agree with either Harley manuscript.[25] The print
is in some respects superior to each of the manuscripts separately, and in a few cases appears to derive from an exemplar better
than either.[26] The format of this exemplar can be precisely
determined from the one large omission in the print, where it is
clear either that the printer inadvertently turned over two leaves
or that his model lacked one folio; there is no conceivable
ideological reason for the omission, an omission which locally
produces nonsense and which leaves chapter IV without an opening or marking in the text, despite being called for in the final
tabula.[27] The printed text is considerably shorter than the version in the extant manuscripts, because it has omitted the Latin
quotations pedantically included in the earlier versions before
the English translations. At the beginning of the text there is a
good deal of minor re-wording that makes little difference to the
sense; at the end there is some sign of abbreviation, probably to
ensure that the text concluded within the quire, an aim effected
somewhat over-zealously. There is some modernization of vocabulary, sometimes done with greater regard for the look of the
individual word than for the overall sense of the passage.[28] But
in general the sense is so well kept that use of this print, together
with Harley 6613, would allow a number of corrections to be

[25] Harley 6613 lacks Swinburn's 14/24–17/1, 21/3–29/8, 31/13–37/18, 48/24–
50/19, and 128/13 to end. For the Claydon trial see the edition of the Chichele
register by E. F. Jacob (Canterbury and York Society, 1938–47) iv. 132–8; no
doubt Claydon's copy was destroyed immediately after the trial.

[26] For instance, the print agrees with Harley 6613 in adding 'nonnes, systers
and spytlers' in 38/17 and in reading *dystynctly* rather than *diligentli* at 56/17;
on the other hand Harley 6613 alone omits 79/30–80/1; the print has a fuller
translation of the Latin quotations, which are omitted from the print itself,
than the available manuscripts at 127/2 and 137/2.

[27] The loss is from 13/19 to 15/5 of the modern edition and is on sig. A8ᵛ of
the print. The amount of text lost, some 46 lines, is a very credible content for
one folio or, if the error were the printer's, one opening; Harley 2324 contains
some 36 lines to a folio, recto and verso, Harley 6613 approximately 58 lines.

[28] For instance, 57/2 *style* for *poyntel*, 51/15 *tarynge* for *terren*, and less
happily 93/22 *nowe* for *wowe*, 16/15 *verefyed* for *waried*, and 108/5, etc. *wyll*
for *nile*.

made to Swinburn's edition. References to affairs of the early
Wycliffite period are hardly changed, though the term *Lollardis*
(11/11) is changed to *heretyckes* (sig. A7); the description of the
persecution of those favouring vernacular scriptures (100/1 ff.,
sig. G5), the account of penance (104/21 ff., sig. G7) and of
Antichrist, the court of Rome its head, the archbishops and
bishops its body, and 'þise (patched and) cloutid sectis . as
mounkis chanouns . and freris ... þe venymous taile' (16/10 ff.,
sig. B1), remain unaltered. As Swinburn said (p. x), the fifteen
points assembled by the trial lawyers at Claydon's investigation
give a fair survey of the heresy in the *Lanterne*; none of these are
mitigated or altered in the print. The only significant change
clarifies an obscure passage, suppressing an allusion to the Eucharist and substituting a clearer exhortation to preaching.[29]

Somewhat further removed from extant medieval English
manuscript versions are the prints of Upland and Thorpe, but in
each case there is good evidence that points towards the authenticity of most of the material introduced. In each case there are
both English and Latin versions surviving from the pre-Refor-
mation period, each preserving slightly different textual traditions; this enables an assessment to be made of the later edition,
and this later edition in turn can be used to remedy defects in the
earlier vernacular version. For the autobiographical account of
Thorpe's trial in 1407 there are three medieval witnesses, the
English account in Bodl. MS Rawl. c.208 (R), and two Latin
versions in Vienna 3936 (V) and Prague Metropolitan Chapter
O.29 (P); there are a number of sixteenth-century versions, Latin
and English, apart from the edition here under discussion (A),

[29] The two Harley manuscripts agree in reading (Swinburn 12/7–9) 'What is
to be sett biforne þe bodi of Crist þat prestis sacren? And siþen þei treten
Cristis bodi. miche raþer seiþ Ierom þei schullen preche & blesse þe peple. Hec
dist. 99.' The print (sig. A7ᵛ) substitutes 'And Seyncte Jerom commendyth in
prestehode prechynge the gospel and blessyng the people before the sayeng of
masse. And Seynct Paull sayth that Christ sent hym to preche & not to baptyse.
So by this it apereth that prechynge the gospel is the hyghest seruyce that may
be done to god.' A marginal note supplies the references 'Dist. 56. I Corin. 1
Non me misit christus baptizare sed euangelizare.'

but they are all derivative, directly or indirectly, from this edition and have no independent value.[30] V and P fairly clearly derive from a common exemplar, presumably the single copy taken abroad to the Hussite area. Whether the original of the text was in English or Latin is not immediately clear, but does not affect the present issue. In general R is much closer to VP than is A. But in cases where error can be established, the value of R against A is more evenly balanced; there are, furthermore, a number of cases where the agreement of A with VP shows that R's apparently acceptable version is probably unoriginal.[31] The main text of the Antwerp print is not modified for doctrinal reasons save possibly in two minor cases: first where the statement 'þe worschipful sacrament of þe auter is *verri Cristis fleisch and his blood in forme of breed and wyne*' (R, f. 41) is amplified by the expansion of the italicized words to 'the sacramente of Christis flesche' (sig. C8ᵛ), and secondly where the less extreme 'it stierith god to take greate vengeaunce both vpon lordis and vpon comons which suffer thes priestes charitably' (sig. E7) is substituted for the interventionist 'it terriþ God to take greet veniaunce boþe vpon lordis and vpon comouns whiche suffren þese prestis to lyuen as þei now done and wolen not bisien hem to amende þese prestis charitabli' (R, f. 66). But the latter, like a number of even more minor changes, is probably a case of inadvertent haplography. However, though the main text is authentically medieval, the same cannot be proved for material that stands after it. The preface (sig. A1ᵛ–A2ᵛ) is declaredly

[30] Again full evidence for these assertions will be given in my edition of the text. A Latin version (now incomplete) in Bale's handwriting was entered into the manuscript of the *Fasciculi Zizaniorum*, Bodl. e Mus. 86, f. 105ᵛ and following five inserted and unnumbered leaves; this was reprinted by Foxe in *Commentarii Rerum in Ecclesia Gestarum* ... (Strasburg, 1554), ff. 118–156ᵛ and in *Rerum in Ecclesia Gestarum* ... (Basel, 1559), pp. 79–96. In his *Actes* Foxes substituted the English from the 1530 print (1563 edn. pp. 143–72).

[31] For instance, in my edition of an extract from R in *Selections from English Wycliffite Writings* (Cambridge, 1978), no. 4/53–4 I should have emended the text in the light of agreement between A and VP to read 'I schulde herþoru3 first [wounde and defyle myn owne soule, and also I schulde herþoru3] 3eue occasioun to many men and wymmen of ful sore hurtynge.'

editorial, and refers to the burning of Thomas Hitton in Maidstone 'now thys yere'. After the trial account appears (sigs. G6–
H2) Thorpe's *testamente*, of which there is no trace in R (nor
any indication that that manuscript is now defective). The *testamente* is dated in the print 20 September 1460, some fifty-three
years, as it observes, after Thorpe's trial. This in itself casts
doubt upon the authenticity of the *testamente*, or at least its
attribution to Thorpe: Thorpe appears to have been instituted
to the vicarage of Marske, Cleveland, in 1395, and would therefore have been at least eighty-five by 1460.[32] In fact, the *testamente* has no connection with the trial or with the interests
shown in it; it deals, after an introduction concerning Christ as
the foundation of all faith, with the evils of the clergy in general
terms. It could be a medieval text, but there is nothing in it to
connect it specifically with Thorpe. The editor of the Thorpe
trial is unusually forthcoming with his comments on his treatment of the language (sig. A2ᵛ):

This I haue corrected and put forth in the english that now is vsed in
Englande/for ower sothern men/nothynge thereto addynge ne yet
therfrom mynysshyng. And I entende hereafter with the helpe of God
to put it forthe in his owne olde english which shal well serue/I doute
not/bothe for the northern men and the faythfull brothern of scot-
lande.

If he carried out his intention, all trace of it has been lost.[33]

The position with regard to Jack Upland is in detail complicated, but in the last resort there seems little evidence that the
print put out by Gough shows substantive sixteenth-century

[32] See *Selections*, pp. 155–7, for some details about Thorpe.
[33] The identity of the editor is a question of considerable obscurity. Foxe,
though he printed the 1530 version in his *Actes*, added a comment to his
introduction in the second edition of this work (1570, i. 629): 'Although for the
more credite of the matter, I rather wished it in his own naturall speache,
wherin it was first written. Notwithstandyng, to put away all doubt and scruple
herein, this I thought before to premonishe and testifie to the reader touchyng
the certeintie hereof: that they bee yet a lyue, which haue seen the selfe same
copy in his own old Englishe, resemblyng the true antiquitie both of the speache
and of the tyme.'

interference. Again, the printed versions of the sixteenth century that survive are all dependent upon Gough (G).[34] But the evidence for the earlier tradition is more varied. In the first place there are two manuscripts, Harley 6641 and CUL Ff.6.2, of which Heyworth provided an edition (E); secondly, there is the indirect evidence of Daw's *Rejoinder* (D), found only in Bodl. MS Digby 41, which, as Skeat perceived and Heyworth confirmed, points to a different version of the questions from that found in E.[35] Unknown to Heyworth, there is a third medieval witness: in MS Bodl. 703 is a text by William Woodford, the Franciscan opponent of Wyclif, setting out a series of 65 questions and answers, the questions being those of Upland, the responses those of Woodford (W).[36] In general G and W agree with each other and against E (D's evidence is only partial, and its text sometimes agrees with E, sometimes with GW).[37] There are a few places where G can be shown to be defective by agreement between E and W, and equally a few places where W can be detected in error by agreement between G and E.[38] W because of its textual proximity to G provides a check on the possibility of G's alterations, suppressions, or additions. In fact in many cases W confirms G's authenticity: G and W contain material not found in E, whilst conversely both G and W omit material found only in E.[39] There are a few instances where W

[34] See Heyworth's paper, (above, n. 12), and edition, p. 29 n. 3.

[35] Skeat, pp. xxxv–xxxvii, and Heyworth, pp. 29–35.

[36] Ff. 41–57; the discovery was made by E. Doyle and is reported in J. Catto, 'William Woodford, O.F.M. (*c.* 1330–*c.* 1397)', University of Oxford D.Phil. thesis (1969), 31.

[37] The fuller comparison allowed by the discovery of W bears out Heyworth's observation that D departs from E principally after l. 285 and that there may have been three versions of Upland (pp. 32–3 and n. 2). G's idiosyncrasies begin at almost exactly the same place, suggesting that there may have been a break in the textual tradition at that point.

[38] For the first instances are at E 371 *causis*, W *causas*, G *cause* or E 390–400, lacking in G; for the second most notably the surviving manuscript of W lacks E 237–43, though it appears in G.

[39] In Skeat's print of G, sections 7–8, 27, 29, 31, most of 37, most of 41, 47, and 50 are all present in W but not in E; in Heyworth's edition of E, ll. 169–73, 182–6, 244–62, 277–81, 291–4 are peculiar to E and missing in both W and G.

does not confirm G's text. One case seems plainly a sixteenth-century sophistication: this is the omission of question 65 (E, 390–400) on the Eucharist, found in both W and E. There are some seven extra questions in G, where the issue is much less clear: after W question 62, E 378, are inserted two questions (sigs. B4–B5), one on the legitimacy of fraternal habits and leaving them and the other on letters of fraternity, whilst at the end are five extra questions (sigs. B5ᵛ–B8). But in all these cases the material added goes over ground that has been covered elsewhere in all versions. The only possibly topical issue is that of the lawfulness of leaving an order, but this, whilst obviously relevant at the time of the disendowment of monastic and fraternal communities by Henry VIII, was a question discussed by the Lollards earlier.[40] Since no good motive can be found for supposing that the independent material in G was supplied by the sixteenth-century editor, it seems wiser, in the light of the evidence where G's text is supported, to withhold condemnation and to conclude that Upland, like Thorpe, is substantively a reliable transcript of a lost medieval exemplar.

John Gough, in his edition of the General Prologue in 1540, asks his readers for an even higher degree of faith. In his long address to the readers he draws their attention to the old-fashioned language 'þe which auntyant wrytynge dyffereth farre from the termys and sentence þat is now in our tyme wryten and spoken' (sig. A3ᵛ). More surprisingly he also draws attention to the more contentious parts of the text (sig. A7):

I humbly requyre you in case ye fynde ony thyng in this boke that shall offend you in the x chapiter or in the xiij I praye you blame not me though I haue folowed myne orygynall and olde copy in worde and sentence. Yet I wrote it not blamyng no person nowe lyuyng, I trust

---

[40] The suppression of the friaries was not effected until 1539, but the matter of dissolution of religious houses had been under discussion for a number of years before the act against the monastic houses gave clear warning to the friars; see S. E. Lehmberg, *The Reformation Parliament, 1529–1536* (Cambridge, 1970), 223–9, and references given. For Lollard discussion see, for instance, T. Arnold, *Select English Works of Wyclif* (Oxford, 1869–71), i. 403/34, ii. 299/5, iii. 432/35.

there be no suche abuses in rulers, gouernours, pastours, curates and preachers, as was in the Romysh church in those dayes (two hundred yeares paste and gone) God forbyd that there shulde be ony suche poysoned stomakes in this Realme.

No doubt, with the *Kynges preuylege* on the title verso, some such disclaimer was prudent.[41] But it is not clear that Gough played entirely fair with the text or his readers. Gough's re-wording of the text, largely no doubt in the cause of moderni-zation of the language, makes it difficult to discover which, if any, of the extant manuscripts of the Prologue he used as his exemplar. None of the ten, however, justify some changes in chapter x, one of those whose text Gough was most anxious to authenticate.[42] Towards the end of the chapter his version re-moves a criticism that linked *lordis* with *prelatis* as indulgers *in wakingis and pleyingis bi niȝt, and in rere-soperis and othere vanites* (l. 34), and, perhaps more dangerously, as the inflicters of inordinate taxes and other extortions on the commons; the sentence is abbreviated and only prelates and curates named (sig. L4ᵛ). Two sentences later again changes are made that eliminate lords from condemnation of the practice of offering to *dede stockes or stones* rather than to *the lyuely ymage of God whiche is a christen man* (sig. L5). That Gough himself was responsible for these alterations is suggested by the wording of this sentence: men 'in tymes past kneled and prayed, and offred fast to dead

---

[41] Gough was also the publisher of Upland, and again there had the royal privilege, though the terms of it are not set out in full in Upland. Heyworth argued (art. cit., pp. 313–14) that Upland was issued as part of Henry VIII's 'calculated campaign of printed propaganda against Rome in his attempt to justify and to secure his claims for royal supremacy'. Heyworth did not mention Gough's 1540 Prologue, and it would be more difficult to argue the king's involvement with this: even though the Prologue is less consistently outspoken than Upland, Henry's conservatism had by that time come to the fore and it is not clear that he would by then have sympathized even with the more moderate work's advocacy of vernacular scriptures for all. It would seem wiser to take the privilege here, at any rate, as 'a perfunctory and permissive formula'. Gough was imprisoned in January 1541 for printing and selling seditious books (see Aston, *Past and Present*, xxx (1965), n. 28).

[42] To the list in Forshall and Madden, i, p. xxxvii, should be added MS 12 in the Scheide collection, Princeton.

ymages, as I am certayne some yet do preuyly' (sig. L5). Rather earlier in the same chapter the editor intrudes more blatantly: after an original comment on the proclamation of papal indulgences at the instigation of secular lords (I. 30), is added 'this hath bene euydently sene of late dayes in our tyme in Englond (for the redresse) laude we God and praye we for our moste noble kynge, that he maye prosperously lyuè and fynysshe the werkes that he hath begonne in God' (sig. K3). In fairness to Gough, it does not appear that his text is consistently unreliable, and it must be admitted that the attentive reader would pick up the contemporary reference from the wording in some cases. But Crowley was wise in 1550 to go back to a manuscript for his edition of the Prologue, rather than reissuing Gough's text.[43]

The remaining text from the first part of my list, the *Compendious treatyse*, is difficult to assess. Bühler in his edition of the medieval tract listed seven manuscripts, to which can be added an eighth; but five of these are post-medieval transcripts, all apparently derived from the same exemplar that seems originally to have been in the library of Worcester Cathedral, and one of the medieval texts is a fragment only consisting of the first thirty-one lines.[44] However, these witnesses, essentially four at best, are in agreement in the version they offer; the only serious discrepancy concerns the position of a passage of twelve lines, at

[43] It is not clear whether Crowley knew of the earlier edition: he does not mention it, but, though he observes (sig. A2ᵛ) 'Many men bistowed muche to haue it copied out to the intent thei might enioye yᵉ frutes of it, in the tyme of errowre and ignoraunce: but thou hast it now offered vnto the for little coste, in a time when true religion biginnith to floryshe. It was at þᵉ fyrste made common to fewe men yᵗ wolde and were able to optayne it. But nowe it is made commen to all menne, that be desyrouse of it', he does not claim his text as the first print.

[44] To Bühler's list may be added Corpus Christi Coll. Cambridge, MS 100, pp. 227-33, a Parkerian collection like 298 and derived from the same source as that, though unlike it corrected from some other source. The other transcripts are Lambeth Palace 594, BL MSS Harl. 425 and Cotton Vitellius D.vii; the incomplete text is in Trinity Coll. Cambridge, MS B.1.26, f. 143ᵛ, where it appears in the inner margin of the final leaf. The only complete medieval texts are Trinity Coll. Cambridge, MS B.14.50, ff. 26-30ᵛ and Pierpont Morgan Library, New York, MS 648, ff. 142-43ᵛ.

the end or in the middle of the text.⁴⁵ The printed version, in all
three issues, omits almost a third of this text, rearranges some,
and adds further material of greater length than that left out.⁴⁶
Some of the omissions could well be accidental, occurring by
haplography either by a medieval scribe or by the printer. The
puzzle derives from the similarity in nature of material omitted
and added: biblical and patristic justifications for scriptural
translation are found in both categories. It is certain that some
revision of the text had occurred: the version found in the
manuscripts must be dated before 1414, since it refers to archbishop Arundel as still alive; on the other hand the printed text
alludes to the *cruell dethe* of Richard Flemyng, bishop of Lincoln, which occurred in 1431.⁴⁷ Some of the added material
would have considerable relevance in the 1520s and 1530s:

And therfore it were good to the Kyng and to other lordes to make
some remedy agaynst this constitucyon of Antechrist that saythe it is
vnlawfull to vs englyshe men to have in englyshe goddes lawe / and
therfore he brennythe and sleythe them that maynteyne thys good
deade / and that is for default that the kyng and lordes knowen not ne
wyll not knowe ther owne office in meantenance of god and hys lawe.
(sig. A5ᵛ)

... it lyethe neu[er] in Antichristes power to destroye all englysshe
bookes / for as fast as he brennethe / other men shall drawe / and thus
the cause of heresy and of þᵉ people that dyethe in heresy is the
frowardnes of byshoppes that wyll not suffer men to haue opyn com-
ounyng and fre in the lawe of gode ... And nowe they turne his lawe

---

⁴⁵ Trinity B.14.50 formed the basis of Bühler's edition; ll. 229–41 of that text
are found in the Morgan manuscript and all the later transcripts (Trinity B.1.26
lacks everything after l. 31) at the end.

⁴⁶ Omitted from Bühler's text are ll. 1–3, 35–9, 45–57, 62–80, 95–9, 207–9,
213–16, 228–76, 299–301; the most substantial additions occur after Bühler's ll.
62, 305, 210, and 213, the last by rearrangement standing at the end of the
treatise.

⁴⁷ The earlier text was itself a reworking of part of a Latin tract which I have
argued elsewhere to be by Richard Ullerston ('The debate on Bible translation,
Oxford 1401', See above pp. 67-84), and the reference to Arundel was added
in that revision. The printed version (sig. A5) omits the words *þat nowe is* (291)
from the story about the archbishop and adds the comment that 'he became
the most cruell enemy that myght be agaynst englyshe bookes' (sig. A5ᵛ).

by ther cruell constitucyons into dampnacion of the people. (sig. A6–
A6ᵛ)

But similar comments had been made from Wyclif's day onwards, even before Arundel's Constitutions had given them full
justification.⁴⁸ What is clear is that if the additions in the printed
edition are editorial then they were made within the same tradition as produced the original tract: a tradition which regarded
the precise citation of biblical, patristic, scholastic, and canonistic passages as the best way of arguing a question.

Something in transition must be said about the *Examination*
of Oldcastle that is appended to the trial of Thorpe. This text
was used in turn by John Bale in *A brefe chronycle concernynge
the Examinacyon and death of ... Syr Johan Oldecastell ...*
([Antwerp?], 1544; *STC* 1276; reprinted in [1545?] and [1548?],
STC 1277–8), a work that I have not considered here because it
does not purport to be a simple reprinting of one medieval text
but declaredly draws on many sources.⁴⁹ The text is an abbreviated and chronologically obscure account of the long process of
investigation that Oldcastle underwent, a process interrupted by
his escape from custody and by the rising of 1413. Parts of it
apparently derive from the same source as the documents recorded in the *Fasciculi Zizaniorum* and Arundel's register.⁵⁰ But

⁴⁸ With the second compare the *Opus Arduum*, dated between Christmas
1389 and Easter 1390 (Brno University Library, MS Mk 28, f. 174ᵛ) where the
prophecy of Revelations 12:4 is said to be fulfilled 'per generale mandatum
prelatorum ad comburendum, destruendum et condemnandum omnes libros,
scilicet omelias ewangeliorum et epistolarum in lingwa materna conscriptos,
suggerendo quasi non liceat nobis Anglicis legem diuinam habere in nostro
vulgari ... Sed quamuis ad hec quantum potuit per se et per suos laborauit
diabolus, non tamen profecit, quia non omnes libri tales sunt destructi, sed
loco eorum alii iam de nouo conscripti sunt ut in breui, Domino fauente
patebit, ipsis multum forciores.'

⁴⁹ Mrs Aston (1964), p. 155 n. 19, suggested that Bale in 1543 did not know
the *Examination*; but side-notes in the *Brefe chronycle* make it plain that he
had used it fully by the following year. For Bale's work on Oldcastle see L. P.
Fairfield, 'John Bale and the Development of Protestant Hagiography in England', *Journal of Ecclesiastical History*, xxiv (1973), 145–60. A reprint of the
Brefe chronycle is in the *Harleian Miscellany*, ii. 233–64.

⁵⁰ *Fasciculi Zizaniorum*, ed. W. W. Shirley (Rolls Series, 1858), 438–9 and
441–2; the material from Arundel's register is printed in Wilkins, iii. 354–5.

no precise parallel is known to the arguments recorded between Oldcastle and Arundel (sigs. H7^v-I4), though it is credible enough that such occurred. Bale maintained (sig. A3^v) that the *Examination* was issued by Tyndale, but observed. 'The which examinacyon was wrytten in the tyme of the seyd Lordes trouble / by a certen frynde of his / and so reserued in copyes vnto this our age. But sens that tyme I haue founde it in theyr owne wryttynges (which were than his vttre enemyes) in a moche more ample fourme than there.' Notwithstanding his reservations about brevity, Bale used the text extensively and treated it as carefully as he did his others, Arundel's register, Netter's *Doctrinale*, and the *Fasciculi Zizaniorum*, and more. Properly, this text belongs with the next group, though it appears as an appendix to one of those for which a medieval exemplar is known. More investigation of the Oldcastle revolt, and of the sources of evidence about it, may throw further light on this enigmatic text;[51] but there is little or nothing in it to suggest a sixteenth-century forgery.

Can any generalizations be made from this mass of detail? It seems to me that it would be fair to say that, with very few exceptions, all the evidence points to a remarkable conservatism in the sixteenth-century handling of the medieval material. There is some variation in the extent to which archaic linguistic forms are retained, but in substantive readings fidelity to the older exemplars can in many cases be established with a high degree of certainty. The fidelity is such that, where material is locally found that has no model, as for instance the extra questions in Upland or the added authorities of the *Compendious treatyse*, it would seem reasonable in default of positive contrary indication to accept that the sixteenth-century editor had an exemplar that differed from those surviving, but an exemplar that was medieval. The exception to this is obviously where the wording of

[51] Though there are references to a book about Thorpe that antedate the printed text (see Foxe, *Actes*, ed. S. R. Cattley (London, 1837–41), iv. 235, 259, 679 and v. 39), I have not come across comparable allusions to a text about Oldcastle.

the edition explicitly refers to contemporary events, or appeals to a contemporary audience—as in the case of the intrusions in Gough's edition of the General Prologue. Where the editors may not be so faithful is over omissions: in particular the topic of the Eucharist produced omission in Upland and re-wording in the *Lanterne of Lyght*. On the other hand, discussion of the Eucharist did not always provoke alteration: the longest treatment of the subject in the texts so far considered is in Thorpe (sigs. C7ᵛ–D2ᵛ), a passage that is unchanged from the version in the surviving manuscript.

In the light of these conclusions we may look briefly at the remaining three texts, the *Ploughman's Tale*, Wyclif's *Wycket*, and the *Praier and complaynte of the ploweman*. The first of these has been examined recently by Andrew Wawn, who concluded that all of the *Tale*, apart from the opening fifty-two lines and ll. 205-28, had 'an early fifteenth-century date of composition'.[52] Whilst I am not entirely convinced by Wawn's dissection of that early poem into a basic debate and a revised version with interpolation, his arguments for an early Lollard origin for the work seem to me entirely persuasive. The evidence that Wawn used was both ideological and linguistic. With regard to the second, the case in the *Ploughman's Tale* is happier than in either of the other two texts: the verse form of the *Tale* makes it possible to argue on strong grounds for the originality of vocabulary in rhyming position. The balance of probability is against the likelihood that the strongly archaic language of the *Praier and complaynte* was composed by a sixteenth-century forger,[53] but this cannot formally be proved. Even less would it be legitimate to dismiss the claims of the *Wycket* to antiquity on the grounds of the more modern language of its editions. In subject matter there seems to me nothing in the *Praier* that would be out

---

[52] Wawn (1972), 39.

[53] The morphology is noticeably archaic, especially in the frequent use of the past participial *y*-prefix; as instances of obsolescent or obsolete vocabulary note *bynemen, dysparpled, fulleden* 'baptised', *gylteth* 'sins', *herynge* 'praise', *sythe* 'afterwards' adv., *vnworshypped, yerners* 'runners'.

of place in a Lollard tract of the early fifteenth century. The case with the *Wycket* is to my mind rather less clear: the terms in which the Eucharist is discussed are not altogether those found in Lollard treatments of that subject and, though biblical passages are amply quoted, there is not the usual Wycliffite citation of patristic proof texts. The *Wycket* was, however, notorious before it was printed: it is mentioned in numerous trials from 1518 to 1532.[54] Bale records that William Grocyn had written a tract against it, and gives the incipit; Bale himself owned a copy of this lost work. This would put the date of composition of the *Wycket* certainly before 1518 and more probably well before this.[55]

From the viewpoint of Robert Crowley, the printer of the latest edition considered here, there is an inexplicable omission from my discussion. The issue of the General Prologue must have been a relatively simple task, and the preparation of the text can have occupied only a small amount of Crowley's time before its appearance in 1550. For in the same year Crowley produced three editions of *Piers Plowman*, editions which, as Kane and Donaldson have been able to deduce from their collations, show successive modifications made as the result of conflation with new manuscripts that came to hand.[56] There is not space here to examine in full Crowley's side-notes, let alone to consider whether any of the idiosyncrasies of his texts reflect his editorial tampering. But it is clear that Crowley linked *Piers Plowman* with the earlier reforming movement: he dated the poem between 1350 and 1409, and most probably in the reign of Edward III, 'In whose tyme it pleased God to open the eyes of many to se hys truth, geuing them boldenes of herte, to open their mouthes and crye oute agaynste the worckes of darckenes, as did John

---

[54] See the registers used by Foxe, *Actes*, iv. 207-8, 226, 234-6, v. 39-40.

[55] Bale, *Scriptorum Illustrium Maioris Brytanniae ... Catalogus* (Basel, 1557-9), i. 707 and ii. 164.

[56] STC 19906, 19907, and 19907a; see G. Kane and E. T. Donaldson, *Piers Plowman: the B Version* (London, 1975), 6-7 and ensuing discussion of textual relations.

Wicklefe, who also in those dayes translated the holye Bible into the Englishe tonge ...' (sig. *ii). The modern reader of the B version might be surprised to learn that passus v contains proof by Reason that 'Abbayes shoulde be suppressed', a subject also argued, we are told, in passus x; but it is clear from Crowley's comment on the second of these that he regarded the whole as a tract for his times: 'Loke not vpon this boke therfore, to talke of wonders paste or to come, but to amende thyne owne misse, which thou shalt fynd here moste charitably rebuked' (sig. *2ᵛ). Modern critics may see a world of difference between *Piers Plowman* and, for instance, Jack Upland or Thorpe's disputations with archbishop Arundel.[57] To the reformers of the sixteenth century all of these texts, along with passages from Chaucer or Gower, were grist to the mill of their argument: to support their own contentions on theological and ecclesiastical questions, and to show that the ideas they put forward were supported by 'a witness preordained by God, so many years before us, for the confirmation of our doctrine'.[58]

[57] I hope to trace elsewhere the fortunes of the ploughman figure, influenced by *Piers Plowman* and by Chaucer's *Canterbury Tales*, in the fifteenth and sixteenth centuries, and to consider the justification for subsequent interpretations in Langland's text. Pamela Gradon has examined the position of Langland in regard to Wyclif's thought in 'Langland and the Ideology of Dissent', *PBA* lxvi (1980), 179-205.

[58] Quoted by Margaret Aston (1964), p. 157, from Luther's preface to the 1528 edition of the Lollard *Opus Arduum*.

CHAPTER 16

Appendix: Additions and Modifications to a Bibliography of English Wycliffite Writings

The lists of manuscripts and early editions in the chapter on "Wyclyf and his Followers" in *A Manual of the Writings in Middle English*, ed. J. Burke Severs (Hamden, Conn., 1970) are in a number of cases incomplete or misleading. The following is intended as a supplement for the items included in this chapter; it does not aim to add to the number of Lollard works, since more study is necessary before the corpus of these writings can adequately be defined. The numeration of the *Manual* has been retained, and the ordering of manuscripts save where this is badly misleading; in order to make the material readily intelligible, some of the more extreme *Manual* abbreviations have been expanded.

[6] This section is particularly muddled. Delete MS. St. John's Cambridge 436 (S.46), a post-medieval collection, and MS. University Library Edinburgh 93 (Laing 140) whose contents are not unorthodox save for one sermon listed under [7]. To British Museum MS. Add. 41321 add Bodleian MS. Rawlinson C.751, ff. 26-110v whose sermons partially overlap and extend the set in the first.

[7] The details given are inaccurate and, since they do not differentiate between defects due to loss of leaves and deliberate omissions, misleading. The following list replaces that given and indicates only deliberate omission; the manuscripts have been re-ordered to bring together those with similar contents. Numbers in brackets refer to the five different sets: (1) Sunday Gospels, (2) Commune Sanctorum, (3) Proprium Sanctorum, (4) Ferial Gospels, (5) Sunday Epistles. For the divergent arrangements of these and their combination in some manuscripts (which make the folio references supplied unhelpful), see *Medium Ævum*, xl (1971), pp. 142-56. 1, MS. Bodley 788 (1-5); 2, British Museum MS. Add. 40672, *olim* Wrest Park 11, (1-5); 3, MS. Pembroke Cambridge 237 (1-5); 4, MS. Leicester Wyggeston Hospital 10.D.34/6 (1-5); 5, Bodleian MS. Douce 321 (1-5); 6, British Museum MS. Cotton Claudius D. viii (1-5); 7, Robert Taylor MS. Princeton, *olim* Wrest Park 32, (1-5); 8, MS. Lambeth 1149 (1-5); 9, Bodleian MS. Don. c. 13 (1–5); 10. British Museum MS. Royal 18 B. ix (1–5, omitting six sermons from the end of 4); 11, MS. St. John's Cambridge C.8 (1-5); 12, MS. Trinity Cambridge B.2.17 (1-4); 13, British Museum MS.

Add. 40671, *olim* Wrest Park 38, (1-4); 14, MS. Trinity Cambridge B.4.20 (1-3, 5); 15, MS. Leicester Old Town Hall 3 (1-3, 5); 16, MS. Wisbech Town Museum 8 (1-3, 5); 17, British Museum MS. Harley 2396 (Advent to 5 Epiphany sermons from 1, 4, 5); 18, MS. Corpus Christi Cambridge 336 (2-4); 19, Magdalene Cambridge MS. Pepys 2616 (2-4, omitting ten sermons from 2); 20, MS. Cambridge University Ii.1.40 (1, 5); 21, MS. Christ's Cambridge 7 (1, 5); 22, Bodleian MS. Laud Misc. 314 (1); 23, Bodleian MS. Add. A. 105 (1); 24, MS. Sidney Sussex Cambridge 74 (1 with independent continuations); 25, MS. St. John's Cambridge G.22 (1 now incomplete, original state doubtful, beginning imperfect in no. 33, ending imperfect in no. 54; see below [11] for other contents); 26, MS. Peterhouse Cambridge 69 (fragments from 1); 27, MS. New College Oxford 95 (4 complete, with seven sermons from 3 and one from 1); 28, MS. Trinity Cambridge B.14.38 (5); 29, British Museum MS. Harley 1730 (5); 30, MS. Hertford Oxford 4 (5, fragments only); 31, MS. Essex Record Office D/DPr 554 (5, single leaf); 32, MS. Edinburgh University Library 93 (one sermon from 3). [The first volume of a new edition of these sermons containing sets 1 and 5 has now been published under the title *English Wycliffite Sermons* I, ed. Anne Hudson (Oxford, 1983). The second volume will contain sets 2 and 3 plus items [9] and [10] below; the third will contain set 4; a commentary will appear in a fourth volume.]

[9] Substitute for this entry on manuscripts: MSS. 1-12 copies of this sermon are found in manuscripts of [7] listed above as nos. 1, 2, 3, 4, 7, 8, 9, 10, 14, 15, 21, 22; 13, MS. St. John's Cambridge G.25, ff. 97-105; 14, MS. Trinity Dublin C.5.6, ff. 96-101.

[10] Substitute for this entry on manuscripts: MSS. 1-14 copies of this sermon are found in manuscripts of [7] listed above as nos. 1, 2, 3, 4, 6, 7, 8, 9, 10, 12, 14, 15, 18, 19; 15, MS. St. John's Cambridge G.25, ff. 102-127; 16, MS. Trinity Dublin C.5.6, ff. 101-116v; 17, British Museum MS. Harley 1203, ff. 91-119v.

[11] Delete "54" from heading; substitute 1, MS. Trinity Dublin C.1.22 (originally a set of 52 sermons on Sunday gospels plus 5 for festivals); 2, MS. St. John's Cambridge G.22, ff. 1-78v (first 25 of those in 1); 3, Cambridge University MS. Add. 5338, ff. 1-67 (seriously damaged at beginning; probably contained first 25 sermons only). These sermons are dependent upon those in [7].

[14] Add 5, Robert Taylor MS. Princeton, *olim* Wrest Park 32, ff. 5-8v; 6, MS. Trinity Cambridge B.14.38, ff. 148v-150 (part only); 7, MS. Cambridge University Nn.4.12, ff. 12v-25v; 8, MS. Norwich Castle Museum 158.926.4g.3, ff. 64v-75.

[15] Add 5, MS. Cambridge University Nn.4.12, ff. 25v-27; 6, MS. York Minister XVI.L.12, ff. 36v-37v.

[16] Add 4, MS. Cambridge University Nn.4.12, ff. 27-29v; 5, MS. York Minster XVI.L.12, ff. 37v-39v.

[19] Add 4, MS. Bodley 938, ff. 73v-117; 5, Harvard University MS. Eng. 738, ff. 31-77.

[20] Delete 2 and renumber; add 4, Harvard University MS. Eng. 738, ff. 77-86v; 5, MS. York Minster XVI.L.12, ff. 39v-50.

[21] Delete 2.

[22] Delete 2 and renumber; add 3, MS. York Minster XVI.L.12, ff. 27-32.

[26] Add 5, MS. Cambridge University Library Ii.6.55, ff. 13-22v; 6, British Museum MS. Harley 2398, ff. 160v-166v; 7, MS. Westminster School 3, ff. 121-132v.

[28] Add 3, MS. Bodley 9, ff. 67-72; 4, Bodleian MS. Eng. th. f.39, ff. 14v-17; 5, MS. Bodley 938, ff. 10v-13; 6, British Museum MS. Harley 2398, ff. 188v-190v; 7, MS. Westminster School 3, ff. 132v-135v.

[35] Add 4, British Museum MS. Add. 37677, ff. 101-105v; 5, MS. Bodley 540, pp. 101-116; 6, MS. Trinity Dublin C.1.14, pp. 76-85.

[40] Add 5, MS. Leicester Wyggeston Hospital 10.D.34/6, ff. 212v-223v.

[43] Add 4, MS. York Minster XVI.L.12, ff. 33v-36v.

[46] Add 4, MS. Pembroke Cambridge 237, f. 217; 5, MS. Leicester Wyggeston Hospital 10.D.34/6, ff. 62v-63.

[51] These are not found as a group elsewhere, so delete "2, 3 not specified"; individual members are known in other manuscripts.

[52] Add 4, MS. Norwich Castle Museum 158.926 4g.3, ff. 1-64.

[[53] Add 4, MS Bodley Lat.th.e.30.]

[55] Delete 6 and renumber; under editions add that a copy is found appended to *A proper dyaloge betwene a gentillman and a husbandman* (1530), STC 6813, facsimile of this (not of STC 3021 as stated) by F. Fry (1863), reprinted Arber Reprints, xviii (1871). See also M. Aston, "Lollardy and the Reformation: Survival or Revival?", *History,* xlix (1964), pp. 149-70.

[58] Add 3, MS. Westminster School 3, ff. 68-72; 4. MS. Norwich Castle Museum 158.926 4g.3, ff. 75-78v.

[65] Expand this confusing entry: Tract 1 *De Salutaribus Documentis*: MSS. 1, British Museum Harley 2330, ff. 1-66v; 2, Cambridge University Ii.6.55, ff. 78-100; 3, All Souls Oxford 24, ff. 61-126v. Edition by S. L. Fristedt, *The Wycliffe Bible,* II Stockholm Studies in English, xxi (1869). Tract 2 *De Vita Christiana*: MSS. 1, British Museum Harley 2330, ff. 66v-97v; 2, Cambridge University Ii.6.55, ff. 42-63v; 3, All Souls Oxford ff. 1-35. Tract 3 *De Creatione*: MSS. 1, British Museum Harley 2330, ff. 97v-100v; 2, Cambridge University Ii.6.55, ff. 63v-66; 3, All Souls Oxford 24, ff. 35-38v; 4, Cambridge University Ii.6.39, ff. 120-122v. Tract 4 *De Duodecim Abusionibus*: MSS. 1, British Museum Harley 2330, ff. 100v-119v (ends incomplete); 2, Cambridge University Ii.6.55, ff. 66-78; 3, All Souls Oxford 24, ff. 38v-59.

[[69] Add to the list of editions that by C. Davidson, *A Middle English Treatise on the Playing of Miracles* (Washington, 1981).]

[73] The text in MS. Trinity College Cambridge B.14.50, ff. 34-35, which is not the same as that in British Museum MS. Add. 24202, is also found in Bodleian MS. Eng. th. f.39, ff. 37-38.

[83] Add 2, MS. Bodley 938, ff. 50-56.

[85] See above p. 9. Re-order the section: Version 1: MSS. 1, Lambeth 551, ff. 2-59v; parts of chapter 7 and the whole of chapters 8-10 and the English appendix of this version were reprinted in *A proper dyaloge* . . . (1530), STC 6813 (see bibliography for this above [55]) and in the probably earlier print ([1529?]) that lacks the addition of [55] found in Bodleian MS. Wood 774 and described by Nijhoff and Kronenberg, *Nederlandsche Bibliographie van 1500 tot 1540* (The Hague, 1919-), no. 4215. Version 2: MSS. 1, British Museum Egerton 2820, ff. 1-121v (ends incomplete); 2, Cambridge University Dd.14.30(2) (defective at both ends); 3, Cambridge University Ff.6.2, ff. 1-70v; 4, Huntington HM 503, ff. 1-129v. On the last see the description and extracts in Quaritch Cat. 328 (1914), no. 585, and the brief account in R. L. Greene, "A Middle English Love Poem and the 'O-and-I' Refrain-Phrase", *Medium Ævum* xxx (1961), p. 170.

[90] Add 2, MS. Trinity Dublin C.5.6, ff. 124-127 (parts only).

[94] Add 2, British Museum MS. Harley 6613, ff. 1-57v (defective); under editions add that printed by Redman [1530?], STC 15225.

[95], [96] The questions in 95 are found in Woodford's *Responsiones ad Quaestiones LXV* preserved in MS. Bodley 703, ff. 41-57; add also the edition by Gough [1536?], STC 5098.

[97]-[103] This section is misleadingly selective; reference should be made to the sources mentioned in Aston (above fn.5) and Thomson (above fn. 33).

[101] Delete "Latin version only"; an English version is found in Bodleian MS. Rawlinson C.208, ff. 1-91v; Latin MSS. are 1, Vienna Nationalbibliothek 3936, ff. 1-22v; 2, Prague Metropolitan Chapter 0.29, ff. 188-209.

[Editions of numbers [9], [29], [51] number 7, [53], [54], [56], and [73] version in Add.24202, and of extracts from numbers [52], [69], [85], [94] and [101] have appeared in Anne Hudson, *Selections from English Wycliffite Writings* (Cambridge, 1978).]

INDEX

Aiscough, William bishop of Salisbury 191; material in his episcopal register 127
Aldbourne (Berks.) 123
Aldbourne (Wilts.) 122
Alfred, alleged biblical translation by him 70, 154
Alington, Robert 13, 78
Alnwick, William bishop of Norwich 97n, 125; abjurations in his courtbook 130, and procedure of investigation 130-1
Ambrose 21, 48, 209; Wycliffite gloss on 211, 214-15; Berengar on 215
Ancrene Riwle, Lollard version 81, 203, 213
Anne, queen of Richard II 71, 108; possession of vernacular scriptures 154
Apocalypse commentary, see *Opus Arduum*
Apology for Lollard Doctrines 166; elements in its vocabulary 177-9
A proper dyaloge... 229, 231, 233-4, 251-2
Aquinas, Thomas 21; *Catena Aurea* 106
Aristotle 21; *Rhetoric* 155
Arius 160
Arundel, Thomas archbishop of Canterbury 58, 71, 81, 83, 88, 243; trial of Oldcastle 244-5; trial of Purvey 87, 96-7, 100; trial of Thorpe 93; authorization of Love's *Mirrour* 155; his *Constitutions* 62n, 67, 69, 77, 129n, 140, 146-9, 156, 159, 168, 244; Lollard references to the *Constitutions* 146n.
Aston, John 13, 86, 89, 116, 150-1, 200, 210; his equivocation on the Eucharist 113, 132n.
Augustine 21, 48, 209
Avignon 195

Bacon, Roger 72
Baker, Joan 191
Baker, John 161n.
Bale, John 47, 67, 93; attributions to Thomas Palmer 82; attribution of *Opus Arduum* to John Purvey 56-7, 99-100; list of Nicholas Hereford's writings 61; on John Purvey 96-100, 109; on *Wycklyffes Wycket* 247; *A brefe chronycle concernynge...Oldcastle* 244-5; *Illustrium Magnae Britanniae scriptorum ... summarium* 96, 98, 100; *Index*

Britanniae scriptorum 98; *Scriptorum illustrium Maioris Brytanniae... catalogus* 98, 100; *Ymage of Both Churches* 99; copy of Thorpe's account of his trial in Bale's hand 237n.
Baron, John, of Amersham; books confiscated from him 142n.
Basil 21
Bath, John of 191
Bath and Wells diocese 115-16
Baxter, Margery 131n.
Beauchamp, Sir William 78
Beaufort, Henry bishop of Lincoln 87
Beccles (Suffolk) 130n.
Becket, Thomas à 144
Bede 21, 48; alleged biblical translation by him 154
Bedman, Laurence 13, 86
Bekynton, Thomas bishop of Bath and Wells; list of questions in episcopal register 127-39; commissary at 1428 meeting of convocation 129
Berengar of Tours 142; regarded as teacher of Wyclif 214-15
Bernard 21, 48
Bible; desire for vernacular version 53; debate on translation 67-84; advocacy of vernacular scriptures not at early stage identified with Lollardy 83, 102; later association of translation with Lollardy 157-8; Lollard texts in favour of translation 83n; restrictions on translation in Arundel's *Constitutions* 147-8
Blackfriars' Council 7, 45
Blandford (Dorset) 123
Blois, Peter of 21
Blythe, John bishop of Salisbury 182, 191
Boethius 21
Books (see also *Lollards* and individual titles); destruction of Lollard books 7, especially when in English 243-4; confiscation of books on suspicion of heresy 125, 142; possession of English books as evidence of heresy 149, 182; mandates against heretical books 150; 'suspect book of commandments' 162; *parchemyners* and scribes amongst early

Lollards 182; *schedulae, quaterni, libri* or *rollis, quairis* 183-6, 199-200

Bottlesham, John bishop of Rochester 87

Boughton, John 118, 191

Boulers, Reginald bishop of Lichfield; material in his register 127, 129

Bowland, Robert 93

Box (Berks.) 122

Boyton (Wilts.) 123

Bradenstoke-cum-Clack (Wilts.) 122

Bradwardine, Thomas 142

Braybrook, Robert bishop of London 58, 87, 97

Braybrook (Northants.) 3, 78-9, 183, 189n, 191, 200

Brethren of the Free Spirit; possible contamination with their views in Ramsbury's beliefs 113-14

Brington, Lincoln diocese 156

Brinkworth (Wilts.) 123

Bristol 95; early centre of Lollardy 87, 95, 115; Purvey's preaching there 89; investigation of Lollards from Bristol 1417 127-8

Brixton Deverill (Wilts.) 122

Brouns, Thomas; Chichele's chancellor 1426-33 and the possible originator of procedural material against Lollards 128-32; his Rochester and Norwich episcopal registers 129

Brut, Walter 28, 55, 145

Bryt, Henry 79

Buckingham, John bishop of Lincoln 86

Bungay (Suffolk) 130-1nn.

Burell, John 131n, 161

Bury, John; *Gladius Salomonis* 160

Butler, William; text on bible translation 67-8, 150, 155-7; relation of this to Ullerston's text 81

Bykenore, Thomas 11n.

Calne (Wilts.) 122

Canon law 21, 214-15; use by Lollards 25

Canterbury; province 147; provincial convocation 1428 128-30

Cassian 21

Cassiodorus 21

Cavell, Robert 131n.

Chastising of God's Children 114

Chaucer, Geoffrey 141, 248; *Canterbury Tales* held on suspicion of heresy 142; *Pardoner's Tale* 104, 149; *Parson's Tale* 149; claimed as author of *Ploughman's Tale* 231, 246; and of *Jack Upland* 232

Chaundler, John bishop of Salisbury 191

Chichele, Henry archbishop of Canterbury 235; alleged trial of Purvey 96-7; investigation of procedure against Lollards 1428 128-30

Chilterns; Lollards in 162

Chippenham (Wilts.) 115, 123

Chipping Warden (Northants.) 61

Christian Malford (Wilts.) 122

Chrysostom 21, 48

Clanvowe, Sir John; *The Two Ways* 54

Claydon, John 95; his copy of *Lanterne of Lyght* 234-5

Clement VII, pope 44, 64

Clifford, Richard bishop of London; notes on procedure of investigating heretics in his register 127, 129-30

Colchester (Essex) 182

Comestor, Peter 21, 49

Commentarius in Apocalypsim see *Opus Arduum*

Compendious olde Treatyse. . . 11, 68, 80, 229, 231, 242-4; attributed to Purvey by M. Deanesly 107; its date 243

Compendium Theologicae Veritatis 21

Constance, Council of 130

Constantine, donation of 197

Constantine, George 228

Courtenay, William archbishop of Canterbury 59-60, 77

Coventry 161

Crashawe, Richard 193

Crashawe, William 193-4, 200; books at St. John's College Cambridge that belonged to him 193

Crowley, Robert 230, 233, 242, 247-8; his edition of *Piers Plowman* 247-8

Crumpe, Henry 45

Cursor Mundi 217-18, 220

Cyprian 21

Cyrcetur, Thomas 32

Daw, Friar; his *Reply* see *Jack Upland*

De Abusiuis; by same author as *Opus Arduum* 54

Deanesly, Margaret; works attributed to Purvey in her *The Lollard Bible* 105-8; on texts concerning the translation of the Bible 67, 80

De Antichristo; by same author as *Opus Arduum* 54

De Heretico Comburendo 1401; its terms anticipated 64-5

Dekyn, Thomas 213

Despenser, Henry bishop of Norwich 45, 64-5, 87, 213

De Versione Bibliorum 69

Dives and Pauper 125, 180, 211-12; vocabulary in 123-4

Donatism; in Lollardy 126

Dore of Holy Scripture see Wycliffite Bible

Drayton, Thomas 109

Dunstable (Beds.) 213

Dymmock, Roger; his objection to Lollard use of the term *prelat* 179

East Anglia; ownership of *Dives and Pauper* there 174
Ederyk, William 88
Edward III 247
Edward VI 227
Edward, John 156
England 194, 197
English language; significance of Lollard use 141-63; knowledge of elements of religion in it as evidence of heresy 161
Erghum, Ralph bishop of Salisbury 118
Eulogium Historiarum continuation; evidence about discrimination of Wyclif's ideas 151
Eusebius 48
Examinacion of Master William Thorpe see Thorpe

Fabian; *Chronicle* 98
Faldo, John; glossary of Quaker terms 167
Fasciculi Zizaniorum 158; Purvey's articles 87; Lavenham's list of Purvey's errors 91-2; Bale's ownership of it and information drawn from it 96-7, 237; Foxe's information from it 101; record of list of questions from Council of Constance 130; material on Oldcastle's trial 244-5
Faulfis, Nicolas 3, 40-41, 45, 78-9, 191
Fifty Heresies and Errors of Friars 108
Fish, Simon 228
Fishbourn, Thomas 115, 119, 121
FitzRalph, Richard 21, 49, 51, 63, 76, 142; regarded by Lollards as saint 49
Flanders Crusade 1383 45, 64-5
Fleccher, Richard 131n.
Fleming, Richard bishop of Lincoln 32n, 68, 243
Floretum 5, 14-29, 31-42, 48, 50, 62, 149; its date 20; English manuscripts 16, 31-4; Bohemian manuscripts 20n, 35; Netter's reference to *author Floreti* 41, 94; relation to 'intermediate' version 15; modified versions 35, 37-8; relation to *Rosarium Theologie* 17-18, 37-8
Foxe, John 96; comments on Purvey 100-101; material on Thorpe 237-8nn; comments on Lollard self-naming 168; *Actes and Monuments* 100-101, 107; *Commentarii in ecclesia gestarum* 99-100; *Rerum in ecclesia gestarum* 100
Friars; their opposition to Wyclif 212-13
Fuller, T., *Church-History of Britain* 102
Fuller, *alias* Heede, William 191
Fyncaisshe, see Piers

Gascoigne, Thomas 77n; on Pecock 160
Gaunt, John of 197

Gawain poet 141
Geoffrey of Pickering 93
Giles of Rome 82
Gilmyn, Richard 161
Glossa Ordinaria 48
Glossed Gospels 9, 62, 107; attributed by M. Deanesly to Purvey 106
Gloucester, Thomas of Woodstock, duke of 196-7
Gloucester, parliament there in 1378 18, 32, 36
Gosele, John 79
Gough (or Gowgh), John 230, 238, 240-2, 246
Gower, John 141, 248
Gratian 214-15
Greatham, Robert of; *Mirror* 107, 141n.
Gregory 21, 48
Gregory XI, pope 195
Gregory Nazianzen 21
Grocyn, William 247
Grosseteste, Robert 21, 49, 76, 144; *Dicta* 39; letter on vernacular teaching 161; regarded as saint by Lollards 49
Guido de Baysio 21
Guilielmus de Monte Lauduno 21

Harley, Robert 88
Hasleton (Gloucs.) 95
Haymo 48
Heede, see Fuller
Henry VI 182
Henry VII 227, 241n.
Hereford, Nicholas 13, 86, 89, 93, 116, 150, 200, 210; Ascension day sermon in Oxford 1382 151; career and possible authorship of *Opus Arduum* 58-61; alleged imprisonment at Saltwood 96, 98; letter upbraiding him after his abjuration of Lollardy 60, 82; letter of Richard II giving him public protection 60; colophon with his name in Bodleian MS Douce 369 104
Heywood, Thomas, dean of Lichfield; probable owner of BL MS Harley 2179 129
Heyworth, William bishop of Lichfield 129
Higden, Ranulph; *Polychronicon* 21, 70-1; comments on dialect 218
Hilton, Walter; *Eight Chapters on Perfection* 114; *Tractatus de Adoracione Ymaginum* 82
Hitton, Thomas 238
Hnatnice, Matthias of 38-41, 45;
Hoccleve, Thomas 145
Hoke, Robert 126n.
Holcot, Robert 21
Honorius Augustodunensis; on *Canticles* 72
Hostiensis 21

Hugh of St. Cher 21
Hugh of St. Victor 21
Hungerford (Berks.) 118, 123, 191
Hus, Jan 34, 41; *De libris hereticorum legendis* 42
Hussite movement; differences from Lollardy 143; naming Wyclif as fifth evangelist 167

Ile, Thomas, of Braybrook 183, 189, 200
Innocent III 88

Jack Upland 10, 12; elements in its vocabulary 180; version printed [1536?] 230, 232, 238-40; textual relations 238-9; purpose of printed edition 241n; *Friar Daw's Reply* 239
James I 193
James, William 58
Jerome 21, 48, 71-2, 152, 209
Jesenice, John of 40
Joachim of Fiore 49
Joannes Andreae 21
John of Rupescissa 49-50, 54
Josephus 48
Joye, George 228

Kemerton 3, 78
Kempe, John archbishop of York 213
Kempe, Margery 114
Kilwardby, Robert 49
Knĕhnic, George of 3, 40, 78-9
Knighton, Henry 53, 57, 59, 115; his chronology 89; on Purvey 89-91, 107-8; on Lollardy 107-8; on Wyclif's part in biblical translation 151; evidence on Lollard language and teaching 165-6

Lambeth Constitutions 161
Lanfranc; *Liber de Corpore et Sanguine Domini* 215
Langdon, John bishop of Rochester 128, 130
Langland, William; *Piers Plowman* 104; Crowley's edition 247-8
Langton, Thomas bishop of Salisbury 162, 191
Language; observations about its nature in debate on biblical translation 153; that heresy may be found in any language 158; northern vocabulary 217-26
Lanterne of Liȝt 27, 50, 166; date 185; elements in its vocabulary 176, 178-9; version printed [1535?] 11, 230, 232, 234-6; relation of printed text to extant manuscripts 235-6
Lateran Council 1215 88, 92, 161
Lathbury (Bucks.) 86
Latimer, Dame Anne 3, 78
Latimer, Sir Thomas 3, 61, 78, 189n

Lavenham, Richard; date of death 91; his list of Purvey's errors 91-2, 96, 98, 108-9; Bale's interpretation of Lavenham's list 99; Lavenham's list in Foxe 100
Lay Folks' Catechism 203, 219n.
Leicester 53, 165, 183; Lollard copyists there 189
Leo 21
Lewis, John; *History of the Life and Sufferings of... John Wicliffe* 102; speculations on Purvey 102-3
Lichfield; connection of Harley 2179 with the place 129; evidence of Lollard vocabulary in courtbook B/C/13 170
Lincoln diocese 168
Littlepage, William 162
Lollard Knights 89; see also Latimer, Sir Thomas, Montague, Sir John and Neville, Sir William
Lollards; name 45, 64, 167, 176; other names for them 166-8; list of questions concerning their beliefs 14, 117, 125-39; comprehensive survey of their beliefs 126, 131; diversity of beliefs 126, 213-14; difficulty of assessing beliefs from abjurations 131-2; conventicles 110; their learning 106; and literacy 145-6, 182; nature of their books 183; Lollard practices from evidence of Ramsbury 115-19; Lollard 'priests' 111; views on church 23, 206; on clergy 88, 205; on clerical temporalities 63; on community of ownership 126; on confession 87, 91, 113, 121, 206; on consecration 112, 120; on Eucharist 63, 87, 90-1, 117-19, 120-1, 209-11; Ramsbury's views 112-13; changes in Reformation editions 209-11, 240, 246; on excommunication 88, 90-1, 121, 126; on fees 90; on friars 48, 63, 90, 203; on images 112, 121, 126; on king in relation to church 197-9; on marriage of religious 121; on oaths 126; on offerings 121; on pilgrimage 126; on pope 23, 88, 91, 205; on predestination 126; on priesthood of predestinate 87-8, 131, 156-7; on priestly obligation to preach 88, 90-1, 121; licenses not necessary to preach 90; on 'private religions' 90, 113, 126, 208-9; on tithes 92, 126; on vernacular Bible 53, 63, 106, 155-8; on war and bishops' involvement in it 47
Lollard Texts; extent of 181; difficulties in discerning 125; late manucripts of 11; 16th-century printing 11-12, 227-48; *Answeris to hem þat seien we schulden not speke of Holy Writte* 183; *Clergy may not hold property* 9-10, 229, 233-4; translation of Wyclif's *Confessio* 183;

and of *De Officio Pastorali* 108; *Dialogue between knight and clerk* 184, 193-200; *Dialogue between Jon and Richerd* 196-7; *Dialogue between Reson and Gabbying* 185, 196; *Dialogue between secular priest and friar* 196; Lollard Disendowment Bill 62, 92, 98, 109; *Great Sentence of the Curse expounded* 108; anonymous Latin text on honour due to images 6; *O and I* poem on Blackfriars' Council 7; *Of the leaven of the pharisees* 108; *Of Ministers in the Church* 185, 200, 202, 250; Lollard sermon-cycle 8, 25-6, 62, 168; manuscripts of it 185-91, 249-50; attributed to Purvey by Workman 108; use of *al ʒif* in manuscripts of it 224-5; its expurgation in Bodleian MS Don.c. 13 201-15, and its language and vocabulary 217-26; *Sex raciones ad probandum quod ad regem secularem pertinet punire clericos* 6; *Tractatus de regibus* 185; *Treatise of Miracle Playing* 251; *Vae Octuplex* 185, 200, 202, 250, and its expurgation in Bodleian MS Don.c.13 203

Lollard vocabulary 10, 28, 52, 54, 62, 109, 113, 165-80, 207-8, 224-5; inadequacy of it as sole test of text's orthodoxy 170; small amount in BL MS Additional 41321 and Bodleian MS Rawlinson C. 751 174

Lombard, Peter 21, 214

London 54, 70, 95, 108, 151, 168, 200; diocese 191; St. Paul's Cross 87, 96, 98; St. Paul's 98, 130, 200, 213; Westminster Hall 98; Westminster Abbey 108

Longbridge Deverill (Wilts.) 123

Longland, John bishop of Lincoln 162, 168

Love, Nicholas; *Mirror* 155

Luther, Martin; edition and preface to *Commentarius in Apocalypsin* 46, 48n, 51, 55, 57, 248; Bale's attribution of text to Purvey 99-100

Lutterworth (Leics.) 90

Lychlade, Robert 3, 78

Lyndwood, William; participation in 1428 Convocation 128; glosses in *Provinciale* to Arundel's *Constitutions* 148

Lyons, Council of, 1274 88, 92

Lyra, Nicholas of 21, 47, 72

Magna Carta 144

Mahomet 160

Maidstone (Kent) 238

Maimonides 81

Malmesbury (Wilts.) 115, 122

Mannyng, M. 140

Marlborough (Wilts.) 122

Marsilius of Padua 142

Marske, Cleveland (N. Yorks) 238

Martham (Norfolk) 130-1nn.

Martinus of Verona 45

Martinus Polonus 24, 49

Mass; Ramsbury's version of 116-18, 121-2

Melksham (Wilts.) 123

Middelworth, William 78

Miroir des Simples Ames 114

Monk, Richard 130

Montague, Sir John; dealings with Nicholas Hereford 59, 61

Morden, James 162

Morden, Marian 162

More, Sir Thomas 155n.

Morgan, Philip bishop of Worcester 95; bishop of Ely 128

Morley, Robert 88

Morton, John archbishop of Canterbury; material in his register 127

Mychel, John 79

Nayland (Suffolk) 130n.

Netheravon (Wilts.) 191

Netter, Thomas 41, 50, 65, 212; on Purvey 10n, 93-5, 107; on Oldcastle 245; evidence on Lollard language 167; evidence on authorship of Lollard sermon cycle 186n; criticism of Wyclif's gloss on Ambrose 214; version of *Doctrinale* used by Bale 96n.

Neville, Sir William; dealings with Nicholas Hereford 59, 61

Northampton 189; Lollard activities there 95, 119, 213.

Nottingham; Purvey imprisoned there 59

Ockham, William of 49-50, 54, 194n.

Oldcastle, Sir John 95, 145; his trial 93, 97n, 130n, 210; revolt 65, 83, 119, 174, 185; Purvey in the revolt 88-9, 109; *Twelve Conclusions* attributed to him by Bale and Foxe 101; account of his trial printed [1530] 12, 230, 244-5; Bale's belief that [1530] print was issued by Tyndale 245

Olivi, Peter John 49-50, 54, 81

Opus Arduum 6, 8-9, 39, 43-65, 152, 154-5, 157, 227n; date 44-5; possible author 54-61; Czech translation 46; Hussite use 46; Bale's attribution of text to Purvey 99-100; abbreviated version published as *Commentarius in Apocalypsin* 46

Origen 21, 48

Orosius 48, 72

Oudin, C.; *Commentarius de scriptoribus ecclesiae antiquis* 102

Oxford 49, 54, 70, 86, 93, 97; Wycliffism in Oxford 75-80; *Floretum* possibly compiled there 21, 23; possible origin of sermon cycle 189; debate on biblical translation 1401 67-84, 150; fire of Wyclif's books 1410 3; dispute over rights of investigation 147; All Soul's College 32; Canterbury Hall 78; Exeter College 79; Lincoln College 32; The Queen's College 79; associates of Wyclif there 78-9; Ullerston's residence 78, 80; Wyclif manuscripts there 78; copy of Butler's tract on biblical translation there in Bale's time 67; St Edmund Hall 79

Palmer, Thomas 82; his text on biblical translation 67-9, 153-4, 157; its relation to Ullerston's text 81; its form and date 81-2; other texts attributed to him 82

Parisiensis, see Peraldus

Parker, John 86

Parker, Matthew archbishop of Canterbury 193

Pater noster commentary 107

Patteshull, Peter 183, 200, 212-13

Payne, Peter 5, 40, 68, 73, 79, 80

Peasants' Revolt 158

Pecham, John archbishop of Canterbury 144; his Lambeth Constitutions 161

Pecock, Reginald 28n, 159-60, 212; importance of his use of English 159-60; his awareness of need to refute Lollardy in English 180; *Repressor* comments on Lollard self-naming 167-8

Peraldus; *De Fide et Legibus* 49

Peter of Poitiers 49

Piers, *alias* Fyncaisshe, John 191

Piers Plowman, see Langland

Ploughman's Tale 227, 231-2, 246-7; its date 246

Polton, Thomas bishop of Worcester; examination material for Lollardy in his register 125-39, 207

Pore Caitiff 106, 125

Poul, John, lector of Reading convent 120

Prague; College of Bohemian nation perhaps owned copy of Ullerston tract 80; copying of Wycliffite texts there 38-41, 45; process of *pronunciacio* there for multiplication of books 39, 45

Praier and Complaynte of the Plowman 227, 230-1, 246-7; its date 246

Pricke of Conscience 218

Pronunciacio 38-9, 45

Purvey, John 10, 150-1, 169; his life and writings 57, 85-110; articles abjured 1401 87-8; Knighton's list of his errors 90; Lavenham's list of his errors 91; involvement in Oldcastle revolt 88-9; Thorpe's comments on him 93; Netter's comments on him 94-5; Netter's attributions to him 57, 94; Bale's comments on him 96-101; Bale's attribution of *Opus Arduum* to him 57, 99-100; alleged connection with Wycliffite Bible 102-8; 'Purvey's Principles' 105; text on biblical translation attributed to him 67, 80; *Sixteen Points* attributed to him 71, 73; *Thirty-Seven Conclusions* attributed to him 103-5; other texts attributed to him 105-8

Ragenhill, Robert archdeacon of Dorset 120

Ramsbury, William; his activities as a Lollard priest and his beliefs 111-123

Ramsbury (Wilts.) 123

Reading; Franciscan convent 120

Reformation; Lollard texts reprinted in the period 227-48

Repingdon, Philip 86, 93, 110, 151, 165, 200, 210

Richard II 144

Richard of St. Victor 21, 49

Richmond, Thomas 213

Rigg, Robert 151

Rochester 129

Rolle, Richard 76, 218; Psalter commentary 73, 154; Wycliffite versions of the Psalter commentary 81, 155, 203

Rome 194-5

Rosarium Theologie 5, 14-29, 32-42, 45, 62, 166, 179; relation to *Floretum* 17-18; English manuscripts 16-17, 33; Bohemian manuscripts 20n, 35; English translation 24

Roye, William 228

Ruysbroek 114

Rymington, William of 10; texts against Wyclif 83

Sabelius 160

Salisbury 49, 54; diocese 111, 115, 118, 191; cathedral 123

Saltwood; archiepiscopal palace there 88, 93, 96, 98, 100

Sampson, Elizabeth 127n.

Sawtre, William 87

Schism 195

Schools; Lollard 28, 109

Scot, Thomas 189

Scryvener, Michael 182n, 189

Selby, Ralph, chancellor of Salisbury diocese 120

Seneca 21

Shenley (Herts.) manor 59

Sherston (Wilts.) 122

Shrewsbury 119

Sixteen Points 25, 71, 107, 196

Slaughterford (Wilts.) 122

Smith, John, of Coventry 161

Smith, William, of Leicester 53, 58, 89, 183, 189

Snappe's *Formulary* 87

Sonning (Berks.) 111, 120
South Creake (Norfolk) 130n.
Speght, William; edition of Chaucer 232
Spencer, see Despenser
Stachdene, John, warden of Reading Franciscan convent 120
Stafford, John bishop of Bath and Wells 128
Steeple Ashton (Wilts.) 123
Stevens, Thomas 129
Stokes, Peter 212
Strood (Kent) 129
Sturminster Marshall (Dorset) 123
Sutton (of dubious location) 122
Swanage (Dorset) 115, 123
Swetstock, John 157n.
Swinderby, William 86, 95
Syon, Bridgettine house 115

Tanner, T.; *Bibliotheca britannico-hibernica* on Purvey 101
Taylor, William 79, 93, 95, 109; his trial 97n, 184
Thirty-Seven Conclusions of the Lollards 71, 166, 172; parallels between them, Wycliffite Bible and General Prologue 103-5; elements in vocabulary 176-80
Thomas of Hales 49
Thomas of Woodstock, duke of Gloucester 97n.
Thoresby, John archbishop of York; *Catechism*, Lollard version of 81, 203
Thorpe, William 55-6, 58, 119, 132n, 210; on Purvey 92-3, 108; texts of his account of his trial 12, 93; version printed [1530] 230-1, 236-8, 244; relation of manuscript versions to each other and to printed edition 236-8; *Testamente* in [1530] edition 238; references to books about him 245n; Bale's version copied into *Fasciculi Zizaniorum* 96; trial in Foxe's publications 100
Thynne, William; his edition of Chaucer 231
Tišnov, Simon of 40
Tissyngton, John 212
Tractatus de Regibus 141; see also Wyclif, *De Officio Regis*
Trefnant, John bishop of Hereford 55
Trevisa, John 83n; *Dialogus inter militem et clericum* 199
True Copye of a Prolog, see Wycliffite Bible
Tunstall, Cuthbert bishop of London 155n, 168
Twelve Conclusions of the Lollards 62, 71, 98-9; originally a *schedula* 183; conjectured by Bale to be by Oldcastle 98n; Foxe's use of text 100-101
Tyndale, William 228; alleged responsibility for edition of *Examination* of Oldcastle 245

Ullerston, Richard 75-83; his text on biblical translation 75-83, 107; his views about translation 150, 152-4, 157-8, 243n; *Defensorium Dotacionis Ecclesie* 75-7, 79; *Petitiones* 75-7; Commentary on Canticles 77n.
Urban VI 44, 60, 64
Ussher, William; *Historia dogmatica* on Purvey 101
Ultraquism 36, 46

Vitae Patrum 48

Wakefield, Henry bishop of Worcester 86
Walcote, John 95
Walsingham, Thomas 59, 213; *Historica Anglicana* evidence on Lollards 111, 115, 119; on the Peasants' Revolt 158
Waltham, John bishop of Salisbury 111, 118; investigation of Ramsbury 111-23
Warminster (Wilts.) 115, 122-3
Warwick, earl of 87
Waterland, Daniel; speculations on Purvey 102-3
Westbury (Wilts.) 123
West Hythe (Kent); Purvey held living there 1401-3 88, 93, 109
West Kington (Berks.) 122
Weston, Nicholas 213
Wharton, H., *Appendix ad historiam literaria. . . G. Cave* 102
Whethamstede, John abbot of St. Albans 125, 149, 174
White, William 93, 95, 109; his trial 97n.
Whitehorne, John 127
Willesthorpe, Matthew 78
William of Malmesbury 49, 70
William of St. Amour 21, 50-51, 54
Winchester diocese 116
Wodard, John 61
Wood, A. à; *History and Antiquities of the University of Oxford* on Purvey 101
Woodford, William 212; *Questiones LXII de Sacramento Altaris* 214; *LXV Questiones* and its relation to *Jack Upland* 10, 239-40, 252
Worcester cathedral lost manuscript of *Compendious treatyse* 242
Worcester diocese 116
Workman, H.B.; works attributed by him to Purvey 108
Wyche, Richard 56, 210; claimed as author of *Opus Arduum* 56
Wyclif, John; place of birth 220n; preaching in London and elsewhere 151; his preaching and that of his followers alleged to be cause of Peasants' Revolt 158; Latin by-name *Doctor Euangelicus* 10, 15, 52, 145, 167; supposed sending

of 'poor preachers' 3-4, 13, 145; his use of term *Ecclesia Anglicana* 143; allusions to him in *Opus Arduum* 50-52; quotations from his works in *Floretum* and *Rosarium* 15; his views on Eucharist 209, and his gloss on Ambrose 214-15; later interest in him in Oxford 77-81; his interest in English 144-5, and his concern for an English Bible 145; alleged authorship of English works 85, 186-7; alleged to be author of Prologue to Wycliffite Bible 230; search for his books 86; prohibition on his writings in Arundel's *Constitutions* 147; link of his works to Lollard writings 13; responsibility for Lollard ways of speech 165, 167; use of *quidam fidelis* for himself 167; use of *fundatus* 172; Latin works 1; importance of Hussite transcripts 2; indexes to his works 4-5, 22-23; *Confessio* (1381) 214; *De Anime Imobilitate* 78; *De Apostasia* 19, 212, 214; *De Blasphemia* 78; *De Civili Dominio* 19, 37n; *De Composicione Hominis* 2, 79; *De Contrarietate Duorum Dominorum* 152; *De Dominio Divino* 3, 78-9; *De Ecclesia* 22, 78; *De Eucharistia* 2, 145, 214-15; *De Eucharistia Confessio* 26; *De Mandatis* 4, 19, 27, 33, 79; index to 4, 22; copy at Queen's Oxford 78; *De Mendaciis Fratrum* 3; *De Nova Prevaricancia Mandatorum* 152; *De Officio Pastorali* 19; vernacular redaction 71; *De Officio Regis* English version 10, 71, 141, 185, 198; *De Paupertate Christi;* 19; *De Potestate Pape* 80; *Descriptio Fratris* 3, 25; *De Solutione Sathanae* 51; *De Statu* version 10, 71, 141, 185, 198; *De Solutione Sathanae* 51; *De Statu Innocencie* 4, 78-9; *De Symonia* 4, 19; *De Tempore* 4, 79; *De Triplici Vinculo Amoris* 154; *De Universalibus* 4, 79; *De Veritate Sacre Scripture* 4, 78, 145; *Dialogus* 19; vernacular derivative 10, 71, 185, 196; *Opus Evangelicum* 5, 19, 214; index to 4-5, 22-3; *Postilla super Totam Bibliam* 2, 50, 77; *Responsiones ad XLIV Conclusiones* 11, 84n; *Sermones* 19, 51; not sole source of English sermons 205; *Sermones Mixti* 19; *Trialogus* 2, 19, 37n, 214, 227n.

Wycliffite Bible 85, 184-5; Wyclif's part in it 102, 151, 247-8; Waterland's speculations on authorship 102-3; Later Version said to be by Purvey 103-8; Forshall and Madden's edition 103-5; Prologue there alleged to be by Purvey 103-5; rarity of quotation from it 104; source of some elements of Lollard vocabulary 176-7; manuscripts 7, 183; ownership of it 182; extra prologues and glosses 105, 152; General Prologue published under title *Dore of holy scripture* 12, 230-2, 240-2; and as *True copye of a prolog* 230-3

Wycliffite Dialect 165-6

Wycklyffe's Wycket 12, 227, 231-2, 246-7; its date 246-7

Wynterton, Thomas 212, 214

Wyring 70

Yatton Keynell (Berks.) 122

York 114, 213

Young, Richard bishop of Bangor 87

INDEX OF MANUSCRIPTS

Documents and episcopal registers are not included in this index. Because many of the manuscripts contain several items, only a general indication of content is given. For the same reason, inclusion or omission of the description 'Wycliffite' should not be taken as a precise indication of the heterodoxy or otherwise of the entire volume.

BERLIN, Deutschstaatsbibliothek

Theol. Lat. fol. 580   Ullerston *Defensiorum Dotacionis Ecclesie* 76n.

BRNO, University Library

Mk 28   *Opus Arduum* and *Rosarium* 6, 8, 20n, 35-9, 41, 44-6, 51n, 55, 69n, 154-5nn, 157n, 244n
Mk 35   *Rosarium Theologie* 20-1nn, 35
Mk 62   *Opus Arduum* 45, 56
Mk 109   Wyclif *Trialogus* extract 19n

CAMBRIDGE, University Library

Additional 5338   English sermons 181n, 250
Additional 6681, 6682 and 6684
   Wycliffite Bibles 7
Dd. 5. 64   Rolle 218n
Dd. 14. 30 (2)   *Clergy may not own property* variant version 10, 185, 208n, 233, 252
Ee. 1. 10   Wycliffite Bible 104
Ee. 6. 32   Lyndwood 149n
Ff. 6. 2   *Jack Upland* and other English Wycliffite tracts 11, 233, 239-40, 252
Ff. 6. 31 (3)   English Wycliffite tracts 117n, 184n, 210n, 215
Ii. 1. 40   English Wycliffite Sermons 250
Ii. 3. 8   anonymous Latin sermons 157n
Ii. 3. 14   Latin archiepiscopal legislation 140n
Ii. 6. 19   *Rosarium* 16
Ii. 6. 26   English tracts on biblical translation 83n, 106-7, 154-7nn, 158, 162n
Ii. 6. 39   English tract 251
Ii. 6. 55   English Wycliffite tracts 27, 251
Ll. 5. 13   Wyclif *De Mandatis* 4, 22
Mm. 2. 15   Wycliffite Bible 233
Nn. 4. 12   English Wycliffite tracts 250

CAMBRIDGE, Christ's College

7   English Wycliffite Sermons 250

CAMBRIDGE, Corpus Christi College

100   *Compendious Treatyse* 11, 242n.
296   English Wycliffite tracts 27
298   *Compendious Treatyse* 242n
336   English Wycliffite Sermons 186n, 250

CAMBRIDGE, Gonville and Caius College

179/212   Wycliffite Bible 189n
217/232   *Rosarium* 16
232/118   *Rosarium* 16
337/565   Wyclif Latin works 2, 4, 79
354/581   English *Rosarium* 24
803/807   Ullerston fragment 74-5

CAMBRIDGE, Jesus College

73   *Rosarium* 33

CAMBRIDGE, Magdalene College

Pepys 2498   English tracts 203
Pepys 2616   English Wycliffite Sermons 250

CAMBRIDGE, Pembroke College

221   Methley Latin translation of *Mirror of Simple Souls* 114
237   English Wycliffite Sermons 200n, 249-51
309   Lyndwood 149n

CAMBRIDGE, Peterhouse

53   Lyndwood 148n
54   Lyndwood 148n
69   English Wycliffite Sermons fragments 250

CAMBRIDGE, St John's College

C. 8   English Wycliffite Sermons 187n, 249

(Cambridge, St John's College, cont.)
C. 21   *Mirror of Simple Souls* 114n
G. 22   English Wycliffite Sermons 181n, 250
G. 25   English Wycliffite tracts 250
S. 46   post-medieval collection 249

CAMBRIDGE, *Sidney Sussex College*

74   English Wycliffite Sermons 188, 250

CAMBRIDGE, *Trinity College*

B. 1. 26   *Compendious Treatyse* 242-3nn
B. 2. 17   English Wycliffite Sermons 187n, 249-50
B. 4. 20   English Wycliffite Sermons 250
B. 14. 38   English Wycliffite Sermons 188n, 250
B. 14. 44   *Rosarium* 16
B. 14. 50   English and Latin Wycliffite material 3, 25-6, 27n, 28, 107, 117n, 184n, 196-7, 208n, 242-3nn, 251
B. 15. 11   Palmer determination 68, 82, 154
B. 16. 2   Wyclif Latin works 4
O. 7. 30   *Rosarium* 16, 33
R. 3. 8   *Cursor Mundi* 217n, 218, 220n, 221-4

CAMBRIDGE, *Mass., Harvard University*

Eng. 738   English Wycliffite tracts 250-1

DRESDEN, *Sächsische Landesbibliothek*

Od. 83   Wycliffite Bible 7

DUBLIN, *Trinity College*

75 (A. 1. 10)   Wycliffite Bible 103
241 (C. 1. 22)   English Wycliffite sermons 181n, 250
242 (C. 1. 23)   Wyclif *Opus Evangelicum* 4, 22, 52n
243 (C. 1. 24)   Wyclif Latin 4
244 (C. 3. 12)   English Wycliffite tracts 27, 183, 196
245 (C. 5. 6)   English Wycliffite tracts 10n, 27, 71n, 117n, 183-5, 196-7, 210n, 215, 250, 252
246 (C. 1. 14)   English Wycliffite tracts 251
775 (D. 3. 4)   transcription of Latin trial material 191n

DURHAM, *University Library*

V. iii. 6   English Wycliffite dialogue 184, 193-

(Durham, University Library, cont.)
200
V. iv. 2   English sermons 163n
V. v. 1   English Wycliffite tracts 41, 81n, 184n

EDINBURGH, *University Library*

93 (Laing 140)   English Wycliffite sermon 249-50

ESSEX RECORD OFFICE, *Colchester*

D/DPr. 554   English Wycliffite Sermons fragment 250

EXETER, *Dean and Chapter Library*

3516   Ullerston *Defensiorum Dotacionis Ecclesie* 76

FLORENCE, *Laurentian Library*

Plut. xix cod. xxxiii   Wyclif Latin works 19n

GÖTTINGEN, *University Library*

theol. 107   *Cursor Mundi* 218, 220n, 221-4

KARLSRUHE, *Badische Landesbibliothek*

346   *Opus Arduum* 6, 45, 51n

KLOSTERNEUBURG, *Stiftsbibliothek*

369   *Floretum* 35, 38

LEICESTER, *Leicestershire County Record Office*

Old Town Hall 3   English Wycliffite Sermons 188-9nn, 223n, 250
Wyggeston Hospital 10 D. 34/6   English Wycliffite Sermons 187n, 189n, 249-51
Wyggeston Hospital 10 D. 34/ 16   *Floretum* 32

LINCOLN, *Cathedral Library*

66   English Sermons 163n
159   Wyclif Latin works 4
241   *Floretum* 34

LONDON, British Library

Additional 10036   *Cursor Mundi* 222n
Additional 10047   Wycliffite Bible 11
Additional 15580   Wycliffite Bible 11
Additional 24202   English Wycliffite tracts
  116n, 175, 178-9, 184n, 186n, 208n,
  251-2
Additional 35205   precedent roll 184n
Additional 37677   English Wycliffite tracts
  251
Additional 37790   *Mirror of Simple Souls*
  114n
Additional 40671   English Wycliffite Sermons
  250
Additional 40672   English Wycliffite Sermons
  188n, 219n, 225n, 249-50
Additional 41321   English Lollard sermons
  156-7nn, 174, 249
Cotton Claudius D. viii   English Wycliffite
  Sermons 187n, 249-50
Cotton Cleopatra B. ii   *O and I* poem 7
Cotton Galba E. ix *Pricke of Conscience* 218n,
  220n, 221-4
Cotton Titus D. i   *Thirty-Seven Conclusions*
  176, 179-80
Cotton Titus D. v   English Wycliffite tract
  146n, 175-80
Cotton Vespasian A. iii   *Cursor Mundi* 217n,
  218, 220n, 221-4
Cotton Vitellius D. vii   *Compendious Treatyse*
  242n
Egerton 617-618   Wycliffite Bible 197n
Egerton 2820   *Clergy may not own property*
  variant version 9-10, 146n, 161n, 175-9,
  233, 252
Harley 272   English Wycliffite tract 27
Harley 401   *Floretum* 5, 16-22, 28, 32
Harley 425   *Compendious Treatyse* 242n
Harley 1203   English Wycliffite tracts 21n, 81n,
  175-6, 178-9, 250
Harley 1205   English collection 220n
Harley 1730   English Wycliffite Sermons 250
Harley 2179   procedural material and questions
  117n, 127-39, 182n, 197n
Harley 2322   English Wycliffite tract 183n
Harley 2324   *Lanterne of Li3t* 234
Harley 2330   *De Salutaribus Documentis* 251
Harley 2385   English Wycliffite tracts 10n
Harley 2396   English Wycliffite Sermons 187n,
  189n, 250
Harley 2398   English tracts 162n, 251
Harley 3226   *Rosarium* 17
Harley 4884   *Rosarium* 17
Harley 6613   *Lanterne of Li3t* 185n, 234-6,

(British Library, continued)
  252
Harley 6641   *Jack Upland* 239-40
Lansdowne 388   Foxe 101
Lansdowne 409   Ullerston *Defenson um*
  Dotacionis Ecclesie 76n
Royal 8 D. ii   *Floretum* 16
Royal 8 F. xii   documents 87n
Royal 9 A. v   Lyndwood 149n
Royal 9 A. xiii   Lyndwood 149n
Royal I1 C. viii   Lyndwood 148n·
Royal 11 E. i   Lyndwood 148n
Royal 18 B. ix   English Wycliffite Sermons
  187n, 213, 249-50

LONDON, Lambeth Palace Library

23   Wyclif works 5
551   *Clergy may not own property* 9,
  233-4, 252
594   *Compendious Treatyse* 242n
1149   English Wycliffite Sermons 187-8nn,
  249-50

LONDON, Westminster Cathedral Archives

B. 2. 8   Norwich courtbook 125-6nn, 130,
  131n, 212n

LONDON, Westminster School Library

3   English tracts 251

LONGLEAT House, Wiltshire

29   Rolle 218n

NAPLES, Biblioteca Nazionale

VII. A. 34   *Opus Arduum* 6, 46-7, 55-6nn

NEW YORK, Pierpont Morgan Library

648   *Compendious Treatyse* 242n

NORWICH, Castle Museum

158. 926. 4g. 3   English Wycliffite tracts 27,
  250-1

OXFORD, Bodleian Library

Additional A. 105   English Wycliffite
  Sermons 250
Additional B. 66   English Wycliffite tract

(Oxford, Bodleian Library, cont.)
183n
Ashmole 789   Pecock's abjuration 159n
Bodley 9   English tracts 251
Bodley 31   *Rosarium* 16, 36
Bodley 55   *Floretum* 16, 18, 21n, 22
Bodley 108   Bury *Gladius Salomonis* 160
Bodley 158   Rymington treatises 11n, 84
Bodley 240   Hereford's sermon 151
Bodley 248   Lyndwood 148n
Bodley 288   English Wycliffite Psalter
   commentary 155-6nn
Bodley 448   *Floretum* 16, 36-7
Bodley 505   *Mirror of Simple Souls* 114n
Bodley 540   *Thirty-Seven Conclusions* 11,
   251
Bodley 626   *Rosarium* 16
Bodley 627   biblical index 23
Bodley 647   English Wycliffite material 183n,
   200n
Bodley 649   macaronic sermons 157n
Bodley 688   biblical index 23
Bodley 703   Woodford texts 214, 239-40, 252
Bodley 709   pseudo-Chrysostom on Matthew
   23
Bodley 716   Wyclif *Postilla* 50n, 77
Bodley 743   pseudo-Chrysostom on Matthew
   23
Bodley 788   English Wycliffite Sermons 187n,
   205n, 218n, 249-50
Bodley 798   Grosseteste *Dicta* 23
Bodley 803   *Rosarium* 17
Bodley 830   Grosseteste *Dicta* 23, 179
Bodley 938   English tracts 250-2
Bodley 959   Wycliffite Bible 104, 106, 176
Digby 41   *Daw's Reply* 239-40
Digby 98   *O and I* poem 7
Don. c. 13   English Wycliffite Sermons in expurg-
   ated version 171, 187-8nn, 201-14, 218-25,
   249-50
Don. e. 151   notes of John Lewis 102n
Douce 53   sermon of William Taylor 175-8
Douce 273   English Wycliffite tracts 10n, 71n,
   141, 185, 198-9
Douce 274   English Wycliffite tracts 198
Douce 295   *Dives and Pauper* 212n
Douce 321   English Wycliffite Sermons
   10, 186-7nn, 202, 249
Douce 369   Wycliffite Bible 104
e Mus. 86   *Fasciculi Zizaniorum* 96-7, 130,
   237n.
Eng. th. f. 39   English Wycliffite tracts 27,
   184n, 251
Fairfax 2   Wycliffite Bible 148n
Fairfax 14   *Cursor Mundi* 217n, 220n, 223n
Holkham Misc. 40   Robert Greatham's *Mirror*

(Oxford, Bodleian Library, cont.)
   in English 141n
Langbaine 5   copy of material from Bodley
   55 16n
Lat. th. e. 30   Dymmok 251
Laud Misc. 200   Latin Wycliffite sermons
   153, 156n
Laud Misc. 210   English Wycliffite tracts
   41, 81n, 184n
Laud Misc. 314   English Wycliffite Sermons
   250
Laud Misc. 608   Lyndwood 148n
Laud Misc. 706   macaronic sermons 157n
Lyell 20   Ullerston on *Canticles* 77n
Rawlinson A. 389   English texts 220n
Rawlinson C. 5   *Rosarium* 17
Rawlinson C. 208   Thorpe trial 93, 119n, 162n,
   230, 236-8, 252
Rawlinson C. 751   English Lollard sermons 174
   249
Rawlinson D. 376   Waterland letters 102n

OXFORD, All Souls College

24   *De Salutaribus Documentis* 251

OXFORD, Balliol College

158   procedural material and questions 140

OXFORD, Corpus Christi College

B. 71   Lyndwood 148n
116   scrapbook of Oxford disputations 79

OXFORD, Hertford College

4   English Wycliffite Sermons fragments
   250

OXFORD, Magdalen College

Lat. 55   Wyclif *Postilla* 50n
Lat. 143   Lyndwood 148n

OXFORD, Merton College

68   Butler determination 67, 82, 156n

OXFORD, New College

49   Olivi on Matthew 50
95   English Wycliffite Sermons 10n, 186n,
   250
320   Wycliffite Bible 11

OXFORD, The Queen's College

453   records of the college 78-9nn

OXFORD, University College

95   *Rosarium* 17

PARIS, Bibliothèque Nationale

fonds latin 15869   Wyclif *De Civili Dominio* 19

POMMERSFELDEN, Schloss

186   *Rosarium* 20n, 35

PRAGUE, Metropolitan Chapter Library

A. 117 (219)   *Opus Arduum* 6, 45, 51n, 55n
A. 163 (269)   *Opus Arduum* 6, 46, 55n
B. 48/1 (351)   *Opus Arduum* 6, 46, 55
B. 48/2 (352)   *Opus Arduum* 6, 46
B. 53 (359)   Wyclif Latin 4
B. 82/2 (395)   *Opus Arduum* 46, 55n
C. 32 (451)   *Floretum* 20-21nn, 35
C. 37/4 (461)   *Floretum* 20-21nn, 35-6
C. 38 (462) Wyclif Latin 4n
C. 73 (504)   Wyclif Latin 4n
C. 118 (550)   Wyclif indexes 5n
D. 16 (582)   *Rosarium* 20n, 35, 38
D. 92/1 (658)   *Rosarium* 20n, 35
D. 92/2 (659)   *Floretum* 20n, 35
D. 105 (674)   *Rosarium* 20n, 35
D. 114 (684)   *Rosarium* 20n, 35
D. 115 (685)   *Rosarium* 20n, 35
0. 29 (1613)   Latin Wycliffe material 93n,
    119, 236-8, 252

PRAGUE, National Museum

X. D., 11   *Rosarium* 35, 38n

PRAGUE, University Library

I. C. 41 (133)   collection 20n, 35
III. B. 5 (414)   Wyclif Latin works 4
III. F. 11 (514)   Wyclif Latin works 4
III. F. 20 (523)   Wyclif *Postilla* 2
III. G. 17 (542)   *Opus Arduum* 6, 46-7, 55n
IV. E. 14 (694)   *Floretum* 20n, 35
IV. G. 19 (751)   *Rosarium* 20n, 35, 38
IV. G. 27 (759)   index of biblical passages
    discussed by Wyclif 5
V. B. 2 (819) *Floretum* 20-21nn, 35, 38
V. E. 3 (895)   *Opus Arduum* 6, 8, 45-6, 51n

(Prague, University Library, cont.)
V. H. 17 (994)   *Rosarium* 20n, 35
VIII. B. 5. (1441)   *Floretum* 20n, 35
VIII. B. 8   (1444)   Grosseteste *Dicta* 39
VIII. B. 18 (1454)   *Floretum* 20n, 35
VIII. F. 9 (1563)   Wyclif *Postilla* 2
VIII. F. 16 (1570)   Wyclif material collected
    by Matthias of Hnatnice 39
IX. D. 6 (1744)   *Floretum* 20n, 35
X. D. 11 (1890)   Wyclif Latin works 4
X. E. 9 (1910)   Wyclif Latin works and
    Wycliffite tract 4, 6, 144n
X. E. 11 (1912)   Wyclif indexes 5
X. H. 4 (1982)   *Rosarium* 20n, 35, 38n
XII. G. 17 (2228)   *Rosarium* 20n, 35
XIII. F. 27 (2365)   *Floretum*   20n, 35, 38

PRINCETON, New Jersey

Scheide collection 12   Wycliffite Bible 241
Robert Taylor collection   English
    Wycliffite Sermons 187n, 249-50

ROME, Vatican

Borghese 29   Wyclif *De Paupertate Christi*
    19n

SALISBURY, Cathedral Library

36   *Floretum* 32, 36

SAN MARINO, Huntington Library

HM 503   *Clergy may not own property*
    variant version 233, 252

SHREWSBURY SCHOOL LIBRARY

X   *Rosarium* 33
XXIII   *Floretum* 33-4

VIENNA, Österreichische Nationalbibliothek

1294   Wyclif Latin 3-5, 78-9
1339, 1340, 1341   Wyclif Latin works 4
1343   Wyclif Latin works 4
1622   Wyclif Latin works 4
1725   Wyclif indexes 5
3927   Wyclif Latin works 4
3928   Latin Wycliffite tract 6, 144n
3929   *O and I* poem and other Wycliffite
    tracts 7
3932   Latin Wycliffite tract 6, 144n
3936   Wyclif Latin works and Thorpe trial
    93n, 119n, 210n, 236-8, 252

(Vienna, Österreichische Nationalbibliothek, cont)
3937 Wyclif Latin works 4
4133 Ullerston tract 69-74, 153n, 156-7
4316 Wyclif Latin works 52n
4488 rewriting of *Floretum/Rosarium* 35n
4492 *Rosarium* 35
4504 Wyclif Latin works 4
4505 Wyclif Latin works 52n
4514 Wyclif Latin works 4
4515 Wyclif Latin works 4
4522 index of biblical passages discussed by
    Wyclif 5
4523 Wyclif Latin works 4
4526 *Opus Arduum* 6, 46, 56n
4527 Wyclif and Wycliffite Latin texts 7
4536 Wyclif Latin works 4
4925 *Opus Arduum* 6, 46, 56n
5204 Wyclif Latin works 4

WISBECH, Town Museum

8 English Wycliffite Sermons 3, 250

WOLFENBÜTTEL, Herzog August Bibliothek

Aug. A. 2 Wycliffite Bible 7
Cod. Guelf (Helmstedt) 306 Wyclif Latin work
Cod. Guelf (Helmstedt) 565 Wyclif Latin work
    5, 23n

WORCESTER, Cathedral Library

Q. 15 *Rosarium* 17, 24n
Q. 68 *Rosarium* 17, 36

WROCLAW, University Library

1302 collection 20n, 35

YORK, Dean and Chapter Library

XVI D. 2 *Glossed Gospels* 9
XVI. L. 12 English Wycliffite tracts 250-1